The Art and Science of Leadership

THIRD EDITION

Afsaneh Nahavandi

Arizona State University West

Prentice
Hall

Upper Saddle River, New Jersey 07458

To my daughters Parisa and Arianne

Library of Congress Cataloging-in-Publication Data

Nahavandi, Afsaneh.
   The art and science of leadership / Afsaneh Nahavandi.—3rd ed.
     p. cm.
   Includes bibliographical references (p.) and index.
   ISBN 0-13-045812-0
    1. Leadership.   2. Leadership—Cross-cultural studies.   I. Title.

BF637.L4 N35 2002
158'.4—dc21   2002066299

Senior Managing Editor: Jennifer Glennon
Editor-in-Chief: Jeff Shelstad
Assistant Editor: Jessica Sabloff
Editorial Assistant: Kevin Glynn
Senior Marketing Manager: Shannon Moore
Marketing Assistant: Christine Genneken
Managing Editor (Production): John Roberts
Production Editor: Kelly Warsak
Permissions Coordinator: Suzanne Grappi
Associate Director, Manufacturing: Vincent Scelta
Production Manager: Arnold Vila
Manufacturing Buyer: Michelle Klein
Cover Design: Kiwi Design
Cover Illustration: Getty Images, Inc.
Composition: BookMasters, Inc.
Full-Service Project Management: BookMasters, Inc.
Printer/Binder: R.R. Donnelley & Sons Company
Cover Printer: Phoenix Color Corp.

Credits and acknowledgments borrowed from other sources and reproduced, with permission, in this textbook appear on appropriate pages within text.

Pearson Education LTD.
Pearson Education Australia PTY, Limited
Pearson Education Singapore, Pte. Ltd
Pearson Education North Asia Ltd
Pearson Education, Canada, Ltd
Pearson Educación de Mexico, S.A. de C.V.
Pearson Education–Japan
Pearson Education Malaysia, Pte. Ltd

10 9 8 7 6 5 4 3 2 1
ISBN 0-13-045812-0

BRIEF CONTENTS

CONTENTS

Contents

CHAPTER 6   Exchange and Relationship Development and Management   160

PART III: CURRENT DEVELOPMENTS AND APPLICATIONS   191

CHAPTER 7   Participative Management and Leading Teams   193

PREFACE

Leading people effectively is a tremendous challenge, a great opportunity, and a serious responsibility. Today's organizations, more than ever, need effective leaders who understand the complexities of our ever-changing global environment; who have the intelligence, sensitivity, and ability to empathize with others; and who can motivate their followers to strive for excellence. We always have been interested in leadership. All civilizations throughout history have focused on their leaders, revering or reviling them. Leaders and followers have existed since humans first organized into groups to accomplish a task. Throughout history, the fate of millions has depended on the leadership qualities of kings and queens and on their battles for succession. Children all over the world learn early, through listening to fairy tales, that the happiness and misery of people depend on the goodness (or evilness) of leaders.

We are truly fascinated by those who lead us. To some, leadership is a magical process. Indeed, when we read about historical figures or meet some of the leaders of our times, we can be transfixed by their seemingly magical exploits. They move armies, create new countries, and destroy whole civilizations through what often appears to be the sheer strength of their will. They affect our very existence on this planet. Although our leaders are the ones who dazzle us, we sometimes fail to consider that leaders alone can accomplish nothing. It is the strength of their followers that moves history. It is the hard work of employees that turns a profit in a faltering company. It is the initiative of volunteers that achieves an institution's goals. We also must remember that many extraordinary leaders have found themselves shunned and rejected by the people who once admired them. President Charles de Gaulle's road to the leadership of France was long, tortuous, and fraught with failure: After coming to office as a hero after World War II, he was forced out of office twice. Winston Churchill was removed from office twice, too, and faced long periods in his life during which his leadership was neither valued nor wanted. Julius Caesar experienced many ups and downs in his battles with the Roman senate. More recently, Margaret Thatcher saw her fortunes come and go with the mood of the British public and the economic upheaval in Europe. Henry Cisneros, once mayor of San Antonio and secretary of housing and urban development under President Clinton, fell into disfavor with the electorate before he regained his popularity. Benazir Butho of Pakistan has moved from national hero to national villain several times. Lee Iaccoca of Chrysler was not always the hero that some consider him to be today. George Watson Jr. was booted out of office after successfully leading IBM for many years. Jack Welch, recently retired from the leadership of General Electric and considered by many to be one of the most successful U.S. CEOs, was nicknamed Neutron Jack in his early days at GE for decimating the company workforce through layoffs. If the powers of these leaders are truly magical, why do they wax and wane? Why are they not effective all the time? This question, along with many others, will be addressed in this book.

For our organizations to be effective and for our society to function successfully, we must be able to select the right leaders and help them succeed. This book presents a broad review and analysis of the field of leadership with application to business and other organizations because the processes of leading others to achieve organizational goals are applicable in any institutional setting. Our current research has done much to demystify leadership and teach it to the rest of us mortals. Although we still come across some leaders whose performance and behavior escape the bounds of scientific explanation, by and large we know a good deal about leadership and how to train people to be leaders. The cornerstone of our new knowledge is that most of us can learn to become better leaders. Maybe only a few of us will someday shape human civilization, but most people are capable of improving their leadership skills and shaping their own organizations and communities.

Despite all the knowledge that various disciplines have accumulated about leadership over the past 70 to 80 years, deep divisions are present in the field. Few scholars and practitioners even agree on how to define leadership and its key elements. Much debate occurs about whether a leader's personality or behavior should be the focus of our inquiry. In addition, the role of followers and their characteristics are the subject of much discussion. These differences and disagreements also are explored in this book, along with a focus on distilling knowledge that can be useful to students and practitioners of leadership.

SOMETHING OLD: KEEPING THE GOOD

The third edition of this book builds on the strengths of the first two editions and introduces new emphases and features. The many debates and controversies within the field of leadership are presented in this edition as they were in the first two. I continue to emphasize integration of the concepts and to distill useful and practical concepts from each theory while taking a cross-cultural perspective. The guiding philosophy and assumption remain the same:

- *We all can learn to become better leaders.* For some of us, the learning will come easier in certain areas than in others, but with practice and support from our organizations, we all can improve our leadership capabilities. Like many readers, I occasionally have come across incredibly charismatic leaders who seem to have special talents at moving others. Although it is tempting to attribute to them a special leadership "gift" that defies systematic explanation, with some effort and critical thinking, one can analyze their style and the situations in which they are effective in an objective manner. Such analysis demystifies their performance. Although it is not easy to teach others to perform the same way, the charismatic leader's actions lose their magical qualities and become understandable and predictable upon analysis.

  Most of us are not trying to change civilizations, although maybe we should be. Instead, we are trying to move our teams, departments, and organizations toward higher levels of effectiveness and efficiency. We want better decision making, more satisfied employees, better-quality products and services, and more satisfied constituencies and customers. These outcomes are difficult to obtain, but no magic is involved in achieving them. We can use the many existing leadership theories to achieve these goals.

- *Application focus*. Along with strong theoretical coverage and analysis, the book continues to be application focused.
- *Cross-cultural focus*. Leadership is not a culture-free process. It occurs within the context of a culture. The styles and behaviors that are considered key to effectiveness differ from one culture to the next. Some common threads do run through different cultures though. Few of the leadership theories presented in this book fully consider the cultural context, either globally or internally within the United States. Issues of race and gender also are rarely addressed. One goal for this book is to include cross-cultural, racial, and gender-based analyses of leadership as a regular part of the discourse about leadership effectiveness. The changing demographics within the United States and the globalization of our economy make such analysis essential.
- *Looking at the future*. I continue to keep an eye on the future by addressing the dramatic changes that organizations are undergoing. Businesses and not-for-profit organizations are being challenged continuously to be more effective. They are reorganizing and redefining the role of leaders. The reliance on teams is a mainstay of our institutions. Quality and customer focus have moved from the academic domain to the everyday language of our organizations. These structural changes and redefinitions of our institutions' focus on their internal and external customers require a new look at the role and functions of leadership. Our old theories do not explain all the current changes adequately. Throughout the chapters, I establish the link between the old and the new and attempt to present how what we have known and used can help the reader deal with the current and future trends in leadership, particularly the focus on teams and nonhierarchical organizations.
- *Exercises and self-assessments*. The end-of-chapter exercises and self-assessments are included again but with some revisions and additions.
- *Three features*. Each chapter continues to include three features from the second edition, although all present new research and examples. "Leadership on the Cutting Edge" presents current empirical or theoretical research studies. "Leading Change" highlights examples of innovative practices in organizations. "Leadership in Action Case" at the end of every chapter presents a short case study of a real-life leader. Four of the cases are new and the others are updated.

SOMETHING NEW: INTRODUCING NEW FOCUS AND NEW FEATURES

Several new themes and features have been added to this third edition, including the following changes:

- Three New Features:
  1. "What Does This Mean for Me?" highlights a managerial application of the concepts presented in each chapter. This feature is intended to provide clear application for students.

2. "Managerial Challenge" at the end of each chapter has replaced the "Ethical Dilemmas" of the second edition. This feature focuses students' attention on the challenging decisions that leaders face by providing a brief scenario to draw out student reactions and discussion.
3. "Surfing the Internet" sources at the end of every chapter allow students to explore the wealth of leadership-related materials available through the World Wide Web.

- Increased cross-cultural examples throughout all the chapters with new examples and presentations of cross-cultural research.
- Expanded discussion of charismatic and transformational leadership in Chapter 8 to present the growing interest in the topic in the past few years.
- More coverage of leadership skills and emotional intelligence in Chapter 3 to reflect the new direction in leadership skills research and the practitioner interest in EQ.
- New real-life examples to continue to illustrate the concepts and theories. I have made a particular effort to include leaders from different levels of organizations and from small as well as large organizations.

WHO SHOULD READ THIS BOOK?

This book is targeted to students of leadership—whether they are advanced undergraduate and graduate students or managers who continue to learn and grow. It is written for those who want not only to understand the various theories and research in the field, but also to apply that knowledge to becoming leaders and to improving the leadership of their organizations. The examples and cases used are from different types of industries and from the private and public sectors. Although the theories often are developed and tested by psychology and management researchers, they have broad applicability to all students of organizational functioning and leadership.

ACKNOWLEDGMENTS

I would like to thank Marty Chemers for putting the leadership bug in my ear when I was a graduate student, and Irv Altman, who taught me to look at any issues from many different perspectives. I owe Carol Werner many thanks for teaching me to organize my thoughts. My research assistant Toncho Keranov's research was invaluable in finding new material for this edition. Many thanks also are owed to my partners at Prentice Hall—Jeff Shelstad, Jennifer Glennon, Kevin Glynn, and Kelly Warsak—as well as Jennifer Welsch of BookMasters, Inc. I also would like to acknowledge Janet Pascal, DeVry Institute of Technology, Kansas City; Dr. Rajnandini Pillai, California State University, San Marcos; Dr. Dong I. Jung, San Diego State University; Dr. Antoinette Phillips, Southeastern Louisiana University; Jennie Carter Thomas, Belmont University; and Kelli J. Schutte, Calvin College for their thoughtful comments in reviewing the book.

Part

I

Building Blocks

*P*art I lays the foundation for understanding the processes of leadership. After studying Part I, you will be able to define the basic elements of leadership and be ready to integrate them to understand more complex leadership processes.

Leadership is a complex process that results from the interaction among a leader, followers, and the situation. All three of these elements are key to the leadership process. Since the formal study of leadership started in the Western world in the late nineteenth century, we have developed many definitions of this concept. As with any social phenomenon, culture strongly influences how we lead and what we expect of our leaders. Furthermore, although leadership evolves and changes, tracing the history of the field can inform us and help us understand leadership today. We also must be aware of how the process of leadership, and our images and expectations of effective leaders, change along with organizational, social, and cultural evolutions.

The first part of the book lays the foundation for understanding leadership. It first provides a history of the field of leadership and a description of its current state and assumptions. Second, the building blocks of leadership are presented. These building blocks include a working definition of leaders and effectiveness, a cultural framework for understanding the process, a definition of leadership roles and functions, a presentation of individual characteristics of leaders, and an analysis of power and its role in leadership. After studying the four chapters in this section, you will be able to define the basic elements of leadership and be ready to integrate them to understand more complex leadership processes.

Chapter 1

Definition and Significance of Leadership

> *Courage, not complacency, is our need today.*
> *Leadership, not salesmanship.*

—JOHN F. KENNEDY

After studying this chapter, you will be able to:

1. Define leadership and leadership effectiveness.
2. Identify the cultural values that have the potential to affect leadership.
3. Discuss the major obstacles to effective leadership.
4. Compare and contrast leadership and management and understand their similarities and differences.
5. List the roles and functions of management and be aware of cultural differences in the use and application of those functions.
6. Summarize the debate over the role and impact of leadership in organizations.

Who is a leader? When are leaders effective? These age-old questions appear simple, but their answers have kept philosophers, social scientists, scholars from varied disciplines, and business practitioners busy for many years. It is easy to define bad leadership; we agree on the characteristics of a bad leader. However, defining and understanding effective leadership is more complex. This chapter

3

defines leadership and its many aspects, roles, and functions, and high-lights the key role of culture in leadership.

WHAT IS AN EFFECTIVE LEADER?

We recognize effective leaders when we work with them or observe them; however, many different ways exist for defining who leaders are and when they are effective.

Who Is a Leader?

Dictionaries define leading as "guiding and directing on a course" and as "serving as a channel." A leader is someone who has commanding authority or influence. Researchers, for their part, have developed many working definitions of leadership. Although these definitions have much in common, they each consider different aspects of leadership. Some researchers define leadership as an integral part of the group process (Krech and Crutchfield 1948). Others define it primarily as an influence process (Bass 1960; Cartwright 1965; Katz and Kahn 1966). Still others see leadership as the initiation of structure (Homans 1950) and the instrument of goal achievement. Several even consider leaders to be servants of their followers (Greenleaf 1998). In spite of the differences, the various definitions of leadership have three elements in common:

A leader is defined as any person who influences individuals and groups within an organization, helps them in the establishment of goals, and guides them toward achievement of those goals, thereby allowing them to be effective.

- First, leadership is a group phenomenon; there can be no leaders without followers. As such, leadership always involves interpersonal influence or persuasion.
- Second, leaders use influence to guide others through a certain course of action or toward the achievement of certain goals. Therefore, leadership is goal directed and plays an active role in groups and organizations.
- Third, the presence of leaders assumes some form of hierarchy within a group. In some cases, the hierarchy is formal and well defined, with the leader at the top; in other cases, it is informal and flexible.

When we combine the preceding three elements, we can define a leader as "any person who influences individuals and groups within an organization, helps them in the establishment of goals, and guides them toward achievement of those goals, thereby allowing them to be effective." Lorraine Monroe, executive director of the School Leadership Academy in New York City, a nonprofit organization she founded in 1997, is surprised at the number of leaders who lack the basic leadership skills. She states: "The job of a good leader is to articulate a vision that others are inspired to follow" (Canabou and Overholt 2001, p. 98). Joyce Wycoff, the 52-year-old founder of the Innovation Network, a company whose goal is to change the way people do business by sharing ideas through newsletters, conferences, and weekly e-mail called "Good Morning Thinkers!", believes that the key to leadership is for people to work together, interact with others, and share and honor ideas (Imperato 1998). As the leader of Innovation Network, her role is to help and guide her followers through a loose but highly complex system that helps other organizations become innovative.

What Is Effectiveness?

What does it mean to be an effective leader? As is the case with the definition of leadership, effectiveness can be defined in various ways. Some researchers, such as Fiedler, whose contingency model is discussed in Chapter 5, define leadership effectiveness in terms of group performance. According to this view, leaders are effective when their group performs well. Other models, for example, House's Path-Goal Theory presented in Chapter 6, consider follower satisfaction as a primary factor in determining leadership effectiveness; leaders are effective when their followers are satisfied. Still others, namely researchers working on the transformational and visionary leadership models described in Chapter 8, define effectiveness as the successful implementation of large-scale change in an organization.

The definitions of leadership effectiveness are as diverse as the definitions of organizational effectiveness. The choice of a certain definition depends mostly on the point of view of the person trying to determine effectiveness and on the constituents who are being considered. For example, Barbara Waugh, a 1960s civil rights and anti-discrimination activist and worldwide personnel manager of Hewlett-Packard Laboratories (often known as the "World's Best Industrial Research Laboratory"—WBIRL), defines effectiveness as "helping people communicate more, collaborate more, and innovate more" (Mieszkowski 1998). For Father Francis Kline, the abbot of Mepkin monastery outside of Charleston, South Carolina, divine service, helping the community, and being self-sufficient are the indicators of effectiveness (Salter 2000). For Michael Price, president of Heine Securities, effectiveness means getting the best deals for himself and his shareholders (Serwer 1996).

Clearly, no one way best defines what it means to be an effective leader. Luthans (1989) proposes an interesting twist on the concept of leadership effectiveness by distinguishing between effective and successful managers. According to Luthans, effective managers are those who have satisfied and productive employees, whereas successful managers are those who are promoted quickly. After studying a group of managers, Luthans suggests that successful managers and effective managers engage in different types of activities. Whereas effective managers spend their time communicating with subordinates; managing conflict; and training, developing, and motivating employees, the primary focus of successful managers is not on employees. Instead, they concentrate on networking activities such as interacting with outsiders, socializing, and politicking.

The internal and external activities that effective and successful managers undertake are important to allowing leaders to achieve their goals. However, Luthans finds that only 10 percent of the managers in his study are effective *and* successful. The results of his study can have grave implications for how we measure our leaders' effectiveness and reward them. In order to encourage and reward performance, organizations need to reward the leadership activities that will lead to effectiveness rather than those that lead to quick promotion. If an organization cannot achieve balance, it quickly might find itself with a majority of flashy but incompetent leaders who have reached the top primarily through networking rather than through taking care of their employees and achieving goals.

Ideally, any definition of leadership effectiveness should take into consideration all the different roles and functions that a leader performs and then factor those into the definition. However, few organizations perform such a thorough analysis, and they often fall back on simplistic measures. For example, stockholders and financial analysts consider the chief executive officer (CEO) of a company to be effective if company stock prices keep increasing, regardless of how satisfied the company's employees are. Politicians are effective if the polls indicate their popularity and if they are reelected. A football coach is effective when the team is winning. Students' scores on standardized tests determine a school principal's effectiveness.

Consider how Linda Wachner, past CEO of Warnaco, the undergarment manufacturer, was considered to be highly effective and not only one of the highest-earning female business executives, but also one of the toughest bosses in the United States. While the company stock performed well and she satisfied her shareholders, her autocratic leadership style was not considered to be a liability. However, when the company found itself in dire financial trouble, Wachner came under attack for being abusive, and her style was blamed for the company's downfall (Kaufman 2001). Politics provides rich examples of the complexity of defining leadership effectiveness. Consider former President Clinton, who despite being tried and impeached in the U.S. Senate, maintained his popularity at the polls in 1998 and 1999; many voters continued to consider him effective.

The common thread in all of these examples of effectiveness is the focus on outcome. We look at the results of what leaders have done to judge how effective they have been. Process issues, such as employee satisfaction, might be measured but are rarely the primary indicator of effectiveness. Linda Wachner delivered the financial results. U.S. voters liked President Clinton because the economy flourished under his administration. Similarly, in a school system, faculty morale and turnover, which are keys to the facilitation of student learning, are not a primary criterion for determining effectiveness; parents look for test scores and graduation rate when evaluating a school.

Although many leadership studies have considered process issues in determining effectiveness, their focus has been primarily on the productivity of the work group. One way to take a broad view of effectiveness is to consider leaders effective when their group is successful in maintaining internal stability and external adaptability while achieving goals. Overall, then, leaders are effective when their followers achieve their goals, can function well together, and can adapt to the changing demands from the external environment. The definition of leadership effectiveness, therefore, contains three elements:

Leaders are effective when their followers achieve their goals, can function well together, and can adapt to the changing demands from external forces.

- Goal achievement, which includes meeting financial goals, producing quality products or services, addressing the needs of customers, and so forth.
- Smooth internal processes, including group cohesion, follower satisfaction, and efficient operations.
- External adaptability, which refers to a group's ability to change and evolve successfully.

LEADING CHANGE
JetBlue David Neeleman Reinvents an Airline

The airline industry in the United States faced considerable challenge and hardship after the September 11, 2001, terrorist attacks. All, except for a few, canceled routes and cut back on personnel. JetBlue, a small carrier that serves mostly the eastern U.S. seaboard and is fast expanding west, was one of the exceptions. The CEO, David Neeleman, successfully navigated the turbulent times with a no lay-offs strategy and expansion plans that targeted routes that other airlines dropped. The company's small size, young fleet, and emphasis on teamwork allowed for quick decisions and implementation. Neeleman has provided the vision, but he also has learned to listen to his people who have, on occasion, vetoed his decisions. Neeleman takes it in stride and states: "I'm being totally deferential and patient. . . . It's because I think the situation demands it. I have to trust the instincts of the people around me" (Judge 2001, p. 131). Those instincts proved to be correct, allowing the airline to serve its customers.

With low fares and unusual routes such as Washington, D.C., to Oakland and Long Beach, California, the airline does things that others in its industry say it should not be doing. What other low-fare carrier provides its coach customers with individual TV sets, blue potato chips, chocolate chip cookies, and a highly likable cabin crew? (Donnelly 2001) What other airline goes against expert advice and buys a fleet of brand new Airbus planes that offer luxury but are not fuel efficient? How can JetBlue afford being the first U.S. national carrier to install bulletproof, dead-bolted doors on cockpits even before a Federal Aviation Administration mandate? JetBlue's attitude and Neeleman's creativity make it work.

Evaluating these unusual decisions, analysts and competitors keep expecting JetBlue to fold; it hasn't yet (Donnelly 2001). As a matter of fact, Jetblue has won several awards for being the best overall airline in 2001 and 2002, and its CEO Neeleman has been recognized as a visionary (www.jetblueairways.com/). Neeleman states:

We aren't waiting. We're small. We're nimble. . . . We do it first because we think it's the right thing to do. But then, for that, you're perceived as a company that can move quickly and that understands what needs to be done. (Judge 2001, p. 132)

Sources: Donnelly, S. B. 2001. Too good to be true. *Time Magazine*, 30 July, 24–27. Judge, P. C. 2001. Suddenly the world changes. *Fast Company*, December; 131–132, www.jetblueairways.com/LearnMore/index.html.

CULTURE AND LEADERSHIP

Leadership is a social and cultural phenomenon. A leader who is considered effective in Singapore might seem too authoritarian in Sweden. The charisma of an Egyptian political leader has no effect on the French or the Germans. Understanding leadership, therefore, requires understanding the cultural context in which it takes place.

Culture consists of the commonly held values within a group of people. It is a set of norms, customs, values, and assumptions that guides the behavior of a particular group of people. Culture gives each group its uniqueness and differentiates it from other groups. We are strongly influenced by our culture; it determines what we consider right and wrong, and it influences what and who we value, what we pay attention to, and how we behave. Culture affects values and beliefs and influences leadership and interpersonal styles. We learn about culture formally through various teachings and informally through observation (Hall 1973).

Levels of Culture

Culture exists at three levels (see Figure 1-1). The first is national culture, defined as a set of values and beliefs shared by people within a nation. Second, in addition to an overall national culture, different ethnic and other cultural groups might live within each nation. Although these groups share national cultural values, they also have their unique culture. Some nations, such as the United States, Canada, and Indonesia, have many such subcultures. Different cultural, ethnic, and religious groups are part of the overall culture of these nations, which leads to considerable cultural diversity. Other subcultures are based on religious, regional, or gender characteristics. For example, as discussed in Chapter 8, religious beliefs in a savior contribute to the rise of charismatic leadership. Similarly, cultural differences based on gender influence whom we consider to be a leader. In particular, widely held gender stereotypes affect our views of leadership (Broverman et al., 1975; Safilios-Rothschild 1977). Many traditional male traits, such as aggression and independence, often are

Figure 1-1
The Three Levels of Culture

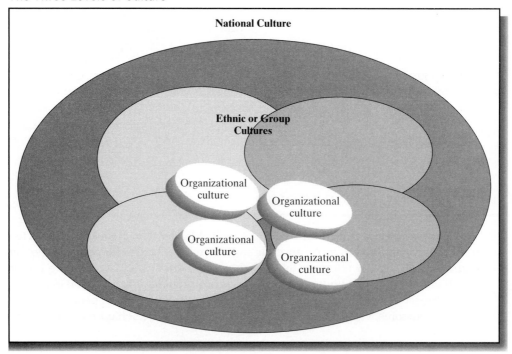

associated with leaders, but traditional female traits of submissiveness and cooperation are not.

The third level of culture is organizational culture—the set of values, norms, and beliefs shared by members of an organization. Given time, all organizations develop a unique culture or character whereby employees share common values and beliefs about work-related issues. These organizational values often include deeply held beliefs about leadership (Schein 1985). In many cases, leaders, and particularly founders, are instrumental in creating and encouraging the culture.

Atlanta-based consulting firm North Highland, which employs 250, has a "no-fly zone" (Canabou 2001). CEO David Peterson was so tired of being constantly on the road and missing out on his family life that he created a company to serve local clients. He considers 50 miles to be the maximum distance people should have to travel for work. His company allows employees to balance their work and home life and provides its clients with consultants who are part of their community. Richard Tuck, cofounder and CEO of Lander International, a company based in El Cerrito, California, encourages his employees to spend less time at work (Fromartz 1998). When Jon Westberg, the company's executive recruiter, hit a performance slump and sought Tuck's advice, Tuck suggested that "maybe he was spending too much time at work, that he needed to devote more time to his art" (Fromartz 1998, p. 125). Tuck wants the people in his company to have outside hobbies and commitments. He hates rules. As a result, the company's culture is loose, with an emphasis on "anything goes." Office manager Helen Winters notes, "I kept waiting for policies to be firmed up, but he just wouldn't do it" (Fromartz 1998, p. 126). Compare Lander's culture with the culture of Atlantic Group Furniture Procurement and Project Management, Inc., an office-furniture distributor in New York City. The company president, Roger Abramson, is obsessed with time and productivity (Fenn 1998). He has announced, "If you are not producing revenue, do not call me during the day" (Fenn 1998, p. 61). Atlantic has a fast-paced culture in which only those who are highly competitive survive. The focus is on pay for performance. The three organizational cultures have different models of leadership effectiveness. At North Highland, balance between work and life is key to effectiveness. At Lander's, the leader is supportive and almost spiritual; at Atlantic, the leader pushes for performance and outcomes.

Because national culture addresses many different aspects of life, it has a strong and pervasive influence on people's behavior in everyday activities and in organizations. The influence of organizational culture generally is limited to work-related values and behaviors. However, national culture strongly influences organizational culture. All French companies, for instance, share some characteristics that make them different from companies in other countries. For example, as compared to their Swedish counterparts, French companies are more hierarchical and status oriented.

All three levels of culture shape our views and expectations of our leaders. Whereas people in the United States do not expect leaders to be failure proof, in many other cultures, leaders' admission of mistakes would be intolerable and a deadly blow to their authority and ability to lead. For example, many U.S. presidents, most recently President Clinton, when faced with no other option, have recognized their mistakes openly and proclaimed to have learned from them. Such admissions are rarely forthcoming in other countries. President Vincente Fox of Mexico has steadfastly refused to admit any error or change course in the handling of his country's economy. He categorically states: "I believe there are no mistakes" (Government in Mexico, 2001, p. 35). When in 1998, Indonesian President Suharto apparently admitted mistakes that contributed to his country's economic crisis, he was seen as weak. Indonesians did not forgive him, and he eventually resigned.

Each country and region in the world has developed a particular organizational and management style based largely on its national culture. This style is called the national organizational heritage. Although there are many differences from one organization to another and from one manager to another, research indicates that this national heritage is noticeable and distinct (Bartlett and Ghoshal 1989, 1992; Bettis and Prahalad 1995).

Models of Culture

Researchers have developed several models to understand national cultures. This section reviews three models that have direct application to organizations and to understanding leadership.

Hall's High-Context and Low-Context Cultural Framework

One of the simplest cultural models focuses on differentiating communication styles within cultures in two groups: one high context and one low context (Hall 1976). In this model, context refers to the environment and the information that provide the background for interaction and communication. Leaders from high-context cultures rely heavily on the context, including nonverbal cues and situational factors, to communicate with others and understand the world around them. They rely on personal relationships to establish communication. Leaders from low-context cultures focus on explicit, specific verbal and written messages to understand people and situations (Munter 1993).

For example, Saudi Arabia, Italy, France, Vietnam, Korea, and China are all high-context cultures, where subtle body posture, tone of voice, detailed rituals, and a person's title and status convey strong messages that determine behavior. Communication does not always need to be explicit and specific. Trust is viewed as more important than written communication or legal contracts. In low-context cultures— such as Germany, Scandinavia, Switzerland, the United States, Great Britain, and Canada—people pay attention to the verbal message. What is said or written is more important than nonverbal messages or the situation. People are, therefore, specific and clear in their communication with others.

The difference between high and low context can explain many cross-cultural communication problems that leaders face when they interact with those who are of a culture that is different from their own. The low-context European and North American leaders might get frustrated working with followers from high-context Asian or Middle Eastern cultures. Whereas the low-context leaders focus on specific instructions, the high-context followers aim at developing relationships. Similarly, high-context leaders might be offended by their low-context followers' directness, which they can interpret as rudeness and lack of respect.

Hofstede's Five Cultural Dimensions

Researcher Geert Hofstede developed one of the best-known classifications of culture, known as Hofstede's dimensions (Hofstede 1980, 1992, 1997, 2001). He originally conducted more than 100,000 surveys of IBM employees in 40 countries, supplemented later by another scale based on Confucian dynamism (Hofstede 1996). He used the results to develop the five basic cultural dimensions along which cultures differ: power distance, uncertainty avoidance, individualism, masculinity, and time orientation (see Table 1-1). The combination of these five dimensions lends each national culture its distinctiveness and unique character.

For example, when compared to 40 other nations, the United States is below average on power distance and uncertainty avoidance, highest in individualism (closely followed by Australia), above average on masculinity, and has a moderate–to–short-term time orientation. These scores indicate that the United States is a somewhat egalitarian culture in which uncertainty and ambiguity are well tolerated; a high value is placed on individual achievements, assertiveness, performance, and independence; sex roles are relatively well defined; and organizations look for quick results with a focus on the present. Japan, on the other hand, tends to be higher than the United States in power distance, masculinity (one of the highest scores), and uncertainty avoidance but considerably lower in individualism and with a long-term orientation. These rankings are consistent with the popular image of Japan as a country in which social structures such as family and organizations are important, power and obedience to them tend to be absolute, risk and uncertainty are averted, gender roles are highly differentiated, and high value is placed on achievement.

Cross-cultural psychologist Harry Triandis has further refined the concept of individualism/collectivism (1995). He argues that different types of collectivist and individualist cultures exist and proposes that by adding the concept of vertical and horizontal, we can gain a much richer understanding of cultural values. Vertical cultures focus on hierarchy; horizontal cultures emphasize equality (Triandis et al., 2001). For example, although Sweden and the United States are both individualist cultures, the Swedes are horizontal individualists (HV) and see individuals as unique but equal to others. In the United States, which is more vertical individualist (VI),

Table 1-1
Hofstede's Five Cultural Dimensions

Power Distance	The extent to which people accept unequal distribution of power. In higher power-distance cultures, a wider gap exists between the powerful and the powerless.
Uncertainty Avoidance	The extent to which the culture tolerates ambiguity and uncertainty. High uncertainty avoidance leads to low tolerance for uncertainty and to a search for absolute truths.
Individualism	The extent to which individuals or a closely knit social structure such as the extended family (collectivism) are the basis for social systems. Individualism leads to reliance on self and a focus on individual achievement.
Masculinity	The extent to which assertiveness and independence from others are valued. High masculinity leads to high sex-role differentiation, and a focus on independence, ambition, and material goods.
Time Orientation	The extent to which people focus on past, present, or future. Present orientation leads to a focus on short-term performance.

Are members of collectivist cultures more likely to be generous when evaluating their in-group versus out-group members? In other words, do they (as compared to individualists) show a bias toward members of their own group? These are questions that researchers Carolina Gomez, Bradley Kirkman, and Debra Shapiro set out to answer (2000). Their focus was specifically on Mexico, where previous research had shown that the sense of family is transferred to employment situations such that Mexican employees will view their work teams as their in-group, or family.

Using a sample of 330 part-time and full-time masters of business administration students (MBA) from Mexico and the United States, the researchers found that Mexicans who are collectivists evaluate their team members significantly higher than U.S. subjects who are individualists. Furthermore, performing group maintenance behavior, as opposed to task behaviors, was found to be more important for Mexicans. In other words,

regardless of actual performance, members of a collectivist culture will show a positive bias toward people they consider to be part of the community.

The researchers suggest that this generosity toward in-group members has positive and negative effects. On the positive side, it can lead to more trust, cooperation, and cohesion within a collectivist team. Managers can use this factor to create cohesive and cooperative teams. Even individuals from diverse backgrounds can be identified as members of the in-group if the focus is building a team identity, and thereby benefit from team cohesion and trust. On the negative side, this bias toward generosity might mask problems and prevent a team from achieving maximum results, as members avoid rating one another negatively. Managers working with collectivistic culture must, therefore, put in place mechanisms to ensure objective peer appraisal systems and fair allocation of rewards.

Source: Gomez, C., Kirkman, B. L., & Shapiro, D. L. 2000. The impact of collectivism and in-group/out-group membership on the evaluation generosity of team members. *Academy of Management Journal* 46 no. 6, 1097–1106.

the individual is viewed not only as unique, but also superior to others. Similarly, in a horizontal collectivistic (HC) culture, such as Israel, all members of the group are seen as equal. In vertical collectivistic cultures (VC) such as Japan and Korea, authority is important, and individuals must sacrifice themselves for the good of the group.

Trompenaars's Dimensions of Culture

Fons Trompenaars and his colleagues provide a complex model that helps leaders understand national culture and its effect on organizational and corporate cultures (Hampden-Turner, F. Trompenaars, and Lewis 2000; A. Trompenaars and Hampden-Turner 2001; A. Trompenaars, Hampden-Turner, and F. Trompenaars 1997). They developed a model based on 15,000 people surveyed in organizations in 47 cultures that suggests that, although understanding national culture requires many different dimensions, cross-cultural organizational cultures can be classified more efficiently based on two dimensions (Trompenaars 1994). These dimensions are (1) egalitarian-hierarchical, and (2) orientation to the person or to the task. When combined, they yield four general cross-cultural organizational cultures: incubator, guided missile, family, and Eiffel Tower (see Figure 1-2). The four general types combine national and organizational cultures. The leader's role in each type differs, as do methods of employee motivation and evaluation.

Incubator cultures are egalitarian and focus on taking care of individual needs. Examples of incubator cultures can be found in many start-up, high-technology firms in the United States and Great Britain (Trompenaars 1994, p. 173). These are typically individualist cultures in which professionals are given considerable latitude to do their jobs. Leaders in such organizations emerge from the group rather than being assigned. Therefore, leadership is based on competence and expertise, and the leader's role is to provide resources, manage conflict, and remove obstacles.

The guided missile is also an egalitarian culture, but the focus is on task completion rather than individual needs. As a result, the organizational culture is impersonal and, as indicated by its name, directed toward accomplishing the job. Trompenaars uses the U.S. National Aeronautics and Space Administration (NASA) as an example of the guided missile. In NASA and other guided-missile organizations, leadership is based on expertise, and follower participation is expected. People work in teams of professionals who have equal status, with performance being the primary criterion for effectiveness.

The family and Eiffel Tower cultures both are hierarchical. Whereas the Eiffel Tower is focused on the task, the family takes care of individuals. As its name indicates, the family culture functions like a traditional family. The leader's role is that of a powerful father figure who is responsible for the welfare of all members. Trompenaars suggests that family organizational cultures are found in Greece, Italy, Singapore, South Korea, and Japan. Finally, the Eiffel Tower is hierarchical and task

Figure 1-2
Trompenaars' Cross-Cultural Organizational Cultures

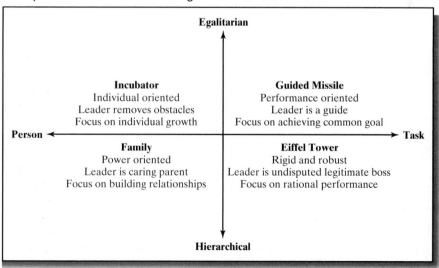

focused. Consistent with the name, many French organizations have an Eiffel Tower culture, characterized by a steep, stable, and rigid organization. The focus is on performance through order and obedience of legal and legitimate authority. The leader is the undisputed head of the organization and has full responsibility for all that occurs.

The three models of culture provide differing ways of understanding national and organizational culture. Each model is useful, but each also can be misapplied if used to stereotype national or organizational cultures. Whereas Hall and Hofstede focus primarily on national culture, Trompenaars provides a model that combines national and organizational cultural characteristics and that addresses leadership more directly. All three models are used throughout the book to provide a cross-cultural perspective on leadership.

OBSTACLES TO EFFECTIVE LEADERSHIP

In all cultures and all organizational settings, being an effective leader is challenging. Even with a clear definition of leadership and what makes a leader effective, being effective is not easy. Meanwhile, organizations pay a heavy price for bad and ineffective leadership (Bedeian and Armenakis 1998). The keys to becoming an effective leader are practice and learning from one's mistakes. Unfortunately, organizations often do not provide an environment in which leaders can practice new skills, try out new behaviors, and observe their impact. In most cases, the price to pay for making mistakes is so high that new leaders and managers opt for routine actions.

Without such practice and without failure, it is difficult for leaders to become effective. The question is, therefore, what are the obstacles to learning to be an effective leader? Aside from different levels of skills and aptitudes that might prevent a leader from being effective, several other obstacles to effective leadership can exist:

- First, organizations face considerable uncertainty that creates pressure for quick responses and solutions. The external factors demand immediate attention. In an atmosphere of crisis, no time or patience is available for learning. Ironically, the implementation of new methods of leadership, if they were allowed, would make dealing with complexity and uncertainty easier in the long run. Therefore, a vicious cycle continues that allows no time for the learning that would help current crises. The lack of learning and experimentation in turn causes the continuation of the crises, which makes it impossible to have time to learn and practice innovative behaviors.
- Second, organizations are often rigid and unforgiving. In their push for short-term and immediate performance, they do not allow any room for mistakes and experimentation. A few organizations, such as W. L. Gore and 3M, that encourage taking risks and making mistakes are the exception. The rigidity and rewards systems of many institutions discourage such endeavors.
- Third, organizations fall back on old ideas about what effective leadership is and, therefore, rely on simplistic solutions that do not fit new and complex

problems. The use of simple ideas, such as those proposed in many popular books, provides only temporary solutions.

- Finally, another factor that can pose an obstacle to effective leadership is the difficulty involved in understanding and applying the findings of academic research. In the laudable search for precision and scientific rigor, academic researchers sometimes do not clarify the application of their research.

The complex and never-ending learning process of becoming an effective leader requires experimentation and organizational support. The inaccessibility of academic research to many practitioners and the short-term orientation of the organizations in which many managers operate provide difficult obstacles to effective leadership. Except for the few individuals who are talented and learn quickly and easily, or those rare leaders who have the luxury of time, these obstacles are not easily surmounted.

Organizations that allow their leaders at all levels to make mistakes, learn, and develop new skills are training effective leaders.

LEADERSHIP AND MANAGEMENT

What is the difference between leaders and managers? Are the two basically the same or do they have sharp distinctions between them? These questions have moved to the forefront of the discussion of leadership in the past few years. Carol Hymowitz, a writer with the *Wall Street Journal*, considers herself lucky to have worked for two bosses who were "leaders more than managers" (Hymowitz 1998a, B1). She believes leaders inspire their followers to take risks. Carol Bartz, chief executive at Autodesk, suggests that managers "know how to write business plans, while leaders get companies—and people—to change" (Hymowitz 1998a, B1).

Whereas leaders have long-term and future-oriented perspectives and provide a vision for their followers that looks beyond their immediate surroundings, managers have short-term perspectives and focus on routine issues within their own immediate departments or groups.

Table 1-2 presents the major distinctions between leadership and management. Whereas leaders have long-term and future-oriented perspectives and provide a vision for their followers that looks beyond their immediate surroundings, managers have short-term perspectives and focus on routine issues within their own immediate departments or groups (Gardner 1986). Zaleznik (1990)

Table 1-2
Management and Leadership

LEADERS	MANAGERS
Focus on the future	Focus on the present
Create change	Maintain status quo and stability
Create a culture based on shared values	Implement policies and procedures
Establish an emotional link with followers	Remain aloof to maintain objectivity
Use personal power	Use position power

further suggests that leaders, but not managers, are charismatic and can create a sense of excitement and purpose in their followers. Kotter (1990) takes a historical perspective in the debate and proposes that leadership is an age-old concept, but the concept of management has developed in the past 100 years as a result of the complex organizations that were created after the industrial revolution. A manager's role is to bring order and consistency through planning, budgeting, and controlling. Leadership, on the other hand, is aimed at producing movement and change (Kotter 1990, 1996).

The debates suggest that for those who draw a distinction between leaders and managers, leaders are assigned attributes that allow them to energize their followers, whereas managers are simply the individuals who take care of the mundane and routine details. Both are necessary for organizations to function, and one cannot replace the other. By considering the issue of effectiveness, many of the arguments regarding the differences between leadership and management can be clarified. Being an effective manager involves performing many of the functions that are attributed to leaders with or without some degree of charisma. For example, are managers who motivate their followers and whose departments achieves all their goals simply effective managers, or are these managers also leaders? The distinctions drawn between leadership and management can be more related to effectiveness than to the difference between the two concepts. An effective manager of people has to motivate them and provide them with a sense of mission and purpose. Therefore, effective managers can be considered leaders (Gardner 1986; Grove 1986).

Based on the definition of leadership presented previously, any manager who guides a group toward goal accomplishment can be considered a leader. Much of the distinction between management and leadership comes from the fact that the title *leader* assumes competence. Therefore, an effective and successful manager can be considered a leader, but a less-competent manager is not a leader. Overall, the debate over the difference between the two concepts does not add much to our understanding of what constitutes good leadership or good management and how to achieve these goals. It does, however, point to the need felt by many organizations for effective, competent, and visionary leadership/management. This book does not dwell on the distinction between the two concepts and uses the terms interchangeably.

ROLES AND FUNCTIONS OF LEADERS

Although leaders in different cultures perform different functions and play different roles, researchers have identified a number of managerial roles and functions.

Managerial Roles

In order to be effective, leaders perform a number of different roles. The roles are sets of expected behavior ascribed to them by virtue of their leadership position. Along with the basic managerial functions of planning, organizing, staffing, directing, and controlling, leaders are ascribed a number of strategic and external roles, as well, which are discussed in detail in Chapter 9. Furthermore, one of the major functions of leaders is to provide their group or organization with a sense of vision and mission.

For example, department managers need to plan and organize their department's activities and assign various people to perform tasks. They also have to monitor their employees' performance and correct their actions when needed. Aside from these internal functions, managers have to negotiate with their boss and other department managers for resources and coordinate decisions and activities with them. Additionally, like managers in many organizations, department managers must participate in strategic planning and the development of their organization's mission.

Researchers have developed different taxonomies of managerial activities (Komaki 1986; Luthans and Lockwood 1984). One of the most cited is proposed by Mintzberg (1973), who adds the 10 executive roles of figurehead, leader, liaison, monitor, disseminator, spokesperson, entrepreneur, disturbance handler, resource allocator, and negotiator to an already-long list of what leaders do. Mintzberg's research further suggests that few, if any, managers perform these roles in an organized, compartmentalized, and coherent fashion. Instead, their days are characterized by a wide variety of tasks, frequent interruptions, and little time to think or to connect with their subordinates. Mintzberg's findings are an integral part of many definitions of leadership and management. The roles he defines typically are considered the major roles and functions of leaders.

Interestingly, research indicates that there are gender differences in how managers perform their roles. In 1990, Sally Helgesen published her book *The Female Advantage: Women's Way of Leadership* and questioned many myths about the universality of management behaviors. Through case studies of five female executives, Helgesen faithfully replicated the methodology used 20 years earlier by Mintzberg in his study of seven male managers. Mintzberg had found that his managers often worked at an unrelenting pace, with many interruptions and few nonwork-related activities. They felt that their identity was tied directly to their job and often reported feeling isolated, with no time to reflect, plan, and share information with others. They also reported having a complex network of colleagues outside of work and preferring face-to-face interaction to all other means of communication.

Helgesen's findings of female managers matched Mintzberg's only in the last two categories. Her female managers also had a complex network and preferred face-to-face communication. However, the other findings were surprisingly different. The women reported working at a calm, steady pace with frequent breaks. They did not consider unscheduled events to be interruptions; they instead viewed them as a normal part of their work. All of them reported having a number of nonwork-related activities. They each had multifaceted identities and, therefore, did not feel isolated. They found themselves having time to read and reflect on the big picture. Additionally, the female executives scheduled time to share information with their colleagues and subordinates.

The gender differences found between the two studies can be attributed partly to the 20-year time difference. However, Helgesen's suggestions about a female leadership style, which she calls "the web," is supported by a number of other research and anecdotal studies. Helgesen's web is defined as a circle with the manager in the center and interconnected to all other parts of the department or organization. This view differs sharply with the traditional pyramid structure common in many organizations (Tropila and Kleiner 1994).

Leaders such as Francis Hesselbein, chief executive of the Girl Scouts; Nancy Bador, executive director of Ford Motor Company; and Barbara Grogan, founder and president of Western Industrial Contractors use the web as their management style. They shun the hierarchical structures for flat webs in which they are at the center rather than at the top. This structure, and their position within it, allows them to be accessible and informed. Whereas top-down and bottom-up information in a traditional hierarchy is filtered and altered as it travels, leaders at the center of the web have direct access to all others in the organization, and their employees have access to them. As a result, the web structure prevents the managers from feeling isolated and out of touch with the needs of their subordinates and their organization. Gerry Laybourne, chairman and CEO of Oxygen Media, is the executive who built the top-rated children's television network Nickelodeon while she was at Viacom. She considers competition to be "nonfemale." When she found out that *Fortune* magazine was ranking women in business, she declared, "That's a nonfemale thing to do. Ranking is the opposite of what women are all about" (Sellers 1998, p. 80).

Many other successful female business leaders, however, do not see their leadership styles as drastically different from that of their male counterparts. Cherri Musser, chief information officer at e-GM or General Motors, recommends "You don't focus on being female—you focus on getting the job done. If you draw too much attention to your gender, you're not a member of the team" (Overholt 2001, p. 66). Darla Moore, president of investment company Rainwater, Incorporated and the first woman to have a business school named after her, argues that women's worse sin is to think, "'You should be a nice girl. You ought to fit in. You should find a female mentor.' What a colossal waste of time" (Sellers 1998, p. 92). Additionally, characteristics typically associated with the female leadership style increasingly are considered necessary regardless of gender (M. Useem 2001).

Functions of the Leader: Creation and Maintenance of an Organizational Culture

One of the major functions of leaders is the creation and development of a culture and climate for their group or organization (Nahavandi and Malekzadeh 1993a; Schein 1985). Leaders, particularly founders, leave an almost-indelible mark on the assumptions that are passed down from one generation to the next. In fact, organizations often come to mirror their founders' personalities. Consider, for example, how Vermont's gourmet ice-cream maker Ben and Jerry's reflects its cofounders', Ben Cohen and Jerry Greenfield, strong beliefs in social responsibility (Welles 1998). The company practices egalitarian management by keeping the difference between managers' and employees' salaries low, encouraging participation, and supporting a lengthy social agenda such as saving the Amazon rain forest. Similarly, Roger Abramson's furniture company discussed previously is a reflection of his frenetic pace and obsession with speed and quick results.

If the founder is control oriented and autocratic, the organization is likely to be centralized and managed in a top-down fashion. If the founder is participative and team oriented, the organization will be decentralized and open. The leaders make most, if not all, of the decisions regarding the various factors that will shape the culture (see Figure 1-3).

Leaders are role models for other organizational members. They establish and grant the status symbols that are the main artifacts of organizational culture.

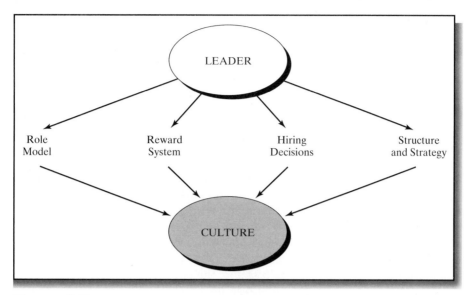

Figure 1-3
Leader's Function in Shaping Organizational Culture

Followers take their cues from the leaders on what behaviors are and are not acceptable. For example, Bob Moffat, who runs IBM's personal computer business, spends 15 and 16 hours per day at the office, coming in at 5 A.M. and rarely going home before 8 P.M. (Fishman 2001). Because IBM is facing tough competition in personal computers, Moffat knows that he, and his division, will have to work hard to stay ahead. His personal work habits and dedication set the pace for others.

One of the key behaviors that leaders need to model is the acceptance of responsibility for one's actions. With the power and status afforded to leaders comes the obligation of accepting responsibility for one's own decisions and the organization's impact on others. The willingness to accept such responsibility often is lacking in many U.S. corporations, where finger pointing takes up more energy than correcting mistakes. The leader's demeanor in this category can set the tone for others in the organization to either accept or shirk responsibility for their actions and decisions.

Other means through which the leader shapes culture are by decisions regarding the reward system (Kerr and Slocum 1987) and by controlling decision standards. In one organization, rewards (financial and nonfinancial) go to only the highest contributors to the bottom line. In another, accomplishments such as contribution to cultural diversity or the degree of social responsibility are also valued and rewarded. Additionally, leaders are in charge of selecting other leaders and managers for the organization. Those selected are likely to fit the existing leader's ideal model and, therefore, fit the culture. Other influential members of the organization provide leaders with yet another opportunity to shape the culture. Many firms, for example, have a nominating committee of the board of directors. In such committees, top managers nominate and select their successors. Therefore, they can not only control the current culture but also have a strong influence on the future of their organization. To select his successor, General Electric's (GE) Jack Welch carefully observed, interacted with, and interviewed many of the company's executives (Charan and Colvin 2001). He sought feedback from top company leaders, and after selecting Jeff Immelt, Welch carefully orchestrated the transition of power. This careful selection assured that the new leader, although bringing about some new ideas, fit the existing culture of the organization (J. Useem 2001).

The power of the leader to make decisions for the organization regarding structure and strategy is another effective means of shaping culture. By determining the hierarchy, span of control, reporting relationship, and degree of formalization and specialization, the leader molds culture. A highly decentralized and organic structure is likely to be the result of an open and participative culture, whereas a highly centralized structure will go hand in hand with a mechanistic/bureaucratic culture. The structure of an organization limits or encourages interaction, and by doing so affects, as well as is affected by, the assumptions shared by members of the organization. Similarly, the strategy selected by the leader or the top-management team will be determined by, as well as help shape, the culture of the organization. Thus, a leader who adopts a proactive growth strategy that requires innovation and risk taking will have to create a different culture than a leader who selects a strategy of retrenchment.

WHAT DOES THIS MEAN FOR ME?
Establishing a Culture

Leaders play a key role in establishing the culture of their department or organization. The following are some things to keep in mind in building the culture:

- In your own mind, clearly define the key elements of the culture that you want to establish. For example, do you value trust and cooperation or competition? Do you seek high performance above all else? Do you want a formal environment? These elements are likely to be based on your own value system and priorities.

- Share your vision with your followers and craft a new one that includes their wishes and aspirations. The resulting "ideal culture" will be owned by all of the department members.

- Keep an eye on the reward system; it can be telling and powerful. In other words, is your reward system encouraging the behaviors that you want and creating the culture that you value?

- Pay attention to big and little things. The formal reward system, as well as the office setting and who has lunch with whom, all contribute to the culture.

- Finally, be aware that you are being watched; your actions always speak louder than your words. Therefore, you must be mindful of the messages that you send, sometimes unconsciously, through your actions and decisions.

DOES LEADERSHIP MAKE A DIFFERENCE?

Open any newspaper or business periodical and you probably will find the profile of a political, community, or business leader or a lengthy article about how an organization is likely to be greatly affected by its new leadership. Company stocks fluctuate as a result of changes in leadership. For example, while the board of directors of American Express was debating the fate of CEO Robinson (he was replaced), the company's stock price plummeted a steep 13 percent in 4 days. Similarly, a new leader can affect a firm's credit rating by affecting the confidence the financial community has in this person. As Xerox weathered considerable financial and leadership problems in 2000 and 2001, the selection of Anne Mulcahy as CEO, a company veteran, helped ease stakeholders' concerns (Bianco and Moore 2001; Hammond 2001). A city or nation might feel a sense of revival and optimism or considerable concern when a new leader is elected. In 1998, Venezuelans elected a former paratrooper and populist leader of a failed coup as president. Despite serious concerns from the business and financial communities, Hugo Chavez energized millions of voters with a party that won 35 percent of congress a year prior to the presidential elections. However, in 2001, Chavez's popularity dropped from a high of 80 percent to 30 percent because of concerns over his authoritarian style and his use of the military (Politics in Venezuela 2001; Venezuela 2002). By and large, we tend to believe that the leadership is an important matter.

Although you might take this assertion for granted, there is considerable debate among leadership scholars concerning whether leadership actually impacts organizations. The following are the key questions:

- To what extent, if at all, does the leadership of an organization affect various organizational elements and organizational performance?
- Does leadership have more impact in certain situations than in others?

Arguments Against the Impact of Leadership

Much of the research about the lack of impact of leadership has roots in the field of sociology. Such an approach asserts that organizations are driven by powerful factors other than their management (Brown 1982; Cyert and March 1963; Hannan and Freeman 1977; Meindl and Ehrlick 1987; Salancik and Pfeffer 1977a). Environmental, social, industrial, and economic conditions, just to name a few factors, are assumed to determine organizational direction and performance to a much higher degree than does leadership. Similarly, the same external factors along with organizational elements such as structure and strategy are assumed to limit the leader's decision-making options, further reducing the leader's discretion. The support for this approach comes primarily from two areas:

- First, a group of researchers studied the impact of change of leadership succession in organizations. Results from studies in the private and public sectors support the notion that the change of leadership does not affect organizational performance strongly. For example, Salancik and Pfeffer (1977a), in a study of the performance of mayors, found that leadership accounted for only 7 percent to 15 percent of changes in city budgets. Similarly, Lieberson and O'Connor (1972) found that, whereas leadership has minimal effects on the performance of large corporations (accounting for only 7 percent to 14 percent of the performance), company size and economic factors have considerable links to firm performance.

- Second, support for the "lack-of-importance" hypothesis is found in an area of research that focuses on the extent of managerial discretion (Finkelstein and Hambrick 1990, 1996; Hambrick and Finkelstein 1987). Although the goal of the research is not to show the insignificance of leadership, some of the results show that CEOs have limited discretion in their choices and activities. The lack of managerial discretion in decision making further reinforces the notion that external environmental elements and internal macro-organizational elements have more impact than does leadership.

Overall, the early evidence from the leadership succession research together with some of the managerial discretion findings can be used to support several suggestions. First, leaders have little impact on organizations. Second, even when leaders do make decisions that affect organizations, their decisions are determined by environmental and organizational factors and are, therefore, not a reflection of the leader's preferences or style. Additionally, some researchers consider leadership to be a simple symbol or myth rather than an objective factor in organizations (Meindl and Ehrlick 1987). Research findings in support of such a view indicate that when asked who is responsible for a group or an organization's success and performance, people are more likely to attribute the success to the leader than to other factors. This occurs even when available data indicate that such attribution to the leader alone is not warranted. Based on these findings, researchers conclude that the effect of leaders, although interesting, is not objective and actual but rather reflects a romantic notion of the role and impact of leaders. Table 1-3 summarizes the arguments regarding the impact of leadership.

Table 1-3
Arguments Over the Impact of Leadership

LEADERSHIP IS INSIGNIFICANT	LEADERSHIP HAS AN IMPACT
• Outside environmental factors affect organizations more than leadership.	• Leadership is one of the many important factors.
• Internal structure and strategy determine the course an organization takes.	• Leadership is key in providing vision and direction.
• Leadership accounts for only 7% to 15% of financial performance.	• Leadership can account for up to 44% of a firm's profitability.
• Leaders have little discretion to make an impact.	• Leadership is critical in orchestrating change.
• Leadership is a romantic myth rather than a real organizational factor.	• Leadership's impact is moderated by situational factors.

Arguments for the Impact of Leadership

Reconsideration of the data and reinterpretation of the findings point to the serious flaws in the research concerning the lack of impact of leadership, reasserting the importance of leadership in organizational performance. (See Table 1-3 for a summary.) For example, in reevaluating Lieberson and O'Connor's 1972 study, Weiner and Mahoney (1981) find that a change in leadership accounts for 44 percent of the profitability of the firms studied. Other researchers (Day and Lord 1988; Thomas 1988) indicate that the early results were not as strong as originally believed. Some studies of school systems show that the principal is the most important factor in the climate of a school and the success of students (Allen 1981). Still other studies find that the leadership is critical to orchestrating and organizing all the complex elements necessary to change an organization (Burke, Richley, and DeAngelis 1985).

Reconciling the Differences

The debates about the impact of leadership make valuable contributions to our understanding of leadership. First, it is important to recognize that leadership is one of many factors that influence the performance of a group or an organization. Second, the leader's contribution, although not always tangible, is often significant in providing a vision and direction for followers and in integrating their activities. Third, the key is to identify situations where the leader does have limited power and discretion over the group and the organization. (These situations are discussed at length in Chapter 6, which discusses substitutes for leadership, and in Chapter 9, which discusses the role of upper-echelon leaders.) Finally, the potential lack of impact of leaders in some situations further emphasizes the importance of followers in the success of leadership and the need to understand organizations as broad systems. Overall, after years of debate, the popular view that leaders impact organizations has received research support, and the focus has shifted from whether a leader has impact to understanding a leader's impact and its consequences.

SUMMARY AND CONCLUSION

A leader is any person who influences individuals and groups within an organization, helps them in the establishment of goals, and guides them toward achievement of those goals, thereby allowing them to be effective. In order to be effective, leaders must help the organization maintain internal health and external adaptability. Despite the apparent simplicity of the definitions of leadership and effectiveness, both are difficult concepts to implement. First, culture can affect whom we consider to be an effective leader. Second, organizations rarely provide their leaders with the opportunity to experiment and improve.

Many have proposed separate definitions for leadership and management. However, the activities performed by leaders are similar to those typically considered the domain of effective managers. Although some have seen the roles of leaders and managers as being different, effective and competent managers are often also leaders within their groups and organizations. In addition to performing the traditional managerial roles and duties, leaders also have a special role in the creation of a culture for their organizations. They can affect culture by making direct decisions regarding reward systems and hiring of other managers and employees, and also by being role models for others in the organization. Notwithstanding the many roles that leaders play in an organization, in some situations they have only limited impact on group and organizational performance. Therefore, it is essential to consider leadership in its proper context and to take into account the numerous factors that can impact group and organizational performance.

Juggling Cultures

Culture, gender, and leadership are closely related. In most cultures, even Western cultures, leadership is associated with males. This is even more the case in many Arab Muslim countries where women play a limited role in public and business life.

As a leader of an organization, you face the choice of selecting the leader of a negotiation team to draft a new deal with a potential Saudi Arabian client. By far your best, most experienced, and most skilled negotiator is one of your female executives. She has, for many years, successfully negotiated deals within the United States and in several Western countries. Her second in command is a promising but relatively young male executive who still needs to develop his skills and experience.

1. Who do you send to Saudi Arabia as head of your team?
2. What cultural factors do you need to consider?
3. What are the implications of your decision for your business and the message you send as a leader?

REVIEW AND DISCUSSION QUESTIONS

1. What are the essential components of the definition of leadership?
2. What are the essential components of the definitions of leadership effectiveness?
3. Provide one example each of an effective leader and a successful leader. Consider how they differ and what you can learn from each.
4. What are the three models of culture, and how do they impact leadership?
5. How would the definitions of leaders and effectiveness differ based on the different cultural values presented by Hofstede and Trompenaars?
6. What are the obstacles to effective leadership? How have the nature and occurrence of such obstacles changed in recent years? Why?
7. Based on your knowledge of the field of management and your personal definition of leadership, how are management and leadership similar or different? How can the differences be reconciled? How do these differences add to our understanding of leadership?
8. What are the ways in which leaders influence the creation of culture in their organizations? Are any additional methods used by top managers? Provide examples.
9. What are the basic assumptions guiding the "insignificant leadership" concept? What is your position on this issue? Document your arguments.

SEARCHING THE WEB

Mintzberg's Research:
sol.brunel.ac.uk/~jarvis/bola/mintzberg/mintzberg1.html
sol.brunel.ac.uk/~jarvis/bola/mintzberg/mintzberg2.html
oak.cats.ohiou.edu/~chappell/Roles.html

Ways Women Lead:
www.emergingleader.com/article9.shtml

Self-Assessment:
www.leaderx.com/tests/testyourlead.html
www.nsba.org/sbot/toolkit/P&LDev.html

Saudi Arabia:
www.executiveplanet.com/community/default.asp?section=Saudi_Arabia

EXERCISE 1-1: WHAT IS LEADERSHIP?

This exercise is designed to help you develop a personal definition of leadership and clarify your assumptions and expectations about leadership and effectiveness.

1. Describe Your Ideal Leader
Individually list five desirable and five undesirable characteristics of your ideal leader.

Desirable	Undesirable
1.	1.
2.	2.
3.	3.
4.	4.
5.	5.

2. Develop Group Definition
In groups of four to five, discuss your list and your reasons and draw up a common definition.
Common definition:

3. Present and Defend Definition
Each group will make a 5-minute presentation of its definition.

4. Common Themes
Discuss various definitions:
A. What are the common themes?

B. Which views of leadership are presented?

C. What are the assumptions about the role of the leader?

EXERCISE 1-2: IMAGES OF LEADERSHIP

One way you can clarify your assumptions about leadership is to use images to describe your ideal leader. Through the use of such images, you can understand your views of the role of leaders in organizations and your expectations and image of leadership. These images are your personal theories of leadership. For example, viewing leaders as facilitators presents a different image from viewing them as parents.

1. Select Your Image

Select the image of your ideal leader. List the characteristics of that image.

2. Share and Clarify

In groups of three or four, share your leadership image and discuss its implications for your own leadership style.

3. Class Discussion

Groups will share two of their individual members' images of leadership.

Discuss implications of various images for:

A. A person's leadership style.

B. Impact on organizational culture and structure.

C. Compatibility with current or past leaders.

D. Potential shortcomings of each image.

The following exercise is a cross-cultural role play designed to allow you to experience the challenges and opportunities of interacting with people from different cultures. The setting is the fictional country of Nari. You will be asked to play the role of either an American or a Narian. Read the exercise carefully; your instructor will provide you with further information and instructions.

Background

Nari is a Middle-Eastern country with an old history and a rich cultural heritage. Through judicious excavation of a number of minerals, the country has obtained considerable wealth, and the stable political and social climate has attracted many foreign investors. As a result, Nari has launched a careful and well-planned development campaign in the past 20 years, which has allowed the country's economy to become the strongest in the region. The per-capita income is the highest in the region, and the literacy rate is more than 80 percent for the population under age 30 (which comprises 53 percent of the total population).

The political system is an authoritarian monarchy. Although there is an elected parliament, its powers are limited to being a consultative body for the king. This political system has been in place for more than 1,000 years. As compared to many of its unstable neighbors, Nari has enjoyed a calm political climate. The current dynasty has been in place for more than 400 years. However, the Western press has been highly critical of the lack of democracy and the authoritarian nature of the government. The king has unceremoniously dismissed the charges as cultural colonialism and has emphasized the need to preserve the Narian culture while welcoming the West and the East's help in economic development.

The culture is warm and generally welcoming of outsiders, although criticism of the culture is poorly accepted and not open for discussion. The extended family remains the core of society, with the father being the unquestioned head. Many younger Narians seek higher education in other parts of the world; however, almost all return eagerly to their country. Although, some rumblings are heard about opening up the political systems and allowing for more democratic participation, the authority of the family, of the community, and of the monarch are rarely, if ever, questioned.

Narian leaders are assigned total and absolute power. Although not viewed as derived from divine rights, leaders are assumed to be infallible. Narian leaders are confident in their complete knowledge of all that they come to face. They do not ask questions and do not seek advice, even from equals. Such potential indication of lack of knowledge or expertise would be seen as incompetence. The Narian leader is expected to take care of loyal followers under any circumstances. Just as followers owe leaders unquestioning obedience, leaders owe followers total devotion. Leaders are fully responsible for all that happens to their followers, in all aspects of their life. Leaders are expected to help and guide followers and come to their rescue when needed. Their primary duty is to take care of their followers.

In return, Narian followers are expected to be loyal, obedient, dutiful, and subservient. They accept their leaders' orders willingly and wholeheartedly, as all Narians are taught from the youngest age that leaders are infallible and that the proper functioning of the social order hinges upon obedience, and loyalty to leaders and elders, and upon fulfilling their responsibility as followers. Dissent and conflict are rarely expressed in the open. When mistakes are made, regardless of where the fault lies, all individuals work on correcting it without assigning blame. If the leader has made a mistake, an event that rarely if ever is brought out in the open, one follower openly accepts the blame to protect the leader's reputation and the social harmony. The person accepting that responsibility is eventually rewarded for the demonstration of loyalty.

The role of women in Narian society has been puzzling to Western observers. For more than 30 years, women have had practically equal rights with men. They can vote, conduct any kind of business transactions, take advantage of educational opportunities, file for divorce, obtain custody of their children, work in any organization. . . . The literacy rate for women is equal to that of men, and although fewer of them have pursued higher education, it appears that most women who are interested in working outside the home have found easy employment in the booming Narian economy. However, the society remains highly patriarchal in its traditions.

Role Play Situation

A U.S. engineering and construction company has won its first major governmental contract for construction of two bridges in Nari. The general terms have been agreed to. The company is working closely with several U.S.-educated Narian engineers who work for the Narian ministry of Urban Development (UD) to draft precise plans and timetables. The minister of UD, Mr. Dafti, is a well-respected civil engineer, educated in Austria in the 1950s. In addition to Narian, he speaks fluent German, English, and French. He has been instrumental in the development of his country. Although a consummate politician and negotiator, and an expert on his country's resources and economic situation, he has not practiced his engineering skills for many years.

Mr. Dafti has decided on the general location and structure of the two bridges to be built. One of the locations and designs has serious flaws. His more junior Narian associates appear to be aware of the potential problems but have not clearly voiced their concerns to the U.S. contractors, who find the design requirements unworkable.

The role play is a meeting with Mr. Dafti, his Narian associates, and representatives of the U.S. engineering firm. The U.S. head engineer requested the meeting, and the request was granted quickly. The U.S. team is eager to start the project. The Nairans also are ready to engage in the new business venture.

Please wait for further instructions.

CASE

Leadership in Action
Alessi Embraces Failure

In 1921, Giovanni Alessi, a skilled lathe turner, established his company in a village on the foothills of the Alps in Novara, Italy. Because of Alessi's skills and creativity, it wasn't long before the household objects the company manufactured from fine metals, such as the nickel-coated brass flask holder and cheese tray, became collectibles all over the world. His son Carlo trained as an industrial designer and moved the company to the forefront of design, not only by putting his own skills to work, but by hiring famous freelance designers who contributed to Alessi's fame for unusual yet practical objects (www.alessi.com/history).

When Alberto Alessi took over his family's business in 1970, he made the company the industry leader in innovation and design. Alessi products, designed by some 500 cutting-edge designers all over the world, are synonymous with style and creativity. They accomplish their goal of perfectly blending form and function. In describing what his company does, Alberto Alessi says:

> Alessi is not a mass-production company. It's a research lab for the applied arts. We are not manufacturers; we are mediators between the expression of creativity and the real things that touch people's hearts. (Kirschenbaum 2001, p. 38)

Objects such as Strack's lemon squeezer, Mendini's corkscrew, and Graves's bird kettle have for many years drawn praise from critics and consumers alike (Alessi SPA 2002). Most recently, Alessi designer Michael Graves's cooperation with the U.S. retailer Target has made the company a household name in the United States.

Alessi's unusual 2,000 objects go hand in hand with the company CEO's belief in the importance of failure. To Alberto Alessi, failure is the source of success. He values it so much that he prominently displays his company's biggest flops in a museum and has published a book about the prototypes that never made it (Kirschenbaum 2001). The failures remind Mr. Alessi and his designers that they are still stretching the limits. He states: "At Alessi, we work as close as we can to the borderline and accept the risk of falling into the other area" (Kirschenbaum 2001, p. 36). Those who try and fail are considered courageous rather than stupid, and the company CEO believes that his customers enjoy taking risks along with him because they know Alessi is sincere in its attempts at creativity and experimentation.

By celebrating failure, Alessi encourages its designers to experiment and focus on pure design, a feature that makes the company unique. The many best-sellers contribute to the $100 million sales and allow company designers to continue to experiment while learning from their mistakes. ■

QUESTIONS

1. How does Alessi define effective leadership? Compare this definition to a traditional view of leadership effectiveness.
2. What impact does culture have on the leadership at Alessi?
3. How successfully could you implement Alessi's leadership in other organizations?

Sources: This case is based on information in: Alessi SPA: The leading company in design. 2002. www.alessi kitchenware.com/alessi2.htm, accessed January 24, 2002; Donaldson-Briggs, A. L. 2002. Embracing the "F" word. www.managementfirst.com/articles/failure.htm, accessed January 24, 2002; www.alessi.com/history, accessed January 24, 2002; Kirschenbaum, J. 2001. Failure is glorious. *Fast Company*, October, 35–38.

Chapter 2

Leadership: Past, Present, and Future

> *Whatever you are, be a good one.*
>
> —ABRAHAM LINCOLN

After studying this chapter, you will be able to:

1. Identify the three major eras in the modern study of leadership.
2. Explain the methods, results, shortcomings, and contributions of the trait and behavior approaches to leadership and identify their impact on current approaches.
3. Present the elements of current contingency approaches to leadership.
4. Discuss the revival of research about individual characteristics for understanding leadership.
5. List the changes in organizations and the new expectations and views of leaders.

The roots of the modern study of leadership can be traced to the western industrial revolution that took place at the end of the nineteenth century. Although scholars throughout history have focused on leadership, the modern approach to leadership has brought scientific rigor to the search for answers. Social and political sciences and management scholars have tried, sometimes more successfully than at other times, to measure leadership through a variety of means. This chapter reviews the history of modern leadership theory and research, and outlines the current popular trends in the field. It further discusses the changes in organizations and their impact on leadership.

A HISTORY OF MODERN LEADERSHIP THEORY

During the industrial revolution, the study of leadership, much like research in other aspects of organizations, became more rigorous. Instead of relying on intuition and a description of common practices, researchers used scientific methods to understand and predict leadership effectiveness by identifying and measuring leadership characteristics. The modern scientific approach to leadership can be divided into three general eras or approaches: the trait era, the behavior era, and the contingency era. Each era has made distinct contributions to our understanding of leadership, and each continues to influence our thinking about the process.

The Trait Era: Late 1800s to Mid-1940s

The belief that leaders are born rather than made dominated much of the late nineteenth century and the early part of the twentieth century. Thomas Carlyle's book *Heroes and Hero Worship* ([1841] 1907), William James's writings about the great men of history (1880), and Galton's (1869) study of the role of heredity were part of an era that can be characterized by a strong belief that innate qualities shape human personality and behavior. Consequently, it was commonly believed that leaders, by virtue of their birth, have special qualities that allow them to lead others. These special characteristics were presumed to push them toward leadership regardless of the context. The historical context and social structures of the period further reinforced such beliefs by providing limited opportunities for common people to become social, political, and industrial leaders. The belief in the power of personality and other innate characteristics strongly influenced leadership researchers and sent them on a massive hunt for leadership traits.

Method

The advent of personality and individual characteristics testing such as IQ in the early twentieth century provided leadership researchers with the tools they needed to identify important leadership characteristics and traits. The major assumption guiding hundreds of studies about leadership traits was that if certain traits distinguish between leaders and followers, then existing political, industrial, and religious leaders should possess them (for a thorough review of the literature, see Bass 1990a). If researchers were then to compare leaders and followers, the differences would become evident. Based on this assumption, researchers identified and observed existing leaders and followers, and collected detailed demographic and personality information about them. They measured hundreds of characteristics, including variables such as age, physical traits, intelligence, motivation, initiative, and self-confidence.

Results

After more than 40 years of study, there is very little evidence to justify the assertion that leaders are born. The results of a large number of studies do not support the suggestion that leadership is a combination of traits.

After more than 40 years of study, there is little evidence to justify the assertion that leaders are born and that leadership can be explained through either one or a collection of traits. Some traits do emerge as important. For instance, much evidence indicates that, on the average, leaders are more sociable, more aggressive, and more lively than other group members. In addition, leaders generally seem to be original, popular, and have a sense of humor. However, which of the traits are most relevant seems to depend on the requirements of the situation. In other words, being social, aggressive, lively, original, and popular or having any other combination of traits does not guarantee that a person will become a leader, let alone an effective one.

As a result of weak and inconsistent findings, the commonly shared belief among many researchers in the late 1930s and early 1940s was that although traits play a role in determining leadership ability and effectiveness, it is minimal, and leadership should be viewed as a group phenomenon that cannot be studied outside a given situation (Ackerson 1942; Bird 1940; Jenkins 1947; Newstetter, Feldstein, and Newcomb 1938; Stogdill 1948). More recent studies in the 1960s and 1970s reinforced these findings by showing that although factors such as intelligence (Bray and Grant 1966) or assertiveness (Rychlak 1963) have some relationship to leadership effectiveness, they alone cannot account for much of a leader's effectiveness.

In his 1990 review, Bass suggests that the findings of the early research of the individual factors related to leadership can be classified into six categories (see Table 2-1). The variables in the six categories cover a broad range of personality traits and individual characteristics. However, recent review again indicates that no single trait or combination of traits was found to have a consistently strong correlation to leadership ability or effectiveness.

The early findings regarding leadership traits clearly show that leadership is much more than a combination of traits. A simple analysis of traits cannot explain or predict leadership effectiveness. Although the trait era's inconsistent findings led researchers to look for other ways of predicting and understanding who will be an effective leader, the inclusion of traits as one of the elements in the leadership equation is well accepted. More recent views of the role of traits and other individual characteristics such as skills have refined our understanding of the role of individual characteristics in leadership (for an example and review, see Mumford, Zaccaro, Harding et al. 2000); these are discussed later in this chapter. The leader's personality, by limiting the leader's behavioral range or by making it more or less difficult to learn certain behaviors or undertake some actions, plays a key role in his or her effectiveness. However, the leader's personality is by no means the only or even the dominant factor in effective leadership.

Behavior Era: Mid–1940s to Early 1970s

Because the trait approach did not yield expected results, and as the need for identification and training of leaders came to the forefront with the advent of World War II, researchers turned to behaviors, rather than traits, as the source of leader effectiveness. The move to observable behaviors was triggered in part by the dominance of behaviorist theories during this period, particularly in the United States and Great

Table 2-1

Six General Categories of Individual Leadership Characteristics

CATEGORY	SINGLE TRAITS OR CHARACTERISTICS
Capacity	Intelligence
	Alertness
	Verbal facility
	Originality
	Judgment
Achievement	Scholarship
	Knowledge
	Athletic accomplishment
Responsibility	Dependability
	Initiative
	Persistence
	Self-confidence
Participation	Activity
	Sociability
	Cooperation
Status	Socioeconomic position
	Popularity
Situation	Mental level
	Interest in followers
	Objectives

Source: Extracted from Bass (1990a).

Britain. Instead of identifying who would be an effective leader, the behavior approach emphasizes what an effective leader does. Focusing on behaviors provides several advantages over a trait approach:

- First, behaviors can be observed more objectively than traits.
- Second, behaviors can be measured more precisely and more accurately than traits.
- Third, as opposed to traits, which are either innate or develop early in life, behaviors can be taught.

These three factors provided a clear benefit to the military and various other organizations that had a practical interest in leadership. Instead of identifying leaders who had particular personality traits, they could focus on training people to perform effective leadership behaviors.

Early Work on Leader Behavior

The early work of Lewin and his associates (Lewin and Lippit 1938; Lewin, Lippit, and White 1939) concerning democratic, autocratic, and laissez faire leadership laid the foundation for the behavior approach to leadership. Democratic leaders were defined as those who consult their followers and allow them to participate in decision making, autocratic leaders as those who make decisions alone, and laissez faire leaders as those who provide no direction and do not become involved with their followers. Although the three types of leadership style were clearly defined, the research failed to establish which style would be most effective or which situational factors would lead to the use of one or another style. Furthermore, each of the styles had different effects on subordinates. For example, laissez faire leadership, which involved providing information but little guidance or evaluation, led to frustrated and disorganized groups that, in turn, produced low-quality work. On the other hand, autocratic leadership caused followers to become submissive, whereas groups led by democratic leaders were relaxed and became cohesive.

Establishing the Two Primary Leadership Behaviors

Armed with the results of Lewin's work and other studies, different groups of researchers set out to identify leader behaviors (e.g., Hemphill and Coons 1957). Among the best-known behavioral approaches to leadership are the Ohio State Leadership Studies. A number of researchers developed a list of almost 2,000 leadership behaviors (Hemphill and Coons 1957). After subsequent analyses (Fleishman 1953; Halpin and Winer 1957), the list was reduced and yielded several central leadership behaviors. Among them, task- and relationship-related behaviors were established as primary leadership behaviors. The Ohio State studies led to the development of the Leader Behavior Description Questionnaire (LBDQ), which continues to be used today. (See Table 2-2 for some sample LBDQ questions.)

The questionnaire focuses mostly on the behaviors of initiation of structure (task) and consideration (relationship). Whereas the initiation-of-structure factor includes a variety of task-related behaviors, such as setting deadlines and clarifying roles, the consideration factor encompasses behaviors that are generally people oriented, and deal with helping and looking out for employees. Researchers suggest that the two sets of behaviors are two different dimensions rather than two ends of the same continuum. As such, a leader can perform both sets of behaviors to varying degrees.

Although the Ohio State research, along with other studies (e.g., Bowers and Seashore 1966), identified a number of leader behaviors, the links between those behaviors and leadership effectiveness were not clearly established. After many years of research, it is still not obvious which behaviors are most effective. It is con-

Table 2-2
Sample LBDQ Questions

Consideration	Initiation of Structure
Treats all work unit members as his or her equal	Lets work unit members know what is expected of them
Is friendly and approachable	Schedules the work to be done
Does little things to make work pleasant	Encourages the use of uniform procedures
Puts suggestions made by the work unit into operations	Assigns work unit members to particular tasks
Looks out for personal welfare of work unit members	Makes his or her attitudes clear to the work unit

sistently agreed though, that considerate, supportive, people-oriented behaviors are associated with follower satisfaction, loyalty, and trust (see, for example, Seltzer and Numerof 1988). Evidence also shows that, although somewhat weak, effective leadership requires both consideration and structuring behaviors (Fleishman and Harris 1962; House and Filley 1971). However, these findings have not received overwhelming support. Furthermore, the leadership dimensions of initiation of structure and consideration do not describe leader behavior adequately for cultures other than the United States that might be less individualistic and have different ideals of leadership (Ayman and Chemers 1983; Chemers 1969; Misumi and Peterson 1985).

Overall, the behavior approach has increased our understanding of leadership by successfully identifying several categories of behaviors. Particularly, task and relationship-oriented behaviors are well established as the primary leadership behaviors (for a recent study, see Casimir 2001). Considering leadership to be an acquired behavior rather than a personality trait has focused attention on leadership training. Another major contribution of the behavior era is the methodology used to measure leader behavior. After close to 30 years, the LBDQ remains a well-accepted and commonly used tool in leadership research.

Similar to the trait approach, the behavior approach to leadership, by concentrating only on behaviors and disregarding powerful situational elements, provides a simplistic view of a highly complex process and, therefore, fails to provide a thorough understanding of the leadership phenomenon.

The Contingency Era: Early 1960s to Present

Even before the behavior approach's lack of success in explaining and predicting leadership effectiveness became evident, a number of researchers were calling for a more comprehensive approach to understanding leadership (Stogdill 1948). Specifically, researchers recommended that situational factors such as the task and type of work group be taken into consideration. However, it was not until the 1960s that this recommendation was applied. In the 1960s, spearheaded by Fred Fiedler, whose Contingency Model of leadership is discussed in Chapter 5, leadership research moved from simplistic models based solely on the leader to more complex models that take a contingency point of view. Other models such as the Path-Goal Theory and the Normative Decision Model, also presented in Chapter 5, soon followed. Such views still dominate current leadership research. The primary assumption of the contingency view is that the personality, style, or behavior of effective leaders depends on the requirements of the situation in which the leaders find themselves.

Basic Assumptions
The majority of the theories presented in this book fall within the contingency framework. Therefore, this framework is discussed at length throughout a number of chapters. The contingency approach includes the following assumptions:

- There is no one best way to lead. Different leadership traits, styles, or behaviors can be effective.
- The situation and the various relevant contextual factors will determine which style or behavior is most effective.

- People can learn to become good leaders. Few of us will become a Joan of Arc, Mahatma Gandhi, or Martin Luther King, Jr., but we can improve and become better leaders in many areas.
- Leadership makes a difference in the effectiveness of groups and organizations. A number of factors affect the course an organization takes and the decisions that are made. Many such factors are as important, if not more important, than a leader. However, the leader of an organization can have a positive or negative impact on the process or outcome in the organization.
- Personal and situational characteristics affect leadership effectiveness. Neither the leader's traits nor the demands of the situation in and of themselves determine leadership effectiveness. Therefore, we need to understand the leader as well as the leadership situation.

Continued Debates

Although many researchers agree about the assumptions of the contingency approach to leadership, the field remains highly divided. Even among contingency theorists, there is little agreement over what constitutes effectiveness, whether leadership style is a trait or a learned behavior, or which situational characteristics are relevant and should be considered when evaluating leadership. Heated debates have occurred over the methodology used by various researchers and the way in which results are interpreted. These debates will be presented when each theory is discussed. Unfortunately such debates often shake the confidence of the application-minded students of leadership who would like to use theoretical models and research findings to improve their leadership skills or select training programs for their organizations. However, aside from and despite all the disagreements about leadership, the existing research and theory have much to offer practitioners.

WHAT DOES THIS MEAN FOR ME?
How to Apply Contingency Principles to Improve Leadership Effectiveness

The current research and practice of leadership is strongly dominated by principles of contingency. Below are some ways you can put these principles to work for you:

- Know yourself: Develop an awareness of your own strengths and weakness, as well your personality traits and styles.

- Understand the key task and relationship behaviors associated with leading groups.

- Identify situations where you have been most and least effective as a leader. Trace common themes among them.

- Acquire tools to analyze the leadership situations you face in terms of the type of followers, the task or problem at hand, organizational support, and so forth.

- Actively seek out training opportunities to learn more about leadership and develop your experience base.

Keep in mind that to be an effective leader, you must consider your own characteristics and the elements of the situation. One or both can be changed to make you more effective.

THE PRESENT: CURRENT TRENDS IN LEADERSHIP PRACTICE AND RESEARCH

Because of the fast pace of cultural, social, and organizational change and perhaps because of the numerous academic debates over methodology and interpretation, academic researchers and practitioners have shown a renewed interest in the topic of leadership. The popular press is now replete with a flurry of practitioner-minded leadership books. The trend started in the 1980s with Peters and Waterman's book *In Search of Excellence* and continues to date. Other such books include *Transforming Leadership (Anderson 1998), Encouraging the Heart: A Leader's Guide to Rewarding and Recognizing Others* (Kouzes and Posner 1999), *Leadership and Spirit: Breathing New Vitality and Energy into Individuals and Organizations* (Moxley 2000), and *The Deep Blue Sea: Rethinking the Source of Leadership* (Drath 2001). Business magazines regularly feature interviews with and articles about business leaders and their successes and failures. The renewed focus on leadership has revived a long-standing interest in leader traits and other personal characteristics.

Leader Characteristics and Traits Revisited

Although strong evidence of a consistent relationship between specific traits and leadership effectiveness is lacking, interest in understanding the personal characteristics of leaders has not subsided. In 1974, a thorough review of traits (Stogdill 1974) together with other findings reestablished the validity of the trait approach, reviving research on the topic. In general, activity level and stamina, socioeconomic class, education, and intelligence, along with a variety of other traits, appear to characterize leaders, and especially effective leaders. However, the role of situational characteristics also is recognized as giving way to the situational and contingency approaches to leadership.

A Fresh Look at Leaders' Individual Characteristics

Kirkpatrick and Locke (1991) have proposed a modern approach to understanding the role of traits in leadership. They propose that although several key traits alone are not enough to make a leader, they are a precondition for effective leadership. They list a number of traits that facilitate a leader's acquisition of needed leadership skills. The key traits are:

- Drive, which includes motivation and energy.
- Desire and motivation to lead.
- Honesty and integrity.
- Self-confidence.
- Intelligence.
- Knowledge of the business.

Some of the traits, namely intelligence and drive, cannot be acquired through training. Others, such as knowledge of the industry and self-confidence, can be acquired with time and appropriate experience. The trait of honesty is a simple choice. Studies of managers and leaders in other cultures have found similar traits present in successful leaders. For example, successful Russian business leaders are characterized by "hard-driving ambition, boundless energy, and keen ability" (Puffer 1994, p. 41). Chinese business leaders value hard work and have an impeccable reputation for integrity.

Consider how many business executives have a reputation for having the traits that Kirkpatrick and Locke propose. Steve Jobs of Apple and Fumio Mitarai of Canon are famous for their drive, energy, intelligence, and self-confidence, as are other business leaders, such as Heidi Miller, chief financial officer of Citigroup, the biggest financial company in the world, and Herb Kelleher, the famous founder of Southwest Airlines. Goran Lindahl, the chief executive of the Swiss-Swedish engineering group ABB, is driven almost to the point of obsession to keep his company's stock prices high (Tomlinson 2000). Other leaders develop knowledge of their business. Emilio Azcarraga Jean, chair of Grupo Televisa SA, the largest Spanish-language media company in the world, had to learn all the details of the family business when he took over for his ailing father (Friedland and Millman 1998). Through his intense drive and motivation, he refocused his organization's culture from loyalty to performance.

Interestingly, integrity, or lack of it, often is cited as a key factor in leadership. Many anecdotes about bad leadership contain elements of lack of trust and dishonesty on the part of the leaders (Carvell 1998). Employees complain bitterly about leaders who abuse their trust, lie to them, or mislead them. For example, former employees of the bankrupt U.S. energy trader Enron complain bitterly about past CEO Ken Lay's betrayal of their trust. Similarly, lack of integrity often is cited as one of the causes of Xerox's financial and leadership crisis (Bianco and Moore 2001; Hammonds 2001).

Just as some traits are necessary for leadership, they can be detrimental when carried to an extreme (Kirkpatrick and Locke 1991). A leader with too much drive might refuse to delegate tasks, and a desire for too much power can work against a leader's effectiveness (Bennis and Nanus 1985). For example, despite continued personal success and the success of Disney, Michael Eisner, the company's president, has not been able to hold on to several talented executives. Eisner's need for control and inability to delegate, which stems in part from his drive and motivation to lead, have been blamed for the high turnover on top.

The current approach to understanding the role of leadership traits suggests that, as many of us believe, leaders are indeed gifted in at least some areas. However, those gifts and talents alone are not enough. Experience, correct choices, and exposure to the right situations are key to allowing those gifts to bloom.

Considering the Demographic Characteristics of Leaders

Another approach to understanding the personal characteristics of leaders is to look at their demographic characteristics. One of the few comprehensive surveys of close to 800 U.S. executives conducted by Kurtz, Boone, and Fleenor in 1989 yielded interesting information about these CEOs' demographic backgrounds. All were male. The majority of executives in their sample were first borns in two-parent,

LEADERSHIP ON THE CUTTING EDGE
A Skill-Based Model for Leadership Performance

Modern leadership theories focus primarily on the leader-follower interaction and relationship, but a group of researchers have taken a different approach and revisited the question of what capabilities a leader must have to be effective (for a review, see Mumford, Zaccaro, Connelly et al. 2000). The skill-based model the researchers developed suggests that leadership depends on an interactive package of complex skills. The three key leadership skills are complex problem solving, solution construction, and social judgment.

Effective leaders have the skills to solve novel and unstructured problems by identifying problems, developing solutions while taking into account complex organizational structures and relationships, and finally motivating their followers and building consensus to work on those solutions (Mumford, Zaccaro, Connelly et al. 2000). Mumford and his associates have found that the leadership skills they propose:

- Can be measured.
- Can predict leadership performance separate from other traits.
- Make a unique contribution to leadership effectiveness.
- Develop as a result of leadership experiences.

Acquisition of the skills is related to underlying characteristics such as achievement orientation, extroversion, and dominance (Mumford, Zaccaro, Johnson et al. 2000).

Early studies that tested the various propositions of the model were supportive, but they relied on limited samples, and further development and testing are needed. However, the skill-based model shows considerable promise as a new perspective for understanding leadership performance.

Sources: Articles about the new leadership skills model can be found in the special 2000 issue of *Leadership Quarterly* 11 no. 1.

middle-class families living in the rust belt. Close to 90 percent were married, with a median age of 58, and many considered themselves to be religious. Eighty percent were right handed; they were taller than and smoked less than the general population, and tended to exercise a fair amount. The CEOs were considerably more educated than the general population, with 47 percent having a graduate degree. The majority studied in public universities, and many contributed to their education, at least to some extent.

The most striking results of Kurtz, Boone, and Fleenor's extensive survey was the homogeneity of the executives, in spite of some differences among industries; for example, banking and utilities have a higher percentage of CEOs from the lower middle classes. Although the survey did not use a randomly selected sample and was therefore subject to bias, the strength and direction of the results provided interesting findings. It appears that U.S. CEOs looked much alike in 1989.

Unfortunately, no comparable recent surveys of U.S. leaders have been completed. It does appear that the homogeneity might be changing, at least in some areas. For example, the number of young entrepreneurs is growing among smaller businesses in the United States. A recent survey indicates that more than one-third of those entrepreneurs are under age 30 and three-quarters are under age 40 when they start their business (Kriss 1998). Women leaders also are making progress; the numbers of female executives and members of boards of directors of large corporations are rising every year (Sellers 1998). The 1997 U.S. census data further indicate that women and minorities own, respectively, 26 percent and 14.6 percent of all businesses (U.S. census, 1997). The high-tech industry also has younger and more educated leaders, with an average age of 42 and nearly 73 percent in one survey having post-graduate training (Paine Weber 2000).

In spite of some changes, the top executives in the United States and in many other parts of the world are still a homogeneous group. The homogeneity in demographic background does not necessarily lead to similar approaches in managing a business and leading followers. However, it is also unlikely to lead to high diversity of thought and approaches to management. Although homogeneity can be a strength if unity of purpose is needed, it can be a weakness where creativity is required. Many studies (e.g., Hackman 1990; Nahavandi and Aranda 1994) propose that lack of support from top management is one of the key obstacles in the implementation of innovative management approaches. With the current state of flux of public and private organizations, the need for diverse and innovative approaches is strong. Given the homogeneity of current business leaders in the United States, it is not surprising that such innovation is sometimes lacking. The homogeneity of U.S. executives might be one of the key factors pointing to the need to further diversify business leadership.

Changes in Organizations and in Expectations of Leaders

To many, a leader is someone who takes charge and jumps in to make decisions whenever the situation requires. This view is particularly dominant in traditional organizations that have a clear hierarchy in which employees and managers have narrowly defined responsibilities. The extent to which a leader is attributed power and knowledge also varies by culture. In high-power distance cultures, such as Mexico, managers are expected to provide all the answers and solutions to work problems and to control the activities of their employees. Although the U.S. mainstream culture is not as authority oriented as some other cultures, a large number of our leadership theories are implicitly or explicitly based on the assumptions that leaders have to take charge and provide others with instructions. For example, the initiation-of-structure concept provides that effective leadership involves giving direction, assigning tasks to followers, and setting deadlines. These activities are considered an inherent part of an effective leader's behaviors. Similarly, the widely used concept of motivation to manage (Miner and Smith 1982) includes desire for power and control over others as an essential component. Students of management still are told that desires for controlling others might be a key factor in determining their motivation to manage, which, in turn, is linked to managerial success.

New Roles for Leaders

With the push for total quality and the use of teams, organizations and their hierarchies are changing drastically. As a result, many of the traditional leadership functions and roles are delegated to subordinates. Figure 2-1 presents the traditional

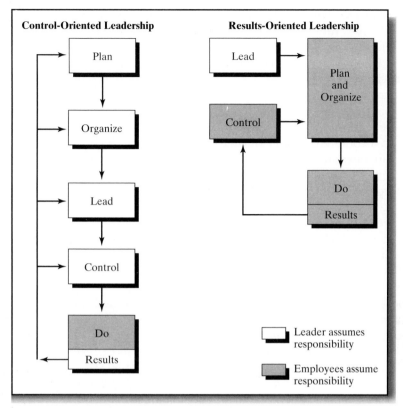

Figure 2-1
Control- vs. Results-Oriented Leadership

model and the new model for the role of leaders in organizations. The focus on quality and teamwork in all aspects of decision making and implementation forces us to reconsider our expectations and requirements for leadership. Effective team leaders are not necessarily in control of the group. They might need facilitation and participation skills much more than initiation-of-structure skills. For example, employees in traditional organizations are responsible only for production; the planning, leading, and controlling functions, as well as the responsibility for results, fall on the manager (see Figure 2-1). However, an increasing number of organizations are shifting the activities and responsibilities typically associated with managers to employees. Managers are expected to provide the vision, get employees the needed resources, act as a support person, and get out of employees' way. The employees, in turn, are learning about the strategic and financial issues related to their job, planning their own activities, setting production goals, producing, and taking responsibility for their results. These changes also are present in local, state, and federal government agencies. In many U.S. cities, for example, principles of total quality management (TQM) are part of all supervisors' training. The result is an attempt to allow government employees to take on more responsibility in responding to citizens' needs.

Effective team leaders are not necessarily in control of the group. They might need facilitation and participation skills much more than initiation-of-structure skills.

Many executives have adopted new management techniques to help them with the challenges inherent in the new roles for leaders. Rick Sapio, the CEO of the 37-employee New York City Mutual.com, a mutual-fund advisory company, admits that his business is high-pressure with little time to stay in touch with his employees (Buchanan 2001). However, recognizing the importance of involving employees, Sapio has created "Hassles," an electronic mailbox where employees can express their concerns and ideas with a guarantee from the CEO that they will be addressed in a week. For those who prefer to see the boss in person, Sapio schedules 1 hour a week in a conference room (rather than his office, which may seem inaccessible) where anyone can drop in to give him input. The Hay Group, a Philadelphia-based management consulting firm, conducted a study that identified elements of an effective corporate culture (Kahn 1998). They found that: "In the most admired companies, the key priorities were teamwork, customer focus, fair treatment of employees, initiative, and innovation" (Kahn 1998, p. 218). Companies such as U.S. Intel, Toyota of Japan, and Asea Brown Boveri of Sweden practice being egalitarian and cooperative. Their priorities are fast decision making, training, and innovation.

The new leadership styles are not limited to business organizations; they also can be seen in government and other nonprofit organizations. Philip Diehl, the director of the U.S. Mint, and his leadership team transformed the stodgy government bureaucracy into an efficient and customer-centered organization by asking questions, listening to stakeholders, creating a sense of urgency in employees, and involving them in the change (Muio 1999). Jane Cummins, president of Hollady Park Medical Center, also works with a large team of people. Her particular skill is being able to establish a one-on-one rapport with many of her peers and subordinates. She spends considerable time walking around, talking to people, and getting direct information about what is going on in her hospital (Weber 1990).

These leaders have moved out of their top-floor offices and are keeping in touch with the members of their organizations. Given the rapid change and complexity of many organizations and the environment in which they operate, having broad sources of information and involving many in the decision-making process are essential. Effective team leaders are not necessarily in control of the group. They might need facilitation and participation skills much more than initiation-of-structure skills.

Factors Fueling Changes

A number of external and internal organizational factors are driving the changes in our organizations and in the role of leaders and managers (see Figure 2-2). First, political changes worldwide are leading to more openness and democracy: These political changes shape and are shaped by images of what is considered to be appropriate leadership. With the fall of the Soviet Union at the end of the twentieth century, the world saw an increase in the use of democratic principles that aim at power sharing. In the United States, the public continues to expect openness in the affairs of the private and the public sectors. Politicians are forced to reveal much of their past and justify to the public many if not all of their decisions. Communities increasingly are demanding participation in the decisions regarding their schools, health care systems, and environment.

Second, increasing global and local competition, and complex and fast-changing technologies are forcing a number of organizations to struggle for their survival and

LEADING CHANGE
Gloria Feldt Takes on Planned Parenthood

Gloria Feldt, Planed Parenthood Federation of America's (PPFA) chief executive, knew she had to change her 85-year-old organization and bring new focus and life to her stakeholders. Facing public controversy and a collection of varied services with different names and limited coordination, the organization was struggling. Feldt's task was to take a group of disparate and geographically dispersed employees, volunteers, and donors who all had a stake in PPFA and help them develop a shared vision, mission, and goals that would carry them for 25 years.

To set the new direction, she brought together 325 PPFA executives from all over the United States in a summit to draft the new vision and goals. Volunteers such as Esperanza Garcia Walters, chair of the visioning committee, conducted focus groups with teen mothers and shared the results. After defining an agenda, the executives returned to their agencies to seek input from their staff members who were encouraged to dream and be as creative as possible. The long, 25-year time frame that Feldt had selected allowed people to move away from immediate problems and focus on possibilities.

The result of the long process was the development of a shared vision and adoption of 10 far-reaching goals for PPFA. Both were wholeheartedly ratified at PPFA's national meeting. Feldt knew that regardless of how good her personal vision was, "these people had to participate or the results would turn to dust" (Hammonds 2002, p. 55). "Creating hope for humanity: The freedom to dream, to make choices, and to live in peace with our planet" is the new shared vision that Feldt believes will inspire the people she leads to take on the challenges they face.

Source: Hammonds, K. H. 2002. Planned parenthood's 25-year plan. *Fast Company*, February, 55–56; www.plannedparenthood.org/vision2025/index.html; www.plannedparenthood.org/vision2025/promise.html.

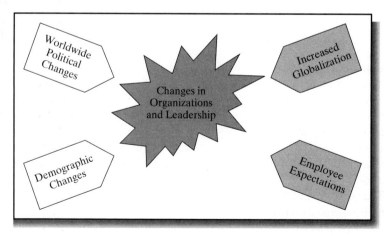

Figure 2-2
Factors Fueling Changes in Organizations and Their Leadership

justify their existence. Many have had to reconsider how they provide goods and services to their customers and to reevaluate the assumptions that they held as basic truths. For example, Bill Ford, Jr., the CEO of Ford Motor, not only is an environmentalist who agreed to speak at a Greenpeace conference, but also comes to union contract negotiations wearing union buttons. Referring to the historical animosity between union and management, Ford states, "I always hated the us versus them" (Morris 2000, p. 136).

The global competition is associated with consumer demands for improved quality in products and services, and the need for flexibility and creativity on the part of organizations. Poor management and lack of leadership often are blamed for the problems facing U.S. organizations. The fierce international competition, together with perceptions of our global competitors' management practices, have pushed us to look for new solutions. Whether it is through restructuring in the private sector or through reinventing government in the public arena, our old institutions need to find new vitality. Many organizations are redefining and reengineering themselves, drastically altering the way employees do their jobs. These practices demand new leadership roles and procedures.

Another key factor fueling changes in leadership is the demographic changes in the United States and many other countries. These demographic changes lead to increased diversity in the various groups and organizations; their leaders have to consider this diversity when making decisions. In some cases, the diversity will be related to age; in others it will be gender, ethnic background, or other factors. Other countries have similar or even greater cultural diversity. For example, Malaysia's population is highly diverse and consists of Malays, Chinese, Indians, Arabs, Sinhalese, Eurasians, and Europeans (Malaysia Yearbook 1996). The majority of Singapore's population of 3 million is Chinese, but it also includes Malays, Indians, and Eurasians. As a result, the country has four official languages: English, Malay, Mandarin, and Tamil. Table 2-3 presents a summary of some of the ethnic and demographic changes in the United States.

Other demographic changes include the increasing number of women in the workforce. Although women currently hold only 10 percent of the executive positions in the United States, they make up half of the lower- and middle-management positions (Himelstein and Forest 1997; Johnson 1996). Similar trends exist all over the world. For example, despite cultural and religious pressures for women to maintain traditional roles in Turkey, 35 percent of professionals are women (Poggioli 1998). As a result, the old ways that were designed for a gender and ethnically homogeneous population do not always work with employees and customers from varied backgrounds and cultures. Much of the burden for devising and implementing these changes falls on the leadership of our organizations. The demand to listen to and address the needs of nonhomogeneous groups requires skills that go beyond controlling and monitoring. Consider how baby boom generation managers often see the Generation Xers as being somewhat detached from their work but at the same time demanding input and participation (Rattan 1993). Leading and motivating these younger workers presents a considerable challenge for the current leadership of our organizations.

Additionally, employees have increased levels of education today, and the younger generation is entering the workplace with expectations for participation and autonomy. They expect fast promotions, challenging learning opportunities, training, and a balance between their home and work lives. The increase in service

Table 2-3
U.S. Demographic Trends

- By 2050, the average age will be close to 40, as opposed to under 35 in 2000.
- The white population growth rate will stay relatively stable, but the number of Hispanics will nearly double by 2050.
- The percentage of whites in the overall population will drop from 72% in 2000 to 64% by 2020.
- The number of households where a language other than English is spoken has increased from 13.6% in 1990 to 17.6% in 2000. In California, Texas and New Mexico, the non-English-speaking households make up more than 39.5%, 35.5%, and 32%, respectively.
- By the year 2050, the average U.S. resident will be from a non-European background.

Source: www.census.gov.

jobs at the expense of traditional manufacturing jobs puts employees in direct contact with customers, and therefore requires changes in how we manage and train employees. This also means that employees must use judgment and make many quick decisions that previously were reserved for management.

As a result of these pressures for change, many organizations find themselves rewriting their policies to address the needs of a diverse community and consumer base. Organizations are building more diversity internally and changing their practices. Ted Childs, IBM's president of global workforce diversity, states:

> You're going to have to sell to people who are different from you, and buy from people who are different from you, and manage people who are different from you. . . . This is how we do business. If it's not your destination, you should get off the plane now. (Swan 2000, p. 260)

One of the leaders at JC Penney, a U.S. retailer, explains, "If we don't have people of diverse backgrounds in back, how in the world can we satisfy the diversity of people coming in through the front door?" (Himelstein and Forest 1997, p. 64). Focusing on addressing the needs of a diverse workforce, along with empowering various people to implement meaningful change, will be key factors in the success of organizations in the future.

Barriers to Change

Despite the factors that are fueling the need for change, few organizations and individuals have adopted new models for leadership painlessly and successfully. In part because of perceived financial pressures and attempts to find a quick way out of them, organizations turn to tough, autocratic leaders whose goals are clearly not employee motivation and loyalty. For example, John Grundhofer, who has been nicknamed "Jack the Ripper," has specialized in implementing massive layoffs and has found his skills in high demand (Duff 1993). Similarly, Al Dunlap, with nicknames such as "Ming the Merciless" and "Chainsaw Al," for a long time moved successfully from the top position of one organization to another before being fired from Sunbeam Corporation in 1998. For many years, the financial community applauded him for his drastic cost-cutting strategies that involved massive layoffs (Sparks 1994).

Another obstacle to the implementation of new models of leadership is that although there are teams in lower and middle levels of organizations, top management still remain a one-person show. The hierarchical structure of many organizations makes change difficult. Old cultures resist change. Few organizations truly reward enterprising employees and managers for crossing the traditional hierarchical barriers. Instead, they continue to reward their leaders for tried-and-true approaches or sometimes for nonperformance and nonproductivity-related behaviors, despite the lack of success (Luthans 1989). Marcus Buckingham, a researcher at the Gallup Organization who has for 15 years studied global leadership practice, suggests: "The corporate world is appallingly bad at capitalizing on the strengths of its people" (LaBarre 2001a, p. 90). Gallup's extensive surveys clearly show that employee engagement can have a considerable positive impact on an organization's performance. However, few organizations take full advantage of their employees' input.

In addition, although they might spend a great deal of time working in teams, employees are still rewarded for individual performance. In other words, our reward structures have not yet caught up with our attempts to increase cooperation among employees and managers. Furthermore, many employees are not willing or able to accept their new roles as partners and decision makers even when they are offered to them. Their training and previous experiences make them balk at taking on what they might consider to be their leader's job.

Even when organizations encourage change, many leaders find giving up control difficult. Although they have been trained in the benefits of empowerment, teams, and softer images of leadership, they simply repeat what seems to have worked in the past, substituting memory for thinking (Pfeffer 1998). Having been trained to be in charge, allowing employees to do more might appear to be a personal failure. Either because of years of traditional training or because of personality characteristics that make them more comfortable with control and hierarchy, the managers' styles often are an obstacle to implementing necessary changes. Research with children's images of leadership indicates that the belief that leaders need to be in control develops early in life. Children, particularly boys, still seem to have a sex-typed schema of leaders: Leaders have male characteristics, including dominance and aggression (Ayman-Nolley, Ayman, and Becker 1993).

SUMMARY AND CONCLUSION

The scientific approach to understanding leadership that started at about the time of the industrial revolution added rigor and attempts at precise measurement to other already-existing views about leadership. The first modern approaches focused on the identification of traits that would distinguish leaders and followers. Although certain traits were found to be associated with leadership, no simple sets of traits can predict who will be an effective leader. Because of inconclusive results, researchers turned their attention to leadership behaviors. The two major categories of initiation of structure and consideration were established as the central leadership behaviors. The switch from simple traits to simple behaviors still did not account for the complex leadership process and, therefore, did not allow researchers to make strong predictions about leadership effectiveness. The most current approach to leadership focuses on understanding characteristics of leaders and the requirements of the situation. By taking a contingency point of view, whereby leadership effectiveness depends on the match between the leader and the situation, we increase our ability to understand complex leadership situations.

The renewed interest in leadership has led to a reconsideration of traits as a factor in leadership, whereby a set of traits is considered necessary but not sufficient in effective leadership. A new definition of the leader's role is further proposed, with an emphasis on results rather than control. As many public and private institutions undergo drastic changes to adapt to demographic and cultural changes, and to revitalize themselves to continue to remain competitive and responsive to their customers, the pressures on leaders are increasing. As a result, the role of leaders is changing from control and hierarchy to the search for innovative solutions. Such solutions more often than not require active employee participation and partnerships and, in some cases, a total reconsideration of the role of leaders. The challenge organizations face is not only to understand the type of leadership needed in turbulent times, but also to develop and train employees who can develop and implement the new concepts.

Selecting Team Members

As the leader of your organization, you have observed a lack of flexibility and a slow decision-making process in many of the departments. You believe that you are not serving your customers well, and have decided to move to a team environment and to push many of the decisions to the lowest possible levels. In other words, you want to create a team-based, empowered organization. Several of your best managers are resisting the idea strongly. They not only feel that many employees are not ready for the change, but they also believe that they personally could never change from a "command and control" style to allowing more participation.

1. How do you deal with the situation?
2. What arguments can you use to persuade your managers?
3. What can you do to help your managers change their style?
4. What are the implications of your actions and decisions?

REVIEW AND DISCUSSION QUESTIONS

1. What are the similarities and differences between the trait and behavior approaches to leadership?
2. What has each approach contributed to our understanding of the process of leadership?
3. What are the major assumptions guiding the contingency approach to leadership?
4. What factors have led to the dominance of the contingency approach in modern leadership?
5. How is the modern trait approach to leadership different from the approach of the early twentieth century?
6. What are the elements of the emerging leadership styles? What are the factors that support such styles?
7. What obstacles do new leadership styles face in traditional organizations?
8. How can obstacles to new models be overcome?

SEARCHING THE WEB

History of Leadership:
www.sedl.org/change/leadership/history.html

History of Management:
sol.brunel.ac.uk/~jarvis/bola/motivation/taylor.html

sol.brunel.ac.uk/~jarvis/bola/competence/fayol.html

sol.brunel.ac.uk/~jarvis/bola/systems/bureau.html

sol.brunel.ac.uk/~jarvis/bola/motivation/masmodel.html

sol.brunel.ac.uk/~jarvis/bola/motivation/mcgregor.html

Self-Assessment:
www.interlinktc.com/assessment.html

EXERCISE 2-1: OLD WINES AND NEW SKINS

This exercise is designed to highlight the changes between new and old leadership styles. The class will be divided into two sections. (Subgroups can be used in each section in classes of more than 20 or 25.) Each section is assigned one of two tasks.

1. **Presentations**

    Prepare a 2- to 4-minute presentation about traditional leadership and management styles, their advantages, and contributions to our institutions. The focus should be on the benefits, although reasons for change should be prepared for discussion.

    OR

    Prepare a 2- to 4-minute presentation about the new leadership and management styles, their potential benefits to our institutions, and the changes that make them desirable. The focus should be on the need to adopt the new methods, although the difficulties and problems should be prepared for discussion.

2. **Class Discussion**

    After presentation of the two sides, the class discussion will focus on:

    - The situations that warrant a change to "New Skins."
    - Situations that make drastic transitions too difficult.
    - Individual students' preferences for "Old Wines" or "New Skins" as:

    A. leaders
    B. subordinates

EXERCISE 2-2: THE TOY FACTORY

The goal of this exercise is for each group to produce as many high-quality toy wolves as possible.

Your instructor will assign you to a group, designate the leader, and provide you with a list of materials needed for making the toy wolves.

Your team leader will give you instructions on how to make the toys.

After a 15-minute production run, each group's productivity will be measured.

Observation and Discussion Questions (See Worksheet)

The Toy Factory Worksheet

1. How would you describe your team leader's style of leadership? Provide several specific behavioral examples.

2. How did you react to your leader's style? How satisfied were you?

3. What suggestions (if any) could you offer your leader?

EXERCISE 2-3: LEADERSHIP AND GENDER

This exercise is designed to explore the relationship between gender roles and leadership.

Your instructor will assign you to one of three groups and ask you to develop a list of characteristics of a particular leader.

Each group will present its list to the class.

Discussion will focus on the similarities and differences between gender roles and leadership.

Leadership and Gender Worksheet

List 8 to 10 characteristics associated with _____ (wait for your instructor's direction). You can use specific personality traits or behavioral descriptions.

1.

2.

3.

4.

5.

6.

7.

8.

9.

10.

CASE

Leadership in Action
The Caring Dictator

By any measure, Jack Hartnett, the president of Texas-based D. L. Rogers Corp., is a successful man. D. L. Rogers owns 54 franchises of the Sonic roller-skating nostalgic hamburger chain, which generate $44 million in revenues for the company. Hartnett's restaurants make 18 percent more than the national average, and turnover is incredibly low for the fast-food industry, with a supervisor's average tenure at 12.4 years. He knows what he wants, how to keep his employees, and how to run his business for high profit.

In a management world where everyone will tell you that you need to be soft, participative, open to ideas, and empower employees, Jack Hartnett appears to be an anachronism. He runs his business on the Sinatra principle, "My Way!" He tolerates little deviance from what he wants, his instructions, and his training. He is absolutely sure he knows the best way, and more than one employee is scared of disagreeing with him. He likes keeping people a little off balance and a little queasy so they will work harder to avoid his wrath. Hartnett even has his own Eight Commandments, and he will fire those who break any one of them twice. The last Hartnett commandment is "I will only tell you one time."

Hartnett restaurants run like clockwork. He does the top-level hiring himself and is reputed to spend as long as 10 grueling hours with prospective managers and their spouses. He wants to know about their personal lives and their financial health, and looks for right responses and any signs of reticence to answer questions. Hartnett says, "I want them to understand this is not a job to me. This is a lifetime of working together. I want partners who are going to die with me" (p. 67). If you are one of the selected few, you are expected to be loyal and obedient. Once a quarter, you also can expect a Hartnett "lock-in" meeting, where Jack will take you away along with other supervisors to a secret location with no chance of escape. You can expect to be blindfolded, put through survival exercises, and sleep in tents before you go to a luxury resort to discuss business.

For all their trouble and unquestioning obedience and loyalty, D. L. Rogers employees and supervisors find a home, a family, a community, and a place to grow. If you have problems with your husband, like Sharon, the wife of one D. L. Rogers supervisor, you can call Jack. He will listen to you, chew your spouse out, and send him home for a while. Hartnett says "I don't want you to come to work unhappy, pissed off, upset, or mad about anything, because I don't think you can be totally focused on making money if you're worried" (p. 63). He pays his employees considerably above national averages, plays golf with them, and gets involved with their personal lives. Hartnett wants to create a bond that lasts. A few years ago, he spent $200,000 to take 254 managers and their families to Cancun, Mexico, for four days. They got training on better time management and marketing techniques, and on how to be a better spouse.

Hartnett also likes to have fun. Practical jokes, including gluing supervisors' shoes to the floor, are common. But he also works hard. Eighty-hour weeks are common, and he starts his days earlier than most. He is not above taking on the most menial jobs in the restaurants and is willing to show the way, no matter what. His presence, his energy, and his unbending confidence in "his way" make converts. Hartnett has created an organization that is consistent and that simplifies everybody's life. ■

QUESTIONS

1. How would you describe Jack Hartnett's leadership style?

2. Why is he successful? Would you work for him?

Source: Based on Ballon, M. 1998. Extreme managing, Inc, July, pp. 60–72.

Chapter 3

Individual Differences and Traits

> He who knows about others may be learned
> But he who knows himself is more intelligent.

—LAO TSU

After studying this chapter, you will be able to:

1. Explain the role of individual difference characteristics in leadership.
2. Describe the difference between the past and current approaches to leadership traits.
3. Identify the impact of values on leadership.
4. Present the potential link between emotional intelligence and leadership.
5. Highlight the role of the "Big Five" and other personality traits in leadership.
6. Understand cross-cultural differences in individual difference characteristics.

*E*ven a quick reading of the history and mythology of any civilization makes it evident that leaders are considered to be special. Their physical characteristics are described in detail, their personalities dissected, and their actions celebrated. Long lists of traits and personal exploits are provided. All of this detailed information about leaders focuses our attention on the person. It also represents a common belief that leaders possess something out of the ordinary—something within them that makes them worthy of our attention. Many believe that good leaders have natural, inborn characteristics that set them apart from others. All of us probably can produce such a list of personal characteristics of effective leaders. Leaders are courageous; they have initiative and integrity; they are intelligent, perceptive, and so forth. However, as discussed in Chapter 2, research findings do not clearly support many popular lay theories about personal characteristics of leaders. The results of hundreds of studies do not yield a specific profile for leaders, despite the fact that certain characteristics are correlated to leadership, if not directly linked to leadership effectiveness.

In recent years, the interest in understanding the individual characteristics and personalities of leaders has been revived. Many new case studies of and interviews with successful business leaders have refocused attention on the role of individual style, demographic background, personality traits, skills, and other individual, rather than situational, characteristics in understanding leadership. For example, Warren Bennis (1992), through numerous interviews and observations, highlights leaders' charisma and personal style and their effects on organizations. Other examples of the continued focus on individual traits are theories of charismatic leadership (Conger 1991), transformational leadership (Bass 1985), and the work of Kouzes and Posner (1993, 1999) about credibility as the heart of leadership. The major difference between earlier work on traits and these recent efforts is the more complex point of view adopted by the researchers. The search is not simply for one individual trait or a combination of traits. Instead, modern theorists also consider the complex interaction among traits, behaviors, and situational characteristics such as expectations of followers. Taken in this light, it is important to understand the role that several personality traits play in leadership style and behavior.

This chapter discusses the role of individual characteristics in leadership by considering values, abilities, skills, and several personality traits. Who the leaders are does not determine how effective they will be. However, individual differences do impact the way leaders think, behave, and approach problems, as well as their interaction with others. No single individual characteristic is a direct measure of leadership style, but each can allow a better understanding of a person's basic approach and preferences.

ELEMENTS OF INDIVIDUAL DIFFERENCES CHARACTERISTICS

What makes every person unique is a combination of many factors, including demographic, physical, psychological, and behavioral differences. These are at the core of who we are. Figure 3-1 shows a framework for understanding individual differences and their complex components. Heredity and environment are the two determinants

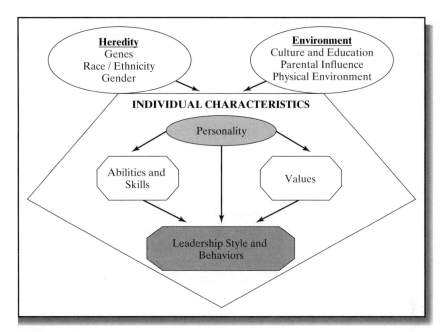

Figure 3-1
Individual Differences Framework

of individual difference characteristics. The interactionist view of individual differences suggests that heredity and the environment interact to influence the development of individual differences. This view is widely accepted, although experts debate the relative influence of each factor. Heredity consists of an individual's gene pool, gender, race, and ethnic background, and it has an early, and some suggest indelible, influence on personality (Keller et al. 1992). Although genetic studies have established a link between heredity and some personality traits, research also shows that the environment strongly affects us. Influences include physical location, parents, culture, religion, education, and friends.

To understand individual differences, we must consider the interaction between heredity and the environment. Environmental and social conditions can reinforce genetic patterns to influence a leader's personality, as can cultural factors, the educational system, and parental upbringing. For instance, in the United States, the genetic traits typically associated with being male are further reinforced by social norms that encourage boys to be competitive and aggressive. Similarly, although female babies tend to develop language skills earlier than males, parents who speak more to their girls, and schools that expect girls to be proficient in language, further reinforce their verbal skills. These genetic and environmental differences often are reflected later in life in leadership styles and behaviors.

As shown in Figure 3-1, three major individual difference characteristics can affect leadership style: personality, values, and abilities and skills. These variables form a pyramid of sorts, with personality at the top. Personality is a stable set of physical and psychological characteristics that makes each person unique. It is made up of a number of personality traits and is the product of interacting biological and environmental factors. It is the primary factor in individual differences and influences the other characteristics. Our personality affects our behavior and our performance in many settings. For an example of the impact of personality traits in interview outcomes, see Cook, Vance, and Spector (2000).

- First, personality is stable. That is, it tends to stay the same over time and across situations. It is not perfectly rigid, however, as it can evolve gradually over the long term.
- Second, personality consists of a set of characteristics rather than one or two traits. This set develops over time and makes the individual unique (McCrae 1993).

The next individual difference characteristic is values. Values are stable, long-lasting beliefs and preferences about what is worthwhile and desirable (Rokeach 1973). Values are closely related to personality. Personality refers to a person's character and temperament, whereas values are principles that a person believes. Like personality traits, values guide a leader's behavior and are influenced by a combination of biological and environmental factors. For example, leaders who hold the value "honesty is the best policy" will attempt to behave fairly and honorably and show integrity in their words and actions. Like personality, values are shaped early in life and are resistant to change. Values also are influenced heavily by one's culture.

Two other related individual differences that play a role in leadership are ability and skill. Ability, or aptitude, is a natural talent for doing something mental or physical. A skill is an acquired talent that a person develops related to a specific task. Whereas ability is somewhat stable over time, skills change with training and experience and from one task to another. You cannot train leaders to develop an ability or aptitude, but you can train them in new leadership skills. Organizations, therefore, recruit and hire leaders who have certain abilities and aptitudes and then train them to acquire needed skills.

Multiple Perspectives and the Impact of the Situation

Although individual characteristics are, by definition, stable, this stability does not mean that leaders cannot behave in ways that are different from their personality. A useful approach is to consider a variety of individual difference factors that explain certain aspects of a person's behavior. Ideally, to understand who people are and what makes them unique, one would have to consider all possible aspects of personality, values, attitudes, abilities, skills, and demographic factors. These multiple perspectives can provide a broad insight. Note that even when considering multiple perspectives, individual difference characteristics do not dictate our behaviors.

Ideally, to understand who a person is and what makes him or her unique, one would have to consider all possible aspects of a personality, values and attitudes the person holds, their abilities and skills, and demographic factors. These multiple perspectives can provide a broad insight.

When situations provide little guidance and are loosely structured, a person's individual characteristics can have a strong impact (Barrick and Mount 1993; Mischel 1973; Weiss and Adler 1984). However, when the situation provides strong behavioral cues—cues that signal what behaviors and actions are expected and appropriate—most people behave according to those cues regardless of their personality traits or other individual characteristics. For example, a highly mechanistic organization with a strong culture that provides detailed, clear rules of behavior will not encourage its managers to express their individuality. In contrast, a loosely structured, organic organization that provides autonomy will allow leaders to experiment and show their individual differences.

Individual Characteristics Set the Limits

Although individual characteristics tend to be stable, that stability does not mean that people cannot behave in ways that are inconsistent with their personality, values, and attitudes. Instead, each characteristic provides a behavioral zone of comfort as presented in Figure 3-2. The zone of comfort includes a range of behaviors that come naturally and feel comfortable to perform because they reflect individual characteristics.

Behaving outside that zone is difficult, takes practice, and in some cases might not be possible. However, although we are at ease in our behavioral comfort zone, we learn and grow by moving to our zones of discomfort. The behaviors outside the comfort zone challenge us and push us to our limits. Therefore, although difficult, an effective learning tool is to move outside the comfort zone. The remainder of the chapter presents various individual difference variables that have the potential to affect leadership or that can help in understanding leadership styles.

VALUES

Values are long-lasting beliefs about what is worthwhile and desirable. They are personal judgments about what is right and wrong, good and bad. Understanding values is important for leaders because they affect how they lead. This section examines two types of values, investigates how culture affects values, and considers the interplay between values and ethics.

Figure 3-2
Individual Characteristics and Behaviors

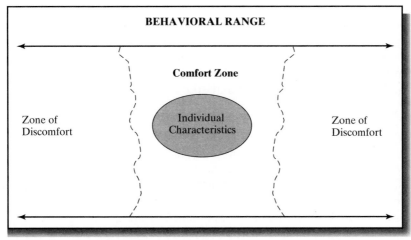

Value System and Culture

The ways in which a person organizes and prioritizes values is that person's value system (see Self-Assessment 3-1). For instance, the value of family might be a top priority for one person in comparison to other issues, such as faith, career, and social relationships. Other people might value their career more than their family or put their faith and spirituality above all else. Each of us has a personal value system prioritized around what we value most. Some people are aware of values and their priorities, whereas others are unclear about their own priorities and become cognizant of them only when conflict results.

Each individual's value system is unique, although members of one family or culture might share certain key values. For example, surveys of political attitude in the United States consistently reveal what some people have called the gender gap, a difference in the value system of men and women. In the United States, many women place a higher value on family and social issues, whereas men focus more on economic problems. These differences are reflected in how they vote. In addition to gender-based differences, many generational and culture-based value systems differences also exist. Leaders must understand their own values and how they influence their styles and behavior, and the values of their followers.

Culture and Values

Cultural values indicate what a cultural group considers to be important, worthwhile, and desirable. We share the values of our culture. The cultural values form the basis for a leader's individual value system. Clearly, not everyone in all cultures holds the same values (Bigoness and Blakely 1996). For example, certain values—fairness, honesty, frugality, compassion, and humility—are universal. In contrast, the value of individual dignity—which refers to placing focus on the uniqueness, self-control, and self-governance of individuals—is more prevalent in individualistic than in collectivistic cultures (Anderson 1997).

In general, the Euro-American cultures within the United States, as well as many other Western cultures, value individuality. As a result, leaders from these cultures rate personal achievement and recognition highly, and organizations select individuals for rewards and recognition. Displays of individuality are welcomed, as evidenced by the respect many people have for entrepreneurs.

By contrast, collectivist cultures place a higher value on the community and a lower value on the individual. For instance, in Japan, conformity to the group is valued and rewarded. Parents teach children not to stand out or draw attention to themselves. A Japanese proverb states that "the nail that stands out will be hammered down." This proverb reflects the individual value system of many Japanese, who believe that they should sacrifice the self for the good of the collective. Leaders are valued for their conformity to the social order as much as their uniqueness.

Several Native American cultures, such as the Navajos, have similar cultural values. Navajos, who are a horizontal collectivistic culture, devalue individualism and standing out in one's community and, indeed, consider such behavior inappropriate. Such cultures value leaders primarily for their contribution to their community. Hofstede's other cultural values of avoidance of uncertainty, power distance, and masculinity similarly affect individuals' value systems (these are discussed in depth in Chapter 1). When a culture emphasizes low-power distance, such as in Sweden, which is individualistic but horizontal, leaders are likely to be cooperative and avoid status symbols and hierarchy. When the culture is masculine, individuals are likely to value honor and self-reliance.

In addition to national cultural differences in value systems, theorists debate the effects of age, ethnic, and other group cultural differences on value systems. Research suggests that many people from the older generation in the United States believe that the young do not value hard work and they lack respect. It also indicates that the younger groups think the older generation's value system is stale and useless. Consultant Regan, who is part of the 20-something generation, talks about what the younger generation wants: "Just tell me what you want me to do and leave me alone." However, he goes on, "Obviously the boss above them wants more direction and control" (Rattan 1993). Table 3-1 presents some value differences based on age.

LEADERSHIP ON THE CUTTING EDGE
Managers' Motivation in Different Cultures

Researchers A. Mathur, Y. Zhang, and J. Neelankavil compared the factors that motivate managers in the United States (176 managers), China (204 managers), India (220 managers), and the Philippines (201). Overall, 784 managers from 209 companies responded to a questionnaire inquiring about safety, social, ego, and self-actualization needs based on Maslow's hierarchy of needs (1943) and Alderfer's ERG theory (1969). The sample included a majority of males (67.3 percent) under age 45 representing a wide selection of businesses and industries.

Financial rewards and self-actualization were least important for the Chinese and most important for U.S. managers. "The need to avoid failure and rejection," social needs, and ego needs (e.g., improving self-esteem and competitive desire to excel) were rated lowest among the Chinese managers, while Indian managers were lowest on "pleasing and meeting the expectation of others" and highest on the need for social status. The researchers explained the low need the Chinese have for financial rewards, achieve-

ments, and social goals based on an image of leadership in that country that suggests that to be effective, leaders must be loyal and devoted to their followers, taking care of them as a father would, and be selfless and trustworthy. Additionally, in collectivistic cultures, social needs are less relevant because individuals are already inherently part of the larger, established, and interdependent social system that reduces the need to strive for additional social affiliation (Mathur et al. 2001, p. 263).

Interestingly, this study showed that the tendency to group all Asian cultures when discussing cultural values might be inappropriate, as researchers found clear differences among China, India, and the Philippines, with the latter two sharing some values with U.S. managers—a factor that might be explained by some similarities in the political and business structures in the three countries. Mathur et al. emphasized the importance of taking motivational and need differences into account when designing human resource systems.

Source: Mathur, A., Zhang, Y., and Meelankavil, J. P. 2001. Critical managerial motivational factors: A cross-cultural analysis of four culturally divergent countries. *International Journal Cross-Cultural Management* 1 no. 3, 251–267.

Table 3-1

Generation-Based Value Differences in the United States

CURRENT AGE RANGE	DEFINING SOCIAL AND HISTORICAL INFLUENCES	DOMINANT VALUE SYSTEM
55+	Raised by Depression-era parents in post-depression period or around WWII	Hard work; frugality; patriotism; Protestant work ethic
40 to 55	Baby boomers raised by WWII parents, grew up during Korean and Vietnam wars, Kennedy assassination and moon landing, rock & roll era, and Woodstock	Nonconformity; idealism; self-focus; distrust of establishment; happiness and peace
30 to 40	Raised by the early hippies; post-Vietnam era; Watergate	The "yuppies;" "me" generation; ambition; material comforts; success driven
up to 30	Peaceful era marked by few major events in the United States; recession and economic changes	Generation Xers; enjoyment of life; jaded; desire for autonomy and flexibility

Sources: Massey, M. E. 1986. The past: what you are is where you were when. Schaumburg, IL: Video Publishing House (videorecording); Cherrington, D. J., Condies, S. J., and England, J. L. 1979. Age and work values. *Academy of Management Journal,* September, 617–623; Ratan, S. 1993. Generational tensions in the office: Why busters hate boomers. *Fortune,* 4 October, 56–70.

Each individual develops a different value system that shapes attitudes and behaviors. Value systems, in turn, affect ethical behavior in organizations, a factor that has critical implications for leaders.

Values and Ethics

Ethics are a person's concept of right and wrong. Two general views of ethics are the relativist and universalist views. Individuals with a relativist view of ethics believe that what is right or wrong depends on the situation or the culture (Donaldson 1994). An index collected by the Berlin Transparency International, an organization that uses a complex set of data to monitor corruption around the world, shows distinct national differences in ethical values. In their June 2001 index, Bangladesh, Nigeria, Uganda, and Indonesia were ranked as some of the most corrupt nations, and Denmark was ranked as one of the least corrupt (Transparency International 2001). To illustrate, businesspeople in many places consider gifts, bribes, or kickbacks acceptable behavior in contract negotiations, although these activities are unethical and illegal based on U.S. values and laws. A person with a relativist view of ethics would take a "when in Rome, do as the Romans do" approach. That is, a U.S. manager who learns that it is generally accepted to bribe officials in Thailand to secure a contract would consider bribing a Thai official acceptable and ethical behavior. Note that it is rarely possible for managers of U.S.-based companies to adopt a relativist view of ethics in business situations because U.S. laws forbid any form of bribery anywhere in the world. In contrast, a person with a universalist view of ethics believes that all activities should be judged by the same standards, regardless of the situation or culture. For example, an oil company based on U.S. laws of equal opportunity and the principles of cultural diversity would appoint a female manager to its Saudi operations, despite the religious and cultural problems it might create.

The value and ethical issues facing leaders are highly complex (Ettorre 1994). Global and cross-cultural issues further add to the complexity of the issues. For example, research by Triandis and his associates (Triandis et al. 2001) indicates that collectivism tends to be related to greater use of deception in negotiation, as well as higher levels of guilt after using deception. Particularly, Koreans and Japanese feel considerable guilt and shame after using deception. Furthermore, based on what each culture values, individuals within that culture might lie for different reasons, such as protecting their privacy in the case of the United States, or benefiting family members in the case of Samoans (Aune and Water 1994). Because of complex cross-cultural and individual differences in values, handling ethical and value-driven issues will continue to be a major part of every manager's job.

ABILITIES AND SKILLS

Much of the early research in leadership characteristics focused on establishing leadership abilities. Although leaders clearly must have some abilities, competencies, and skills, these do not have high correlations to leadership effectiveness (for a review of the early research, see Bass 1990a). Intelligence, technical, interpersonal, and cognitive skills have received particular attention.

Intelligence and Emotional Intelligence

The research on the link between intelligence and leadership shows a clear relationship between the two. However, the correlations vary (Bass 1990a). To date, only one major leadership theory, the Cognitive Resource Model (Fiedler and Garcia 1987a, b), has used intelligence specifically as a major factor. Reviews of the link between general intelligence and leadership indicate that it is an important aspect of leadership (Cornwell 1983; Lord, DeVader, and Alliger 1986). However, the relationship may be moderated by many factors. For example, when being competent at a task is key, leaders who are more intelligent might do better. However, in situations that require interpersonal skills, general intelligence might not be sufficient. The level of leadership also may be a factor. In particular, intuition may be especially important for leaders at upper organizational levels (Bruce 1986). Furthermore, some early research shows that a curvilinear relationship may exist between intelligence and leadership (Ghiselli 1963). Those with either low or high scores are less likely to be effective and successful leaders. Both, for different reasons, might have difficulty communicating with their followers and motivating them to achieve the task.

Consider Scott Rudin, producer of hit movies such as *The Truman Show* and *In and Out*. Some of the people who work with him consider Rudin to be "one of the smartest and most clever and witty guys I have ever met" (Carvell 1998, p. 201). He is bright and creative, and many admire his work. However, his intelligence and creativity are not enough. As one of Rudin's ex-assistants states: "I think the people that work there—most of them hate him. Nobody likes him. Everybody's miserable" (Carvell 1998, p. 201). As this example illustrates, being intelligent is not sufficient for being an effective leader. Many other characteristics play important roles.

Emotional Intelligence

In the past few years, a new perspective has been added to the concept of intelligence. Whereas intelligence generally is defined in terms of mental abilities, some have argued that the ability to relate interpersonally contributes another type of intelligence (see Goleman 1995). The ability to interact well with followers, satisfy their emotional needs, and motivate and inspire them is another key to effective leadership. (For more on this, see the discussion of charismatic leadership in Chapter 8.) Table 3-2 summarizes the five elements of emotional intelligence, or EQ.

> The ability to interact well with followers, satisfy their emotional needs, and motivate and inspire them is key to leadership.

Individuals with high EQ are in touch with their emotions and demonstrate self-management in their ability to control their moods and feelings productively and in staying motivated and focused even when facing obstacles. They can calm themselves when angry and stay balanced. They also are able to read others' emotions, feel empathy for them, and put themselves in their place. The last component of EQ is having the ability to develop productive and positive interpersonal relationships through understanding, conflict resolution, and negotiation (Goleman 1998; see Self-Assessment 3-2).

Psychologist Daniel Goleman argues that EQ might play a key role in the success of managers and leaders. He states: "The rules for work are changing, and we're all being judged, by a new yardstick—not just how smart we are and what technical skills we have, which employers see as givens, but increasingly by how well we handle ourselves and one another" (Fisher 1998, p. 293). Although competence and cognitive ability might be keys for success when working alone, leadership requires successful interaction with others and the ability to motivate them to accomplish goals.

Table 3-2

Components of Emotional Intelligence

Component	Description
Self-awareness	Being aware of and in touch with your own feelings and emotions
Managing emotions	Being able to manage various emotions and moods by denying or suppressing them
Self-motivation	Being able to remain positive and optimistic
Empathy for others	Being able to read others' emotions accurately and putting yourself in their place
Interpersonal skills	Having the skills to build and maintain positive relationships with others

Source: Based on Goleman (1995) and Goleman, Boyatzis, and McKee (2002).

Therefore, EQ might be a central factor in several leadership processes, particularly in the development of charismatic and transformational leadership, where the emotional bond between leaders and followers is imperative. Being able to empathize with followers can further allow a leader to develop followers and create a consensus. Some researchers suggest that emotional intelligence contributes to effective leadership because an emotionally intelligent leader focuses on followers, on inspiring them, and on developing enthusiasm (George 2000). Whereas leaders with a high IQ lead with their head, leaders with a high EQ lead with their heart and address their followers' emotional needs.

Ken Chenault, CEO of American Express (Amex) and one of only a handful of black leaders of Fortune 500 companies, is able to win his employees' trust and build cohesion. He is described as understated and modest, with quiet warmth and a style that makes people want to be on his team (Schwartz 2001). Tom Ryder, who competed with Chenault for the top Amex job, states: "If you work around him, you feel like you'd do anything for the guy" (Schwartz 2001, p. 62). Dan Hanson, president of the Land O'Lakes' fluid-dairy division, also leads with his heart. His focus is on building relationships inside and outside his organization. He states: "One important thing I've learned is that people want to be challenged as well as appreciated" (Row 1998, p. 192).

Many organizations are finding that developing their managers' emotional intelligence can have a positive impact on performance. The U.S. Air Force Recruiting Service successfully used EQ to identify recruiters who would meet their quotas and considerably reduced the turnover of their recruiters (Schwartz 2000). American Express insurance division similarly found that focusing on emotional intelligence and training their financial advisors on how to understand their emotions better led to increased sales performance (Schwartz 2000). In spite of many anecdotal reports about EQ's benefits, its increasing popularity as a leadership training tool, and some research supporting its validity (Ciarrochi, Chan, and Caputi 2000; Sosik and Megerian 1999), much more research is needed about its effect on improving leaders' performance (Newsome, Day, and Catano, 2000).

WHAT DOES THIS MEAN FOR ME?
Applying Emotional Intelligence

EQ can be a useful tool for self-development. Here are some areas to work on:

- Learn about your strengths and weaknesses by taking self-assessments, engaging in honest reflection, and seeking and listening to feedback.

- Work on controlling your temper and your moods; stay composed, positive, and tactful when facing difficult situations.

- Integrity is a choice; stay true to your word and your commitments.

- Set challenging goals and be willing to work hard to achieve them; admit your mistakes and learn from them.

- Build relationships with others and develop your network.

- Pay attention to those around you; be concerned about their well-being and their feelings.

Creativity

A leader's ability to be creative is increasingly important, given the uncertainty that many businesses face (Horton 1986). Creativity—also known as divergent thinking or lateral thinking—is the ability to combine or link ideas in new ways to generate novel and useful alternatives (Boden 1994). Lateral thinking focuses on moving away from the linear approach advocated by rational decision making (DeBono 1992). Philippe Gaulier, a professional clown who runs L'Ecole Gaulier, a nontraditional leadership school in London, has a similar approach. He focuses on teaching leaders to go past their rational minds, and connect with their emotions and on reaching a "heightened energy state" (Rubin 2000). Through creative acting methods, Gaulier helps his students find a strong stage presence and their true inner self. They learn to be passionate, use drama and emotions, forget appearances, and leave self-consciousness and old habits behind.

Creative leaders listen intently to all sources, especially to bad news, in order to know where the next problem is emerging. They value subjective as well as objective information. They turn facts, perceptions, gut feelings, and intuitions into reality by making bold and informed decisions. These executives do not rely solely on the rational decision-making models. Creative leaders share four characteristics (Sternberg and Lubart 1995):

- *Perseverance in the face of obstacles and self-confidence.* Creative individuals persevere more in the face of problems and have strong beliefs in the correctness of their ideas.
- *Willingness to take risks.* Creative individuals take moderate to high risks rather than extreme risks that have a strong chance of failing.
- *Willingness to grow and openness to experience.* Creative individuals are open to experiences and are willing to try new methods.
- *Tolerance of ambiguity.* Creative individuals tolerate lack of structure and not having clear answers.

As this list suggests, creative leaders tend to be confident in the paths they select and are willing to take risks when others give up. They also focus on learning and are willing to live with uncertainty to reach their goals. As with any other characteristics, the organizational setting can have a great impact on allowing creativity to flourish (Ekvall and Ryhammar 1999; Zhou and George 2001).

Skills

The research on leadership skills is considerably clearer and more conclusive than that on leadership abilities. Leadership skills generally are divided into three categories: technical, interpersonal, and conceptual (see Table 3-3).

As leaders and managers move up in their organization, they rely less on technical skills and increasingly on interpersonal and conceptual skills. Company CEOs, school principals, or hospital administrators do not need to be able to perform various jobs in detail. However, they should be able to negotiate successfully and effectively various interpersonal relationships inside and outside the organization. Furthermore, top executives more than lower-level leaders and managers need to

Table 3-3
Leadership Skills

Skills Category	Description
Technical skills	Knowledge of the job processes, methods, tools, and techniques
Interpersonal skills	Knowledge of interpersonal relationships including communication, conflict management, negotiation, and team building
Conceptual skills	Knowledge of problem solving, logical thinking, decision making, creativity, and reasoning in general

read and analyze their internal and external environments, and make strategic decisions that require considerable problem-solving skills.

The impact of ability and skills on leadership depends to a great extent on the situation. Situational factors such as the type of organization, level of leadership, ability and needs of followers, and type of task at hand all play a role in what abilities and skills leaders will need in order to be effective. The recent approach to leadership skills presented in Chapter 2 further emphasizes that key skills of complex problem solving, solution construction, and social judgment develop as a result of experience (Mumford, Zaccaro, Johnson et al. 2000).

LEADING CHANGE
Learning in Organizations

Judy Rosenblum is a learning expert. She teaches leaders and companies how to learn. She has worked with companies such as Coca-Cola and Coopers & Lybrand as vice president and chief learning officer, and vice chair for learning and education. The focus on learning is increasingly important in a fast-changing environment. Rosenblum believes that leaders play a key role in learning in their organization. ". . . learning is a strategic choice; it doesn't just happen. Learning is a capability. It requires skills. It requires processes. And it requires leaders who value it" (Webber 2000, p. 274).

Rosenblum proposes some key factors that allow members of organizations to learn. First, leaders have to become champions of learning; they have to believe in it and drive the process from the top. Second, models of leadership that require the leader to provide all of the information and instructions prevent followers from learning. Instead, they simply rely on the leader to make decisions. Therefore, leaders must provide direction and encourage followers to learn solutions. Third, learning requires that people interact formally and informally. Fourth, learning skills have to be taught and valued. Finally, although some short-term results occur, learning is a long-term process that requires long-term commitment. Fundamentally, the culture of an organization must support learning. "Learning is a marathon, not a sprint" (Webber 2000, p. 282).

Source: Webber, A. 2000. Will companies ever learn? *Fast Company,* October, 275–282.

Although a review of early trait research, summarized in Chapter 2, indicates that no specific traits can allow us to predict who will become a leader or which leader will be effective, traits do play a role in leadership in several ways.

- First, as discussed in Chapter 2, researchers have identified some traits that are consistently associated with leadership.
- Second, a leader's personality influences his or her preferences, style, and behavior.
- Third, personality may impact the ease with which a leader learns skills and is able to implement them.
- Finally, being aware of key personality traits that have been shown to affect work-related behaviors can help leaders develop their self-awareness and aid them in their learning and development.

The next section presents six personality traits that have implications for leadership.

The Big-Five Personality Dimensions

Over time, organizational behavior and human resource management researchers have condensed countless personality traits into a list of five major personality dimensions, known as the Big Five (Barrick and Mount 1991; Digman 1990; Norman 1963). Researchers have found that these five dimensions are consistent components of personality not only in the United States, but in several other cultures, as well (Blumberg 2001; Rust 1999). Table 3-4 summarizes the key elements of the Big Five personality dimensions.

Table 3-4
Big Five Personality Dimensions

PERSONALITY DIMENSIONS	DESCRIPTION
Conscientiousness	Degree to which a person is dependable, responsible, organized, and plans ahead
Extraversion/Intraversion	Degree to which a person is sociable, talkative, assertive, active, and ambitious
Openness to experience	Degree to which a person is imaginative, broad minded, curious, and seeks new experiences
Emotional stability	Degree to which a person is anxious, depressed, angry, and insecure
Agreeableness	Degree to which a person is courteous, likable, good natured, and flexible

Sources: Based on descriptions provided by Norman (1963), Digman (1990), and Barrick and Mount (1991).

The Big-Five dimensions allow the grouping of many different traits into a meaningful taxonomy for studying individual differences. These five dimensions are relatively independent and have several implications for management.

A number of the Big-Five personality dimensions have links to work-related behaviors such as career success (Judge et al. 1999; Seibert and Kraimer 2001) and the performance of managers who work abroad (Caligiuri 2000). However, none alone is a strong predictor of performance or leadership. Of the five dimensions, conscientiousness is the most strongly correlated to job performance. This makes sense: Individuals who are dependable, organized, and hard working tend to perform better in their job (Barrick and Mount 1991; Frink and Ferris 1999; Hayes, Roehm, and Catellano 1994). Most managers would agree that a good employee is dependable, shows up on time, finishes work by deadlines, and is willing to work hard. For instance, Andy Grove, former CEO of Intel and management guru, used to make a list of which of his employees showed up on time. He believes that dependable employees perform better.

Extraversion is the Big-Five dimension with the second-highest correlation to job-related behaviors, and is particularly important in jobs that rely on social interaction, such as management or sales. It is much less essential for employees working on an assembly line or as computer programmers (Hayes, Roehm, and Catellano 1994). Unlike conscientiousness, which can apply to all job levels or occupations, extroversion is not an essential trait for every job, and individuals can succeed without being extroverted. In fact, one of the U.S.'s most-admired business leaders, Lew Platt, previous CEO of Hewlett-Packard, is not an extravert. "Lew Platt isn't a loud, extroverted guy, but he is . . . in his own quiet, blushing way getting his colleagues not only to understand but to agree [with his way]" (Stewart 1998, p. 82).

Openness to experience can help performance in some instances, but not in others. For example, being open to new experiences can help employees and managers perform well in training because they will be motivated to explore fresh ideas and to learn (Goldstein 1986), and it might help them be more successful in overseas assignments (Ones and Viswesvaran 1999). Bill Gates, CEO of Microsoft, is legendary for his intelligence and his thirst for new ideas (Gimein 2001). After his travel to India in 1997, he observed: "Even though 80 percent of what you hear from customers is the same all over the world, you always learn something you can apply to our business elsewhere" (Schlender 1997, p. 81). But the same eagerness to explore new ideas and ways of doing things can be an impediment to performance on jobs that require careful attention to existing processes and procedures.

As one would expect, emotional stability also is related to job behaviors and performance. At the extreme, individuals who are neurotic are not likely to be able to function in organizations. However, some degree of anxiety and worrying can help people perform well because it spurs them to excel. Andy Grove's book, *Only the Paranoid Survive: How to Exploit the Crisis That Challenges Every Company and Career,* is an indication of the sense of anxiety he instills at Intel to make sure employees perform and the organization excels.

Finally, although agreeableness is a highly desirable personality trait in social situations, it generally is not associated with work-related behaviors or performance. The most important managerial implication of the Big-Five dimensions is that despite the reliability and robustness of the Big Five as measures of personality, no single trait is linked strongly to how well a leader or manager will perform in all types and levels of jobs.

Other Individual Personality Traits

Another approach to understanding the role of traits in leadership is to take into consideration general personality traits that have an impact on the way a person leads. As is the case with the Big-Five dimensions, many of the traits fit into the framework and categories proposed by Kirkpatrick and Locke (1991) discussed in Chapter 2.

Locus of Control

The concept of locus of control, introduced by Rotter in 1966, is an indicator of an individual's sense of control over the environment and external events. People who have a high internal locus of control (i.e., a high score on the scale; see Self-Assessment 3-3) believe that many of the events around them are a result of their actions. They feel a sense of control over their lives. They attribute their successes and failures to their own efforts. Because of this attribution, individuals with an internal locus of control are more proactive and take more risks (Anderson, Hellreigel, and Slocum 1977). As such, they demonstrate the motivation, energy, and self-confidence proposed by Kirkpatrick and Locke (1991) to be central leadership traits. Research indicates that internals are less anxious, set harder goals, and are less conforming to authority than externals (for a review of the literature, see Spector 1982). In addition, internals make greater efforts to achieve their goals and tend to be more task oriented than externals. They also have been found to be more ethical in their decision making and harsher on bribery (Cherry and Fraedrich 2000)

Individuals with an external locus of control attribute the events in their lives to forces external to them—to factors such as luck, other powerful people, or a deep religious faith. They attribute their success to luck and interpersonal skills rather than to their intelligence and ability (Sightler and Wilson 2001). In other words, they do not generally perceive that they have a high degree of control over their lives. Therefore, they are more reactive to events and less able to rebound from stressful situations. They rely on others' judgments and conform to authority more readily than internals (Spector 1982). As leaders, externally controlled individuals are likely to use more coercive power, a factor that stems from projecting their own sense of lack of control onto others. Because they do not feel they control events and because they tend to be reactive, they believe others will do the same, and they overcontrol their followers to compensate for how they perceive others.

Several studies have explored the link between leadership and locus of control. Some findings indicate that internals are more likely to emerge as group leaders, and that groups led by internals perform better than those headed by externals (Anderson and Schneier 1978). Other research has looked at the effect of locus of control on CEOs' behaviors and choices of strategy for their organizations. The results indicate that internally controlled CEOs select risky and innovative strategies for their firms to a higher degree than do externals (Miller and Droge 1986; Miller, Kets de Vries, and Toulouse 1982). They also tend to be more proactive and future oriented.

Although research is limited, the pattern of results is highly consistent. A clear difference is evident between the behavior and decision-making patterns of internally and externally controlled leaders. Such patterns are not the only determinant of a leader's behavior, but they have the potential to affect a leader's actions.

Type A

Since the late 1960s, researchers have focused on the concept of the Type A behavior pattern as a risk factor for coronary disease (Glass 1983; Rosenman and Friedman 1974). Psychologists and management researchers also have become interested in the Type A personality (Baron 1989). Generally, Type A's are described as trying to do more in less and less time. As compared to Type B's, they are involved in a whirlwind of activity. At the heart of the Type A construct is the need for control (Smith and Rhodewalt 1986; Strube and Werner 1985). As opposed to Type B's, who tend to have less need for control, Type A individuals have a high need for control, which manifests itself in four general characteristics (see Figure 3-3).

The first Type A characteristic, time urgency, leads Type A individuals to be concerned with time. Being in a hurry, impatience with delays, and worries about time are aspects of time urgency. The second Type A characteristic is competitiveness. Type A individuals are generally highly competitive in work, social, and sport situations. They measure their outcomes against others and keep track of their performance; getting ahead and winning are major concerns. The third characteristic, polyphasic behaviors, involves doing several things at once. Although everyone is likely to undertake several activities when pressured, Type A's often do so even when not required to by work or other deadlines. For example, they might make a

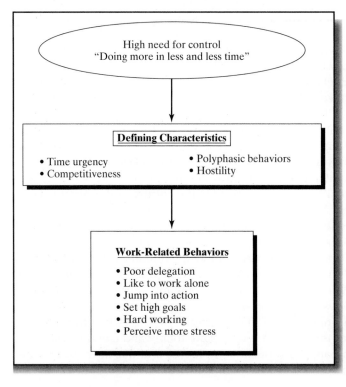

Figure 3-3
Type A Characteristics and Behaviors

list of specific activities they think they have to undertake during a vacation. The last Type A characteristic is hostility. It is the only characteristic still found by researchers to be tied to coronary problems. It is manifested in explosive speech; diffused anger; intolerance for delays or mistakes; and a generally fiery, aggressive (Baron, Neuman and Geddes 1999), and sometimes malicious style of interaction (Strube et al. 1984).

These four sets of characteristics are triggered by the Type A's need for control and are aimed at providing the Type A with a sense of control over the environment (see Self-Assessment 3-4). Interestingly, although the Type A and locus of control concepts use the construct of control as a key defining element, the two scales are not related. Internally controlled individuals feel they control their lives; Type A's need an increasing amount of control over events even when they exhibit internal locus of control. Type A characteristics are neither bad nor good. Type A's and Type B's have certain traits and behaviors that can either be helpful or provide obstacles to being effective leaders; situational requirements are the key.

The relationship of Type A to leadership has not been established specifically, but a number of findings that link Type A behavior to work-related behaviors provide interesting insights. The results of one study suggest that being Type A affects the way CEOs approach organizational strategy (Nahavandi, Mizzi, and Malekzadeh 1992). Type A executives see more threats in the environment of their organizations and set challenging strategies that still provide them with a sense of control. Furthermore, as compared to Type B's, Type A's tend to be poor delegators and generally prefer to work alone (Miller, Lack, and Asroff 1985). They like to maintain control over all aspects of their work. The lack of delegation can be damaging to a leader, as it often is considered a major pitfall of management. Furthermore, with the increasing focus on cooperation, use of teams, and empowerment as a leadership style, the inability to delegate can prove to be an obstacle to successful leadership.

Type A's tend to set high performance goals and have high expectations for themselves and those around them. Such high expectations lead faster promotions at lower organizational levels (Stewart-Belle and Lust, 1999). When taken in a leadership context, such high expectations can lead to high performance and high quality, as well as to overload and burnout when carried to an extreme. Along with high expectations, Type A's also do not recognize and admit that they are tired. They are hard workers who might not understand other people's less-intense approach to work. Chapter 1 considered the culture of the Atlantic Group, the New York furniture distributor, and the role of its leader, Roger Abramson, in creating that culture. Abramson is an excellent example of a Type A person. He is tireless, obsessed with time, loses his temper easily, is focused on measuring performance, and keeps numerous balls in the air at any given time (Fenn 1998). Gerard Mestrallet, the CEO of the French utilities company Suez Lyonnaise des Eaux, is obsessed with his company's performance so much so that he interrupts interviews to check on stock prices (Tomlinson 2000). Tom DeMarco, a high-tech consultant, suggests that many companies believe that they are ". . . effective only to the extent that all their workers are totally and eternally busy" (Anders 2001b, p. 28). Such an approach pushes employees and managers to take on many Type A characteristics.

> Type A's tend to set high performance goals and have high expectations for themselves and those around them. When taken in a leadership context, such high expectations can lead to high performance and high quality, as well as to overload and burnout when carried to an extreme.

As is the case with locus of control, the Type A construct has been related directly to leadership in only a few studies. However, the consistency of the findings that Type A's like to maintain control, are active and hard working, and tend to be impatient with delays and with their coworkers allows us to consider the potential implications for leadership. These behaviors are similar to the high energy and motivation that Kirkpatrick and Locke (1991) propose as central leadership traits. Type A leaders are likely to be intense and demanding, set high performance standards, and be intolerant of delays and excuses. They also might have trouble delegating tasks or working in a team environment. Interestingly, although some Type A characteristics appear to define effective leaders (such as drive, ambition, and energy), others, such as impatience with delays and a tendency to jump into action, are characteristics that do not serve leaders well.

Self-Monitoring

When observing some leaders, we can identify their style easily and in some cases even their personality traits. They seem to be an open book, and their behavior is consistent in many different situations. For example, Herb Kelleher, founder of Southwest Airlines, has a forceful but open style in all settings, whether he is dealing with the Southwest employees or stockholders, or presenting at a business conference. Other leaders are harder to read, or their behaviors appear to change from one situation to another.

One reason it might be easy to read some people and establish their style but difficult to do so for others is the concept of self-monitoring. Developed by Snyder (1974), the self-monitoring (SM) scale identifies the degree to which people are capable of reading and using the cues from their environment to determine their behavior. Individuals who score high on the scale (see Self-Assessment 3-5) are able to read environmental and social cues regarding what is appropriate behavior and use those cues to adjust their behaviors. They can present themselves and manage impressions (Turnley and Bolino 2001). Those scoring lower on the scale either do not read the cues or do not use them to change their behavior. For high SMs, behavior is likely to be the result of a perception of the environment and is therefore likely to change depending on the situation. Low SMs' behaviors are more internally determined and are likely to appear constant across different situations. This internal focus also seems to make them more accurate decision makers regarding performance ratings and personnel decisions (Jawahar 2001).

As will be seen in Part II, many leadership theories rely on the assumptions that leaders (1) have the ability to evaluate various situations and (2) can change their behaviors to match the requirements of the situation. In that context, being a high SM might become a key leadership trait. Being a high self-monitor should help a leader better perceive and analyze a situation. Furthermore, given self-monitors' higher ability to adjust their behaviors, it is reasonable to suggest that, at least in situations that are ambiguous and difficult to read, they might be more effective leaders. Some studies have supported these ideas (e.g., Dobbins et al. 1990). Researchers have found that high SMs emerge as leaders more frequently than do low SMs, leading to the hypothesis that self-monitoring is a key variable in leadership. Interesting findings also have emerged regarding the link between Type A and SM, as well as the role that gender might play in SM.

Several studies have looked at the impact of gender, self-monitoring, and Type A on conflict management and leadership in organizations (Baron 1989; Becker, Ayman, and Korabik 1994; Dobbins et al. 1990). The results indicate the following:

- High self-monitors emerge as leaders more often than do low self-monitors.
- Men emerge as leaders more often than do women.
- Type A's are in conflict more often than are Type B's, particularly when dealing with their subordinates.
- High self-monitors resolve conflicts cooperatively when dealing with their subordinates and their supervisors.
- Women generally report lower levels of conflict with both their subordinates and their supervisors.
- High self-monitoring women are especially sensitive to various organizational cues and seem to perceive more conflict.

Overall, self-monitoring has interesting applications to leadership, many of which remain unexplored. Little doubt remains, however, that being a high SM can be a useful characteristic in helping leaders adjust their behaviors and perhaps even in learning new skills. It has been suggested that high SMs are better able to cope with cross-cultural experiences because such situations are ambiguous and require the ability to interpret environmental cues. Similarly, the changing leadership roles are making leadership situations considerably less routine and more uncertain than they were 20 years ago. Modern leaders have to deal with diverse cultures and followers' demands for participation and autonomy, and they also have to understand an increasingly complex global environment. Self-monitoring might be a key characteristic in these new tasks.

Myers Briggs Type Indicator

Although the research about its robustness is contradictory, the Myers Briggs Type Indicator (MBTI) is one of the most widely used personality tests in organizations for leadership training and team building (Caggiano 1998; Hammonds 2001). Its primary use has been to help teams and work groups understand and capitalize on the individual approaches to decision making. As an aid to decision making and team building, the MBTI has enjoyed tremendous success. The scale classifies individuals along four bipolar dimensions that are combined to provide a profile for each person. The first two major dimensions, sensing/intuition and thinking/feeling, relate to information gathering and information interpretation (see Figure 3-4). The other two are perception/judgmental (P/J) and extrovert/introvert (E/I).

People with different styles approach problem solving and decision making differently. Some studies have linked MBTI to behaviors such as time urgency, academic problems, and even the selection of functional areas. For example, most scientists are sensation thinkers (STs) or intuitive thinkers (NTs), whereas research and development managers tend to be either sensation feelers (SFs) or intuitive feelers (NFs). (For a review of behaviors related to MBTI, see Furnham and Stringfield 1993.) People with different dominant styles prefer a certain type of information, have different time orientation, and generally approach problems in different ways. The MBTI is used as a leadership training tool in several major leadership training programs, most notably in the Center of Creative Leadership (Conger 1992). The assumption is

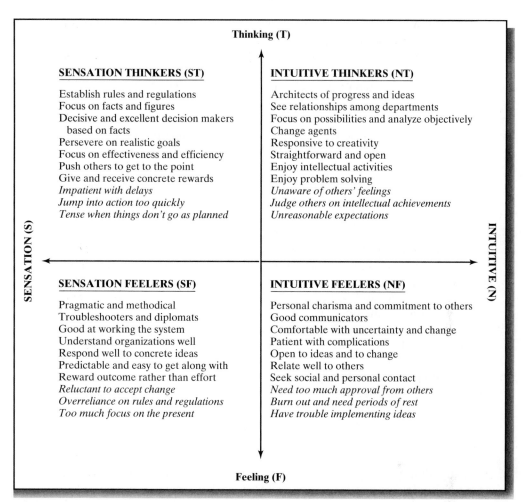

Figure 3-4
Four MBTI Categories

Sources: Extracted from Furnham and Stringfield (1993), Haley and Stumpf (1989), and Moore (1987).

that individuals with different MBTI styles are likely to approach their tasks and their groups differently. For example, a sensing-thinking (ST) leader is likely to require his or her group to seek out and provide facts and figures, and concrete alternatives and solutions. Because the feeling (F) dimension is secondary for that leader, focus on interpersonal issues is likely to be absent or not a primary factor, which might hinder resolution of interpersonal conflict in some situations. An intuitive-feeler (NF) leader will have little interest in the group's factual analysis and is likely to prefer to hear about possibilities and creative alternatives to problems.

Interesting cross-cultural studies point to national differences regarding the MBTI. For example, Chinese managers are higher in introversion, sensing, thinking, and judgment than their European counterparts (Furnham and Stringfield 1993). The Chinese management profile appears to be ISTJ (introverted-sensor-thinker-judgmental) as compared to the Europeans' ESTJ (extroverted-sensor-thinker-judgmental). For

European and Chinese groups, managers' extroversion is linked to better performance and higher satisfaction.

The MBTI also has been applied to executive leadership (Haley and Stumpf 1989; Henderson and Nutt 1980; Nutt 1986, 1988). In general, the findings show that STs are risk averse, whereas SFs tolerate risk better. The MBTI seems particularly applicable to upper-echelon research because the strategic domain is to a great extent a decision-making environment in which the CEO and top-management team analyze the environment and make decisions regarding the best strategies to take advantage of that environment. (See Chapter 9 for further discussion of the role of CEOs.)

Overall, the MBTI has been a useful tool in understanding the way individuals think and make decisions. Given that the latter two activities are key to leadership, knowledge of their MBTI score and its related behavioral correlates can help people understand their own actions as leaders and help them prepare for areas that might be difficult to undertake. For example, the MBTI score can be the basis for the selection of leadership training and development. An NF leader, for instance, is less likely to need training on interpersonal relations than an ST leader. However, the NF's lack of interest in facts and figures and logical problem solving can become a major impediment when making a presentation to an ST-dominated board of directors. In such a situation, training NF leaders in logical problem solving might help them become more effective with some of their constituents (see Self-Assessment 3-6).

Machiavellian Personality

Do you believe that the end justifies the means? Are you skilled at manipulating others to get what you want? Are you a ruthless, skilled negotiator? If you answer positively to these questions, chances are you have some elements of a Machiavellian personality (see Self-Assessment 3-7). The concept of the Machiavellian personality, developed by Christie and Geis (1970), is based loosely on Niccolo Machiavelli's work *The Prince*. The Machiavelli (Mach) scale measures an individual's willingness to put self-interests and his or her preferences above the interests of the group, and an individual's ability to influence and manipulate others for personal gain (Jaffe, Nebenzahl, and Gotesdyner 1989; Panitz 1989).

Individuals with a high score on the scale are comfortable using various means to achieve their personal goals. A high Mach has a cynical view of human nature (Corral and Calvete 2000), few scruples, and is willing to step outside the bounds of formal authority. These individuals might lack the honesty and integrity that are requirements of effective leadership. On the other end of the scale, low Machs tend to be overly naive and trusting. Although no formal linkages have been established, it can be assumed that high Machs' political and manipulation skills allow them to be successful if not effective leaders (Luthans 1989). Their aim is to promote themselves rather than supporting their followers. Low Machs, on the other hand, might not demonstrate enough political savvy and therefore might be unable to provide their group with the necessary resources and visibility.

Neither the high Machs nor those scoring low on the scale are likely to be effective leaders. High Machs are too focused on their personal goals; low Machs are not skilled at the legitimate influence tactics essential for effective leadership. In general, individuals who are medium Machs tend to be the most effective leaders. Such people are good negotiators and savvy about manipulation of others to reach goals. However, they do not abuse their power, and they focus on achieving organizational rather than personal goals. Medium Machs are the ones who are capable of being successful and effective (Luthans 1989).

As can be expected from a concept that relates to perception and use of power, cross-cultural differences exist with regard to Mach scores. For example, Hong Kong and People's Republic of China (PRC) managers score higher on the Mach scale than do their U.S. counterparts. It appears that the Chinese are more willing to use social power to accomplish their goals (Ralston, Gustafson, Cheung et al. 1993; Ralston, Gustafson, Terpstra et al. 1993). This finding fits with the concept of high-power distance, where authority is broad and respected.

Our popular press is full of examples of ruthless leaders from the private and public sectors, who wheel and deal their way to achieving their goals with considerable disregard for their subordinates. Some are admired for what they can achieve; others are simply feared. Several publications prepare regular lists of these tough bosses. In many cases, as long as the bottom line is healthy and key constituents, such as the board of directors or stockholders, are satisfied, the means used by these leaders are tolerated.

Each of the preceding individual characteristics and traits plays a role in how leaders interact with others or make decisions. Any one trait alone, or even a combination, cannot explain or predict leadership effectiveness. However, these characteristics can be useful tools for self-awareness and understanding, and as guides to leadership development. Certain characteristics, though, have been found to be detrimental to effective leadership.

What about Leaders Who Fail?

Another way to learn about leaders' individual characteristics is to evaluate leaders who are not successful and who derail. Do they have some common characteristics? Are they any different than those who succeed? The Center for Creative Leadership has conducted research tracking leaders who derail (McCall and Lombardo 1983), and many anecdotal accounts report characteristics of leaders who do not succeed (Hymowitz 1988a; Nelton 1997). The following are the primary reasons for derailment:

- An abrasive, intimidating style.
- Coldness and arrogance.
- Untrustworthiness.
- Self-centeredness and overly political actions.
- Poor performance.
- Inability to delegate.

As the list shows, lack of people skills and the inability to manage relationships are central issues. Leaders who are good with followers and other constituents have a better chance of success. Pam Alexander is the CEO of Ogilvy Public Relations Worldwide, a public relations firm that concentrates on building relationships. She states: "To build trust, invest in your relationships constantly. Don't sweat the ROI [return on investment]; help people, whether or not they can return the favor. Connect them to appropriate opportunities whenever you can" (Canabou and

Overholt 2001, p. 100). John Chambers, the CEO of Cisco Systems, led his company out of the 2000 dot.com slump by providing a vision and setting a direction, helping his employees, preparing them for disruption, and listening to his customers (Anders 2001a). Increasingly, leaders who rule with an iron fist, exercise power without accountability, and are unwilling or unable to allow followers to contribute and develop are rated poorly (Russell 1990).

USING INDIVIDUAL CHARACTERISTICS

The various individual characteristics presented in this chapter do not allow us to develop a clear leadership profile. We still do not know what makes an effective leader, although we have some indications about undesirable characteristics. The different characteristics are generally independent from one another. In other words, an individual might have an internal locus of control, be a Type B, NF, moderate Mach, and high self-monitor. Although certain combinations are intuitively more likely to occur, the scales are not statistically correlated. Research in the area is minimal, and it is reasonable to assume that some combinations of traits make certain traits and behaviors more salient and dominant. For example, a low self-monitor Type A who also happens to be an ST with internal locus of control is likely to have a highly proactive and aggressive style in many situations. On the other hand, a high self-monitor Type B with high scores on the feeling dimension of the MBTI is likely to come across as low key, interpersonally oriented, and socially sensitive, especially if the person believes that the situation requires such behavior.

Despite the validity of the constructs presented, it is important to limit the use of the scales to the purpose for which they were developed until further research evidence allows for broader application. The scales are all good self-awareness and self-development tools. The issue of self-awareness, through various means, is becoming key in many organizations (Caggiano 1998). The first step to leadership effectiveness is being aware of one's strengths, weaknesses, and personality characteristics. These characteristics explain in part why learning certain new behaviors is harder for some people than for others; they are not selection tools and should not be used for promotional or other job-related decisions. However, several organizations, ranging from Dell Computers to General Electric to Bristol-Myers and Hewlett-Packard, require candidates for top leadership positions to undergo hours of psychological testing, spending upwards of $5,000 for each evaluation (Daniels 2001). These companies claim that the results of such tests help them pick leaders who fit well with their culture.

The self-awareness trends in the business sector are leading to the use of 360-degree feedback, which allows managers to receive feedback about their behaviors, style, and performance not only from their bosses but also from their peers and subordinates. Although the results are sometimes painful, they are a helpful step in overcoming weaknesses. Another self-awareness tool that has gained popularity with companies such as AT&T and PepsiCo is the use of meditation and self-reflection as a means of increasing self-awareness and of managing stress (Sherman 1994). These individual tools often are combined with seminars such as that presented in Covey's *The Seven Habits of Highly Effective People* (1989), where the focus is on self-mastery and positive thinking. In times of change and with increasing pressure on leaders to be flexible, creative, and to deliver high performance, the push toward better self-knowledge allows for necessary self-development. Although it used to be assumed that leaders needed little training, the current trend brings continuous improvement down to the individual level.

SUMMARY AND CONCLUSION

This chapter presents the current thinking on the role of traits in leadership effectiveness and identifies several individual differences and personality characteristics that impact a leader's style and approach. Although these individual differences do not dictate behavior, they establish a zone of comfort for certain behaviors and actions. Values are long-lasting beliefs about what is worthwhile. They are strongly influenced by culture and are one of the determinants of ethical conduct. Intelligence is one of the abilities that most impacts leadership. Although being intelligent is related to leadership to some extent, it is not a sufficient factor to predict effectiveness. On the other hand, the recently proposed concept of emotional intelligence might have more direct impact on leadership as it relates to interpersonal skills. Creativity is another ability that might be important in leadership effectiveness, especially in situations that require novel approaches.

One of the most reliable sets of personality traits is called the Big Five. Although the conscientiousness and extraversion dimensions in the Big Five have some links to work-related behavior, the traits are not linked directly to leadership. Several other individual traits do have links to leadership. Locus of control is an indicator of the degree to which individuals perceive that they have control over the events around them. Individuals with internal control have been found to be more proactive, more satisfied with their work, and less coercive. Type A behavior also deals with issues of control but focuses on the need for control as demonstrated through a person's time urgency, competitiveness, polyphasic behaviors, and hostility. The Type A's need for control makes it difficult to delegate tasks and pushes the individual toward short-term focus and selection of strategies that will maximize control. Another relevant personality characteristic, self-monitoring, is the degree to which individuals read and use situational cues to adjust their behavior. High self-monitors have a degree of flexibility that might be helpful in leadership situations.

One of the most-used personality variables is the MBTI, which focuses primarily on the way a person gathers information and uses it to make decisions. The various MBTI types approach situations differently and have been found to focus on different factors as leaders. The last characteristic presented, Machiavellianism, focuses on the use of social power to achieve goals. High Machs are adept at manipulating others to achieve their personal goals. All of the concepts presented allow for better self-understanding and awareness. Although none is a measure of leadership style, they all relate to many leadership behaviors, such as delegation and decision making. The measures are well validated, but they are not meant to be used for selection or promotion decisions. Interestingly, cross-cultural research has indicated many differences on the scales in terms of gender and national cultures. These differences point to the potential role of culture in an individual's personality characteristics.

Using Psychological Testing

Organizations are relying increasingly on psychological tests to select, evaluate, promote, and develop their employees and managers. Although many of the tests are reliable and valid, many others are not. Additionally, tests developed in one culture do not always apply or have predictive validity in other cultures. However, such tests do provide a seemingly quick and efficient way to get to know people better.

As a department manager, you are faced with the selection of a new team of 10 members to run the marketing research and advertising campaign for a new product. The ideal employee profile includes: intelligence, creativity, assertiveness, competitiveness, ability to persuade others and negotiate well, and ability to work with a team. Your human resource department has conducted extensive testing of 50 inside and outside applicants for the new team. As you review the candidates' files, you notice that the majority of candidates who fit the profile best are young, Caucasian males while women and minorities tend to have low scores, particularly on assertiveness and competitiveness.

1. How much weight do you give the psychological tests? What factors do you need to consider?
2. Who do you select for the team?

REVIEW AND DISCUSSION QUESTIONS

1. What is the impact of individual characteristics on behavior?
2. How do values impact behaviors, and what impact does culture have on our value system?
3. How do emotional intelligence and general intelligence impact leadership?
4. What role does productivity play in leadership? Can a leader be effective with only average creativity?
5. Describe the six personality traits and their implications for leadership.
6. In your opinion (or based on your experience), do certain characteristics and traits have a greater impact than others on a person's leadership style? Explain your answer.
7. What are the limitations of the personality approach presented in this chapter, and how should the information about personal characteristics be used in leadership?
8. After completing the personality self-assessment surveys at the end of this chapter, consider your personal profile. What is the impact of this profile on your leadership style?

SEARCHING THE WEB

Machiavelli:
sol.brunel.ac.uk/~jarvis/bola/ethics/mach.html

Self-Assessments:
inst.santafe.cc.fl.us/~mwehr/X9PerT.htm
(Big Five)

psychology.about.com/library/jv/
bljv_pers.htm (Type A)

EXERCISE 3-1: YOUR IDEAL ORGANIZATION

This exercise is designed to help you understand the way different individuals perceive and define organizations.

Part I: Individual Description

Think of working in the organization of your dreams. What would it look like? How would it be organized? How would people interact? Your assignment in this part of the exercise is to provide a description of your ideal organization. In doing so, consider the following organizational characteristics and elements.

What industry would it be?

What is the mission of your ideal organization?

What is the culture? What are the basic assumptions? What are the behavioral norms? Who are the heroes? How do people interact?

How would people be organized? What is the structure? Consider issues of centralization, hierarchy, formalization, specialization, span of control, departmentation, and so on.

What is the role of the leader? What is the role of followers?

Describe the physical location, office spaces, office decor, and so on.

Consider issues such as dress code, work schedules, and others that you think are important in describing your ideal organization.

Part II: Group Work

Your instructor will assign you to a group and provide you with further instructions.

SELF-ASSESSMENT 3-1:   VALUE SYSTEMS

Rank the values in each of the two categories from 1 (most important) to 5 (least important to you).

Rank	Instrumental values	Rank	Terminal values
_____	Ambition and hard work	_____	Contribution and a sense of accomplishment
_____	Honesty and integrity		
_____	Love and affection	_____	Happiness
_____	Obedience and duty	_____	Leisurely life
_____	Independence and self-sufficiency	_____	Wisdom and maturity
_____	Humility	_____	Individual dignity
_____	Doing good to others (Golden Rule)	_____	Justice and fairness
		_____	Spiritual salvation

Scoring key: The values that you rank highest in each group are the ones that are most important to you. Consider whether your actions, career choices, and so forth are consistent with your values.

Source: Based on Anderson, C. 1997. Values-based management. *Academy of Management Executive* 11 no. 4, 25–46; Rokeach, M. 1973. *The nature of human values.* New York: Free Press.

SELF-ASSESSMENT 3-2: EMOTIONAL INTELLIGENCE

Indicate whether each of the following statements is true or false for you.

Self-Awareness
_____ 1. I am aware of how I feel and why.
_____ 2. I understand how my feelings affect my behavior and my performance.
_____ 3. I have a good idea of my personal strengths and weaknesses.
_____ 4. I analyze things that happen to me and reflect on what happened.
_____ 5. I am open to feedback from others.
_____ 6. I look for opportunities to learn more about myself.
_____ 7. I put my mistakes in perspective.
_____ 8. I maintain a sense of humor and can laugh about my mistakes.

Managing Emotions and Self-Regulation
_____ 9. I can stay calm in times of crisis.
_____10. I think clearly and stay focused when under pressure.
_____11. I show integrity in all my actions.
_____12. People can depend on my word.
_____13. I readily admit my mistakes.
_____14. I confront the unethical actions of others.
_____15. I stand for what I believe in.
_____16. I handle change well and stay the course.
_____17. I can be flexible when facing obstacles.

Self-Motivation
_____18. I set challenging goals.
_____19. I take reasonable and measured risks to achieve my goals.
_____20. I am results oriented.
_____21. I look for information on how to achieve my goals and improve my performance.
_____22. I go above and beyond what is simply required of me.
_____23. I am always looking for opportunities to do new things.
_____24. I maintain a positive attitude even when I face obstacles and setbacks.
_____25. I focus on success rather than failure.
_____26. I don't take failure personally or blame myself too much.

Empathy for Others
_____27. I pay attention to how others feel and react.
_____28. I can see someone else's point of view, even when I don't agree with it.
_____29. I am sensitive to other people.
_____30. I offer feedback and try to help others achieve their goals.
_____31. I recognize and reward others for their accomplishments.
_____32. I am available to coach and mentor people.
_____33. I respect people from varied backgrounds.
_____34. I relate well to people who are different from me.
_____35. I challenge intolerance, bias, and discrimination in others.

Social Skills

___36. I am skilled at persuading others.

___37. I can communicate clearly and effectively.

___38. I am a good listener.

___39. I can accept bad as well as good news.

___40. I can share my vision with others and inspire them to follow my lead.

___41. I lead by example.

___42. I challenge the status quo when necessary.

___43. I can handle difficult people tactfully.

___44. I encourage open and professional discussions when disagreements arise.

___45. I look for win-win solutions.

___46. I build and maintain relationships with others.

___47. I help maintain a positive climate at work.

___48. I model team qualities such as respect, helpfulness, and cooperation.

___49. I encourage participation from everyone when I work in teams.

___50. I understand political forces that operate in organizations.

Scoring key: For each of the 50 items, give yourself a 1 if you have marked "true" and 0 if you have marked "false." Consider your total for each of the subscales and your overall total score:

> Self-awareness: _____ out of 8
> Managing emotions: _____ out of 9
> Self-motivation: _____ out of 9
> Empathy for others: _____ out of 9
> Social skills: _____ out of 15
> Overall total: _____ out of 50

Those with higher scores in each category and overall demonstrate more of the characteristics associated with high emotional intelligence.

Source: Based on information in: Goleman, D. 1998. *Working with Emotional Intelligence.* New York: Bantam; Rosier, Richard H. ed. 1994, 1995. *The Competency Model Handbook,* Vol. 1, 2. Boston: Linkage.

Read the following statements and indicate whether you agree with Choice A or Choice B

A	B	
Making a lot of money is largely a matter of getting the right breaks.	Promotions are earned through hard work and persistence.	____
I have noticed a direct connection between how hard I study and the grade I get.	Many times, the reactions of teachers seem haphazard to me.	____
The number of divorces indicates that more and more people are not trying to make their marriages work.	Marriage is largely a gamble.	____
It is silly to think that one can change another person's basic attitudes.	When I am right, I can convince others.	____
Getting promoted is a matter of being a little luckier than the next person.	In our society, a person's future earning power depends on his or her ability.	____
If one knows how to deal with people, they are easily led.	I have little influence over the way other people behave.	____
The grades I make are the results of my own efforts; luck has little or nothing to do with it.	Sometimes I feel I have little to do with the grades I get.	____
People like me can change the course of world affairs if we make ourselves heard.	It is only wishful thinking to believe that one can readily influence what happens in our society at large.	____
A great deal that happens to me is probably a matter of chance.	I am the master of my fate.	____
Getting along with people is a skill that must be practiced.	It is almost impossible to figure out how to please some people.	____

Scoring key: Give yourself 1 point for each of the following selections: 1B, 2A, 3A, 4B, 6A, 7A, 8A, 9B, and 10A. Scores are interpreted as follows:

8–10 = High internal locus of control	5 = Mixed
6–7 = Moderate internal locus of control	3–4 = Moderate external locus of control
	1–2 = High external locus of control

Source: Adapted with permission from Rotter, Julian B. 1971. External control and internal control. *Psychology Today,* June, 42. Copyright 1971 by the American Psychological Association.

SELF-ASSESSMENT 3-4: TYPE A BEHAVIOR PATTERN

Indicate whether each of the following items is true or false for you.

_____ 1. I am always in a hurry.
_____ 2. I have a list of things I have to achieve on a daily or weekly basis.
_____ 3. I tend to take on one problem or task on at a time, finish, then move to the next one.
_____ 4. I tend to take a break or quit when I get tired.
_____ 5. I am always doing several things at once at work and in my personal life.
_____ 6. People who know me would describe my temper as hot and fiery.
_____ 7. I enjoy competitive activities.
_____ 8. I tend to be relaxed and easy going.
_____ 9. Many things are more important to me than my job.
_____ 10. I enjoy winning at work and at play.
_____ 11. I tend to rush people along or finish their sentences for them when they are taking too long.
_____ 12. I enjoy "doing nothing" and just hanging out.

Scoring key: Type A individuals tend to indicate that questions 1, 2, 5, 6, 7, and 10 are true and questions 3, 4, 8, 9, and 12 are false. Type B individuals tend to answer in the reverse.

Indicate the degree to which you think the following statements are true or false by circling the appropriate number. For example, if a statement is always true, you should circle the 5 next to that statement.

5 = Certainly always true
4 = Generally true
3 = Somewhat true, but with exceptions
2 = Somewhat false, but with exceptions
1 = Generally false
0 = Certainly always false

1. In social situations, I have the ability to alter my behavior if I feel that something else is called for.	5 4 3 2 1 0
2. I am often able to read people's true emotions correctly through their eyes.	5 4 3 2 1 0
3. I have the ability to control the way I come across to people, depending on the impression I wish to give them.	5 4 3 2 1 0
4. In conversations, I am sensitive to even the slightest change in the facial expression of the person I'm conversing with.	5 4 3 2 1 0
5. My powers of intuition are quite good when it comes to understanding others' emotions and motives.	5 4 3 2 1 0
6. I can usually tell when others consider a joke in bad taste, even though they may laugh convincingly.	5 4 3 2 1 0
7. When I feel that the image I am portraying isn't working, I can readily change it to something that does.	5 4 3 2 1 0
8. I can usually tell when I've said something inappropriate by reading the listener's eyes.	5 4 3 2 1 0
9. I have trouble changing my behavior to suit different people and different situations.	5 4 3 2 1 0
10. I have found that I can adjust my behavior to meet the requirements of any situation I find myself in.	5 4 3 2 1 0
11. If someone is lying to me, I usually know it at once from the person's manner of expression.	5 4 3 2 1 0
12. Even when it might be to my advantage, I have difficulty putting up a good front.	5 4 3 2 1 0
13. Once I know what the situation calls for, it's easy for me to regulate my actions accordingly.	5 4 3 2 1 0

Scoring key: To obtain your score, add up the numbers circled, except reverse the scores for questions 9 and 12. On those, a circled 5 becomes a 0, 4 becomes 1, and so forth. High self-monitors are defined as those with a score of approximately 53 or higher.

Source: Lennox, R. D. and Wolfe, R. N. 1984. Revision of the self-monitoring scale. *Journal of Personality and Social Psychology,* June, 1361. Copyright © 1984 by the American Psychological Association. Reprinted with permission.

SELF-ASSESSMENT 3-6:   MBTI

The goal of this exercise is to identify your cognitive style. There are no right or wrong answers. Please respond to the following 16 items. After you have completed all items, use the scoring key to identify your style.

Part I. Circle the response that comes closest to how you usually feel or act.

1. Are you more careful about:
   - A. People's feelings
   - B. Their rights
2. Do you usually get along better with:
   - A. Imaginative people
   - B. Realistic people
3. Which of these two is the higher compliment:
   - A. A person has real feeling
   - B. A person is consistently reasonable
4. In doing something with many other people, does it appeal more to you:
   - A. To do it in the accepted way
   - B. To invent a way of your own
5. Do you get more annoyed at:
   - A. Fancy theory
   - B. People who don't like theories
6. It is higher praise to call someone:
   - A. A person of vision
   - B. A person of common sense
7. Do you more often let:
   - A. Your heart rule your head
   - B. Your head rule your heart
8. Do you think it is worse:
   - A. To show too much warmth
   - B. To be unsympathetic
9. If you were a teacher, would you rather teach:
   - A. Courses involving theory
   - B. Fact courses

Part II. Circle the word in each of the following pairs that appeals to you more.

10. A. Compassion   B. Foresight
11. A. Justice   B. Mercy
12. A. Production   B. Design
13. A. Gentle   B. Firm

14. A. Uncritical   B. Literal
15. A. Literal   B. Figurative
16. A. Imaginative   B. Matter of fact

Scoring key: To categorize your responses to the questionnaire, count one point for each response on the following four scales and total the number of points recorded in each column.

Sensation		Intuition		Thinking		Feeling	
2B.	_____	2A.	_____	1B.	_____	1A.	_____
4A.	_____	4B.	_____	3B.	_____	3A.	_____
5A.	_____	5B.	_____	7B.	_____	7A.	_____
6B.	_____	6A.	_____	8A.	_____	8B.	_____
9B.	_____	9A.	_____	10B.	_____	10A.	_____
12A.	_____	12B.	_____	11A.	_____	11B.	_____
15A.	_____	15B.	_____	13B.	_____	13A.	_____
16B.	_____	16A.	_____	14B.	_____	14A.	_____
Totals:	_____		_____		_____		_____

Part III. Identifying Your Style

If your intuition score is equal to or greater than your sensation score, select intuition. If sensation is greater than intuition, select sensation. Select feeling if feeling is greater than thinking. Select thinking if thinking is greater than feeling. When thinking equals feeling, you should select feeling if you're a male and thinking if you're a female.

My style is (circle the two dimensions based on the instructions above)

Sensation **or** Intuition   Thinking **or** Feeling

Source: Slocum, J. W. Jr. and Hellreigel, D. 1983. A look at how managers' minds work. *Business Horizons,* July–August, 58–68. With permission.

Part IV. Interpreting Your Style

The MBTI is an indicator of the way people gather and use information. Each of the four styles views problem solving, decision making, use of information, and time, and provides a general view of how things should be done differently. Each style has strengths and weaknesses, with no one style being the best. The MBTI is used extensively in a number of organizations as part of team building to allow team members to assess their strengths and weaknesses.

SELF-ASSESSMENT 3-7: MACHIAVELLIANISM

For each statement, circle the number that most closely resembles your attitude.

	Disagree			Agree	
Statements	A lot	A little	Neutral	A little	A lot
1. The best way to handle people is to tell them what they want to hear.	1	2	3	4	5
2. When you ask someone to do something for you, it is best to give the real reason for wanting it rather than giving reasons that might carry more weight.	1	2	3	4	5
3. Anyone who completely trusts anyone else is asking for trouble.	1	2	3	4	5
4. It is hard to get ahead without cutting corners here and there.	1	2	3	4	5
5. It is safest to assume that all people have a vicious streak, and it will come out when they are given a chance.	1	2	3	4	5
6. One should take action only when it is morally right.	1	2	3	4	5
7. Most people are basically good and kind.	1	2	3	4	5
8. There is no excuse for lying to someone else.	1	2	3	4	5
9. Most people more easily forget the death of their father than the loss of their property.	1	2	3	4	5
10. Generally speaking, people won't work hard unless they're forced to do so.	1	2	3	4	5

Scoring key: To obtain your Mach score, add the number your have circled on questions 1, 3, 4, 5, 9, and 10. For the other four questions, reverse the numbers you have circled: 5 becomes 1, 4 is 2, and so forth. Total your ten numbers to find your score. The higher your score is, the more Machiavellian you are. Among a random sample of American adults, the average was 25.

Source: Excerpt from *Studies in Machiavellianism* by Richard Christine and Florence L. Geis, copyright 1970, Elsevier Science (USA), reprinted by permission of the publisher.

CASE

Leadership in Action
Bonnie Reitz—Helping to Fly Continental

The story of the success of Continental Airlines over the past 10 years is already part of business and management legend. The airline moved from last place to first place in less than 5 years: from losing $204 million in 1994, to earning $556 million in 1996; from rated the worst airline based on mishandled baggage and customer complaints in 1994, to being voted the best airline in customer surveys in 1997. Much of the miraculous turnaround is attributed to CEO Gordon Bethune and President and COO Greg Brenneman (Bethune and Huler 1998).

Just as Continental was basking in its success, the terrorist attacks of September 11, 2001, plunged the airline industry in crisis in 2001 and 2002. Watching the national tragedy unfold, Bonnie Reitz, Continental's senior vice president for sales and distribution, also watched all the hard work of her company's employees disintegrate. Describing the layoffs that followed September 11 at Continental, Reitz states: "I walked around the cubicles, watching people pack their boxes. We were all hugging, crying. . . . It just broke your heart. We had worked so hard" (Hammonds 2001d, p. 98). The airline took special care to communicate with its employees while it let go nearly one-fifth of its workforce.

Reitz had been instrumental in regaining the customer base back in the mid-1990s. Her leadership in building the company Web page along with other programs brought customers back to Continental (www.continental.com/press/press_2000-08-08-01.asp). After September 11, she once more had to get people back on the planes. Her success in keeping the customer focus that is essential to Continental's success, is attributable to constant conversations with employees and customers. She states: "Listening is the key to knowing if what we're doing is right. . . . there's always something to be learned" (Hammonds 2001d, p. 100).

Gordon Bethune, Continental's CEO, describes Reitz as "a very tenacious person" (Hammonds 2001d, p. 98). She is a tough negotiator and a no-nonsense manager, who considers herself to be primarily focused on the airline's operations. Reitz says: "What's gets measured gets done. I believe in unshakable facts. Get as many facts as you can" (Hammonds 2001d, p. 100). Along with the strong task focus, Reitz has a warm side that somehow allows her to establish a personal relationship with people she meets, especially with her customers. She knows that she needs to take care of her team:

> "My people know that no matter what they do, I will be right there next to them. . . . Have strength of character in good times and in bad. If you do those things—and people know that's how you operate—that's how they start to lead. (Hammonds 2001d, p. 100)

The work of rebuilding Continental for a second time, after so much success, is grueling. Somehow, though, the long hours and the late-night meetings seem to energize Reitz. Her personal guide is: "You have to be able to look at yourself in the mirror every day and say, 'I did the best I could.'" (Hammonds 2001d, p. 100). ∎

QUESTIONS

1. What are Reitz's key defining individual characteristics?

2. What makes her an effective leader?

Sources: Based on Bethune, G. and Huler, S. 1998. *From worst to first: Behind the scenes of a remarkable comeback.* New York: John Wiley & Sons Inc.; Hammonds, K. H. 2001. Continental's turnaround pilot. *Fast Company,* December, 96–101; www.continental.com/press/press_2000-08-08-01.asp.

Chapter 4

Power and Leadership

> *Nearly all men can stand adversity, but if you want to test a man's character, give him power.*

—ABRAHAM LINCOLN

> *Power tends to corrupt and absolute power corrupts absolutely.*

—LORD ACTON

After studying this chapter, you will be able to:

1. Define power and its key role in leadership.
2. Understand the cross-cultural differences in the definitions and use of power.
3. Identify the individual and organizational sources of power available to leaders, and describe their consequences for followers and organizations.
4. Understand the role of power in the leadership and effectiveness of teams.
5. Identify the power sources available to top executives.
6. Explain the sources of power corruption and present ways to prevent its occurrence.
7. Trace the changes in use of power and explain their consequences for leadership.

*A*n integral part of the study of leadership is the understanding of power and how leaders use it. Leaders need power to fulfill the primary goal of leadership. Without power, they cannot guide their followers to achieve their goals. We expect great things from our leaders and provide them with wide latitude and power to accomplish their goals. Department heads, CEOs, and city mayors can order the layoffs of thousands. In many states, employment-at-will laws allow managers to fire employees without much reason or notice. All societies shower their leaders with great privilege. In addition to high salaries and other financial incentives (some of the highest in the world, in the case of U.S. business executives), organizations provide their leaders with many luxuries, such as company cars and planes, lavish offices, generous expense accounts, and access to subsidized or free housing, just to name a few.

By and large, we accept the power of our leaders and the privileges that it carries. This is even the case in a culture such as the United States where power distance is low. In recent years, the new management philosophies such as teaming, empowerment, and the focus on quality have led organizations to question the role of and need for centralized and concentrated power. As a result, we have changed the way we view power and how leaders use it. Additionally, research concerning the potential for power to corrupt power holders points to the need to consider and use power with caution.

This chapter examines the various approaches to power and their implications for leadership. It presents the sources of power for individuals and groups, and discusses the potential detriments of excessive and concentrated power. Finally, it analyzes current views of power in organizations in light of cultural differences and the changes in our management philosophies and organizational structures.

POWER IN ORGANIZATIONS: DEFINITION AND CONSEQUENCES

The terms *power, authority,* and *influence* often are used interchangeably. In its most basic form, power is the ability of one person to influence another. As such, power is not exclusive to leaders and managers. Individuals at all levels inside an organization, as well as outsiders to an organization—namely, customers or suppliers—can influence the behavior and attitudes of others. Authority, on the other hand, is the power vested in a particular position, such as that of a CEO or hospital manager. Therefore, whereas people at all levels of an organization have power to influence others, only those holding formal positions have authority.

Consequences of Using Power

The reaction to the use of power depends to a great extent on the source and manner in which leaders use it. The three most typical reactions to use of power are commitment, compliance, and resistance. Commitment happens when followers welcome the influence process and accept it as reasonable and legitimate. Consider the employees of PeopleSoft, a California-based software company. David Duffield, the company's CEO, is so popular with employees that they have created a musical band called the "Raving Daves" (Lieber 1998). The employees believe in their leader and are fully committed to his ideas. As a result, the changes he proposes are accepted enthusiastically at PeopleSoft (Roberts 1998).

Another potential reaction to power is compliance. In this case, although followers accept the influence process and go along with the request, they do not feel any personal acceptance or deep commitment to carry out the order. Subordinates go along with the leader simply because they have to. An example of this would be the imposition of unpopular new rules by a school administrator. Because of the administrator's authority, the faculty and staff have to implement the rules. However, they do so without any personal commitment; they simply comply.

The third possible reaction to power is resistance. The target in this case does not agree with the attempt at influence and either actively or passively resists it. Examples of resistance to a leader's authority abound in our institutions. The most dramatic ones occur in the labor-management disputes, whereby employees who typically either accept or comply with management's requests refuse to do so and take overt or covert action against management. The 1998 to 1999 National Basketball Association (NBA) basketball players' strike offers a twist on the labor-management conflict and resistance. In that case, player union members went against the recommendation of their own president, Patrick Ewing, and other union leaders and voted to accept the owners' final offer.

A leader's power increases when employees have personal commitment and acceptance of the leader's ideas and decisions. However, many leaders rely excessively on simple compliance, which can have dire consequences.

As a general rule, a leader's power increases when employees have personal commitment and acceptance of the leader's ideas and decisions. However, many leaders rely excessively on compliance, which, as you will read in this chapter, can have dire consequences. In understanding the sources of power, it is important to evaluate individual factors and organizational elements. Power can be drawn from what a person does or is, and from the structure of an organization.

Distribution of Power

Traditional organizations typically concentrate power in a few positions. Authority is vested in formal titles, and nonmanagers have limited power to make decisions. Their role is primarily the implementation of the leaders' decisions. Despite the vast amount of publicity about the use of empowerment and teams, the majority of U.S. organizations are still traditional in their approach to management (Lawler and Mohrman 1987). However, even before empowerment and teaming became fashionable, research about the effect of the distribution of power in organizations suggested that concentrated power can be detrimental to organizational performance (Tannenbaum and Cooke 1974). The more equal the power distribution is throughout the organization, the higher the performance of the organization is. This research further reinforces the need to distribute power as evenly as possible within organizations.

However, it is important to consider various cultural factors in the distribution of power, because the perception of power differs considerably based on cultures. For example, employees in the United States respond well to managers they like, but Bulgarian employees follow directions when their managers have legitimate power or authority (Rahim et al. 2000).

Based on research by Hofstede (1997, 2001) and others regarding different cultural values in management, the United States tends to be a low to medium power-distance culture. The differential of power between the highest and lowest levels of the organization is not great (although the salary differential is one of the highest in the world). The low power distance allows employees in the United States and in other low power-distance cultures such as Australia to call their bosses by their first name, interact with them freely, and express their disagreement with them. In addition, employees in low power-distance cultures do not expect their managers and leaders to have all the answers; they accept the fact that leaders, too, can make mistakes (Adler 1991; Laurent 1983). Low power distance further facilitates the implementation of participative management and other power-sharing management techniques.

In cultures with high power distance, employees have limited expectations for participation in decision making and expect leaders to be somewhat infallible. For example, many Chinese business leaders who operate from a variety of locations around the Pacific Rim have highly authoritarian-oriented, family controlled organizations (Kraar 1994). These leaders make all decisions without questions or challenges from followers. Contrary to current U.S. thinking regarding management and leadership, their organizations are successful despite continued reliance on hierarchical structures. Their structure and power distribution fit their culture. The Chinese value order, hierarchy, and a clear delineation of power. Their organizations function in accordance with those cultural values.

Similarly, the French, Italians, and Germans expect their managers to provide answers to subordinates' questions and problems (Laurent 1983). The organizational cultural model of Eiffel Tower used by the French, for example, concentrates power at the top of the organization. French managers report great discomfort at not knowing who their boss is. This need for a clear hierarchy is likely to make it more difficult for the French than for Swedes or North Americans to function in a leaderless, self-managed, team environment. In other countries, such as Japan and Indonesia, people value clear hierarchy and authority. Similarly, the Mexican culture—with a family type of organization culture, its strong paternalistic tradition, and the presence of the machismo principle—also expects leaders to be strong, decisive, and powerful. Leaders, like powerful fathers, must provide answers, support the family, and discipline members who stray (Teagarden, Butler, and Von Glinow 1992).

The combination of the culture's power distance and its tolerance for uncertainty determines part of the power structure of an organization. The higher the power distance is and the lower the tolerance for uncertainty is, the more likely it is that leaders will hold a high degree of power and that subordinates will expect them to use it. In such cultures, the implementation of power sharing is likely to face more obstacles than in cultures where subordinates do not rely heavily on their supervisor. The following section considers the sources of power for leaders.

SOURCES OF POWER

Alan Greenspan, the chairman of the U.S. Federal Reserve (Fed), is reputed to be the most powerful executive in the United States. As chairman, Greenspan has been able set policies to sustain low to moderate economic growth, assuring that the U.S. economy expands but does not overheat, thereby avoiding high inflation. In a 1996 survey of 1,000 CEOs of the largest U.S. companies, 96 percent wanted him to be reappointed as the leader of the Fed (Walsh 1996). Greenspan has considerable power to chart the course of the U.S. and world economy. He is a well-known economist, a consummate relationship builder, and described as low key and down to earth. Greenspan has no executive power, he cannot implement a single decision, and he has only a few staffers reporting to him. Nevertheless, Greenspan is powerful. He is able to convince the U.S. president, the Congress, other members of the Fed board, and the financial markets that his policies are devoid of politics and in the best interests of the United States. Where does Greenspan get his power? He relies on individual and organizational sources of power.

Sources of Power Related to Individuals

One of the most widely used approaches to understanding the sources of power comes from the research by French and Raven (1968). These researchers propose five sources of power vested in the individual: legitimate power, reward power, coercive power, expert power, and referent power (see Table 4-1).

Sources and Consequences

The first three sources of power—legitimate, reward, and coercive—are position powers. Although they are vested in individuals, the individuals have access to them because of the position they hold (Davis, Schoorman, and Donaldson 1997). For example, a manager's legitimate power disappears if the title or position is taken away. Subordinates comply, but no commitment occurs (Yukl and Falbe 1991). Alan

Table 4-1
French and Raven's Sources of Individual Power

Legitimate Power	Based on a person holding a formal position. Others comply because they accept the legitimacy of the position of the power holder.
Reward Power	Based on a person's access to rewards. Others comply because they want the rewards the power holder can offer.
Coercive Power	Based on a person's ability to punish. Others comply because they fear punishment.
Expert Power	Based on a person's expertise, competence, and information in a certain area. Others comply because they believe in the power holder's knowledge and competence.
Referent Power	Based on a person's attractiveness to and friendship with others. Others comply because they respect and like the power holder.

Greenspan holds considerable legitimate power, although his power to reward and punish is limited. Managers and executives generally hold all three of these sources of power. Examples of managers being sent to "corporate Siberia" illustrate well the limitations of position power. Once managers lose their prestigious position, they lose their means of influencing others. Similarly, in order to reward or punish, a person needs to have access to resources. As is the case with legitimate power, such access comes from holding a position within the organization.

Those who have formal positions have access to rewards and coercive power. In addition, some employees might have access to rewards that others want, and sometimes they can even punish their colleagues indirectly. In all cases, once the access to rewards or punishment is taken away by the organization, a leader or individual relying on such sources loses power. Because the source of power is related to the individual's position, followers are most likely to react by complying or resisting, as illustrated in Figure 4-1. Generally, the harsher the source of power that is used, the less willing subordinates will be to comply (Schwarzwald, Koslowsky, and Agassi 2001).

The last two sources of power—expert and referent—are personal (Davis, Schoorman, and Donaldson 1997). Access to these two sources of power does not depend solely on the organization. In the case of expert power, people have influence over others because they have special expertise, knowledge, information, or skills that others need. People will listen to the experts, follow their advice, and accept their recommendations. Alan Greenspan provides an excellent example of expert power. In addition to his title, knowledge, and expertise, his established record of success forms the basis of his power. In other cases, those who have expert power might not hold official titles or any legitimate power. However, people will bypass their manager and their organization's formal hierarchy and structure in order to seek help from those who have some expertise they need. For example, a department's computer expert has power even if the person is young and relatively inexperienced.

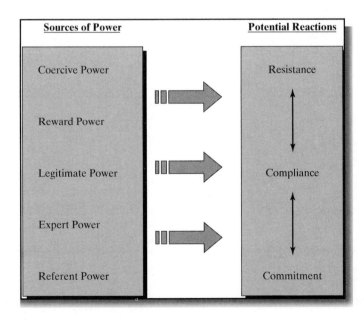

Figure 4-1
Potential Reactions to Individual Sources of Power

Referent power operates in much the same way. Individuals with referent power have power because others like and respect them. As with expert power, this power does not depend on the position or the organization. The person has power because he or she is a role model for others. Greenspan is well liked for his ability to work with others. PeopleSoft employees admire Duffield. The respect and friendship comes on top of other considerable sources of power. In the cases of expert and referent power, followers welcome the influence process and in many cases seek it, and they generally respond with commitment and acceptance. The use of expert and referent power also is related to higher follower satisfaction and performance (Yukl and Falbe 1991).

Using Individual Sources of Power

Although power and influence are closely related, some research indicates that the two can be treated as separate concepts. A leader who has power might not be able to influence subordinates' behaviors, or influence can occur without a specific source of power. Several researchers, most notably Kipnis and his colleagues (Kipnis, Schmidt, and Wilkinson 1980) and Yukl along with several others (Yukl and Falbe 1990, 1991), have identified various influence tactics. The result of their work is the classification of influence tactics into nine categories (see Table 4-2). Each tactic relies on one or more of the sources of power related to the individual. Each is appropriate in different situations and has the potential for leading to commitment on the part of the person being influenced. For example, personal appeal relies on referent power and tends to be appropriate when used with colleagues; it is not likely to lead to a high degree of commitment. Inspirational appeal, which also relies on referent power, leads to high

Table 4-2

Using Power: Influence Tactics and Their Consequences

Influence Tactic	Power Source	Appropriate to Use With	Effectiveness and Commitment
Rational persuasion	Expert and access to information	Supervisors	Moderate
Inspirational appeal	Referent	Subordinates and colleagues	High
Consultation	All	Subordinates and colleagues	High
Ingratiation	Referent	All levels	Moderate
Personal appeal	Referent	Colleagues	Moderate
Exchange	Reward and information	Subordinates and colleagues	Moderate
Coalition building	All	Subordinates and colleagues	Low
Legitimate tactics	Legitimate	Subordinates and colleagues	Low
Pressure	Coercive	Subordinates	Low

commitment. Rational persuasion relies on expert power and is appropriate to use when trying to influence superiors. The commitment tends to be moderate.

Although leaders must rely on all sources of power to guide and influence their followers and others in their organization, they often have to adjust how they use power throughout their career. J. P. Kotter, a well-respected writer on issues of leadership and managerial power, suggests that in the early stages of a manager's career, the manager must develop an adequate base of power (Kotter 1985). A manager can accomplish this by relying on the various bases of personal power. In particular, young leaders must develop a broad network of interpersonal relationships and establish credibility through information and expertise. Other means involve becoming visible by volunteering for challenging and high-visibility projects.

The demonstration of competence and skills is key to the development of power in the early stages of a leader's career. In mid career, most successful leaders have developed some degree of legitimacy through formal titles and have accumulated other status symbols that demonstrate their power. Their early efforts are likely to have established their credibility and competence within a well-developed network of loyal subordinates, peers, and bosses (Kotter 1985). Therefore, leaders in mid-career stage already have considerable power. The challenge at this point is to use the accumulated power wisely and ethically to achieve organizational goals and personal benefits.

Finally, leaders during the late-career stage must learn to let go of power gracefully. By the time they reach retirement age, successful leaders in thriving U.S. public and private organizations enjoy considerable power and influence. In order to use power well at this career stage, a leader needs to plan for its orderly transmission to others while simultaneously finding new personal sources of power and fulfillment.

WHAT DOES THIS MEAN FOR ME?
How to Use Power Wisely

Judicious use of power can contribute greatly to a leader's effectiveness. Below are some guidelines for developing and using power.

- Develop your competencies and expertise. Expert power is one of the strongest sources; no one can take it away from you, and it leads to commitment from others.

- Develop good working relationships with a broad base of people inside and outside your organization. These professional and personal friendships provide you with a wide base of influence.

- Be generous in handing out rewards when you have access to them. Rewards are not only a source of power, but your generosity will help you build other relationships that will outlast your access to rewards.

- Apply coercive power with great care. As others comply to you out of fear, giving you short-term results, you will lose their long-term commitment.

- Make those around you feel powerful. The more power you give away and share with others, the more powerful you will become.

Sources of Power Related to Organizational Structure

The differences between organizational and individual sources of power are not always obvious. The structure of an organization provides sources of power to individuals and groups over and above those listed in Table 4-1. Although individuals also can rely on organizational sources of power, these sources are particularly important when considering the use of teams. Aside from the expertise of their members, teams have access to power in organizations mainly because of their control of strategic contingencies.

Teams have access to power in organizations mainly because of their control of strategic contingencies.

The concept of strategic contingencies originally was developed to understand the distribution of power across departments (Hickson et al. 1971; Salancik and Pfeffer 1977b); however, it also has direct application to teams. Strategic contingencies suggest that individuals, teams, or departments gain power based on their ability to address issues that are instrumental to reaching organizational goals. For example, if a team removes obstacles for others and helps them achieve goals, its leader and members will accumulate power. Mervyn's, a California-based retailer, uses special teams that rush into stores in response to management requests to solve critical problems quickly. These teams, called SWAT after the police fast-response units, have highly trained members with broad expertise who can deal with crises that could impact the organization (Carbonara 1998). Because of their ability to deal with many problems, these teams are highly regarded and have considerable power. Table 4-3 summarizes the four strategic contingencies that form the basis of organizational sources of power.

Coping with Uncertainty

The first source of power for teams is their ability to help others cope with uncertainty. With the increased competition and constant changes in the political and economic environments facing many institutions, having information about the changes and alternatives for dealing with them becomes key to performance. For example, the leader and members of a cross-functional team designed to provide an organization with market information regarding future products and competitors will gain considerable influence by virtue of the fact that others need that information. The team's product or service reduces uncertainty. A case in point is governmental liaison teams and lobbyists in the United States in a time of change in the health industry. These groups have acquired particular power because they help others within the organization reduce or manage the uncertainty they face.

Teams and their leaders can reduce uncertainty through three interrelated methods (Hickson et al. 1971). First, they can obtain information that others need. This can be achieved through market research, polls, contact with key constituents, focus groups, or reliance on external experts. The second method is uncertainty prevention, which focuses on the prediction of upcoming changes. For example, a team can research and predict the moves of competitors. Public university administrators can rely on their legislative liaison team to predict the mood of the legislature regarding funding of universities. Third, a team can reduce uncertainty for others through absorption. In this situation, the team will take certain steps to prevent the change from affecting other teams or departments. The university administrator who had information about the legislative mood might try to forestall budget cuts through lobbying. However, if the cuts happen

Table 4-3
Organizational Sources of Power: Strategic Contingencies

Coping with Uncertainty	Power based on the ability to reduce uncertainty for others. This can be achieved by obtaining information they need, making predictions and engaging in forecasting, or by preventing the effect of change on others. Others comply because the power holder helps them achieve their goals by reducing uncertainty.
Centrality	Power based on being central to how the organization achieves its mission and goals. Others comply because the power holder provides key organizational activities.
Dependency	Power based on others depending on power holder to get their work done. Others comply because they cannot accomplish their goal without the power holder's help.
Substitutability	Power based on providing a unique and irreplaceable service or product to others. Others comply because they cannot find what the power holder provides elsewhere.

Source: Hickson et. al (1971).

anyway, various groups within the university might undertake less painful internal budget-reduction mechanisms, such as nonreplacement of retiring employees, thereby preventing more drastic measures to be imposed by outside sources and absorbing uncertainty. Through the use of these three methods, a team and its leader can reduce uncertainty for others and thus acquire power.

Centrality
Another organizational source of power is the centrality to the production or service delivery process. This factor relates to how a team's activities are key to the mission and goals of the organization. Teams closest to the customer, for example, will gain power. Members of an executive team who work closely with the CEO of the organization also will gain power via their access to the CEO. For example, the librarian team at Highsmith reports directly to the company's executives—a factor that give its members further power (Buchanan 1999). Another case in point is the management of diversity in organizations. One of the many recommendations for the successful implementation of diversity plans in organizations involves making diversity central to the organization and to the organization's leaders. The most successful programs put the individuals and teams in charge of diversity planning and implementation in strategic positions within organizations, reporting directly to the CEO.

Dependence and Substitutability
A final structural source of power available to teams and their leaders closely resembles the reward and expert power of individuals. This source of power depends on the extent to which others need a team's expertise. If employees depend on a team to provide them with information and resources, the team's power will increase. The larger the number of departments and individuals who depend on the team is, the

greater the team's power will be. In addition, if the tasks performed by the team are unique and nonreplaceable in the organization, the dependence on the team and its power will increase. However, if the team's collective expertise is duplicated in others and its function can be performed easily by another individual or group, the team is likely to have little influence to obtain needed resources and implement its ideas. For example, despite the widespread use of personal computers, many individuals still require considerable assistance in order to use computer resources well. This factor allows information technology departments to gain power, obtain resources, and implement new technologies.

Interestingly, the major complaint from teams in many organizations is their lack of power to obtain resources or implement their ideas (Nahavandi and Aranda 1994). In the new organizational structures, team leaders often do not have any of the formal powers traditionally assigned to managers. In the best of cases, team members respect their leader because of personal relationships or expertise. However, these individual sources of power do not translate to power in the organization. As a result, many team leaders express anger and frustration at their lack of ability to get things done. Recommendations on how to make teams more effective often include making them central to the mission of the organization, assigning them to meaningful tasks, and providing them with access to decision makers (Katzenbach and Smith 1993; Nahavandi and Aranda 1994).

Special Power Sources of Top Executives

Top executives of our institutions hold tremendous power. One obvious source of power is the legitimacy of their position. A number of symbols establish and reinforce their legitimate power: They have separate executive offices, pictures of past executives hang in public hallways, they eat in separate dining facilities, and they are able to maintain privacy and distance from other employees (Hardy 1985; Pfeffer 1981). However, the Enron fiasco in the United States demonstrated how easily power can be abused, and it brought to our attention the lack of accountability of many executives. Other executives, such as the past CEO of Coca-Cola, Doug Ivester, have lost their positions partly because of their arrogance (Sellers, 2000). Top executives have considerable power and are well protected. Along with the sources of power we discussed earlier, top executives have four other sources of power:

- *Distribution of Resources:* Top managers, either alone or in consultation with a top-management team, are responsible for the distribution of resources throughout the organization. This access to resources is a key source of power.
- *Control of Decision Criteria:* Another unique power source available to executives is the control of decision criteria (Nahavandi and Malekzadeh 1993a; Pettigrew 1973). By setting the mission, overall strategy, and operational goals of organizations, top executives limit other managers' and employees' actions. For example, if a city mayor runs his or her campaign on the platform of fighting crime and improving education, the city's actions and decisions during that mayor's term will be influenced by that platform. Crime reduction will be one of the major criteria used to evaluate alternatives and make decisions. For instance, funding requests for increased police training or for building a neigh-

borhood park will be evaluated based on the crime-fighting and education values of the proposals. If they address the decision criteria set by the mayor, they will have a better chance of passage, having the mayor's weight behind them. If they do not, such proposals might not even be brought up for consideration.

- *Centrality in Organization:* Another source of executive power is a top manager's centrality to the organizational structure and information flow (Astley and Sachdeva 1984). Whether the organization is a traditional hierarchical pyramid or a web, CEOs are strategically placed for access to information and resources. Indeed, new top managers often bring with them a group of trusted colleagues who are placed in strategic locations throughout the organization to ensure their access to information.
- *Access:* A final source of power for top executives is their access to all levels of the organization so that they can build alliances that further enhance their power. The most obvious example is the change in personnel in Washington with the election of a new president. Similar personnel changes occur on different scales in all organizations when a new leader is selected. University presidents bring with them several top assistants and create new positions to accommodate them. Other members of top university administration are slowly replaced with those selected by the new leader. In the private sector, the changes designed to put key people in place are even more drastic and obvious. Within a month of becoming CEO of Gulf & Western, Martin Davis placed his own team in key positions. At General Electric, the selection of Immelt to succeed Jack Welch as CEO led to the turnover of several top-management team members who had been contenders for the position. Whether new leaders force out several individuals to make room for their own team or whether they leave on their own, the outcome of the personnel shuffle is to allow new leaders access to trustworthy people and information.

In addition to having considerable power, top executives are often not accountable for their actions. This lack of accountability can lead to abuse and corruption, the topics considered next.

THE DARK SIDE OF POWER: CORRUPTION

Having power allows leaders to influence others and help their team, department, or organization achieve their goals. However, too much power without accountability can lead to many negative consequences. The old adage "power corrupts" continues to be true. The privilege associated with power and leadership has come under attack as being at best unnecessary and at worst dysfunctional (Block 1993). Power without accountability is blamed for many excesses, ranging from financial waste to fraud to sexual harassment. For example, unchecked power was blamed for one of Europe's biggest financial scandals, which involved the Paris-based Credit Lyonnais and executives in several countries (McClintick 1997). All the legal requirements and checks and balances did not prevent Enron executives from operating without accountability for a long period of time.

Power, whether legitimate or excessive, increases the distance between leaders and followers and thereby removes leaders from the inner workings of their organizations. Such separation can lead to uninformed, unrealistic, and in some cases unethical decision making.

Power, whether legitimate or excessive, increases the distance between leaders and followers and thereby removes leaders from the inner workings of their organizations. Such separation can lead to uninformed, unrealistic, and in some cases unethical decision making. In most cases, the excessive concentration of power is more a function of the social and class structure than a function of organizational performance needs. In other words, the power structure is a reflection of social and cultural factors not related to organizational strategic factors. The following sections consider the cause, consequences, and potential solutions to abuse of power.

Causes

The causes of power corruption stem from leaders distance from others and developing an inflated view of themselves, which is the starting point of the corruption cycle depicted in Figure 4-2. The sources of such a perception not only relate to the leaders themselves but also to the organizational structure and the behavior of subordinates. First, having power, by definition, means that others comply with the power holder (Kipnis 1972). In some cases, subordinates follow leaders because of personal commitment and acceptance of their decisions, or they might truly respect their leaders' expertise and personal integrity. In other cases, the compliance is simply due to fear of retribution or the desire to obtain certain rewards (Prendergast 1993). The subordinates' continued compliance can cause leaders to believe that their actions and decisions are always correct. If they are not, why won't anyone say so?

In addition to compliance, subordinates often adopt flattery and ingratiation as a means of influencing their leader concerning their ideas or for obtaining the personal or departmental resources that they need. Few dare argue and disagree with

Figure 4-2
Power Corruption Cycle

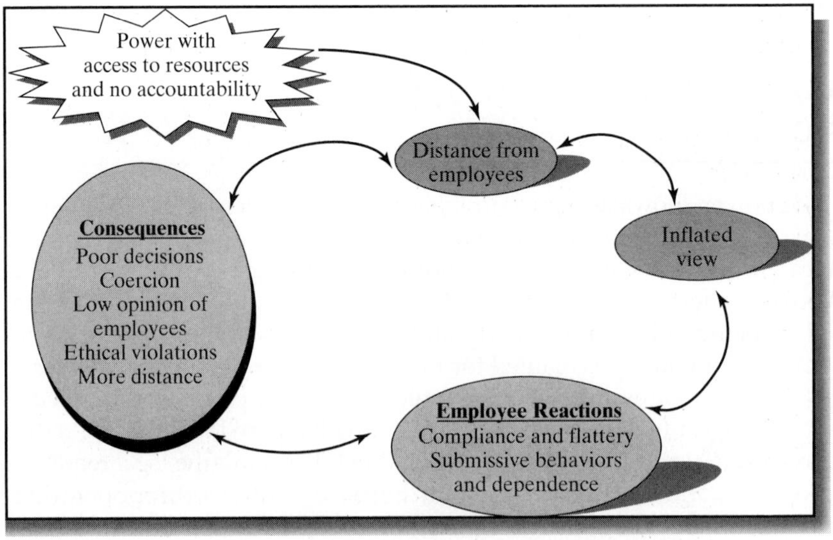

the leader. Even when they express disagreement, they do so in the softest, most roundabout ways, after praising the leader's ideas and painstakingly recognizing that the leaders are correct. Most of us have witnessed or even been party to such political behavior, which is considered essential to obtaining needed resources. However, such flattery can lead to a perception on the part of leaders that they are always right.

Another factor that contributes to the development of leaders' inflated views of themselves is the distance between leaders and followers. By virtue of the hierarchical structure of many organizations, power holders are separated from those they lead. Although many changes have been made in recent years, leaders still have offices on separate floors, park their cars in reserved areas, eat in executive dining rooms, and spend a great deal of their time with other power holders. All of these symbols of power increase the legitimacy of leaders. The distance and separation can be justified further based on the need to protect the leaders' valuable time and to allow them access to other power holders with whom they need to work to make decisions. However, these symbols also can corrupt the leaders by providing them with an overly inflated view of themselves.

Finally, the leaders' access to resources without much accountability continues to reinforce their view that they are special, deserve special treatment, and are above the rules applied to others. Consider the case of Richard Scrushy, the CEO of HealthSouth Corporation, a multibillion-dollar health care company, and also CEO of MedPartners, Incorporated, another health-related company. Scrushy wields tremendous power. One of the ways he uses this power is to intimidate his employees, going as far as sending them out of meetings if he does not like their clothing (Jones 1998). As another example, Andre Harrell, the flamboyant CEO of the Motown record label, spent $200,000 in an advertising campaign promoting himself while the company was facing financial troubles (Johnson 1997). His actions led to his resignation a few months later.

Another classic tale of corruption and a leader who was out of touch with the organization and its needs is that of Philip Agee, most recently CEO of Morrison Knudsen Corporation (MK) (O'Reilley 1995). Although Agee joined MK with a strong reputation and an impressive background, MK employees quickly decided that he was looking for personal glory and was unresponsive to the culture of their organization. He made unilateral decisions and was perceived as expecting to hear only good news. Those who disagreed with him faced firing, and he gained a reputation of being afraid to develop talent around him. Agee is accused of appointing people to the board of directors who were so similar to him that they would be highly unlikely to challenge him. He went as far as to snub Boise, Idaho, where the corporation's headquarters were located. In addition to allegations of misuse of power and company resources, Agee's numerous bad business decisions caused a group of MK executives and other constituents to document his incompetence, overly high salary, and abuses to the board, which led to his ultimate firing (O'Reilly 1995).

Consequences

As the preceding examples and Figure 4-2 show, the excessive power and accompanying corruption of leaders can have serious consequences for an organization. On a general level, leaders' distance from others in the organization can lead to poor decision making because leaders will lack the information needed to make good judgments. Employees filter information, avoid giving bad news, and hide their mistakes, providing an overly rosy picture of the organization. As a result, leaders lose touch with their organization and its customers. Because of the compliance of followers, leaders might see their followers as dependent and incapable of autonomous behavior and decisions. Leaders then come to see themselves as the source of all events in the organization and consequently might rely less on persuasion and more on coercive methods to get followers to comply. These processes are supported further by a general devaluation of followers. Leaders come to see their subordinates as less than competent and therefore unable to function without the leader's strong guidance.

Another consequence of excessive power is the potential development of a separate sense of morality. Leaders might see themselves as subject to different rules than their subordinates. As a result, they might engage in unethical and illegal activities while expecting their subordinates to follow a set of rules that does not apply to them. Consequently, the leaders become poor role models and lose their credibility and their ability to be effective. Amiable negotiation and win-win strategies to resolve conflict and disagreements are replaced with executive fiats and intolerance of diverse opinions. This, in turn, can lead to bad decisions, to follower resistance and reactance, and to followers' unwillingness to take any risks.

A final consequence of corruption is the devaluation of followers, with the potential for a self-fulfilling prophecy. The leader continues to maintain total control, not allowing followers' input into decisions. The followers comply and encourage such behavior, further proving to the leader the futility of power sharing. The leader sees such compliance as evidence of subordinates' weakness and incompetence, thereby centralizing decision making even further. This self-fulfilling prophecy can become a major obstacle to the successful implementation of programs such as total quality management (TQM) and empowerment that require broad power distribution and decentralized decision making.

Solutions

No magic formula will prevent the excessive centralization of power, abuse, and corruption. Following are factors that can help:

- *Involving the leader in day-to-day activities.* The closer the leader is to the day-to-day activities of followers and to the organization's customers, the less potential there is for corruption (Block 1993; Prendergast 1993).
- *Reducing the followers' dependency on the leader.* The more independent the followers are, the less likely they are to contribute—intentionally or unintentionally—to the corruption cycle. If a person's pay, promotion, and career depend entirely on the manager's subjective opinion and rating, a person is more likely to comply with that manager (Prendergast 1993).
- *Using objective measures of performance.* Having objective measures of performance, either through precise measurement or based on direct feedback from relevant constituents, is one way to curtail the excessive power of the leader and ensure proper and accurate information flow. The subordinate can act for

Can one leader be so powerful and so destructive as to be an impediment to change and success in an organization? Do truly "evil" leaders survive? Unfortunately, management scholar Andre Delbecq has found them to be common in today's organizations (Delbecq 2001). The destruction they bring often is detected when it is too late, and many individuals as well as the organization as a whole already has paid a heavy price in productivity, morale, and personal suffering.

Delbecq describes the evil leaders as sharing the following characteristics. They are bright but highly controlling, rigid, inflexible, and unable to compromise. They present themselves as the standard bearer of quality, equating all those who challenge them with poor performers. Their world is divided into those who agree with them and enemies who oppose them. They are vicious and ruthless, particularly with colleagues who are junior and vulnerable. They are manipulative, cunning, hypercritical, self-aggrandizing, and lack empathy. However, these evil managers are shrewd in manipulating upward information, can charm their superiors, and succeed in appearing reasonable. These evil managers bring devastation to their organization by terrifying their colleagues through ruthless and assured retribution, and destruction of trust and collegiality. Morale and productivity suffer as employees are intimidated into silence, have to focus on self-protection, and withdraw by not engaging fully in the organization.

Because the evil managers' behaviors are so far outside the norm, many hesitate to address the problem, and they often escape discovery. Although not easy to stop once they gain power, the key factor in preventing the destructive effect of evil managers is to establish a strong culture of collegiality, civility, and respect. Delbecq recommends that organizations pay attention to the early warning signals, investigate them, and take action quickly.

Source: Delbecq, A. 2001. "Evil" manifested in destructive individual behavior: A senior leadership challenge. *Journal of Management Inquiry* 10 no. 3, 221–226.

the benefit of the customers with feedback from them, rather than for the benefit of the boss.

- *Involving outsiders in decision making.* By opening up the decision making process to outsiders, an organization can get an objective view and prevent inbreeding. Outsiders can bring a fresh perspective that can break the corruption cycle. For example, the presence of outsiders on a company board of directors has been found to help keep executive salaries more in line with company performance (Conyon and Peck 1998).
- *Changing the organizational culture.* The most difficult and most effective solution to preventing power corruption is a change in the culture and structure of organizations. The change should focus on performance, productivity, and customer service rather than on satisfying the leaders.

Partly because of many abuses of power and partly as a result of philosophical and structural changes in our organizations, the face of power is changing in many of today's organizations.

EMPOWERMENT: THE CHANGING FACE OF POWER

One of the major forces for cultural and structural changes in organizations has been the empowerment movement. Empowerment involves sharing power with subordinates and pushing decision making and implementation power to the lowest possible level. Its goal is to increase the power and autonomy of all employees in organizations. It has roots in perceptions of Japanese management, the quality circle efforts of the 1970s and the quality of work life (QWL) approach (Lawler and Mohrman 1987), and the psychological concept of self-efficacy (Bandura 1977). The underlying theme of empowerment is the giving away and sharing of power with those who need it to perform their job functions. Such power sharing provides people with a belief in their abilities and enhances their sense of effectiveness. Research on the distribution of power (Tannenbaum and Cooke 1974) together with observations of many leaders (Bennis and Nanus 1985; Block 1987) strongly suggests that equal power sharing contributes to an organization's effectiveness.

Empowerment of employees can be a powerful motivational tool because it provides them with control and a sense of accomplishment. Key to empowerment are giving employees control over how they perform their work and over their work environment, and building a sense of self-efficacy or competence by providing them with opportunities to succeed. Additionally, encouraging participation in goal setting is likely to lead followers to internalize the goals and build commitment to them, a key factor in producing a feeling of empowerment (Menon 2001).

When Linda Ellerbee, television reporter and CEO of Lucky Duck Productions, an award-winning television production company, found out she had cancer, she was forced to give up the reins of her company to her employees. Although she previously had been involved in every aspect of her company, she found out that "I had hired really good people who were good at their job, and what they needed was for me to get out of their way. The company continued to thrive in my absence. I never tried to micromanage again" (Ellerbee 1999, p. 81).

Steps to Empowerment

Once managers and leaders decide to adopt and implement empowerment as a management technique, they must adjust the culture and structure of their organization. Many managers talk about empowerment, but few have fully accepted the concept and implemented it completely. Several leadership and organizational steps must be taken to implement empowerment (see Table 4-4).

The Leadership Factors

When empowering employees, the role of the leader is to provide a supportive and trusting atmosphere that encourages them to share ideas, participate in decision making, collaborate with one another, and take risks. The leader can achieve this through various means, such as role modeling, openness to others, and enthusiasm. Leaders who want to implement empowerment successfully must "walk the talk," be aware of their verbal and nonverbal signals, and be believers in the empowerment

Table 4-4

Leadership and Organizational Factors in Empowerment

LEADERSHIP FACTORS	ORGANIZATIONAL FACTORS
• Creating a positive emotional atmosphere	• Decentralized structure
• Setting high performance standards	• Appropriate selection and training of leaders
• Encouraging initiative and responsibility	• Appropriate selection and training of employees
• Rewarding openly and personally	• Removing bureaucratic constraints
• Practicing equity and collaboration	• Rewarding empowering behaviors
• Expressing confidence in subordinates	• Fair and open organizational policies

Sources: Based on information in Block (1987); Conger (1989b); Conger and Kanungo (1988).

process. They must encourage experimentation and tolerate mistakes. Leaders can further encourage an atmosphere of openness by increasing their informal interaction with subordinates in and out of the workplace.

High work and productivity standards, clarification of organizational missions and goals, and clear and equitable rewards for proper behaviors and proper productivity outcomes must accompany the positive atmosphere the leader creates. Empowerment does not mean a lack of performance or standards. Rather, it involves providing employees with many opportunities to set high goals, seeking out resources that they need, supporting them in their decisions and actions, and rewarding them when the goals are achieved. The leader needs to have high standards of expectation and express confidence in the followers' ability to deliver high performance.

Roy Vagelos, CEO of Merck, a drug manufacturer, insisted on the impossible when he set out to eradicate river blindness, a disease that had long gone without a cure. The price of the project was an apparently unmanageable $200,000 for a drug whose customers were unlikely to be able to afford it. Vagelos forged ahead and continued to expect that the project would succeed. His high expectations paid off when the drug was developed and distributed to reach 19 million people (Labarre 1998).

The Organizational Factors

In addition to the leader's role in empowerment, the organization also needs to take steps to empower employees (see Table 4-4). First and foremost, the structure of the organization has to allow for power sharing by breaking down formal and rigid hierarchies and by decentralizing decision making. It is difficult for a leader to empower employees to make decisions when the organizational structure does not recognize the empowerment. The traditional lines of authority and responsibility do not lend themselves well to the empowerment process, so before new techniques can be implemented, organizations must evaluate their structure with an eye for removing bureaucratic barriers. In many cases, the physical office space must be changed to accommodate the new way people will be working. Formal offices and cubicles indicate hierarchy and individual work, so encouraging interaction will require a different work space that encourages flexibility and cooperation. Several organizations have found that changing their office layout is the key to better performance (Goldstein 2000).

Another organizational step is the selection of leaders and employees who are willing to share power. The change in structure and empowerment can be difficult for leaders and followers who are not comfortable with such a process (Frey 1993). Along with proper selection, appropriate training has to be provided to teach the new behaviors of collaboration, encouragement, participation, and openness. Finally, just as leaders have to "walk the empowerment talk," so do organizations by implementing appropriate reward structures and fair policies that allow for experimentation, initiative, making mistakes, and collaboration. Intense focus on the short-term financial outcomes can be deadly to an empowerment process that needs time to take hold. One of the ways organizations can start the process of empowerment is by recognizing and identifying the potential blocks to empowerment. Some consultants and academics even recommend that organizations and employees be encouraged to outright reject authority. Jim Dator, director of the University of Hawaii Research Center for Futures Studies, suggests: "Reject pronouncements that sound reasonable, comfortable, or familiar" (Olofson 1998). Dator considers broad access to information to be one of the tools people can use to make independent decisions.

LEADING CHANGE
The New Scientists at Roche

The Swiss pharmaceutical giant founded in 1896 brought the world drugs such as Valium and the antibiotic Bactrim by relying on its old, highly competitive culture that pitted each scientific team against the others, discouraged interaction, and focused on individual performance. The culture obviously worked; the company not only has a long list of successful products, but also many awards including the Nobel prize and several others for its discoveries (www.roche.com/). However, as even the scientific world became more complex, particularly with the explosion of genetic research and the availability of massive amounts of computer data, the old structure needed to change. "The competing-team approach can work. But if you have a large number of targets, it can't work" states Nader Fotouhi, Roche's vice president for discovery chemistry (Anders 2002, p. 66).

Lee Babiss, head of preclinical research at Roche's Nutley, New Jersey, headquarters, saw an opportunity by observing his scientists interacting informally in the hallways. He pushed for the creation of the first cross-functional team called the Genomics Oncology (GO) team (Anders 2002). The new team model became the standard at Roche after 1999. German Juergen Hammer heads the GO team, which hired on a highly diverse group of scientists from all over the world. The new team members do not always have the best scientific résumé, but they are creative and flexible. They can deal with the new, extremely fast-paced genomics research paradigms, embrace the need to interact with scientists from different disciplines, and focus on what Babiss calls "failing fast," which involves cutting down the time it takes to consider wrong solutions (Anders 2002, p. 66).

Source: Anders, G. 2002. Roche's new scientific method. *Fast Company,* January, 60–67; www.roche.com/.

Impact of Empowerment

Empowering employees is a difficult process, but it continues to be recognized as a key factor in today's new structures and a requirement for leaders. Leaders in large and small organizations are encouraged to give up power to their followers, and many case examples and anecdotes illustrate that empowerment can be a motivational tool and lead to increased performance. It might even be that empowerment (or its opposite, too much control) can create a self-fulfilling prophecy (Davis, Schoorman, and Donaldson 1997). On the one hand, the less a leader controls employees, the more likely they are to accept control and responsibility. On the other hand, increased control can cause followers to become passive, and in the extreme can lead to corruption. The idea of self-leadership, which is discussed in Chapter 7, is partially based on the concepts of empowerment.

Interestingly, despite the many reported positive benefits of empowerment, research on the subject is scarce and mixed. Although research has been conducted on the benefits for high-involvement organizations that use empowerment and employee participation to various degrees (Lawler, Mohrman, and Ledford 1995), few direct empirical tests of the various elements of empowerment are available. Nevertheless, despite the many obstacles and difficulties and the limited empirical evidence, empowerment has become a permanent feature of many organizations in the United States and many other Western countries. When applied well and in culturally compatible institutions, empowerment can have a powerful impact on a leader's and an organization's effectiveness.

SUMMARY AND CONCLUSION

This chapter focuses on the link between power and leadership. Having power to influence others is the key to a leader's ability to achieve goals and to being effective. In this influence process, a leader has access to a number of personal and organizational sources of power. The more leaders rely on power sources vested in themselves, the more likely it is that subordinates will be committed to the leader's decisions and actions. Reliance on organizational sources of power such as legitimacy, reward, or punishment at best leads to temporary employee commitment and at worst to resentment and resistance. Given the increasing use of teams in U.S. organizations, it is also important for teams and their leaders to develop sources of power by coping with uncertainty, becoming central to their organization's mission and goals, and providing unique products or services that make them indispensable to others in their organization.

Although power is necessary in order to accomplish organizational goals, power also has many potential negative effects. Excessive power can cause leaders to develop inflated views of themselves due to compliance of the followers, flattery and compliments, the separation of leaders from their subordinates, and their access to too many resources without much accountability. In addition to the ethical consequences, such excessive power also can lead to poor decision making, reliance on authoritarian leadership, poor information flow, adversarial interactions, and ultimately, subordinate reactance and resistance.

The face of power is changing in many organizations. The key aspect of this change is the sharing of power to allow subordinates to participate in decision making, thereby leading to higher-quality decisions and subordinates' sense of accomplishment. This empowerment movement has many successes. It depends on the leader and the organization creating a positive atmosphere in which structures are decentralized and employees are encouraged to experiment and innovate; employees also must be well trained and supported. In addition, high performance standards need to be set and rewards have to be tied clearly and fairly to performance. Despite the bad press the abuse of power has received recently, its proper application in organizations is key to a leader's effectiveness. As part of the process of influencing others, power is at the core of the leadership interaction.

How Much Is Enough?

Business executives, particularly in the United States, commandeer incredibly high salaries and compensation packages. The numbers are approaching and surpassing the $100 million mark, in some cases in companies that are performing poorly. A number of arguments explain the rise in compensation packages, including market forces and competition for the few talented executives. Where do you draw the line? If you were offered an outrageous compensation package to join a company that is laying off employees, declaring bankruptcy, and performing poorly overall, would you take it?

1. What factors contribute to high compensation packages?
2. What are the personal and organizational implications of your decision?

REVIEW AND DISCUSSION QUESTIONS

1. Provide examples for each personal source of power. Why are some forms of power more influential than others?
2. Provide scenarios for the appropriate use of each source of power.
3. Provide examples of how teams can use the sources of power available to them.
4. How are the team sources of power different from those available to individuals?
5. Provide examples of the use of different influence tactics.
6. What is the impact of too much power on organizations? Provide examples.
7. What are the key roles of a leader in implementing empowerment?
8. Where does the additional power to be given to subordinates come from?
9. Could empowerment lead to powerless leaders? Why or why not?

SEARCHING THE WEB

Power and Influence:
www.gov.sk.ca/psc.mecentre/
Impact_Influence.htm

sol.brunel.ac.uk/~jarvis/bola/motivation/
etzioni.html

Corruption:
www.transparency.org/
www.worldbank.org/fandd/english/0398/
articles/010398.htm

Leader Compensation:
www.fortune.com/indexw.jhtml?channel=/
editorial/mag_archive/2001/mag_archive.
6.25.01.html (cover stories on executive pay)
www.asaenet.org/newsroom/faq2/
0,2412,,00.html

EXERCISE 4-1: RECOGNIZING BLOCKS TO EMPOWERMENT

This exercise is designed to help you recognize organizational readiness for empowerment and the potential blocks to its implementation.

For each question, think about the current state of your organization or department and check the appropriate box.

Questions	Yes	No
1. Is your organization undergoing major change and transition?	☐	☐
2. Is your organization a start-up or new venture?	☐	☐
3. Is your organization facing increasing competitive pressures?	☐	☐
4. Is your organization a hierarchical bureaucracy?	☐	☐
5. Is the predominant leadership in your organization authoritarian and top down?	☐	☐
6. Is there a great deal of negativism, rehashing, and focus on failures?	☐	☐
7. Are employees provided with reasons for the organization's decisions and actions?	☐	☐
8. Are performance expectations and goals clearly stated?	☐	☐
9. Are goals realistic and achievable?	☐	☐
10. Are rewards clearly tied to performance or the accomplishment of organizational goals and missions?	☐	☐
11. Are rewards based on competence and accomplishments?	☐	☐
12. Is innovation encouraged and rewarded?	☐	☐
13. Do many opportunities arise for participation?	☐	☐
14. Are most tasks routine and repetitive?	☐	☐
15. Are resources generally appropriate for performing the tasks?	☐	☐
16. Are opportunities for interaction with senior management limited?	☐	☐

Scoring key: For items 1 through 6 and 14 and 16, give a score of 1 if you have marked Yes, 0 if you have checked No. For items 7 through 13 and item 15, reverse scoring, giving a 0 to Yes and 1 to No.

Interpretation: The maximum possible score is 16. The closer you have rated your organization to that maximum score, the less ready it is for implementation of empowerment. An analysis of individual items can point to specific blocks to the implementation of empowerment.

This self-assessment is designed to provide you with insight into your attitude regarding power.

Questionnaire

Indicate your opinion on each question by using the following scale:

1 = Strongly agree	4 = Somewhat disagree
2 = Somewhat agree	5 = Strongly disagree
3 = Neither agree nor disagree	

Questions   **Your Score**

1. It is important for leaders to use all power and status symbols that the organization provides in order to be able to get their job done.   ____
2. Unfortunately, for many employees, the only thing that works is threats and punitive actions.   ____
3. In order to be effective, a leader needs to have access to many resources to reward subordinates when they do their job well.   ____
4. Having excellent interpersonal relations with subordinates is essential to effective leadership.   ____
5. One of the keys to a leader's influence is access to information.   ____
6. Being friends with subordinates often reduces a leader's ability to influence them and control their actions.   ____
7. Leaders who are reluctant to punish their employees often lose their credibility.   ____
8. It is difficult for a leader to be effective without a formal title and position within an organization.   ____
9. Rewarding subordinates with raises, bonuses, and resources is the best way to obtain their cooperation.   ____
10. In order to be effective, leaders need to become experts in the area in which they are leading.   ____
11. Organizations need to ensure that a leader's formal evaluation of subordinates is actively used in making decisions about them.   ____
12. Even in most enlightened organizations, a leader's ability to punish subordinates needs to be well preserved.   ____
13. The dismantlement of formal hierarchies and the removal of many of the symbols of leadership and status have caused many leaders to lose their ability to influence their subordinates.   ____
14. Leaders need to take particular care to be perceived as experts in their area.   ____
15. It is key for a leader to develop subordinates' loyalty.   ____

Scoring key: Reverse scoring for item 6 (1 = strongly agree, 5 = strongly disagree), then add your scores on each item as follows:

Legitimate power:	Add items 1, 8, and 13	Total: _____
Reward power:	Add items 3, 9, and 11	Total: _____
Coercive power:	Add items 2, 7, and 12	Total: _____
Referent power:	Add items 4, 6, and 15	Total: _____
Expert power:	Add items 5, 10, and 14	Total: _____

Interpretation: Your total in each of the preceding five categories indicates your belief and attitude toward each of the personal power sources available to leaders.

CASE

Leadership in Action

The Most Powerful Woman in Banking

"Toughest babe in business" (*Fortune*, 1997), "a cross between the Terminator and Kim Basinger" (Sellers 1997, p. 64), and "Banking's best paid woman," (money.cnn.com) are some of the labels used to describe Darla Moore, considered to be one of the most powerful women in U.S. business (Folpe 1999). Charlotte Beers, chairman and CEO of the advertising firm of Oglivy and Mather, says Moore is mysterious. Martha Stewart, the world's most famous gracious living adviser, describes her as: "a cutthroat killer underneath, which makes her really exciting" (Sellers 1996). Those who worked for Moore are likely to agree. Several years ago, when she worked at Chemical Bank in New York City, her entire group quit because she was too tough. Moore explains that her employees thought she was too demanding and intolerant (money.cnn.com). She still considers her intolerance and extremely high standards to be one of her weaknesses. Although Moore has learned to tone down her expectations and has become a better manager of people, she continues to be a ruthless and demanding negotiator.

After having graduated from the University of South Carolina, she worked for Chemical Bank, where she developed the reputation of being a tough businesswoman with no management skills. After marrying Richard Rainwater, who paid her the ultimate compliment by calling her his best investment, and successfully implementing several high deals, Moore become CEO of Rainwater Incorporated in 1994. Even before becoming CEO, she was one of the highest paid women in banking. Moore is also the first woman to endow and have a college of business named after her; the University of South Carolina Business school is now called the Darla Moore School of Business after her $25 million endowment.

Moore and her husband are in the investment business. He finds the places to invest and she executes the deals. As one analyst describes them: "They work with so much capital—often hundreds of millions of dollars—that people pay attention to what they want, even though they don't appear on management charts or take seats on boards of directors" (money.cnn.com). Moore describes her style as follows: "We pick great managers and we back them. Then we get out of the way. If, over time, they don't perform, we replace them" (money.cnn.com). Moore has gained notoriety for ousting several powerful executives after investing in their firms. She considers this simply a matter of good business. She says "No one felt good about this. You feel bad. But you get through that because the stakes are too high and something has to be done and it's your responsibility" (money.cnn.com).

Moore's strengths come from "an ability to withstand great stress without tearing or breaking" (money.cnn.com) and "seeing through the smoke into chaos, and operating where everything is exploding" (Sellers 1997, p. 65). Moore says "I used to love a good fight. As long as you stay on the facts and information and keep the emotional stuff out of it" (money.cnn.com). She shuns much of the advice women get and give about networking and finding mentors. She thinks women in business are "outliers, mavericks, misfits" (Sellers 1998, p. 92). She says women "really aren't powerful if they don't have personal power" (Sellers 1998, p. 92). Her advice is "to find a niche then become the best there is in that field. If you perform, you'll get recognized" (Sellers 1996, p. 57). ■

QUESTIONS

1. What are Darla Moore's strengths and weaknesses? What are the individual and organizational sources of her power? Which sources of power does she not have?

2. Why is she effective?

Sources: This case is based on information in Folpe, J. 1999. *Fortune*'s 50 most powerful women. *Fortune,* (www.business2.com/articles/mag/print/0,1643,5757,FF.html); Sellers, P. 1996. Cocktails at Charlotte's with Martha and Darla. *Fortune,* 134 no. 3, 56–57; Sellers, P. 1997. Don't mess with Darla. *Fortune* 136 no. 5, 62–72; Sellers, P. 1998. The fifty most powerful women in American business. *Fortune* 138 no. 7, 76–98; and information in money.cnn.com/1998/06/17/Fortune_promo/.

Part II

Contingency Models

*P*art II presents the contingency theories of leadership that have dominated the field for the past 40 years. After studying Part II, you will
be able to describe the individual and situational variables of each of the
models, list their similarities and differences, understand their contributions and limitations to our understanding of leadership, and be able to
use the different models in improving leadership effectiveness.

The contingency view suggests that no one best way to lead has
been found, but rather the type and style of leadership that are effective
depend on various situational contingencies. From a contingency point
of view, neither autocratic leadership, which was predominant in the
early part of the twentieth century, nor participative leadership, which
was the focus in the 1960s and 1970s, is effective all of the time. As
early as the 1930s, studies by Lewin and his associates (Lewin and
Lippit 1938; Lewin, Lippit, and White 1939) suggested that both autocratic and democratic styles of leadership can be effective. In the late
1940s, Stogdill proposed the concept of contingency, although he was
not able to convince fully the leadership behavior researchers of his era.
It was not until the mid-1960s that the contingency approach to leadership was fully developed and eventually adopted by the majority of
scholars in the field. Although, as will be discussed in Part III, a movement away from contingency views of leadership might be occurring,
such views continue to dominate current management and leadership
thought.

The contingency theories presented in Chapters 5 and 6 have many
differences; however, they all suggest that effective leadership is a

function of the leader and the situation. The theories are divided into two general categories (Chemers 1993). The first group considers how leaders use resources; these are discussed in Chapter 5. The second group focuses on how leaders develop and maintain relationships with subordinates; they are presented in Chapter 6.

Part II   Contingency Models

Chapter 5

Contingency Models:
Using Resources Effectively

> *A pretzel-shaped world needs a pretzel-shaped theory.*

—FRED FIEDLER

After studying this chapter, you will be able to:

1. Explain the importance of the effective use of resources to leadership.
2. Distinguish between a task-motivated and a relationship-motivated leader and identify the elements of situational control used in Fiedler's Contingency Model of leadership.
3. Present the Contingency Model's predictions and explain how to use the model to improve leadership effectiveness.
4. Present the four decision styles used in the Normative Decision Model of leadership.
5. Understand the role of decision quality and follower acceptance in the choice of leadership styles and how to use the Normative Decision Model to improve leadership effectiveness.
6. Discuss the Cognitive Resource Theory and its implications for leaders.

An effective leader must know how to use available resources to achieve goals. The effective use of resources helps translate the leaders' and followers' efforts into performance (Chemers 1993).

125

Understanding how leaders use the resources available to them is, therefore, essential. Resource utilization models allow us to answer questions such as the following: When should the leader use the group as a resource? Under which circumstances should leaders rely on their own experiences and expertise? When should more training be sought? When should leaders exercise their power and authority fully? The successful use of each of these resources depends on (1) an understanding of the leadership situation—that is, the contingency factors, (2) the identification of the leader's style or behavior, and (3) a match between the situation and the leader.

This chapter presents two of the most well-established contingency models of leadership. Fiedler's Contingency Model and the Normative Decision Model focus on the way a leader uses resources to achieve effectiveness. A third, more recent view, the Cognitive Resources Theory, also is discussed.

FIEDLER'S CONTINGENCY MODEL

Fred Fiedler was the first researcher who took Stogdill's advice about adopting a contingency view of leadership to heart and proposed a contingency approach to leadership. His Contingency Model is the oldest and most highly researched contingency approach to leadership (Fiedler 1967). Fiedler's basic and relatively simple premise is that leadership effectiveness is a function of the match between the leader's style and the leadership situation. If the leader's style matches the situation, the leader will be effective; if the leader's style does not match the situation, the leader will not be effective.

Leadership effectiveness is a function of the match between the leader's style and the leadership situation. If the leader's style matches the situation, the leader will be effective; if the leader's style does not match the situation, the leader will not be effective.

Leader's Style

To determine a leader's style, Fiedler uses the least-preferred coworker (LPC) scale, a measure that determines whether the leader has a task or relationship motivation. Fiedler's research shows that people's perceptions and descriptions of their least-preferred coworker provide insight into their basic goals and priorities toward either accomplishing a task or maintaining relationships (see Self-Assessment 5-1).

According to Fiedler, people with low LPC scores—those who give a low rating to their least-preferred coworker (describing the person as incompetent, cold, untrustworthy, and quarrelsome)—are task motivated. Task motivation means that the person is motivated primarily by task accomplishment. Task-motivated individuals draw their self-esteem mostly from accomplishing their task well (Chemers and Skrzypek 1972; Fiedler 1967; Fiedler and Chemers 1984; Rice 1978a, 1978b). When the task-motivated leaders or their groups fail, they tend to be harsh in judging their subordinates and are often highly punitive (Rice 1978a, 1978b). When the task is going well, however, the task-motivated leader is comfortable with details and with monitoring routine events (Fiedler and Chemers 1984).

People who have high LPC scores rate their least-preferred coworker relatively positively (describing that person as loyal, sincere, warm, and accepting); they are relationship motivated. Relationship motivation means that interpersonal relations is the primary motivator for the person. For the most part, relationship-motivated individuals draw their self-esteem from having good relationships with others. To such people, the least-preferred coworker is often someone who has been disloyal and unsupportive rather than incompetent (Rice 1978a, 1978b). This finding further reinforces the suggestion that relationships are more important than task accomplishment. Relationship-motivated persons are easily bored with details (Fiedler 1978; Fiedler and Chemers 1984) and focus on social interactions (Rice 1978a, 1978b) (see Table 5-1).

Marilyn Moats Kennedy, managing partner of Career Strategies, a consulting firm based in Wilmette, Illinois, is a task-motivated low-LPC leader. She describes her leadership style:

> Leaders can't succeed if they care more about how people feel than how they perform. So focus on output, not on attitude. Sincerity and competence rarely share a soul. Reward the latter and forget the former. (Kennedy 1997, p. 98)

Contrast her views with those of Mort Meyerson, chairman of Perot Systems, a computer firm based in Dallas, Texas, who is a relationship-motivated, high-LPC leader:

> Most companies are still dominated by numbers, information, and analysis. That makes it much harder to tap into intuition, feelings, and nonlinear thinking—the skills that leaders will need to succeed in the future. If you work with the whole person, and their whole mind, you will reach a better place—for them and the company. (Meyerson 1997, p. 99)

Individuals who fall in the middle of the scale have been labeled socio-independent. They tend to be less concerned with other people's opinions. Depending on how close their score is to the high or the low end of the scale, they might belong to either the task-motivated or relationship-motivated groups (Fiedler

Table 5-1
Differences between Task- and Relationship-Motivated Individuals

Task Motivated (Low LPC)	Relationship Motivated (High LPC)
• Draws self-esteem from completion of task	• Draws self-esteem from interpersonal relationships
• Focuses on the task first	• Focuses on people first
• Can be hard on failing employees	• Likes to please others
• Considers competence of coworkers to be key trait	• Considers loyalty of coworkers to be key trait
• Enjoys details	• Gets bored with details

and Chemers 1984). The task-motivated person's focus on tasks and the relationship-motivated person's concern for relationships are most obvious in times of crisis when the person is under pressure.

Despite some problems with the validity of the LPC scale, it has received strong support from researchers and practitioners and has even translated well to other cultures for use in leadership research and training (Ayman and Chemers 1983, 1991). A key premise of the LPC concept is that because it is an indicator of primary motivation, leadership style is stable. Leaders, then, cannot simply change their style to match the situation.

Situational Control

Fiedler uses three factors to describe a leadership situation. In order of importance, they are: (1) the relationship between the leader and the followers, (2) the amount of structure of the task, and (3) the position power of the leader. The three elements combine to define the amount of control the leader has over the situation.

According to Fiedler, the most important element of any leadership situation is the quality of the relationship, and the cohesion between the leader and the followers and among the followers (Fiedler 1978). Good leader-member relations (LMR) mean that the group is cohesive and supportive. In such a case, leaders have a high degree of control to implement what they want. When the group is divided or has little respect or support for the leader, the leader's control is low.

Task structure (TS) is the second element of a leadership situation. It refers to the degree of clarity of a task. A highly structured task has clear goals and procedures, few paths to the correct solution, one or few correct solutions, and can be evaluated easily (Fiedler and Chemers 1974). For instance, making a blueprint based on specifications is a highly structured task. An unstructured task is one in which the goals are not clear, few or no procedures are available for how to do the task, many different viable procedures and possible solutions exist, and no easy way is known to check results. For example, developing a public relations campaign is unstructured. The degree of task structure affects the leader's control. Whereas the leader has considerable control when doing a structured task, an unstructured task provides little sense of control. One factor that moderates task structure is the leader's experience level (Fiedler and Chemers 1984). On the one hand, if leaders have experience with a task, they will perceive it as more structured. On the other hand, not having experience will make any task appear to be unstructured.

The third and least influential element of the leadership situation is the leader's position power (PP), which refers to the leader's official power and influence over subordinates to hire, fire, reward, or punish. The leader who has a high amount of formal power feels more in control than one who has little power. For example, managers in most organizations have considerable position power, whereas a coordinator in charge of volunteers has little.

By analyzing these three elements, leaders can determine how much control they have over a situation. The combination of LMR, TS, and PP yields the amount of situational control (Sit Con) the leader has over the situation. At one end of the continuum, good leader-member relations, a highly structured task, and high position power for the leader provide the leader with high control over the leadership situation. In this case, the leader's influence is well accepted. In the middle of the continuum are situations whereby either the leader and the followers do not get along, or the task is unstructured. In such situations, the leader does not have full control over the situation and the leadership environment is more difficult. At the other end of the situational control continuum, the leader-member relations are poor, the task is unstructured, and the leader has little power. Such a situation is chaotic and unlikely to continue for a long period of time in an organization. Clearly, this crisis environment does not provide the leader with a sense of control or any ease of leadership (see Self-Assessment 5-2 for Sit Con).

Predictions of the Contingency Model

At the core of the Contingency Model is the concept of match. If the leader's style matches the situation, effectiveness will result. Because Fiedler suggests that the leader's style is constant, a leader's effectiveness changes as the situation changes. The Contingency Model predicts that low-LPC, task-motivated leaders will be effective in high- and low-situational control, whereas high-LPC, relationship-motivated leaders will be effective in moderate-situational control. Figure 5-1 presents the predictions of the model.

In high-control situations (the left side of the graph in Figure 5-1), task-motivated, low-LPC leaders feel at ease. The leader's basic source of self-esteem, getting the task

LEADING CHANGE
Seeing the World from a Different Perspective

Donald Winkler has a unique perspective on his company. He is the chairman and CEO of Ford Motor Credit Company. He is also dyslexic, a disability that causes him to struggle with how he processes the world, to wander, and that makes it difficult for him to focus. However, he believes it also lets him see the world from a unique perspective.

Winkler believes that people don't fail—events do. He does not let his employees point fingers and blame, does not like to hear about "we" and "they," and does not let anyone use the term *but*—*and* is an acceptable replacement. What he does like is straight talk and a collective effort. He faces challenges with the key phrase "up until now." His energy and passion about getting things done, accountability, and the style he calls

breakthrough leadership have changed the culture of his organization. Employees have adopted his language; they have even made buttons featuring the key phrases. Winkler states: "Leadership is about taking people to places that they wouldn't have gotten to by themselves" (Hammonds 2000, p. 266) He encourages followers to ask "power questions." To move ahead, Winkler believes that people have to focus on the future; trust and equality must exist, and people must listen to every idea intensely and maintain constant dialogue. By setting clear priorities, being accountable, making tough decisions, paying attention to detail, stressing fairness, and seeing failure as a stepping stone, Winkler has created major change.

Source: Hammonds, K. 2000. How do we break out of the box we're stuck in? *Fast Company* (November), 260–268.

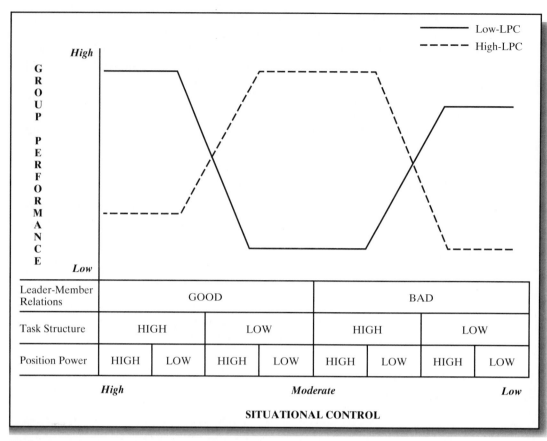

Figure 5-1
Fiedler's Contingency Model

done, is not threatened, so the leader can relax, take care of details, and help the followers perform. The same high-control situation has a different effect on relationship-motivated, high-LPC leaders. They are likely to be bored, and feel that there is nothing to do or that nobody needs them. Because the group is cohesive and the task is clear, the leader is needed mainly to get the group the resources it needs, take care of details, and remove obstacles—all activities that are not appealing to high LPCs, who might, therefore, start being overly controlling and interfere with the group's performance to demonstrate that they are needed (Chemers 1997; Fiedler and Garcia 1987a). See Table 5-2 for a summary of the leaders' behaviors in each situation.

Moderate situational control (the middle of graph in Figure 5-1) stems from lack of cohesiveness or lack of task structure. In either case, the situation is ambiguous or uncertain, and task completion is in jeopardy. The relationship-motivated, high-LPC leader's skills at interpersonal relationships and participation are well suited for the situation. This type of leader seeks out followers' participation and focuses on resolving task and relationship conflicts. The high-LPC leader uses the group as a resource to accomplish the task. The same elements that make moderate control attractive to relationship-motivated leaders make the situation threatening to the

Table 5-2

Leader Style and Behaviors in Different Levels of Sit Con

	HIGH SIT CON	MODERATE SIT CON	LOW SIT CON
Task-Motivated (low-LPC) Leader	Confident; considerate and supportive; removes obstacles and stays out of the way	Tense; task focused; overbearing and overcontrolling; insists on getting things done	Directive; task focused; serious; little concern for others
Relationship-Motivated (high-LPC) Leader	Bored; aloof and self-centered; somewhat autocratic; can interfere with group	Considerate; open to ideas and suggestions; concerned with resolving conflicts	Tense and nervous; hurt by group's conflict; indecisive

Sources: Partially based on Fiedler, F. E. 1978; Fiedler, F. E. and M. H. Chemers. 1974. *Leadership and effective management.* Glenview, Ill.: Scott-Foresman; Fiedler, F. E. and M. H. Chemers. 1984. *Improving leadership effectiveness: The leader match concept.* 2d ed. New York: Wiley.

task-oriented, low-LPC leader. The lack of group support, the ambiguity of the task, or both make the low LPC feel that the task might not be completed. The task-oriented leader becomes autocratic, ignores the task and relationship conflicts, and tries simply to complete the task to get a sense of accomplishment (Fiedler 1993). The inappropriate use of resources is likely to worsen the group's lack of cohesion and prevent the exploration of creative solutions to an unstructured task. As a result, the task-motivated leader's group performs poorly in moderate control.

Consider the example of several recent U.S. presidents. Former Presidents Nixon and Carter were task-motivated leaders. Both were highly intelligent, focused on the task, and able to analyze large amounts of detail. Both needed to stay in control, had uncompromising views and approaches to issues, and could be harsh toward failing subordinates. They performed well in high control. Nixon had considerable success in foreign policy, where he was respected, the task was clear, and he held power tightly. As his legitimate power and popularity decreased—leading to moderate control—he became controlling, punitive, and ineffective. Carter's effectiveness followed a similar pattern, although he never faced a high-control situation, a factor that might explain his overall poor effectiveness ratings. Almost immediately after being elected, he found himself in moderate control with poor relations with the U.S. Congress and an unstructured task exacerbated by his limited experience in foreign policy. His single-minded focus on human rights and his inability to compromise made him ineffective.

At the other end of the continuum are former Presidents Reagan and Clinton, both high LPCs who focused on interpersonal relations; were bored with details; and had an apparently unending ability to compromise, a desire to please others, and the ability to perform and "put on a show" for their public. Both enjoyed working with people and were popular with crowds. Reagan was well liked but faced an unstructured task with moderate power. Clinton faced a novel and unstructured situation but continued to enjoy unprecedented support of the electorate. Both relationship-motivated presidents were in moderate control where, by many accounts, they performed well.

As a situation becomes chaotic and reaches a crisis point with no group cohesion, no task structure, and no strong position power (the right side of the graph in Figure 5-1), the task-motivated, low-LPC leaders' need to complete the task pushes them to take over and make autocratic decisions without much concern for followers. As a result, although performance is not high and followers might not be satisfied, in a chaotic crisis situation, groups with a low-LPC leader get some work done. For the relationship-motivated, high-LPC leader, the low Sit Con environment is a nightmare. The group's lack of cohesion is further fueled by its inability to perform the task and makes efforts at reconciliation close to impossible. The high-LPC leader's efforts to gain support from the group, therefore, fall on deaf ears. In an attempt to protect their self-esteem, high LPC leaders withdraw, leaving their group to fend for itself and causing low performance. The data for the socio-independent leaders are less clear. Fiedler (1978) suggests that they generally perform better in high-control situations, although more research is needed to predict and explain their performance.

Evaluation and Applications

Although a large number of studies have supported the Contingency Model over the past 40 years, several researchers have voiced strong criticisms. In particular, the meaning and validity of the LPC scale (Schreisheim and Kerr 1977; Yukl 1970), the predictive value of the model (Vecchio 1983), and the lack of research about the middle-LPC leaders (Kennedy 1982) have come under attack. Thirty years of research has addressed the majority, although not all, of the concerns. As a result, the Contingency Model continues to emerge as one of the most reliable and predictive models of leadership, with a number of research studies and meta-analyses support-

WHAT DOES THIS MEAN FOR ME?
Taking Advantage of Training Programs

Fiedler's Contingency Model strongly suggests that leaders cannot and should not change their styles. Instead, they must learn to recognize and manage the situation. However, much of the available popular leadership training teaches leaders how to change. Following are some guidelines regarding how to use those training programs, even if your leadership style will not change.

- Focus on behaviors. Regardless of what your motivation and leadership style are, you can benefit from expanding your behavioral range.

- Although some behaviors might be hard or even close to impossible to master, you can always push yourself a little farther and learn new behaviors and skills.

- The training will, either by design or by default, expose you to many different leadership situations. This is a good opportunity to practice analyzing situations to ascertain the degree of situational control they provide.

- Don't expect miracles or even quick change. Increasing your effectiveness as a leader is a long journey, not a destination.

ing the hypotheses of the model (see Ayman, Chemers, and Fiedler 1995; Chemers 1997; Peters, Hartke, and Pohlmann 1985; Strube and Garcia 1981).

Overall, the direction of the research findings is as Fiedler predicted. The LPC scale, despite its apparent lack of face validity (i.e., it might not be obvious that it is measuring what it is supposed to measure), has been found to be valid and reliable (Rice 1978a, b). Most importantly, for the practitioner of leadership, the model has been tested extensively not only in laboratory settings but in a variety of field settings, ranging from the military to volunteer groups. In most cases, the predictions were supported. In-match leaders performed better than out-of-match leaders. In addition, the basic definition of effectiveness used by the contingency model ("group productivity") has been broadened to include constructs such as employee satisfaction (Nahavandi 1983) and leader stress (Chemers et al. 1985).

It is important to note that a person's LPC is not the only or the strongest determinant of a leader's actions and beliefs. Although the focus has been on the description of stereotypical task-motivated and relationship-motivated leaders, a person's behavior is determined by many other internal and external factors. It would, therefore, be inappropriate to carry the task or relationship orientation considerably beyond its use in the Contingency Model. It is a reliable predictor of leadership effectiveness within the model but not necessarily beyond it.

Using the Contingency Model

Fiedler's Contingency Model helps individuals recognize and understand their leadership style and the leadership situation they face. The major training tool developed based on this model is called Leader Match (Fiedler and Chemers 1984), which first teaches leaders to recognize their own style (LPC) and then to evaluate the various leadership situations they face. Situations are often dynamic and can move a leader from an in-match situation to an out-of-match one. For example, relationship-motivated leaders who effectively lead their group in moderate control by getting them to solve the problems associated with the task or by creating cohesion and good leader-member relations will effectively have put themselves out of match by moving the situation to high control. Similarly, task-motivated persons who get assigned a new, more difficult task because of their past success will face an unknown task that will put them out of match. Leader Match coaches leaders on how to change situations, whenever necessary, to match a person's leadership style (Fiedler and Chemers 1984). Compared to other leadership training models, Fiedler does not encourage changing the leader's style to match the situation because one's LPC score is long lasting and stable. The Contingency Model advocates changing the situation, and in effect training the leader in better use of resources (see Exercise 5-1). Much of the focus when using the Contingency Model to increase leadership effectiveness is on job and task rotation (Fiedler and Chemers 1984).

The Contingency Model has several practical implications for managers:

- Leaders must understand their style and the situation to predict how effective they will be.
- Leaders should focus on changing the situation to match their style instead of trying to change how they act.

A good relationship with
followers is key to a
leader's ability to lead, and
it can compensate for lack
of power.

- A good relationship with followers is key to a leader's ability to lead, and it can compensate for lack of power.
- Leaders can compensate for ambiguity of a task by getting training and experience.

Fiedler's focus on changing the situation rather than the leader is unique. The Normative Decision Model considered next, along with many other leadership models, assumes that the leader can change styles depending on the situation.

THE NORMATIVE DECISION MODEL

Should a leader make decisions alone or involve followers? What factors can help a leader determine how to make decisions? The Normative Decision Model, developed by researchers Victor Vroom, Philip Yetton, and Arthur Jago, answers these questions (Vroom and Jago 1988; Vroom and Yetton 1973). The model takes a contingency view of leadership decision making rather general leadership style. It is called normative because it recommends that leaders adopt certain leader styles based on the prescriptions of the model.

Like Fiedler, Vroom and his associates recommend matching the leader and the situational requirements. However, they differ on several points:

- The Normative Decision Model is limited to decision making rather than general leadership.
- The Normative Decision Model assumes that leaders can adopt different decision making styles as needed.
- The Normative Decision Model is concerned mostly with the quality of the decision rather than group performance.

The Normative Decision Model relies on two well-established group dynamic principles: first, that groups are wasteful and inefficient, and second, that participation in decision making leads to commitment. Based on these principles, the model recommends that leaders adjust their decision style depending on the extent to which it is important that the decision be high quality and the likelihood that employees will accept the decision.

Leader's Decision Styles

The Normative Decision Model identifies four decision methods available to leaders (Vroom and Jago 1988). The first method is autocratic (A), in which the leader makes a decision with little or no involvement from followers. The second decision method is consultation (C), which means that the leader consults with followers yet retains the final decision making authority. The third decision method is group (G). Here, the leader relies on consensus building to solve a problem. The final method involves total delegation (D) of decision making to one employee. The decision styles and their subcategories are summarized in Table 5-3.

A leader must decide which style to use depending on the situation that the leader and the group face and on whether the problem involves a group or one

Table 5-3

Decision Styles in the Normative Decision Model

DECISION STYLE	AI	AII	CI	CII	GI	GII	DI
Description	Unassisted decision	Ask specific information but make decisions alone	Ask for specific information and ideas from each group member	Ask for information and ideas from whole group	Ask for one person's help. Mutual exchange based on expertise	Group shares information and ideas and reaches consensus	Other person analyzes problem; makes decision
Who makes the decision	Leader	Leader	Leader	Leader with considerable group input	Leader and one other person	Group with leader input	Other person
Type of problem	Group and individual	Group and individual	Group and individual	Group	Individual	Group	Individual

Key: A = Autocratic, C = Consultative, G = Group

Sources: Vroom, V. H. and A. G. Jago. 1988. *The new leadership: Managing participation in organizations.* Upper Saddle River, NJ: Prentice Hall; Vroom, V. H. and P. W. Yetton. 1973. *Leadership and decision making.* Pittsburgh: University of Pittsburgh Press.

individual. Individual problems affect only one person, whereas group problems can affect a group or individual. For example, deciding on raises for individual employees is an individual problem, whereas scheduling vacations is a group problem. Similarly, deciding on which employees should receive training or go to an overseas assignment is an individual problem, whereas moving a business to another state or cutting down a city service are group problems. The distinction between the two is not always clear; individual problems can affect others, and group problems can have an impact on individuals.

Contingency Variables: Defining the Problem

The two central contingency factors for the Normative Decision Model are the quality of the decision and the need for acceptance and commitment by followers. Other contingency factors to consider are whether the leader has enough relevant information to make a sound decision, whether the problem is structured and clear, the likelihood that followers will accept the leader's decision, whether the employees agree with the organizational goals, whether employees are cohesive, and whether they have enough information to make a decision alone. Table 5-4 presents the eight contingency factors.

The various combinations of the eight contingency factors create different leadership situations. Each situation requires a different decision-making style to ensure that a quality decision is made and implemented by followers within the required time frame. The next section considers the model's predictions of the best match between the leader's decision-making style and the situation.

Table 5-4
Contingency Factors in the Normative Decision Model

CONTINGENCY FACTOR	QUESTION TO ASK
Quality requirement (QR)	How important is the quality of the decision?
Commitment requirement (CR)	How important is employee commitment to the implementation of the decision?
Leader information (LI)	Does the leader have enough information to make a high-quality decision?
Structure of the problem (ST)	Is the problem clear and well structured?
Commitment probability (CP)	How likely is employee commitment to the solution if leader makes the decision alone?
Goal congruence (GC)	Do employees agree with and support organizational goals?
Employee conflict (CO)	Is there conflict among employees over solution?
Subordinate information (SI)	Do employees have enough information to make a high-quality decision?

Sources: Vroom, V. H. and A. G. Jago. 1988. *The new leadership: Managing participation in organizations.* Upper Saddle River, NJ: Prentice Hall; Vroom, V. H. and P. W. Yetton. 1973. *Leadership and decision making.* Pittsburgh: University of Pittsburgh Press.

The Normative Decision Model's Predictions

The Normative Decision Model is a decision tree, as shown in Figure 5-2. Leaders ask the series of questions listed in Table 5-4; the questions relate to the contingency factors and should be asked sequentially. By responding "yes" or "no" to each question, managers can determine which decision style(s) are most appropriate for the problem they face. Figure 5-2 presents the most widely used Normative Decision Model. This model is labeled "time efficient," based on the assumption that consultation and participation require time and are not efficient (Vroom and Jago 1988). Therefore, whenever appropriate, the model leans toward more autocratic decision making. A second version of the model, labeled "time investment," focuses on the development of followers at the expense of efficiency. This version recommends more participative decision making whenever possible.

Figure 5-2
Normative Decision Model

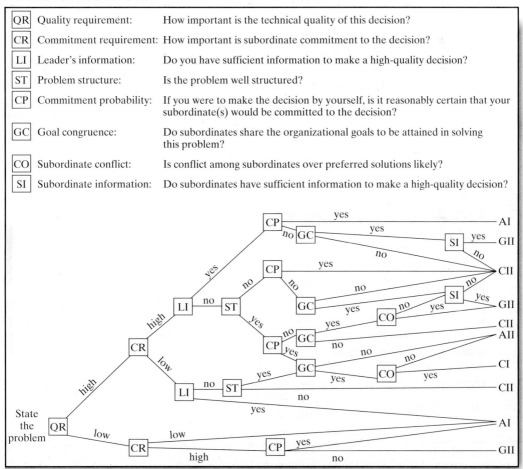

QR	Quality requirement:	How important is the technical quality of this decision?
CR	Commitment requirement:	How important is subordinate commitment to the decision?
LI	Leader's information:	Do you have sufficient information to make a high-quality decision?
ST	Problem structure:	Is the problem well structured?
CP	Commitment probability:	If you were to make the decision by yourself, is it reasonably certain that your subordinate(s) would be committed to the decision?
GC	Goal congruence:	Do subordinates share the organizational goals to be attained in solving this problem?
CO	Subordinate conflict:	Is conflict among subordinates over preferred solutions likely?
SI	Subordinate information:	Do subordinates have sufficient information to make a high-quality decision?

Source: Adapted and reprinted from *Leadership and Decision-Making* by Victor H. Vroom and Philip W. Yetton, by permission of the University of Pittsburgh Press. Copyright © 1973 by University of Pittsburgh Press.

An autocratic decision-making style is appropriate in the following situations:

- *When the leader has sufficient information to make a decision.* If the leader has sufficient information, it is usually more efficient to use an autocratic style. This is especially true in cases where subordinates are cohesive, agree with the organization's goals, and are likely to implement decisions despite a lack of involvement in decision making.
- *When the quality of the decision is not essential.* Generally, it is more efficient to allow the leader to make a decision that does not need to be high quality. For example, group involvement is unnecessary when deciding where to buy a pack of pencils to restock the office cabinet.
- *When employees do not agree with each other.* If employees cannot agree, then a decision might never be made unless the leader takes charge.
- *When employees do not agree with the goals of the organization.* In this case, even when leaders do not have all of the information, they need to make the decision alone because the employees' decision might not benefit the organization.

A consultative style of decision making is appropriate in the following situations:

- The leader has sufficient information, but the employees demand participation to implement the decision.
- The leader has insufficient information, and employee consultation will help the leader gather more information as well as develop commitment.
- When followers generally agree with the goals of the organization.

A group-oriented decision style should be used when the leader does not have all the information, quality is important, and employee commitment is essential. Delegation is used to assign the decision to a single individual who has the needed information, competence, and organizational commitment to make and implement it.

Evaluation and Application

Several research studies have provided support for the Normative Decision Model (Crouch and Yetton 1987; Jago and Vroom 1980; Tjosvold, Wedley, and Field 1986). The decision methods are clearly defined, and the contingency factors included are based on extensive research about group dynamics and participative management (Maier 1963).

Some practitioners and theorists argue, however, that the model has two main weaknesses. First, it is too complex to have practical value. Few managers have the time to work their way through the decision tree to conclude which style to use in a given situation. Second, the assumption that leaders have the ability to use any of the decision styles equally well might be flawed. Not all leaders can be autocratic for one decision, consultative for another, and group oriented for still others. Although this might constitute an ideal for leadership effectiveness, it might not be possible given differences in personality and personal style preferences, as well as each person's behavioral range.

Knowledge of the problem-identification questions and familiarity with the decision styles can help leaders make higher-quality decisions by using the group as a resource.

The Normative Decision Model, compared to Fiedler's Contingency Model, has a narrower focus on leadership decision making. Within that limited focus, the model works well and can be a helpful tool for leaders. Knowledge of the problem-identification questions and familiarity with the decision styles can help leaders make higher-quality decisions by using the group as a resource. It is also important for leaders to recognize that some decision styles might be harder to master due to their personality traits and behaviors patterns. For example, delegation might be difficult for a Type A, ST leader who needs to maintain control. By the same token, making autocratic decisions could take considerable practice for an NF leader who likes to please others.

The Normative Decision Model suggests several practical implications:

- Leaders must understand the situation and understand how and when to use the different decision methods.
- Participation is not always desirable as a leadership style.
- Leaders must pay particular attention to their followers' needs and reactions when making a decision.

The Normative Decision Model offers practical and useful recommendations regarding which situational factors leaders must consider, and it assumes that the leader can learn to change styles based on those factors. The next section presents a recent model of leadership that considers the importance of a leader's cognitive resources and the impact of stress on leadership effectiveness.

COGNITIVE RESOURCES THEORY

Do situations arise in which the leader's intelligence and other cognitive abilities can be a disadvantage? How does stress impact a leader's effectiveness? The most recent resource utilization contingency model of leadership addresses these questions. Developed by Fred Fiedler and Joseph Garcia (1987a, b), the Cognitive Resources Theory (CRT) considers situations in which the leader's cognitive resources can be an asset or a liability to the leader and to group performance.

Leader Characteristics and Contingency Factors

CRT considers two leader characteristics: intelligence and experience. Intelligence is defined as "an overall effectiveness in activities as measured by standardized intelligence tests" (Fiedler 1995; Fiedler and Garcia 1987a, b). Experience includes learned behavioral patterns and skills acquired through performing various tasks. These two leader characteristics have different impacts on leader and group performance depending on the level of stress, which Fiedler defines primarily as "interpersonal conflict and concerns about performance" (Fiedler 1995). When leaders have concerns about their performance or are experiencing conflict with their own superiors, they are likely to experience stress. Other stressful situations include periods of organizational change and upheaval, such as times of mergers or reorganization.

CRT's Predictions

CRT considers leader intelligence, experience, and the stressfulness of the situation, and proposes several hypotheses. First, the leader's intelligence can contribute positively to group performance when the leader is directive. In other words, the group can benefit from a leader's intelligence only if the leader guides followers. This is particularly relevant when the group is performing complex tasks. Second, CRT proposes that stress moderates the relationship between intelligence and performance: When the situation is not stressful, a leader's intelligence is an asset; in times of high stress, it can either detract from or have no impact on group performance. Third, CRT proposes that a leader's experience is positively related to performance in high-stress situations but not in low-stress situations. When facing high-stress situations, leaders with experience can fall back on tried-and-true approaches they have acquired and, therefore, help their group perform better. However, the same experienced leader can rely too much on experience in low-stress situations. In low-stress situations, intelligence rather than experience is helpful to leaders (Fiedler 1995; Fiedler and Garcia 1987a, b). Fiedler suggests that "intelligence and experience interfere with one another" (Hooijberg and Choi 1999, p. 658).

Examples of CRT hypotheses at work can be seen in many organizations. When faced with crises, most organizations look for leaders who have faced similar crisis situations. For example, several organizations sought the help of Al Dunlap, nick-named "Chainsaw Al" and "Rambo in Pinstripe," when they faced business down-turns. Companies such as Scott Paper and Sunbeam considered Dunlap's considerable experience in downsizing and layoffs to fit their situation. Similarly, when Xerox faced considerable upheaval in the late 1990s and early 2000s, it turned to one of its own experienced veterans, Anne Mulcahey, to run the company.

Evaluation and Application

The CRT is relatively recent, and despite some support for its various propositions, it still requires considerable testing before it is fully developed. Early studies provide support for different parts of the theory (see Fiedler 1992, 1995; Fiedler and Garcia 1987a, b; Gibson 1992). The new skill-based models of leadership developed by Mumford and his associates (see Chapter 2), if integrated with CRT, are likely to bring a new perspective to the model. In the meantime, however, several issues need further clarification. In particular, definitions and measures of experience must be more precise, other cognitive abilities must be considered, and the leader's tolerance for stress and the possibility of the relationship between intelligence and experience must be addressed. For example, CRT does not predict how groups led by leaders who are intelligent *and* experienced will perform. With these limitations in mind, CRT suggests the following implications for organizations and their leaders:

- The role of stress in leadership situations must be considered and assessed. Whereas other leadership theories suggest looking at the task complexity and follower characteristics, the level of stress is another factor that leaders and organizations should consider. This further suggests that stress management is an important part of leadership training. In particular, leaders with high levels of cognitive resources can be encouraged to manage stress better so that they can lead their groups through stressful times more effectively.
- Intelligence and experience play a role in performance. Organizations and their leaders cannot and should not ignore either of these variables when selecting and training leaders.

Contingency Models and Culture

Contingency views of leadership such as the three reviewed in this chapter have dominated U.S. views of leadership for more than 40 years. But how well do they travel? As is the case with many U.S. management theories, outright application to other cultures is not possible. The key to applying the models across cultures is to take into consideration cultural factors (Ayman 1993; Early and Mosakowski 1996). These cultural values influence cultural images of ideal leaders. A good leader in a collectivist culture is likely to be supportive and nurturing, and play the role of a father figure. For example, a longitudinal study done in Japan found that a good

LEADERSHIP ON THE CUTTING EDGE
Cross-Cultural Differences in Following Directions

Do cultural differences exist in the extent to which people follow directions from their supervisors? Researchers Bu and associates set out to address this question by using samples from Taiwan (184 respondents) and the People's Republic of China (PRC) (106 respondents)—two countries with similar cultural background and facing the challenge of meshing cultural traditions and modern development—and the United States (67 respondents). In Taiwan and the PRC, individuals are expected to bow to hierarchical pressure, but the United States represents the other extreme, with a strong value for individual rights and independence. The researchers hypothesized that compliance will be strongest among PRC employees, followed by the Taiwanese, and finally U.S. employees. They further predicted that employees from all three countries will comply more readily when they feel that they are following company policy, when there is pressure from peers, and when they feel that compliance will benefit the company.

The researchers asked participants to indicate degree of compliance when reading vignettes describing a supervisory request that caused either minor or major disruption to the employees. The vignettes also provided different information regarding company policy, peer pressure, and benefit to the company. The results indicate that PRC and Taiwanese employees were significantly more likely to comply to the supervisor's request than U.S. employees, especially when compliance created a major disruption for the employee. Furthermore, in spite of similarity of cultures, the Taiwanese were more inclined to resist supervisory authority than PRC employees (Craig and Peng 2001). PRC employees were willing to resist when they felt that they were justified in doing so by company policy; for the Taiwanese and U.S. employees, merit of the request played a key role.

Overall, the researchers found clear cultural differences in the degree of compliance and concluded that managers have considerably more discretion in PRC and Taiwanese business cultures, a factor that can be advantageous in the fast-growing business environments in those countries.

Source: Bu, N., T. J. Craig, and T. K. Peng. 2001. Acceptance of supervisory direction in typical workplace situations: A comparison of U.S., Taiwanese and PRC employees. *International Journal of Cross-Cultural Management* 1 no. 2, 131–152.

leader in that culture is production oriented and nurturing (Misumi 1985). On the other hand, in individualist cultures such as the United States or Australia, a good leader is one who provides autonomy.

Almost all contingency models have been developed within the context of Western individualistic cultures. Unfortunately, limited information is available about their application to other cultures (for some exceptions, see Ayman and Chemers 1983, 1991). Based on the limited data, some researchers have suggested that due to the power of the collectivity and the importance of harmony and good interpersonal relations in collectivist cultures, the leader always needs to be nurturing and supportive (Triandis 1993). Focus on the task while ignoring interpersonal relations would not be acceptable, regardless of the situation. Therefore, the concept of contingency leadership might have broad application only in individualist cultures.

SUMMARY AND CONCLUSION

The Contingency and Normative Decision Models are two of the best-supported and best-researched models of leadership. Both models focus on the need to match the leader's style to the situation in order to achieve effectiveness. Whereas the Contingency Model assumes that the leader's style (LPC) is determined by internal traits and therefore difficult to change, the Normative Decision Model relies on decision-making methods that are assumed to be learnable. CRT uses a combination of internal traits and experience. The models also differ in their criteria for effectiveness. The Contingency Model and CRT, both developed by Fiedler, focus primarily on group performance; the Normative Decision Model has a narrower focus on decision quality as a main leadership effectiveness criterion.

Despite these differences, the models have much in common, each considering how a leader can use the available resources to be more effective. For example, they all address when and to what extent the group's participation should be sought or when leaders should rely on their own training and expertise. In addition, the Contingency and Normative Decision Models focus on the nature of the task and the degree to which it is structured as a major contingency factor. Perhaps the Contingency and Normative Decision Models' most interesting contribution to leadership application and training is that both have a series of well-defined variables that can be used to improve leadership effectiveness. In addition, both have practical guidelines that can be followed by leaders and help them in better identifying situations and deciding on their own behaviors. The CRT introduces an interesting twist to the contingency model and begs for further research.

Creating Crisis: Performance vs. Morale

One of the team leaders in your departments has an extremely strong performance track record. His team always pulls through, especially in times of crisis. The team also has a much higher-than-average turnover rate. As you conduct exit interviews with the latest three bright team members who have recently resigned, you notice an interesting pattern to their comments. It seems that your effective team leader thrives on chaos and crisis. The team members strongly suggest that he purposefully and consciously creates a sense of extreme urgency and crisis by encouraging conflicts among members, withholding or selectively sharing information, and even misguiding the team members. The team leader always manages to pull the team out of the crisis that was partly his creation, and performs well.

1. What could be some possible explanations for the team leader's behavior?
2. Should you intervene? Why or why not?
3. If you decide to intervene, what can you do?

REVIEW AND DISCUSSION QUESTIONS

1. What is the focus of the resource utilization models of leadership?
2. What does the LPC measure? What are the differences between the two major styles?
3. After assessing your own style, interview several people who have worked with you to determine whether their perceptions match your score based on the LPC.
4. Which element of situational control is most important? Why?
5. Provide two examples each of a structured and unstructured task. Which ones would you prefer to do? Why?
6. How does changing the situation alter the effectiveness of a leader? Provide examples.
7. Provide examples for the situations in which each of the major decision styles of the Normative Decision Model would be appropriate.
8. How can the CRT be used to improve leadership effectiveness?
9. Compare and contrast the three models presented in this chapter. How are they different and how are they similar?

SEARCHING THE WEB

Further Information about Fiedler's Model:
www.stfrancis.edu/ba/ghkickul/stuwebs/btopics/works/fied.htm

Further Information about the Normative Decision Model:
www.css.edu/users/dswenson/web/LEAD/vroom-yetton.html

Mary Kay Cosmetics Company:
www.marykay.com/

EXERCISE 5-1: CHANGING THE LEADER'S SIT CON

This exercise provides you with a checklist for changing situational control based on Fiedler's Contingency Model. Fiedler recommends that in order to be effective, leaders change the situation to match their style. You can use Self-Assessments 5-1 and 5-2 as the basis for determining whether you are in match with your leadership situation. The changes you would undertake in each area depend on whether you need to increase or decrease your level of situational control. The various recommendations can be used alone or in combination with others. In addition, each situation is different and is likely to require different solutions. Use your own creativity and problem-solving skills to come up with other alternatives.

Changing Leader-Member Relations

To increase:

- Spend more time with subordinates.
- Organize activities outside of the workplace.
- Transfer troublesome members out of your team.
- Raise morale by obtaining more rewards and resources for your group.
- Obtain training on interpersonal skills.

To decrease:

- Decrease time you spend with your subordinates.
- Make yourself less available to them.
- Volunteer to direct competent but difficult subordinates.

Changing Task Structure

To increase:

- Request transfer to jobs with which you have some familiarity.
- Avoid transfers to highly different jobs.
- Volunteer for long-range assignments that allow you to develop in-depth expertise.
- Ask for clear tasks or more instructions.
- Learn the task yourself first by asking an expert or obtaining training either from inside or outside the organization.
- Actively seek and use all organizational documentation that is available.
- Break down the task into smaller, simpler parts.
- Develop your own step-by-step procedures and records.

To decrease:

- Request frequent transfers to keep jobs fresh.
- Volunteer to troubleshoot unusual situations.
- Ask for new and unusual tasks.

- Bring problems to the group and ask for suggestions and ideas.
- Include more people in discussions.

Changing Position Power

To increase:

- Improve interpersonal relations with your subordinates.
- Exercise full power of organization.
- Become an expert at the job.
- Centralize information flow.
- Request increases in authority.

To decrease:

- Increase member participation in decision making.
- Decentralize information flow.
- Delegate responsibility.

Source: This exercise is based on information from Fiedler, F. E. and M. M. Chemers. 1984. *Improving Leadership effectiveness: The leader match concept.* 2nd ed. New York: Wiley.

EXERCISE 5-2:   USING THE NORMATIVE DECISION MODEL

This exercise is based on the concepts and principles presented in the Normative Decision Model of leadership. Use the contingency factors presented in Table 5-4 to analyze each case. Figure 5-2 along with Table 5-3 then provides a guide to the appropriate decision styles for each case.

Case 1: Centralizing Purchasing

You are the western regional manager in charge of purchasing for a group of hospitals and clinics. Your territory includes eight western states. You have joined the group recently, but you have close to 10 years of experience in purchasing with one of the company's major competitors. One of your major achievements in your previous job was the implementation of a highly efficient, companywide purchasing system. The health group has more than 30 associated health clinics and hospitals in your region alone. Each center has been operating somewhat independently without much control from the regional purchasing manager. Several of the clinics are cooperating and have informal arrangements that allow them to get better prices from suppliers. The purchasing managers from the larger hospitals in your region, on the other hand, have almost no contact with one another or with you. As a result, they often are competing for suppliers and fail to achieve economies of scale that would allow them to save considerable costs on their various purchases. In other cases, the managers rely on totally different suppliers and have managed to obtain advantageous contracts.

With the pressure to cut health care costs, the health group's board of directors and the group's president have identified purchasing as one area where savings need to be achieved. You have been charged with centralizing purchasing, and you are expected to reduce the costs of purchasing by at least 15 percent within a year.

You have not had a chance to meet many of the purchasing managers who are supposed to report to you. Your appointment was announced through a memo from the group's president. The memo also mentioned the need to cut costs in all areas and indicated the need to focus on purchasing as the first step. The purchasing managers you have met or contacted were civil but not overly friendly. Having only 6 months to show the first results, you need to start planning and implementing changes as soon as possible.

Centralizing Purchasing: Analysis and Recommendation

Using the problem requirements, decision rules, and leadership styles of the Normative Decision Model, indicate which decision style(s) would be most appropriate.

   1. What type of problem is it?
      Group   Individual

2. Contingency Factors:
   Is there a quality requirement?

   Does the leader have enough information to make a high-quality decision?

   Is the problem clear and structured?

   Is employee acceptance of the decision needed for its implementation?

   Would subordinates accept the decision if the leader makes it alone?

   Do subordinates share the organization's goals for the problem?

   Is there conflict among subordinates (are they cohesive) regarding the problem?

3. What are acceptable decision styles? Why?

4. What are unacceptable decision styles? Why?

Case 2: Selecting the Interns

You are the manager of the public relations and advertising department of a large electronics plant. Through your contacts with a local university, you have made an arrangement for your department to hire several interns in public relations and marketing every summer. Your company has been supportive of the idea, because ties with universities are important to you. The interns provide support to your department and work directly with your assistant and report to him. They spend most of their time observing various activities and helping where needed. The interns you have had over the past years have all been excellent and helpful. Your assistant enjoys working with them and has helped several of them find jobs after they graduated, some within your company.

This year, you have received more than 20 applications and you have funds for only two interns. You need to decide which two to hire.

Selecting the Interns: Analysis and Recommendation

Using the problem requirements, decision rules, and leadership styles of the Normative Decision Model, indicate which decision style(s) would be most appropriate.

1. What type of problem is it?
   Group   Individual
2. Contingency factors:
   Is there a quality requirement?

   Does the leader have enough information to make a high-quality decision?

   Is the problem clear and structured?

   Is employee acceptance of the decision needed for its implementation?

   Would subordinates accept the decision if the leader makes it alone?

   Do subordinates share the organization's goals for the problem?

   Is there conflict among subordinates (are they cohesive) regarding the problem?

3. What are acceptable decision styles? Why?

4. What are unacceptable decision styles? Why?

Case 3: Moving to a New Location

You are the manager of a medium-sized city in the Midwest. Through a number of exchanges between the state, local cities, and several businesses, the city has just acquired a building that could house several departments. The building is within one-half mile of other major municipal offices. Although the building is newer than most of the other city buildings and offers larger offices, it is relatively sterile and does not have the charm of many of the older buildings. You have inspected the building and also have just received the report of the space allocation committee that had been working on the problem of overcrowding of several departments. You have identified five departments that could move to the new location. After the initial disruption caused by the move, neither the departments' employees nor their constituents would be affected by the move. Due to the demand for office space, you have less than 2 days to make the decision. You are aware that considerable disagreement is arising among the various departments' employees as to which building is a better location and who would be less negatively affected by the move. Everyone agrees that overcrowding is a problem.

Moving to a New Location: Analysis and Recommendation

Using the problem requirements, decision rules, and leadership styles of the Normative Decision Model, indicate which decision style(s) would be most appropriate.

1. What type of problem is it?
   Group   Individual
2. Contingency factors:

   Is there a quality requirement?

   Does the leader have enough information to make a high-quality decision?

   Is the problem clear and structured?

   Is employee acceptance of the decision needed for its implementation?

   Would subordinates accept the decision if the leader makes it alone without input?

Do subordinates share the organization's goals for the problem?

Is there conflict among subordinates (are they cohesive) regarding the problem?

3. What are acceptable decision styles? Why?

4. What are unacceptable decision styles? Why?

EXERCISE 5-3: CREATING AN ATMOSPHERE THAT ENCOURAGES PARTICIPATION

This exercise provides you with a checklist for encouraging participation in groups. Keep in mind that subordinate participation is not always the most desirable and effective leadership style.

Step 1: Before a Meeting:

- Determine your own level of commitment and comfort with the group's participation.
- Practice nondefensive listening skills.

Step 2: During a Meeting:

- Don't state your position or opinion early. Allow group members to talk first.
- When presenting your ideas, be tentative and present them as a proposal.
- Listen to and record all suggestions from the group.
- Be tactful in critiquing group members' suggestions. (This can even be left until after all ideas have been collected.)
- Provide constructive feedback and build on members' suggestions.
- Provide positive feedback and express appreciation for suggestions.

SELF-ASSESSMENT 5-1: DETERMINING YOUR LPC

To fill out this scale, think of a person with whom you have had difficulty working. That person can be someone you work with now or someone you knew in the past. This person does not have to be the person you like the least well, but should be the person with whom you have had the most difficulty working. Rate this person on the following scale.

				Score
Pleasant	8 7 6 5 4 3 2 1	Unpleasant	_____
Friendly	8 7 6 5 4 3 2 1	Unfriendly	_____
Rejecting	1 2 3 4 5 6 7 8	Accepting	_____
Tense	1 2 3 4 5 6 7 8	Relaxed	_____
Distant	1 2 3 4 5 6 7 8	Close	_____
Cold	1 2 3 4 5 6 7 8	Warm	_____
Supportive	8 7 6 5 4 3 2 1	Hostile	_____
Boring	1 2 3 4 5 6 7 8	Interesting	_____
Quarrelsome	1 2 3 4 5 6 7 8	Harmonious	_____
Gloomy	1 2 3 4 5 6 7 8	Cheerful	_____
Open	8 7 6 5 4 3 2 1	Guarded	_____
Backbiting	1 2 3 4 5 6 7 8	Loyal	_____
Untrustworthy	1 2 3 4 5 6 7 8	Trustworthy	_____
Considerate	8 7 6 5 4 3 2 1	Inconsiderate	_____
Nasty	1 2 3 4 5 6 7 8	Nice	_____
Agreeable	8 7 6 5 4 3 2 1	Disagreeable	_____
Insincere	1 2 3 4 5 6 7 8	Sincere	_____
Kind	8 7 6 5 4 3 2 1	Unkind	_____
		Total	_____

Scoring key: A score of 57 or below indicates that you are task motivated or low LPC. A score of 64 or higher indicates that you are relationship motivated or high LPC. If your score falls between 58 and 63, you will need to determine for yourself in which category you belong.

Source: Fiedler, F. E. and M. M. Chemers. 1984. *Improving leadership effectiveness: The leaders match concept.* 2d ed. New York: Wiley.

SELF-ASSESSMENT 5-2: ASSESSING
A LEADERSHIP SITUATION

This exercise is based on Fiedler's Contingency Model and is designed to allow you to assess a situation you have faced as a leader. In order to complete the questions in each category, think of current or past situations at work, in sports, or at social or church events where you have been the formal or informal leader of a group of people. You might have been successful or not so successful. Rate the situation by answering the questions below; use the same situation to answer all the questions. You will evaluate your effectiveness, relationship with your followers, the structure of the task, and the power you had.

Self-Rating of Effectiveness

1. Considering the situation and task, how effective were you as a leader? (circle one)

3	2	1
Very effective	Moderately effective	Not at all effective

2. How effective was your group in completing its task? (circle one)

3	2	1
Very effective	Moderately effective	Not at all effective

3. How would you rate the overall performance of your group? (circle one)

4	3	2	1
Very high performance	Moderately high performance	Somewhat low performance	Poor performance

Total of the three questions   _____

The maximum score is 10; minimum is 3. A high-performance score would indicate effectiveness. A score between 7 and 10 indicates high performance; a score between 6 and 4 is moderate performance; a score of 3 and lower indicates poor performance.

Leader-Member Relations Scale (LMR)

Circle the number that best represents your response to each item using the scale below:

Strongly agree	Agree	Neither agree nor disagree	Disagree	Strongly disagree
1	2	3	4	5

1. The people I supervise have trouble getting along with each other.	1 2 3 4 5
2. My subordinates are reliable and trustworthy.	5 4 3 2 1
3. There seems to be a friendly atmosphere among the people I supervise.	5 4 3 2 1
4. My subordinates always cooperate with me in getting the job done.	5 4 3 2 1
5. There is friction between my subordinates and myself.	1 2 3 4 5

6. My subordinates give me a good deal of help and support
   in getting the job done.   5 4 3 2 1
7. The people I supervise work well together in getting the job done.   5 4 3 2 1
8. I have good relations with the people I supervise.   5 4 3 2 1

Scoring key: Add up your scores for all eight questions.
Total LMR score: _____

Task Structure Rating Scale—Part I (TS—Part I)

Circle the number that best describes your group's task using the following scale:

0 = seldom true
1 = sometimes true
2 = usually true

Goal clarity

1. There is a blueprint, picture, model, or detailed description available
   of the finished product or service.   2   1   0
2. There is a person available to advise and give a description of the
   finished product or service, or how the job should be done.   2   1   0

Goal-path multiplicity

3. There is a step-by-step procedure, or a standard operating procedure
   that indicates in detail the process that is to be followed.   2   1   0
4. There is a specific way to subdivide the task into separate parts
   or steps.   2   1   0
5. There are some ways that are clearly recognized as better than others
   for performing this task.   2   1   0

Solution specificity

6. It is obvious when the task is finished and the correct solution
   has been found.   2   1   0
7. There is a book, manual, or job description that indicates the best
   solution or the best outcome for the task.   2   1   0

Availability of feedback

8. There is a generally agreed understanding about the standards
   the particular product or service has to meet to be considered
   acceptable.   2   1   0
9. The evaluation of this task is generally made on some quantitative
   basis.   2   1   0
10. The leader and the group can find out how well the task has been
    accomplished in enough time to improve future performance.   2   1   0

Scoring key: Add up your scores for all 10 questions.
Total TS score (Part I): _____

Chapter 5   Contingency Models: Using Resources Effectively   155

Task Structure Rating Scale—Part II (TS—Part II)

Only complete if your score on TS—Part I is higher than 6.

Training and experience adjustment (circle a number for each of the following questions)

1. Compared to others in this or similar positions, how much training have you had?

3	2	1	0
No training at all	Very little training	A moderate amount of training	A great deal of training

2. Compared to others in this or similar positions, how much experience do you have?

6	4	2	0
No experience at all	Very little experience	A moderate amount of experience	A great deal of experience

Add the numbers you circled for the two questions—*Total TS—Part II:* _____

Scoring for TS: _____

Total from TS—Part I: _____

Subtract Total from TS—Part II– _____

Total TS score: _____

Position Power Rating Scale (PP)

Circle the number that best describes your answer.

1. As the leader, I can directly or by recommendation administer rewards and punishments to my subordinates.

2	1	0
Can act directly or can recommend with high effectiveness	Can recommend but with mixed results	Cannot recommend

2. As the leader, I can directly or by recommendation affect the promotion, demotion, hiring, or firing of my subordinates.

2	1	0
Can act directly or can recommend with high effectiveness	Can recommend but with mixed results	Cannot recommend

3. As the leader, I have the knowledge necessary to assign tasks to subordinates and instruct them in task completion.

2	1	0
Yes I have knowledge	Sometimes or in some aspects	No I do not have knowledge

4. As the leader, it is my job to evaluate the performance of my subordinates.

2	1	0
Yes	Sometimes or in	No
I can evaluate	some aspects	I cannot evaluate

5. As the leader, I have some official title of authority given by the organization (for example, supervisor, department head, team leader).

2	0
Yes	No

Scoring key: Add your scores for the five PP questions.
Total PP score: _____

Situation Control Score (Sit Con)

Enter the total score for each of the LMR, TS, and PP scales in the following spaces. Using the ranges provided below, evaluate the situational control you had as the leader in the situation you described.

_____ + _____ + _____ =
LMR + TS + PP = Sit Con

Total score	51–70	31–50	10–30
Amount of Sit Con	High control	Moderate control	Low control

Source: Adapted from Fiedler, F. E. and M. M. Chemers. 1984. *Improving leadership effectiveness: The leader match concept.* 2d ed. New York: Wiley.

Evaluation and Discussion

Self-Assessment 5-1 provided you with your LPC score; Self-Assessment 5-2 helped you assess the situational control you have as a leader. Fiedler's Contingency Model suggests that if you are a low-LPC, task-motivated leader, you and your group will perform best in high- and low-situational control. If you are a high-LPC, relationship-motivated leader, you and your group will perform best in moderate-situational control. If the leader is in match, the group will perform best.

1. Where you in match with the situation you described?

2. To what extent did your level of effectiveness match Fiedler's predictions? Why or why not?

C A S E

Leadership in Action

The Cosmetic Queen and the Software King

Leaders come in many different shapes, sizes, and colors, but despite sometimes considerable differences, they all can command the respect of their followers. Consider two completely different leaders: Mary Kay Ash of Mary Kay Cosmetics and Bill Gates of Microsoft. It is rare to find two CEOs who are more different yet equally effective. Ash and Gates came from different generations and different socioeconomic and educational backgrounds, have practiced different approaches to their businesses and different leadership styles, and even focused on different goals. However, they both have been described as highly intelligent, passionate about their business, energetic, driven, and extremely well-regarded leaders in their respective industries.

Mary Kay Ash, who died in November of 2001, created Mary Kay Cosmetics in 1963 when she was in her forties with $5,000 in savings and the help of her family. Her organization puts God and family ahead of career while providing career opportunities for women. With $1.4 billion in sales, more than 500,000 part-time and full-time employees, and one of the best-selling skin care and color cosmetics lines in the United States, the company is undoubtedly successful (dallas.about.com/library/weekly/aa09100a.htm?terms=mary+kay+ash). Staying close to one's family and providing support during personal crises are concepts that are at the core of the organization, along with a focus on fairness and balance. She stated: "Many women have made the mistake of changing their beliefs to accommodate their work. It must be the other way around" (McGarvey, 2002). While she ran her company, Mary Kay Ash played the role of mother figure, maintaining her image as an accessible, nurturing, and successful woman.

The highly emotional company conventions are further evidence of the desire to build a successful family. While the mostly female Mary Kay consultants participate in training and seminars, their husbands take classes on how to support their spouse. During the Las Vegas-style events, the company gives away pink Cadillacs, lavish trips, and jewelry to its top performers to recognize their achievements. Mary Kay is a cosmetics company that is on a mission to create opportunities to allow women to be successful, and its leader was proud to admit that caring about people was what she was all about. The concern for people and a keen business and marketing savvy helped Mary Kay stay on top in a highly competitive industry.

Bill Gates has built Microsoft on intelligence and continual learning (Gimein 2001). His company dominates the world's software industry, and he is one of the richest men in the world. Highly intelligent and curious, Gates states: "The key point is that you've got to enjoy what you do every day. For me, that's working with very smart people and it's working on new problems" (Schlender 1998, p. 53). He has been described as acerbic, confrontational, condescending, rude, completely task focused, and one of the hardest-working executives in the world. Nothing gets done and no new ideas get developed without Gates's approval (Nocera 2000). Gates is known for his cunning business sense and his cognitive abilities. He keeps a close eye on his own performance. For example, Gates spends a quarter of his time on the road, preaching the "Microsoft gospel." During these trips, he evaluates his performance by keeping track on how full his schedule is. After one such trip that included 14 speeches, more than a dozen personal meetings, and 25,000 miles of air travel, Gates stated, "It was a great trip. The guys filled my time up really well" (Schlender 1997, p. 81). A focus on performance, intense competition, and technological innovation drive Microsoft. Little concern is given for an individual's balance and nonwork-related life. The strong culture built around competence and dominating competitors has helped keep Microsoft the leader in its industry. ∎

QUESTIONS

1. How would you describe each of the two leaders? How are they similar? How are they different?

2. What makes each effective?

Sources: This case is partially based on research done by Anne Crowley, Colin Halbig, and Rich White for an MBA leadership elective course. Other sources include Andrews, P. and S. Manes. 1993. *Gates.* New York: Doubleday; Ash, M. K. 1981. *Mary Kay.* New York: Harper and Row; McGarvey, Candice, "Christian Businesswoman Mary Kay Ash Dies," Christianity.com, accessed February 28, 2002; Farnham, A. 1993. Mary Kay's lessons in leadership. *Fortune* 128, no. 6, 68–76; Gimein 2001; Kirkpatric, D. 1997. He wants all your business—and he's starting to get it. *Fortune* 135, no. 10, 58–68; Schlender, B. 1997. On the road with Chairman Bill. *Fortune* 135, no. 10, 72–81; Schlender, B. 1998. The Bill and Warren show. *Fortune* 138, no. 2, 48–64; dallas.about.com/library/weekly/aa09100a.htm?terms=mary+kay+ash, accessed April 16, 2002.

Chapter 6

Exchange and Relationship Development and Management

> *Why are the people rebellious? Because the rulers interfere too much. Therefore, they are rebellious.*
>
> —LAO TSU

After studying this chapter, you will be able to:

1. Explain the key role of relationship development and management in effective leadership and use the concepts in improving leadership effectiveness.
2. Discuss the Path-Goal Theory of leadership and explain the role of the leader in removing obstacles in followers' paths.
3. Understand the role of attribution in the relationship between leaders and followers and how it can be used to manage relationships.
4. Present the Leader-Member Exchange Theory of leadership, and clarify how the creation of in-groups and out-groups affects the leadership process.
5. Summarize the impact of leadership substitutes and identify situations in which the leader's impact is decreased.

The previous chapter considered three contingency models that hinge on how leaders use various resources to be effective. The present chapter reviews several contingency approaches that focus on the exchange between leaders and their followers, and on the ways in which the leaders and followers establish, develop, and manage their relationship (Chemers 1993). The concept of contingency remains at the heart of this group of theories. However, the theories use different definitions of effectiveness and focus on different situational variables. Most importantly, they focus on the process by which the leader guides subordinates to become effective rather than on how resources are used. All the models presented in this chapter assume that the leaders understand the task and are able to alter their behavior to address the needs of subordinates.

The following models will be considered here: Path-Goal Theory, attributional models, the Leader-Member Exchange Model (LMX), substitutes for leadership, and the Situational Leadership Model. The limitations and applications of each model will be discussed.

PATH-GOAL THEORY

The Path-Goal Theory of leadership, developed in the early 1970s, proposes that the key role of the leader is to clear the paths subordinates have to take in order to accomplish goals (House 1971; House and Dessler 1974; House and Mitchell 1974). By doing so, leaders allow subordinates to fulfill their needs and as a result, leaders reach their own goals, as well. The concept of exchange between leaders and subordinates, whether it is an implicit or explicit contract, is at the core of this model. The leader and followers establish a relationship that revolves around the exchange of guidance or support for productivity and satisfaction.

The Framework

The major conceptual basis for the Path-Goal Theory is the expectancy model of motivation (Porter and Lawler 1968; Vroom 1964). Expectancy theory describes how individuals make rational choices about their behavior based on their perceptions of the degree to which their effort and performance can lead to outcomes they value. The key to motivation, then, is to remove the various obstacles that can weaken the linkages between effort and performance and between performance and outcomes. Accordingly, in the Path-Goal Theory, the role of leaders is to help strengthen linkages among effort, performance, and outcome through their own behavior.

The nature of the task and follower characteristics determine which leadership behavior contributes to subordinate satisfaction (see Figure 6-1). If the task is new and unclear, the followers are likely to waste their efforts due to lack of knowledge and experience. They might feel frustrated and unmotivated. In such a situation, the leader must provide instructions and training, thereby removing obstacles to followers' performance and allowing them to do their job. On the other hand, if a task is routine and has been performed by subordinates successfully a number of times, they might face an element of boredom. This situation, according to the Path-Goal Theory, requires the leader to show consideration, empathy, and understanding toward subordinates.

Original versions of the Path-Goal Theory relied on the two leader behaviors of supportive and directive leadership. Supportive leadership is similar to consideration behaviors, whereas directive leadership is comparable to initiation of structure.

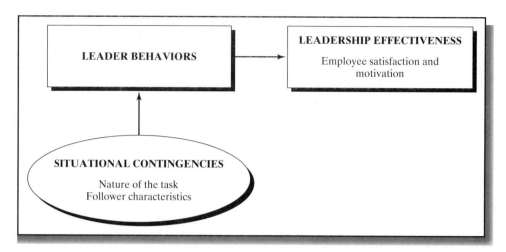

Figure 6-1
Path-Goal Theory of Leadership

With further research, participative and achievement-oriented leadership were added to the model (House and Mitchell 1974). Participative leadership involves consultation with followers; achievement-oriented behaviors include setting challenging goals and boosting followers' confidence.

The Path-Goal Theory assumes that leaders can (1) correctly analyze the situation, (2) decide which behaviors are required, and (3) change their behavior to match the situation. The Path-Goal Theory proposes the following general hypotheses:

- When the task is unambiguous, boring, or stressful, the leader must be supportive and considerate in order to increase subordinate satisfaction. The leader's consideration and supportive behaviors remove the blocks to satisfaction.
- When the task is unstructured, complex, or novel, or when subordinates lack skills or experience, the leader's directive behaviors are key. In such situations, the followers need instructions and direction. By providing such direction, the leader can remove the major obstacles to employee motivation and satisfaction.
- When the task is unstructured, participative leader behaviors can further increase follower satisfaction by helping clarify the task.
- When the task is unstructured, achievement-oriented leadership can challenge followers, increase their self-confidence, and therefore increase satisfaction.

Behaviors the leader uses to motivate employees also depend on the employees themselves (Griffin 1979; Stinson and Johnson 1975). Some employees need guidance and clear instructions; others like to be more challenged and seek autonomy to do their own problem solving. The followers' need for autonomy and other personal characteristics such as locus of control are factors that the leader needs to consider before selecting an appropriate behavior. For example, a follower who likes challenges and needs autonomy will not need or want the leader to be directive even during an unstructured task. For that employee, leader directiveness can be irrelevant or even detrimental because it might reduce satisfaction.

Limitations and Applications

Although several supportive research studies have been conducted (House and Mitchell 1974; Schriesheim and Kerr 1974), the empirical support for the Path-Goal Theory has been mixed (Downey, Sheridan, and Slocum 1975; Szilagyi and Sims 1974). Several reviews (e.g., Evans 1996; Podsakoff et al. 1995; Wofford and Liska 1993) have found inconsistent support for the theory. In many instances, for example, consideration for employees leads to higher employee satisfaction regardless of the task (Johns 1978). In other cases, contrary to Path-Goal Theory predictions, leaders successfully used structuring behavior in structured situations (Bass et al. 1975). Recent additions to the theory have clarified some of the limitations related to the definitions of leader behavior (House 1996).

The Path-Goal Theory contributes to our understanding of leadership by once more focusing attention on the behavior of providing guidance and support to followers.

Notwithstanding contradictory findings, the Path-Goal Theory contributes to our understanding of leadership by once more focusing attention on the behavior of providing guidance and support to followers. It adds to resource utilization models such as Fiedler's Contingency Model by including followers' perceptions of the task (i.e., does the follower know how to do the job?) and the role of the leader in removing blocks to task accomplishment. The Path-Goal Theory's use of employee satisfaction as a criterion for leadership effectiveness broadens our view of leadership. The model's suggestion that not all behaviors will be effective with all subordinates points to the importance of an employee's need for challenge and desire to be autonomous as a determinant of a leader's behavior. Interestingly, the role of the leader in the Path-Goal Theory is that of an obstacle remover, which is a role similar to that ascribed to team leaders (see Chapter 7). In addition to further emphasizing the need to use different behaviors depending on the situation, the following are recommendations for effective leadership based on the Path-Goal Theory:

- Leaders must understand their followers' perception of the task.
- Leaders must take their followers' need for challenge and autonomy into consideration.
- When subordinates need to be challenged, even when the task is complex, leaders must avoid being directive.
- When the task is routine and boring, or stressful, leaders must be supportive to motivate their followers.

The next section reviews a leadership model that focuses on how leaders interpret their followers' actions and use that information as the basis for their relationship with them.

Attributional Models

A component of the exchange between leaders and followers is the way the leader perceives and interprets followers' behaviors and uses those interpretations to make decisions regarding future actions. For example, when an employee fails to contact a key potential client and, as a result, causes the loss of that client to a competitor, the manager will attempt to understand the cause of the error in order to decide what needs to be done. Whether the manager perceives the cause to be the employee's laziness or lack of concern for the job, or whether the problem as caused by his or her own failure to communicate the importance of the client will determine future actions. In the first case, the employee is to blame, and a reprimand or more serious disciplinary action might be appropriate. In the second case, because the manager shares the blame, he or she is not likely to reprimand the employee.

A number of research studies have focused on understanding the processes described in the preceding example (Green and Mitchell 1979; Mitchell and Wood 1980; Offermann, Schroyer, and Green 1998). Social psychologists have for many years studied the process by which we attribute cause of behavior (Jones and Davis 1965; Kelley 1967). Such processes are called attribution and focus on explaining the way we interpret the cause of others' behaviors and our own. Our interpretations depend on many factors, including our analysis of the situation, as well as national culture.

Two factors come into play in leadership situations. First, the leader must determine whether the cause of the error is internal to the employee (e.g., lack of ability or effort) or external to the employee (e.g., task difficulty, lack of training or support, bad luck, etc.). Second, the leader must decide on a corrective course of action. The degree to which the employee's actions impact on goal accomplishment and productivity (i.e., the seriousness of the consequences) provides further information to determine subsequent action. The employee is much more likely to be blamed and held responsible for the following types of errors:

- When the consequences are severe (for example, the loss of an important client or the anger of a major constituent).
- When the employee has a mediocre track record on similar and different types of tasks and other employees are successful under similar circumstances.
- When the employee shows defensiveness in responding to the manager's inquiry.
- When the manager's success depends on the employee's good performance.

One factor that can further impact how leaders make attributions is national culture. Consider the following example. A Canadian expatriate manager working in Jordan asks the advice of his Jordanian assistant before he makes a decision on the purchase of new equipment from a local manufacturer. The Jordanian assistant appears noncommittal and provides no concrete answers but seems to suggest that one manufacturer would be better than the other. The Canadian manager orders from that manufacturer. The decision turns out to be costly and disastrous. The Canadian manager interprets his assistant's behavior as uncooperative, indicating a lack of initiative, or even as incompetent and disloyal. The Jordanian assistant is puzzled by his leader's lack of confidence and inability to lead. Leaders, after all, are supposed to have the answers.

This scenario illustrates typical misattributions that occur when people interpret behaviors across cultures. The leader in this case is interpreting his subordinate's response from his own cultural framework. The Canadian culture is low-power distance; therefore, it is acceptable and desirable to request feedback from one's subordinate when a leader does not have all the information. A subordinate who refuses to help appears to be incompetent or disloyal. The Jordanian assistant also is interpreting behavior within his own cultural context, which includes high-power distance and a strong paternalistic tradition. To him, a leader who does not have solutions and must ask for his employees' help is incompetent and weak.

The potential for bias and misinterpretation is greatly increased when individuals from one culture have to interpret and make attributions about the behavior of individuals who are from a different culture. However, even within the same cultural context, attributions are subject to considerable biases.

Limitations and Applications

The attributional model of leadership is based on well-established psychological principles whose application to leadership situations has been supported by research. However, it is not a broad model of leadership and is concerned with only a particular aspect of the relationship between leaders and followers—namely, how a leader interprets followers' behaviors and actions, and how such interpretations affect their interactions.

Despite their limited scope, the propositions and findings of attributional models have many applications to leadership situations. In particular, because the issue of interpretation and evaluation of followers' actions is a central part of leadership activities, understanding these processes can be helpful to leaders. As is the case with all processes that involve social perception, evaluating followers can be subject to biases. Among these biases are the potential effect of stereotypes, the self-serving bias that leads people to accept credit for success and reject blame for failure, ego defensiveness, and actor-observer differences. For example, leaders can easily attribute the lack of performance of a subordinate they like to external factors, and blame the mistakes of someone they do not like on the subordinate's laziness. Similarly, leaders' stereotypes of a particular group can affect the way they interpret the actions of their followers. The female employee who is hard driving might be seen as pushy and overly aggressive, whereas the same behavior from a male employee is considered appropriately competitive. Because of racial stereotypes, an African-American employee's mistakes might be attributed to laziness, whereas the same mistake is overlooked for a white employee.

The primary key to a leader's correct interpretation of subordinates' actions is to be aware of the potential effect of various biases. Recognition of one's stereotypes and other personal biases is also key.

The attribution process, by definition, is subject to bias. The primary key to a leader's correct interpretation of subordinates' actions is to be aware of the potential effect of various biases and to recognize one's stereotypes and other personal biases. In addition, relying on clear behavioral descriptions and objective measures such as the ones used in well-designed performance appraisal systems, rather than on impressions and feelings, is another way leaders can help assure that their interpretations are correct. Another key factor is open and honest communication with subordinates before assigning blame. The subordinates might have access to information that can explain their behaviors. Leaders need to use that information together with the data they have gathered whenever possible before an attribution is made.

Similar to attributional models, the next model considered focuses on the dyadic relationship between leaders and their followers.

WHAT DOES THIS MEAN FOR ME?
Avoiding Biases

Research on social perception, attribution theory, and attributional models of leadership indicate that what we perceive is often more important than objective reality. It is, therefore, essential that as leaders and followers we carefully manage perception, considering the following points:

- Awareness of our biases is key to getting as close to an objective evaluation and judgment as possible.
- Depend on objective, reliable measures of performance when available.

- Keep notes about your own work and reactions, as well as the work and reactions of your followers; few of us have good recall.
- Actively seek all sides of an issue; listen to your followers to hear their side of events. There is always more than one perspective and explanation.
- Do reality checks with your close associates, but also with others whom you respect but who might not be close to you or the problem you have encountered.

LEADER-MEMBER EXCHANGE (LMX)

Many of us experience leadership, either as leaders or followers, as a personal relationship between a leader or a subordinate rather than a group phenomenon. We interact daily with our managers and forge an individual relationship with them. As leaders, we do not have the same relationship with all of our followers. Each dyadic relationship is different and a leader establishes a one-on-one relationship with each follower (see Figure 6-2). Each relationship varies greatly in terms of the quality of the exchange. These concepts are at the core of the LMX model, which was called the Vertical Dyad Linkage Model in its earlier versions (Dansereau, Graen, and Haga 1975; Graen and Shiemann 1978). LMX is defined as a unique, relationship-based exchange between a leader and followers (Graen and Uhl-Bien 1995).

In each exchange, the leader and follower establish a role for the follower. Those followers who have a high-quality relationship are in the in-group. High-quality LMX is defined as mutual respect, anticipation of deepening trust, and expectations of continued and growing professional relationships and obligations. In-group followers enjoy their leader's attention, support, and confidence and receive challenging and interesting assignments. The leader might overlook their errors (Duarte, Goodson, and Klich 1994) and attribute them to factors outside of the followers' control.

In exchange for the in-group status, the followers' role is to work hard, be loyal, and support the leader. They are likely to work beyond their formally prescribed job duties (Liden and Graen 1980) and increase their commitment to their goals (Klein and Kim 1998). For the members of the in-group, high-quality exchange is likely to become a self-fulfilling prophecy and lead to high performance, high satisfaction, and low stress. Studies extend the impact of a positive LMX to safety communication,

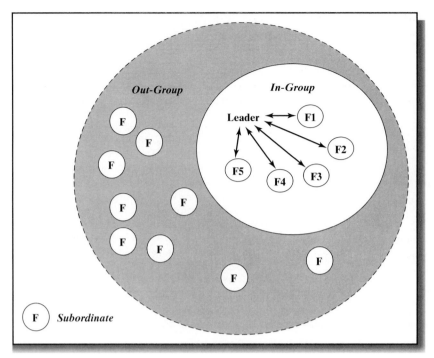

Figure 6-2
Leader-Member Exchange (LMX) Model

commitment, and reduction of accidents (Hofmann and Morgeson 1999). Recent conceptual extensions of the model suggest that the positive work relationship might even extend to social networks, whereby leaders sponsor members of their in-group into various social networks (Sparrowe and Liden 1997). Other research indicates that having a positive exchange with a leader is a factor in the extent to which employees feel the organization supports them (Wayne, Shore, and Liden 1997).

The followers in the out-group face a different situation. The leader might perceive them as less motivated or less competent, interact with them less, provide them with few opportunities to perform, and promote them less often (Wakabayashi et al. 1988). Their role tends to be limited to that defined by formal job descriptions, and there is little or no expectation of high performance, commitment, or loyalty. Regardless of whether the leader's perception and expectations are accurate and fair, members of the out-group are likely to live up, or down, to them. As result, out-group members who have a low-quality LMX will perform poorly and experience more stress. They also are more likely to take retaliatory actions against the organization (Townsend, Phillips, and Elkins 2000) and file for grievances more often (Cleyman, Jex, and Love 1993).

The relationship between the leader and each follower forms early. The LMX model suggests that development of the leader-follower relationship takes place in stages summarized in Table 6-1. Culture also can play a key role in how in-group membership is assigned. In achievement-oriented cultures such as the United States and Germany, individuals are evaluated based on their performance and achievement

Table 6-1

Stages of Relationship Development Between Leaders and Their Followers

STAGE	DESCRIPTION
Testing and assessment	No relationship is formed yet. Leaders consider followers who do not yet belong to a group in terms of objective and subjective criteria for inclusion in either the in-group or out-group. Followers' potential, ability, skills, and other psychological factors such as loyalty might be tested. Group assignments are made. The relationship with out-group followers does not progress beyond this stage.
Development of trust	This stage exists only for in-group members. Leader provides in-group followers with challenges and opportunities to perform that reinforce development of trust. In return, followers perform and demonstrate their loyalty to the leader.
Creation of emotional bond	In-group followers who have a well-established relationship might move to this stage, where the relationship and the bond between them becomes strong and emotional. Followers are highly committed to the leader's vision.

Source: Partially based on information in Graen, G. B. and M. Uhl-Bien. 1991. The transformation of work group professionals into self-managing and partially self-designing contributors: Toward a theory of leadership-making. *Journal of Management Systems* 3, no. 3, 33–48.

rather than on their past or their membership in certain castes (Trompenaars 1994). In ascriptive cultures, such as many in the Middle East or France, the evaluation is based on issues such as social class and birth (Trompenaars 1994). In achievement-oriented cultures, it is expected that leaders will select their in-group members based on competence, performance, and commitment to the organization rather than based on a personal relationship. Anything else would be called favoritism and nepotism. As a result, formal human resource policies and procedures, as well as day-to-day personnel practices, in such cultures focus on fairness, equal opportunity, and on hiring those who are most qualified for the jobs based on their personal competence.

> In achievement-oriented cultures such as the United States and Germany, individuals are evaluated based on their own performance and achievement rather than based on their past or their membership in certain castes. In ascriptive cultures, such as many in the Middle East or France, the evaluation is based on issues such as social class and birth.

The concepts of nepotism and inappropriate favoritism to one's in-group do not apply readily in ascriptive and collectivist cultures, where loyalty to one's village, clan, or family is the primary concern. In such cultures, managers hire those they know and who are recommended by others they know. Skills and competence are secondary to such personal recommendations. In Hong Kong and Malaysia, for example, leaders are obligated to take care of their own people first (Adler 1991). In many Middle Eastern countries, including various Arab countries and non-Arab ones such as Afghanistan and Iran, leaders surround themselves with family and clan members who can be trusted and who are loyal. Doing otherwise would be disloyal and even foolish. A wise leader does not allow strangers into the in-group, no matter how competent and qualified they are. Outsiders are hired to help, but access to the in-group is based on community factors.

Reseachers Adrienne Colella and Arup Varma studied the impact of subordinate disability on the quality of the LMX using an organizational simulation and a field study of 41 supervisors and their 220 subordinates. Their hypotheses were based on research that shows the impact of similarity on LMX and other theories that suggest that nondisabled persons have ambivalent feelings of compassion, aversion, and hostility toward those with disabilities. The researchers proposed that not only will nondisabled supervisors form lower-quality LMX with subordinates with a disability than those without a disability, but that when disabled employees perform well, there will be a more positive impact on the LMX than for nondisabled employees. They also proposed that ingratiation—making special efforts and statements to get on the super-visor's good side—will lead to more positive LMX for disabled employees than nondisabled employees.

The results of their study supported their hypotheses. Supervisors were found to have significantly lower-quality LMX with disabled employees, particularly when the disabled employees did not engage in ingratiating behaviors toward the supervisors. In fact, engaging in ingratiation behaviors had more impact for disabled than nondisabled employees. Researchers suggest that based on their findings, "It is more important for people with disability to engage in upward influence tactics than others. . . . [individuals with disability] must take it upon themselves to make others comfortable and initiate interaction" (Colella and Varma 2001, p. 313).

Source: Colella, A. and A. Varma. 2001. The impact of subordinate disability on leader-member exchange relationships. *Academy of Management Journal* 44, no. 2, 304–315.

Limitations and Applications

There has been general support in a number of studies for different aspects of the LMX model, while some criticism also has been fueled by a recent revival of interest in the model. (For recent examples, see Brower, Schoorman, and Tan 2000; and Schriesheim, Castro, and Yammarino 2000.) The model still needs clarifications on a number of points. Specifically, the adequacy of the theory, the multiple measures, and the methods used to test the concepts have been questioned. (For a detailed review, see Schriesheim, Castro, and Cogliser 2000.) Additionally, the factors that lead to the development of an in-group versus an out-group relationship need more attention. Some research suggests that similarity in regard to personality plays a key role early in the relationship (Dose 1999; Murphy and Ensher 1999), whereas performance matters more as time goes on (Bauer and Greene 1996). More research needs to be conducted in other areas, as well, including identifying factors that impact the development of the LMX, assessing the desirability of having the two groups or the conditions under which subordinates move from one group to the other, and exploring the cultural factors that are likely to impact the decision on who belongs to the in-group. The research on the impact of gender similarity on the development of LMX, for example, has been mixed and requires further clarification (see McAllister 1995; Tsui and O'Reilly 1989). However, the results of at least one study in Mexico show gender similarity to be related to lower absenteeism, particularly with female leaders (Pelled and Xin 1997) and higher trust (Pelled and Xin 2000).

From a practitioner and application point of view, the LMX model has considerable appeal. Given some experience in organizations, all of us have experienced the feeling of being part of either the in-group or the out-group. Many have seen the departure of a well-liked manager, who is replaced with someone who has their own team. The quick movement from in-group to out-group is felt acutely. The concept of in-group and out-group also can be perceived as violating the norm of equality (Scandura 1999), which is highly valued in the many Western cultures including the United States. As leaders, most of us can identify our in-group (see Self-Assessment 6-1). These are the people we trust. They are our right-hand assistants. We can give them any assignment with confidence. They will get the job done without us having to check up on them. We also know the members of our out-group. Toward some, we feel neutral; others we dislike and might be trying to get transferred. In both cases, those individuals do not get many chances to interact with us, and they are not provided with many opportunities to demonstrate their competence on visible and key projects.

The development of an individual exchange with others is a natural part of any interaction. Such a situation can be highly positive for an organization, allowing for the identification of competent individuals and ensuring that they achieve organizational goals. However, the creation of in-groups and out-groups also can be highly detrimental, leading to feelings and accusations of unfair treatment (Scandura 1999). The key issue is the basis upon which such relationships are formed. Researchers have suggested that personal compatibility and employee ability are the basis for selection (Graen and Cashman 1975). Unfortunately, organizational reality does not always match theory. Most of us can identify, or have been part of, LMX relationships that have been based on either positive or negative personal feelings, stereotypes, and interpersonal conflicts. Many highly competent and qualified employees have been excluded from a leader's in-group based on personal dislike or organizational politics. After all, leaders are subject to human error just like the rest of us.

Abuse of power (discussed in Chapter 4) and membership of some top-management teams (discussed in Chapter 9) are examples of the potential negative effects of in-groups. Being able to work with people you trust and agree with and who share your vision for the organization sounds like an ideal situation for any leader, who would then not have to face unnecessary arguments and delays. Decisions would be made quickly and efficiently, and goals would be achieved. This ideal situation is exactly what many top-level executives attempt to set up when they select their top-management team and the members of their board of directors. They pick people they trust and can work with. Executives rarely consciously and willingly pick members with whom they have major conflicts and differences. The goal is to create a workable team—a team made up of in-group members. For example, when Daimler Benz merged with Chrysler in 1998, Daimler Chrysler CEO Jurgen Schrempp's allies were awarded many of the top jobs in the new company, and most of the company is now run by former Daimler executives (Taylor 1999).

Research on friendship patterns and attraction to others indicates that people tend to associate with those who are like them, have similar backgrounds, and share their values and beliefs. To counteract this potential bias, Maggie Widerotter of Wink Communication makes a point of taking time to look for employees she does not see on a regular basis. She takes time to get out of her office and go on a "lion hunt" (McCauley 2000, p. 114). She says:

> That gives me a chance to connect with employees who I don't usually talk to. . . . I always walk away from the experience having learned something: I have a renewed understanding of what we're doing at my company. (McCauley 2000, p. 114)

Without a conscience effort to seek out new people, the in-group for most CEOs includes people who are like them, with similar backgrounds and views. This homogeneity in top-management teams and board of director members has been blamed recently for many of the problems in U.S. businesses. Industrial giants such as General Motors, AT&T, and IBM suffered from the lack of initiative and creativity of their top-management teams. The members worked well together and disregarded input from outsiders. As a result, they failed to foresee the problems and full consequences of their decisions or inaction.

The ease, comfort, and efficiency of working with an in-group that is cohesive are usually due to the similarity, on many dimensions, of its members. However, these advantages are sometimes offset by a lack of creativity and limited decision making. In an ideal case, no in-group or out-group should exist. All of a leader's subordinates should have equal access to the leader and to projects and resources. Those who do not perform well should be helped or moved out of the group altogether. However, reality is different, and avoiding the creation of in-groups and out-groups is difficult. One of the key issues then becomes how members are selected to be in each group. In order for the individual relationship to be productive, leaders should follow some general principles in creating in-groups and out-groups and in selecting their membership. It is important to note that these guidelines apply mostly to achievement-oriented rather than ascriptive cultures:

- Pick in-group members based on competence and contribution to the organization.
- Periodically evaluate your criteria for in-group and out-group membership.
- Assign tasks to persons with the most applicable skills regardless of group membership.
- Set clear, performance-related guidelines for in-group membership.
- Avoid highly differentiated in-groups and out-groups.
- Keep membership fluid to allow movement in and out of the groups.
- Maintain different in-groups for different activities.

Whereas LMX focuses on the importance of the quality of the relationship between a leader and individual followers, the next model identifies situations in which leadership is not needed.

SUBSTITUTES FOR LEADERSHIP

In some situations, a relationship with a leader is not needed to satisfy followers' needs. Various aspects of the work environment provide enough resources and support to allow the subordinates to achieve their goals without having to refer to their leader. For example, an experienced team of pharmaceutical salespeople who spend a considerable amount of their time on the road and who have control over their commissions are not likely to rely much on their manager. Their job provides them with challenges, and their experience allows them to make many decisions on their own. The office is not accessible, and they often rely on other salespeople for help and information. In such circumstances, various situational factors replace the leader's functions of providing structure, guidelines, and support to subordinates.

Situations such as these have led to the development of the Substitutes-for-Leadership Model (SLM) (Kerr and Jermier 1978). SLM proposes that various organizational, task, and employee characteristics can provide substitutes for the traditional leadership behaviors of consideration and initiation of structure (see Table 6-2). In general, if information about the task and its requirement is clear and available to the subordinates through various means such as their own experience, their team, or through the organization, they are not likely to need the leader's structuring behaviors. Similarly, when support and empathy are not needed or are available through other sources such as coworkers, the subordinates will not seek the leader's consideration behaviors.

In addition to substituting for leadership, some situations can neutralize the effect of the leader. Most notably, the leader's lack of power to deliver outcomes to followers and an organization's rigid culture can prevent a leader's consideration and structuring behaviors from impacting subordinates. For example, a subordinate whose manager is in another state or who does not value the rewards provided by the manager, or who has a powerless leader who cannot deliver on any promises, is not likely to be affected by the leader's behaviors (see Table 6-2). Consider how

Table 6-2
Leadership Substitutes and Neutralizers

SUBSTITUTES OR NEUTRALIZERS	CONSIDERATION	STRUCTURING
Follower Characteristics		
1. Experience and training		Substitute
2. Professionalism	Substitute	Substitute
3. Lack of value for goals	Neutralizer	Neutralizer
Task Characteristics		
1. Unambiguous tasks		Substitute
2. Direct feedback from task		Substitute
3. Challenging task	Substitute	
Organizational Characteristics		
1. Cohesive team	Substitute	Substitute
2. Leader's lack of power	Neutralizer	Neutralizer
3. Standardization and formalization		Substitute
4. Organizational rigidity		Neutralizer
5. Physical distance between leaders and followers	Neutralizer	Neutralizer

Source: Based on Kerr, S. and J. M. Jermier. 1978. Substitutes for leadership: Their meaning and measurement. *Organizational Behavior and Human Performance* 22, 375–403.

Ricardo Semler, president of the Brazilian firm Semco, author and proponent of open-book management (Semler 1993) and management guru, has set up his company so that it runs with few managers. Workers are trained carefully; provided with considerable information, including detailed financial data and salary information; and left to set their own hours, evaluate and vote for their managers, and make most of the decisions. The workers' training and experience have allowed the company to function with only a half dozen senior managers (Colvin 2001b).

Limitations and Applications

The leadership substitute model has not been tested extensively, and considerable clarification is needed regarding the nature of the various substitutes and neutralizers and the situations to which they might apply. The results have not been consistently supportive, and the few studies performed in non–U.S. cultural settings have not yielded support to the model (Farh, Podsakoff, and Cheng 1987). However, several recent studies have improved some of the psychometric properties of the measures used to test the model (Podsakoff and MacKenzie 1994, 1996; Podsakoff, MacKenzie, and Bommer 1996) and conducted large-scale organization-based tests of the model (reported in Podsakoff, MacKenzie, and Bommer 1996). Some of the results are promising and indicate support for the role of various substitutes (Gronn 1999; Podsakoff and MacKenzie 1998; Trevelyan 2001). However, considerable clarification and development are needed. (For some suggestions, see Podsakoff and MacKenzie 1997.)

Like the LMX, however, the Leadership Substitutes Model is intuitively appealing and addresses processes not taken into account by other leadership models. In particular, it questions the need for leadership in certain situations and points to the difficulty of being an effective leader when many neutralizers are present (Howell et al. 1990). Depending on the culture, strategy, and goals of an organization and on a specific leader's personality, the leader might want to set up or remove leadership substitutes. For some control-oriented leaders or in organizations that have traditional structures and hierarchies in place, the presence of substitutes could be perceived as a loss of control and authority.

Given the flattening of many organizations and the push toward empowerment and use of teams, judicious use of substitutes can free up the leader for other activities, such as strategic planning, and still allow the organization to achieve its objectives. The use of information technology tools that make information widely available and support work structures such as telecommuting and outsourcing further reduces the need for leadership in some situations (Howell 1997). An interesting application of the Leadership Substitutes Model is to autonomous and self-managed teams. The goal of such teams is to be able to function without supervision. The team becomes a substitute for leadership. Extensive technical and team-building training, selection of team members with a professional orientation, and intrinsically satisfying tasks for which team members have considerable autonomy and direct feedback can be used as substitutes for leadership structuring behaviors. Similarly, a cohesive team replaces the leader's supportive behaviors. The factors identified as substitutes can be used as a guide in setting up such autonomous work teams (see Self-Assessment 6-2).

One final implication of the Leadership Substitutes Model is for leadership training. Based on this model, leadership training might need to focus on teaching the

It isn't that Medtronic is changing the way it's doing business that gets the company and its past CEO, Bill George, a lot of attention. It is the way it always has done business. Medtronic, a Minnesota-based company worth more than $60 billion, invented the battery-powered pacemaker and is the leading producer of pacemakers, neuro-stimulators, and other medical devices. However, it is equally well known for its unique, employee and customer-centered culture and management practices, and it has been rated a number of times as one of the 100 best companies to work for in the United States (Levering and Moskowitz, 2001). From the annual holiday party where people who are alive because of Medtronic devices give testimonials drawing emotional responses from all employees—to its soft-spoken past CEO and now chairman of the board, to empowering employees, well-designed jobs, a learn-ing culture, and flexible schedules that allow people to balance their lives, Med-

tronic serves as a role model for many other companies.

Bill George the chairman of the board states:

> The best path to long-term growth in shareholder values comes from having a well-articulated mission that employees are willing to commit to, a consistently practiced set of values, and a clear business strategy that is adaptable to changing business conditions. (George 2001, p. 40)

He recognizes that employees spend a good part of their lives at work and believes that their work should have meaning and purpose. He wants to create a workplace where people can balance their life and their work. As a result, he has created a "human" workplace (Whitford 2001). Medtronic's financial performance and employee satisfaction levels indicate that he has succeeded. Survey results indicate that close to 90 percent are proud to work there, understand the mission, and feel that it is consistent with their personal values (George 2001, p. 45).

Sources: Levering, R., and M. Moskowitz. 2001. The 100 best companies to work for. *Fortune* (January 8), 166; Whitford, D. 2001. A human place to work. *Fortune* (January 8), 108–122; George, W. 2001. Medtronic's Chairman William George on how mission-driven companies create long-term shareholder value. *Academy of Management Executive* 15, no. 4, 39–47.

leader to change the situation as much as it focuses on teaching effective leadership behaviors. Leaders can be taught how to set up substitutes and avoid neutralizers. Such a recommendation is similar to recommendations made based on Fiedler's Contingency Model discussed in Chapter 5.

SITUATIONAL LEADERSHIP

A final model based on the relationship between the leader and followers is the Situational Leadership Model, originally called the Life Cycle Theory (Hershey and Blanchard 1977). This model is widely used in a number of leadership training programs in many public- and private-sector organizations even though it has few theoretical bases and little research support. Its popularity with many practitioners earns it coverage here. The model can be credited with popularizing the concept of contingency. The basic premise, as with other models covered in this chapter and in Chapter 5, is that different leader behaviors are effective in different situations; therefore, leadership is situational. The Situational Leadership Model proposes that leaders need to change their behavior based on the ability and willingness of subordinates to complete the task. The combination of ability and willingness demonstrates various levels of employee maturity. As with other models, the leader's key behaviors are task and relationship, which are combined here to form four behaviors: telling (high task, low relationship), selling (high task, high relationship), participating (low task, high relationship), and delegating (low task, low relationship). Depending on the subordinate's maturity level, the leader needs to use one of the four behaviors. For example, when the subordinate is mature (both willing and able), the leader can delegate. If the subordinate is able but not willing, the leader needs to be considerate and sell. Interestingly, according to the model, if the subordinate is immature (neither able nor willing), the leader needs to tell the person what to do rather than attempt to build motivation.

Limitations and Applications

Although the Situational Leadership Model is used widely in leadership training, it suffers from serious flaws. It does not include a number of situational variables such as task structure, even though they are likely to have more impact than follower maturity. The concept of maturity itself is not well defined. Furthermore, the components that are emphasized change from one situation to another without any clarification (Nicholls 1985). In addition, it is not clear how a leader is to assess the followers' maturity levels, and once maturity is assessed, the matching leader behaviors are not defined consistently from one situation to another (Graeff 1983). Several of the predictions of the model are inconsistent with widely supported research on motivation and leadership. Finally, the questionnaire that is used to assess leader behavior in this model suffers from serious methodological flaws and biases.

Because of methodological and theoretical flaws and lack of empirical support, the Situational Leadership Model is one of the weakest contingency models. However, it has impacted the practice of leadership more than many of the other theories. The intuitively appealing concept that leaders need to adjust their style to followers' abilities and motivations, along with the apparent simplicity of the recommended behaviors, has made this model popular with practitioners and trainers. The positive results of training with the model, however, are not well documented beyond anecdotal accounts and post-training testimonials (House and Aditya 1997). Results seem to have little, if any, long-lasting impact on a leader's effectiveness.

SUMMARY AND CONCLUSION

This chapter discusses contingency models that focus on the relationship between leaders and followers. The Path-Goal Theory proposes that the leader's main function is to remove obstacles in the subordinates' path in order to allow them to perform their jobs and to be motivated and satisfied. According to this model, the leader needs to use either task or relationship behaviors, depending on the task and follower characteristics. The attributional models consider the way in which a leader interprets performance information about followers. Various factors in the relationship between leaders and followers affect the leader's interpretation and subsequent action. The

LMX Model focuses on the dyadic relationship between a leader and each follower and proposes the concept of in-groups and out-groups as the defining element of that relationship. The Leadership Substitutes Model considers situations in which a relationship between the leader and subordinates is not needed and is replaced by various individual, group, and organizational factors. Finally, the Situational Leadership Model focuses on follower maturity as the factor that determines the relationship between leaders and followers and the leader's behavior.

All the models use a contingency view of leadership, and in all of them, the leader's behavior depends on the requirements of the situation. In addition, the models all focus on the way leaders develop, manage, and maintain relationships with subordinates. Although the concept of task and relationship orientation continues to be dominant, several of the models consider other factors as well, thereby expanding our views of leadership. The structure and routineness of the task continue to be key situational factors, although other variables such as follower independence and maturity also are considered. (The concept of exchange in the leadership interaction is expanded and developed further in a more recent model of leadership, Transactional-Transformational Leadership, covered in more detail in Chapter 8.)

The contingency models of leadership presented in Chapters 5 and 6 continue to dominate the field of leadership. Their impact on our understanding of leadership processes has been great. The models differ in the factors they use to describe the leader's style or behavior, and elements of the leadership situation that are considered (for a summary, see Table 6-3).

Table 6-3

Comparison of Contingency Models of Leadership

	LEADER CHARACTERISTIC	FOLLOWER CHARACTERISTIC	TASK	OTHER FACTORS	EFFECTIVENESS CRITERIA
Fiedler's Model	LPC based on motivation; not changeable	Group cohesion	Task structure	Position power	Group performance
Normative Decision Model	Decision-making style; can be changed	Group cohesion	Available information	Agreement with goals; Time	Quality of the decision
Path-Goal Theory	Leader behavior; can be changed	Individual follower need to grow	Clarity and routineness of task		Follower satisfaction and motivation
LMX					Quality of relationship with follower
Substitutes	Leader behavior; can be changed	Group cohesion	Clarity of task; availability of information	Organization culture, structure, and processes	Need for leader
Situational Leadership	Leader behavior; can be changed	Follower ability; motivation and maturity			Unclear

For each, however, whether in resource utilization or in exchange and relationship development models, the focus is on the match between the leader and the situation. The extensive research about the various contingency models that is presented in Part II, although not always consistent and clear, has led to the broad acceptance and establishment of the concept of contingency in leadership. Clearly, no one best way to lead exists. Effective leadership is a combination of and match between the leader and the leadership situation.

The In-Group Applicant

You are an expatriate manager sent to work in the Indian operation of your company. As you get settled in, one of your first decisions is to hire an assistant manager. Your efficient office manager, who has been extremely helpful to you already and has been with the company for many years, quickly suggests one of his relatives, whom he tells you would be perfect for the job. According to him, his cousin just graduated from a top business school and, most importantly, is trustworthy, loyal, and eager to work and learn. Your office assistant tells you that his cousin will be coming shortly to introduce himself. He tells you that don't have to be inconvenienced any further and won't need to waste your time and risk having an unreliable stranger become your assistant.

1. How do you interpret and explain your office manager's actions?
2. Will you hire the "cousin?"
3. What factors do you need to consider before making your decision?

REVIEW AND DISCUSSION QUESTIONS

1. Provide examples of how the Path-Goal Theory of leadership can be used to improve leadership effectiveness.
2. How can leaders' knowledge of attributional processes increase their leadership effectiveness?
3. How does the LMX Model differ from all the other contingency theories of leadership?
4. How can leaders use the LMX Model in improving their effectiveness?
5. What are positive and negative impacts of substitutes on leaders and organizations? Provide examples.
6. Compare and contrast the contingency models of leadership. How are they similar? How are they different? How do they each contribute to our understanding of leadership?

SEARCHING THE WEB

Path-Goal Theory:
www.css.edu/users/dswenson/web/
LEAD/path-goal.html

Leader-Member Exchange:
www.siop.org/Instruct/LMXTheory/
sld001.htm

Substitutes for Leadership:
www.css.edu/users/dswenson/web/
LEAD/substitutes.html

Commander Abrashoff:
www.watsonwyatt.com/strategyatwork/
articles/2001/2001_05_tl.asp

EXERCISE 6-1:   REMOVING OBSTACLES

This exercise is designed to provide you with a way to identify the task that subordinates are performing and their need for autonomy. Your instructor may provide you with vignettes to use for this exercise or ask you to rate your current job. Once the task and subordinate characteristics are identified, the proper leadership behavior can be used to remove obstacles.

Step 1: Identifying the Task

Using the following scale, rate the task that subordinates are performing:

1	2	3	4	5
Strongly disagree	Somewhat disagree	Neither agree nor disagree	Somewhat agree	Strongly agree

_____ 1. My subordinates have performed the task many times before.
_____ 2. Clear instructions are available on how to perform the task.
_____ 3. The task has clearly identifiable solutions.
_____ 4. The task is relatively new.
_____ 5. Many written procedures explain how to do this task.
_____ 6. Feedback about the task is quickly and easily available.

Scoring key: Reverse score item 4 (1 = 5, 5 = 1). Add up your score for all six items. The maximum score is 30; the higher the score is, the more structured the task is.

Total: _____

Step 2: Identifying Subordinates' Need for Autonomy

Using the following scale, rate the extent to which the majority of your subordinates need autonomy:

1	2	3	4	5
Strongly disagree	Somewhat disagree	Neither agree nor disagree	Somewhat agree	Strongly agree

_____ 1. My subordinates have extensive job experience.
_____ 2. My subordinates require little instruction in order to perform their job.
_____ 3. My subordinates rarely ask for new responsibilities.
_____ 4. My subordinates are professionals.
_____ 5. My subordinates work well without me.
_____ 6. My subordinates require extensive training every time they start a new task.

Scoring key: Reverse score items 3 and 6 (1 = 5, 5 = 1). Add up your score for all six items. The maximum score is 30. The higher the score is, the more autonomy your subordinates are likely to require.

Total: _____

Step 3: Selecting a Leadership Behavior

The task structure is (circle one):

    High   Moderate   Low

My subordinates' need for autonomy is (circle one):

    High   Moderate   Low   Depends greatly on the person

Based on the recommendations of the Path-Goal Theory of leadership, what would be the appropriate leadership behaviors? Consider the following additional factors in selecting a style: the extent to which your employees differ from one another and how you might want to approach each subordinate differently.

EXERCISE 6-2: IN-GROUP/OUT-GROUP

This exercise is designed to help you identify the emotions and behavioral reactions associated with being a member of an in-group and an out-group.

Step 1: Being in the In-Group

Think of a situation where you belonged to your manager's in-group, enjoyed the manager's confidence and trust, and were given challenging assignments. Describe the elements of that situation.

What factors caused you to be in the in-group?

Describe your boss's behavior toward you.

What impact did it have on your motivation?

What impact did it have on your performance?

Step 2: Being in the Out-Group

Think of a situation where you did not belong to your manager's in-group, did not enjoy your manager's confidence and trust, and were not given challenging assignments. Describe the elements of that situation.

What factors caused you to be in the out-group?

Describe your boss's behavior toward you.

What impact did it have on your motivation?

What impact did it have on your performance?

Discussion Questions

1. What are the major differences between the two situations?
2. How did having an in-group and an out-group affect the groups and the organization?
3. To what extent was membership in either the in-group or the out-group based on performance and task and organizationally relevant factors? What nontask factors entered into the decision?
4. What are the implications for leadership and a leader's relationship with followers?

This exercise is designed to help you identify the members of your in-group and out-group and your own behavior toward members of each group.

Step 1: Identify the Members

Make a list of the subordinates (or team members) you trust. Select people who work for you (or with you) whom you like and respect—people who enjoy your confidence.

Make a list of the subordinates (or team members) you do not trust. Select people who work for you (or with you) whom you do not like or respect.

Step 2: Membership Factors

What are the commonalities among the group members in each group? What are the factors that caused them to be in each group? Consider behaviors, personalities, and demographic factors, as well as any other factors that were relevant.

Step 3: How Did You Treat Them?

Describe your own behavior as a leader toward each group and its members.

Leader Behaviors	In-Group Members	Out-Group Members
Amount of at-work interaction		
Type of interaction		
Type of assignments given		
How was feedback provided?		
Amount of out-of-work interaction		
Performance expectations		
Other factors: List		

Step 4: Self-Evaluation

1. What does it take for a person to move from your in-group to your out-group?

2. How does having two groups affect your group or department and the organization?

3. To what extent is group membership based on organizational versus personal factors?

4. What are the implications for you as a leader?

SELF-ASSESSMENT 6-2: LEADERSHIP SUBSTITUTES

This exercise is designed to help you identify the leadership substitutes and neutralizers that might be present in the group you lead. Consider the team, group, or department you are leading. Rate it on the following factors using this scale:

1	2	3	4	5
Never	Occasionally	About half the time	Most of the time	Always

____ 1. My subordinates have considerable training and experience in their jobs.
____ 2. My subordinates have a professional orientation.
____ 3. The rewards that the organization provides are valued by my subordinates.
____ 4. Most of the tasks my group performs are clear and routine.
____ 5. My subordinates can get direct and timely feedback about the tasks/ services they perform.
____ 6. The tasks that my subordinates perform are challenging.
____ 7. My subordinates get along and are a cohesive team.
____ 8. As the leader, I do not have much power to influence my subordinates.
____ 9. I have access to many rewards for my subordinates.
____ 10. The organization has many rules and regulations about behaviors and tasks.
____ 11. My subordinates can rely on written procedures to do their job.
____ 12. The organizational structure is rigid and bureaucratic.
____ 13. I do not have direct daily contact with my subordinates.

Scoring key:

Overall presence of substitutes: Add items 1, 2, 4, 5, 6, 7, 10, and 11.

Total: _____

Overall presence of neutralizers (same score for consideration and structuring behaviors): Reverse items 3 and 9. Add items 3, 8, 9, 12, and 13.

Total: _____

Substitutes for consideration behavior: Add items 2, 6, and 7.

Total: _____

Substitutes for structuring behavior: Add items 1, 2, 4, 5, 7, and 11.

Total: _____

Discussion Questions

1. Is the presence of substitutes desirable?

2. What can be done to increase or decrease their impact?

3. How can neutralizers be removed?

CASE

Leadership in Action

The Caring Navy Commander

Under the leadership of Commander Michael Abrashoff, the *U.S.S. Benfold*, one of the U.S. navy's most modern warships, became a model of performance. It was ranked as having the best combat readiness in the Pacific fleet and achieved the highest gunnery score and lowest rate of key equipment failures. The ship's crew completed several of its training exercises in record time, and 100 percent of its career sailors signed on for an additional tour of duty as opposed to the 54 percent average for the rest of the navy. The *Benfold* returned $600,000 of its $2.4 million maintenance budget and reduced its spending every year during Abrashoff's command. Morale was excellent and Commander Abrashoff's future promotion was guaranteed.

Much of the ship and the crew's outstanding performance can be attributed to Abrashoff's leadership. His focus was on his crew. He stated:

> When you shift your organizing principle from obedience to performance, the highest boss is no longer the guy with the most stripes—it's the sailor who does the work . . . my job was to listen . . . to see the ship from the eyes of the crew. (Labarre 1999, pp. 116–118)

One of the commander's first steps after joining the ship was to interview every crew member and ask each what they liked about their ship and what they wanted to change. He then identified nonvalue-added tasks that caused the most dissatisfaction and proceeded to tackle them.

Several steps were taken to address problems. The metal parts of the ship were replaced with stainless steel bolts and a specially coated metal that did not require constant painting; the youngest sailors who dreaded the constant chipping and painting were delighted. An agreement with an SAT administrator allowed sailors who wanted to go to college to take the SAT in Bahrain. Because the crew spends so much time away from their families and often felt cut off, Abrashoff set up a special account through America Online to allow his sailors to stay in touch with their families. He disregarded strict navy rules for shore leave and rented minivans to allow his sailors to have more freedom on shore leave in Dubai under the supervision of senior petty officers. Another sore spot for the crew was the food. The commander rejected naval provisions, switched to purchasing lower-cost, brand-name products, and used the savings to send his ship's cooks to culinary school. The *Benfold's* crew had pumpkins during Halloween, they projected music videos on the side of their ship, and their chief navigator was known for his Elvis impersonations.

Abrashoff knew every one of his crew by name. He wanted to help them "chart a course through life . . . I consider my job to improve my little 300-person piece of society" (LaBarre 1999, p. 119). Interestingly, although the *Benfold* and its commander did not focus on strict discipline, there was no lack of respect and cohesion on the ship. The crew willingly saluted its commanding officer, and a strong sense of duty and cooperation prevailed. One indicator of the positive culture was the results of the ship surveys, which indicated that only 3 percent of minorities reported prejudice, and only 3 percent of the female sailors reported any sexual harassment.

Abrashoff stated:

> I have to prepare higher-level people to step into leadership roles. If all you do is give orders, then all you'll get are order tak-

ers. Removing many of the nonreadiness aspects of the job—from chipping paint to cleaning—lets us spend more time on learning. (LaBarre 1999, p. 124)

Abrashoff's care for his crew, his ability to listen to them, his relative disregard for rules while focusing on performance and problem solving, and his focus on improving the quality of life created enviable results.

When Abrashoff left command of the *Benfold* for a post at the Space and Naval Warfare Systems Command, his legacy continued. The *Benfold* continues to be rated as one the best ships in the U.S. Navy; it has been nominated for the highest award in combat readiness (Dahle 2000). Abrashoff credits the beginning of his leadership style to an epiphany when he observed sailors on the *Benfold* cheer the departure of his predecessor (Abrashoff 2001). He decided then that he would lead differently. Instead of the traditional command and control, he focused on seeing the ship through the eyes of his crew, removing obstacles, and freeing his crew to perform their job. Commander Abrashoff has retired from the navy and now runs a leadership consulting firm. ■

QUESTIONS

1. What are the elements of Abrashoff's leadership style? What factors contribute to his effectiveness?

2. What models can be used to explain his performance?

Sources: Abrashoff, D. M. 2001. Giving up control to gain command. www.watsonwyatt.com/strategyatwork/articles/2001/2001_05_tl.asp, accessed April 15, 2002; Dahle, C. 2000. Updating the agenda. *Fast Company* (April), 206–208; LaBarre, P. 1999. Grassroots leadership. *Fast Company* (April), 115–126.

Part III

Current Developments and Applications

*P*art III focuses on recent views of leadership in light of the popularity of teams, participative management, and empowerment in today's organizations. After studying Part III, you will be able to understand the challenges of managing teams, the role of cultural factors in such a setting, the key role of leaders in implementing change in organizations, and the role of upper-echelon leaders.

The management of organizations has changed considerably in recent years. To be successful and remain competitive, organizations must be able to change and respond quickly to increasing environmental pressures. Many organizations have adopted new management models to address the new demands. The use of teams and increased employee involvement in decision making and implementation are central themes in organizations' attempts to remain effective. Accordingly, there has been a revived interest in industry in the topic of leadership, and new leadership models also have evolved. The various leaders who have succeeded in changing their organizations by pulling them out of stagnation have become heroes in the business and other industry press. The revived interest in the role of leaders is related closely to the concept of empowerment and borrows much from existing concepts of participative management and delegation. The focus in this section, however, is on change-oriented leadership and on the upper level of leadership in organizations. This view considers the ability to enact large-scale changes to be the major role and effectiveness criterion of leadership.

Chapters 7 and 8 focus on teams and change-oriented leadership models. Although the concepts presented in this part have many ties to the contingency theories presented previously, the major difference with the concepts covered in these chapters is the relative absence of a contingency approach. In addition, in the case of change-oriented leadership, the concepts focus as much on upper-echelon and organizational leaders as on small-group and department leaders. Chapter 9 focuses exclusively on understanding the challenges and roles of upper-echelon strategic leaders.

Chapter 7

Participative Management and Leading Teams

> Do you have as much sense as a goose? When geese fly in the "V" formation, the whole flock adds considerably more to its flying range than if each bird flew alone. Whenever a goose falls out of formation, it suddenly feels the drag and resistance of trying to fly alone and quickly gets back into formation to take advantage of the power of the formation. When the lead goose gets tired, it rotates back in the wing, and another goose flies point. The back geese honk from behind to encourage those up front to keep up their speed. Finally, when a goose gets sick and falls out, two geese fall out of formation with it until it is either able to fly or it is dead. They then launch on their own, or with another formation, to catch up with the group.
>
> —ANONYMOUS

After studying this chapter, you will be able to:

1. Understand when and why participation should be used to improve leadership effectiveness.
2. Explain the role of culture in the use and success of participative leadership.
3. Specify the elements of effective delegation.
4. Clarify the role of leadership in self-managed teams.
5. Explain the principles of super- and self-leadership.

Employee participation has been a central issue in leadership for many years. Almost all of our past and current models address this issue in some form. For example, Theory Y of management recommends a higher level of employee participation than Theory X does. The Theory Y manager allows employees to decide their own development and provides them with support, whereas the Theory X manager controls employees rather than involving them in decision making. Similarly, the initiation-of-structure construct from the behavioral approach assumes that the leader is the one who provides the structure; no mention is made of subordinate participation in the development of the structure. The consideration behaviors in the same model have a stronger participation component. Fiedler's task-motivated leader makes decisions alone; the relationship-motivated leader involves the group. Finally, the Normative Decision Model is built around the degree of follower participation in decision making.

This chapter focuses on the concept of participative management in its past and current uses in leadership. It discusses the use of participation and delegation and the challenges they present for leaders, and it considers the special characteristics of teams and the importance of super- and self-leadership.

WHEN SHOULD PARTICIPATION BE USED?

Participation is a continuum. On one end, the leader retains all control and makes all the decisions without any consultation or even information from the subordinates; on the other end, the leader delegates all decision making to followers and lets them have the final say. Few leaders use extreme autocratic or delegation styles; most use a style that falls somewhere in between. Similarly, few organizations today are entirely team based or make no use of teams at all. Most fall in the middle of the continuum, with some use of teams and some traditional hierarchical structures (see Figure 7-1). For example, although still maintaining many elements of traditional structures, Ford Motor Company relies on teams for many tasks. Talking about hiring people with diverse backgrounds, Mary Ellen Heyde, line director of lifestyle vehicles in Ford's Dearborn, Michigan, plant states: "... we realize that good ideas come when people with different perspectives work together on the same problem" (Rosenfeld 2000, p. 102). About the value of teams, Nancy Gioia, a chief program engineer at Ford, says: "Work in groups and leverage the variety of perspectives that you'll find in those groups . . . bounce your ideas off of your colleagues. Share your ideas and your energy" (Hammonds 2000, p. 143).

Longitudinal research about employee involvement conducted by researchers at the University of Southern California indicates that organizations can reap many benefits from a variety of types of employee participation and involvement (Lawler, Mohrman, and Ledford 1995). These programs include such methods as information sharing; group decision making; and the use of teams, empowerment, profit sharing,

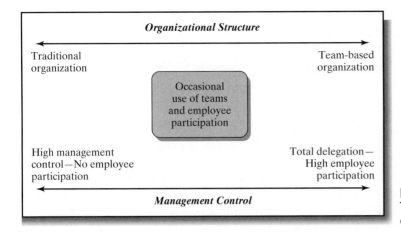

Figure 7-1
The Continuum
of Participation

and stock option plans. These programs increase employee involvement and participation in the organization. The study results show that the adoption of such programs has clear, positive impact on performance, profitability, competitiveness, and employee satisfaction (Lawler, Mohrman, and Ledford 1995).

Joe Gerra, CEO of American Golf and operator of 300 public and private golf courses, knows how important it is to involve all employees in decision making. To encourage employee input:

> several times a year we do a departmental "workout" session, where supervisors leave and the group creates a list of ideas for improvement . . .
> One result has been that we've saved hundreds of man-hours. . . . (Guerra 2001, p. 84)

Consider how US AirWays, one of the largest air carriers in the United States, used a team to design a new, low-fare airline, initially called US2 (Carey 1998). Rakesh Gangwal, president of US AirWays, asked two dozen of his employees without any start-up experience to find the best way to compete with Southwest Airlines. A catering truck driver and baggage handler in Baltimore, an aircraft cleaner in Pittsburgh, and a ramp supervisor were among the two dozen other airline specialists who joined the design team that spent 4 months investigating the competition. The team traveled extensively on Southwest, Shuttle by United, Alaska Airlines, and Delta Express with the goal of learning what makes each competitor efficient and effective. The members then assembled in Arlington, Virginia, and worked on their start-up idea. After 4 months of intensive work, MetroJet was selected as the start-up's name. Gangwal announced that MetroJet would take off June 1, 1998. After the announcement, the team was disbanded and members sent back, reluctantly, to their regular jobs. "It's kind of like letting your child be married off," noted ramp supervisor Greg Solek (Carey 1998, p. B2). By using a team to make an important decision, Gangwal received input from many employees who otherwise would not be involved, and in so doing built their commitment to the success of the new operation.

LEADING CHANGE
From Old Style Manufacturing to "Biological Cells"

"Delivery used to take 21 days. But now, if you order on Monday, we can deliver on that precise order by Friday. Go look at other plants. There aren't many out there that have reached that magnitude" (Dorsey 2000, p. 212). "I've been here 26 years. This place used to be nothing but conveyers. Now it's down to about 200 feet. We've become lean" (Dorsey 2000, p. 224). These are some examples of the major changes that have occurred at Delphi Automotive Systems in Oak Creek, Wisconsin, a plant that makes catalytic converters. Delphi used to be part of General Motors (GM) before it split off and went public in 1999. As clients demanded customized converters and relied on fewer suppliers, and with independence from GM, Delphi employees reinvented their work.

Peter Wood, Delphi manufacturing-systems manager, considers himself to be a change agent as well as a manager. He repeatedly encourages employees to be proud of their accomplishments. One of the most visible signs of the change is a lot of empty space—equal to about two ice-hockey rinks—where old conveyer belts that fed the assembly lines used to be. "I often take employees out here to remind them of how proud they should be" (Dorsey 2000, p. 217). People, not machines, have become the center of the work. Delphi employees now work in small groups of up to four they call a biological cell. Everything is modular and portable, with people-centered work practices. The cell members establish the speed, determine their own schedule, inspect their own work, discover flaws, change the work flow, adjust tooling, check for quality, keep tabs on supplies, and communicate directly with customers.

The new working method allows everyone to take ownership of the work process and the products. Employees lead themselves. Because they work on the whole converter, workers have responsibility for what they make. They also have the opportunity to own stock and can monitor their stocks' performance on monitors throughout the plant.

Source: Dorsey D. 2000. Change factory. *Fast Company* (June), 210–224.

Criteria for Participation

If the organization, its leaders, and employees are ready for participative management and there is no strong time pressure, the task is complex, and employee commitment is important, leaders should rely on employee participation in making decisions. However, if there is genuine time pressure or the leader, followers, or organization are not ready, then participation is not likely to yield many benefits.

Despite its many potential benefits, participation is not a cure-all. Its use is more appropriate in some situations than in others. After many years of debate and research about participative management in social sciences and management, there are clear criteria for when it is most effective to use groups in decision making (see Table 7-1).

Overall, if the organization, its leaders, and the employees are ready for participative management and there is no strong time pressure, the task is complex, and employee commitment is important, leaders should rely on employee participation in making decisions. However, if time pressure is genuine or the leader, followers, or organization are not ready, then participation is not likely to yield many benefits. For example, if leaders have a high need for control, are highly task oriented, and have been successful in using an autocratic style of leadership, they are unlikely to be able to

Table 7-1

Criteria for Use of Participation

CRITERIA	DESCRIPTION
• When the task is complex and multifaceted and quality is important	Complex tasks require input from people with different expertise; people with different points of view are more likely to deliver a quality decision.
• When follower commitment is needed in successful implementation	Follower participation increases commitment and motivation.
• When there is time	Using participation takes time; legitimate deadlines and time pressures preclude seeking extensive participation.
• When the leader and followers are ready and the organizational culture is supportive	Participation can succeed only if both leader and followers agree to its benefits, are trained in how to use it, and are committed to its success. The organizational culture has to encourage or at least tolerate employee participation.
• When interaction among leader and followers is not restricted by the task, the structure, or the environment	Participation requires interaction among leaders and followers; such interaction is possible only if no restrictions exist due to factors such as geographic location, structural elements, or task requirements.

implement participation easily. In addition, if followers have either little need to participate or are willing to trust the leader, participation might not be required or at least might not lead to better results. Similarly, some organizational cultures are more supportive of participation than others.

Another factor in using participation is whether the task or the structure limits its use. If followers cannot interact easily with one another and with the leader, either because of task or geographic restrictions, participation might not be appropriate. In some instances, legal and confidentiality requirements may preclude participation, such as in personnel decisions.

The case of Kiwi Airlines presents an interesting example of the potential pitfalls of mismanaged participation (Bryant 1995). When Kiwi Airlines was founded in 1992, it quickly became the symbol of all that is good about participative and egalitarian leadership. Created by a group of ex–Eastern Airline pilots and other employees, Kiwi promised not to repeat any of Eastern's mistakes and aimed at creating a family atmosphere for all of its employees. The employees were all owners with varying degrees of shares and the corresponding pride and desire for involvement, control, and commitment that come from ownership. All decisions were made with full participation. All employees, regardless of levels, pitched in to get the job done and deliver the quality service that soon earned Kiwi honors in surveys of airline quality. The airline quickly grew to more than 1,000 employees with more than 60 daily flights. One of the pilot-founders and then chairman of Kiwi, Robert W. Iverson, attributed the stunning growth and success to the employees' commitment and the organization's egalitarian culture. Kiwi was truly a symbol of the benefits of participation and involvement.

In 1994, the bubble burst. Kiwi's board, which included fellow founders and owners, booted Iverson out of office. This event revealed serious management and organizational deficiencies within the airline. The dark side of participation was an amazing lack of concern for management decisions. Many employee-owners failed to follow management directives if they did not agree with them. Employees demanded input in every decision, a factor that led to stagnation in decision making and an inability to act to solve problems. Iverson admitted, "One of the stupidest things I ever did was call everybody owners. An owner is somebody who thinks he can exercise gratuitous control." The case of Kiwi Airlines demonstrates the ineffective use of participation. A few managers could have handled many of the decisions more effectively and efficiently than the employees did through participation.

LEADERSHIP ON THE CUTTING EDGE
Heterogeneous Members and Cooperation

One of the widely held assumptions about group composition is that team members' demographic heterogeneity tends to have a negative effect on team cooperation and performance. However, studies about the topic have been somewhat contradictory. Researchers Jennifer Chatman and Francis Flynn proposed that although heterogeneity might be related negatively to cooperation in teams, such an effect is likely to decrease over time and with increased contact among team members (2001). They further proposed that the development of cooperative norms is related to higher member satisfaction, more contributions to group objectives, and overall effectiveness. In effect, they suggest that the potential negative effects of member heterogeneity can be overcome through the development of a norm for cooperation.

Using samples of 110 MBA students and through a field study of 160 officers in a financial services firm, the researchers indeed found that although demographic heterogeneity led to the development of norms for lower cooperation, the effect weakened such that over time, those who were different were more positively affected by contact, and they developed even more cooperative norms than those who were similar. It appears that members with different backgrounds try to compensate for their differences by focusing more on the group objectives and on developing cooperation. The study further found that a norm of cooperation, as opposed to one of independent work, is related to setting meetings early in the project, more satisfaction, better individual performance, and more effective teams (Chatman and Flynn 2001, p. 971).

The researchers concluded that heterogeneity in and of itself is not a negative factor. What is more important is the mediating effect of a norm for cooperation.

Source: Chatman, J. A., and F. J. Flynn. 2001. The influence of demographic heterogeneity on the emergence and consequences of cooperative norms in work teams. *Academy of Management Journal* 44, no. 5, 956–974.

The Role of Culture

An additional factor when considering the use of participation is national cultural values. Factors such as collectivism, power distance (Hofstede 2001), and cross-cultural organizational cultures (Trompenaars 1994) impact whether leaders can use participation successfully. For example, Japanese culture, with its strong emphasis on conformity, consensus, and collectivity at the expense of individual goals (Chen 1995), supports the use of participative management despite relatively high power distance. Participation in Japan is a mix of group harmony and consensus, with elements of directive leadership (Dorfman et al. 1997). Being a vertical collectivistic culture, individuals are expected to sacrifice their personal goals for the good of the group. Mexico is also relatively high on collectivism, power distance, and masculinity. The Mexican culture, however, has a well-established tradition of autocratic leadership without a history of participative leadership (Dorfman et al. 1997). In such a cultural context, neither the leader nor the followers find participation desirable. Similarly, in the cross-cultural organizational cultures, which Trompenaars labels the Eiffel Tower—France, for example—the focus is on performance through obedience and respect for legitimate authority (Trompenaars 1994). In such an environment, a leader is ascribed great authority and is expected to know much; asking for subordinate participation easily can be perceived as weakness and lack of leadership ability.

Cultures such as the United States and Australia that have relatively egalitarian power distributions but are vertical individualist, pose a different challenge. The low power distance allows for participation, but the value placed on individual autonomy and individual contribution can be an obstacle to cooperation in a team environment. In horizontal individualist cultures such as Sweden, participation and team cooperation are much easier because all individuals are equal.

Furthermore, appropriate team behaviors vary considerably from one culture to another (Kanter and Corn 1993). An effective team member in Japan is above all courteous and cooperative; members avoid conflict and confrontation (Zander 1983). In the United States, effective team members speak their mind, pull their weight by contributing equally, and participate actively, yet they expect to be recognized individually. German employees are taught early in their careers to seek technical excellence. In Afghanistan, team members are obligated to share their resources with others, making generosity an essential team behavior. In Israel, a horizontal collectivistic culture, values of hard work and contribution to the community drive kibbutz team members. The Swedes are comfortable with open arguments and will disagree publicly with one another and with their leader. Each culture expects and rewards different types of team behaviors.

These cross-cultural differences in team behavior create considerable challenges for the leadership of culturally diverse teams. Success depends on accurate perceptions and careful reading of cross-cultural cues. Leaders must be flexible and patient, and be willing not only to listen to others, but also to question their own assumptions. Additionally, they must keep in mind that many behavioral differences have individual rather than cultural sources. The only constant in the successful implementation of teams is the leader's sincere belief in the team's ability to contribute to the organization (Marsick, Turner, and Cederholm 1989). Such belief is necessary regardless of the cultural setting.

THE ISSUE OF DELEGATION

Delegation differs from participation in a number of ways, although many managers consider it to be an aspect of participation. For example, many leaders define themselves as participative managers if they delegate tasks to their subordinates. Although this might lead to more subordinate participation in decision making, the goal of delegation is not necessarily to develop employees or create more commitment. Neither does delegation always involve power sharing with employees. The goal of delegation can be as simple as helping a leader with an excessive workload. In its most basic form, delegation is a simple application of participation concepts; in its most complex form, delegation can resemble participative management.

Benefits of Delegation

The proper delegation of tasks to followers is becoming more important as managerial ranks are thinned and managers see their workloads increase.

The proper delegation of tasks to followers is becoming more important as managerial ranks are thinned and managers see their workloads increase. Production managers find themselves with twice as many subordinates to supervise; sales managers see their territories double in current attempts to develop leaner structures. Many organizations undergoing such restructuring are testing team-based approaches. Until such techniques are well accepted and implemented, however, judicial delegation is still a basic tool for a leader's success. The potential benefits of delegation include the following:

- Freeing up the leader's time for new tasks and strategic activities.
- Providing employees with opportunities to learn and develop.
- Allowing employees to be involved in tasks.
- Allowing observation and evaluation of employees in new tasks.
- Increasing employee motivation and satisfaction.

Aside from being a time- and stress-management tool for leaders, delegation allows subordinates to try new tasks and learn new skills, thereby potentially enriching their jobs and increasing their satisfaction and motivation. When employees perform new tasks, the leader also has the opportunity to observe them and gather performance-related information that can be used for further development, evaluation, and preparation of employees for promotions. As such, delegation can be one of the tools available to leaders for succession planning in their organizations. Employees who consistently perform well on new tasks and are willing to accept more responsibility could be the future leaders of the organization. Without the opportunity to grow outside of their current job, no data are available for accurate forecasting of their performance in higher-level positions.

The final benefit of delegation is, as is the case with participation, increased employee involvement and commitment. Job enrichment and participative management research (Hackman and Oldham 1980) indicates that employees who are interested in growth quickly feel stifled and unmotivated if they do not have the opportunity to participate in new and challenging tasks. Delegation of such tasks to them helps increase their motivation and commitment to the organization.

Guidelines for Good Delegation

As with any tool, misuse and misapplication of delegation can be disastrous. Leaders must take into account some relatively simple principles (see Table 7-2 for a summary). One of the major issues for leaders is to separate delegation from dumping. Leaders need to delegate easy, hard, pleasant, and unpleasant tasks to their subordinates. If only unpleasant, difficult, and unmanageable tasks are assigned consistently to subordinates, while leaders complete the high-profile, challenging, and interesting projects, delegation becomes dumping. One of the major complaints of subordinates regarding delegation is this exact issue. In order to reap the benefits of delegation, a variety of tasks should be delegated, and the leaders should pay particular attention that their delegation is viewed as balanced.

Effective delegation requires more than handing off a task. Leaders must be clear about their expectations and support their followers while they perform the task. The support might include informing department members and others outside the department that the task has been delegated. Another aspect of support involves providing training and other appropriate resources that allow the subordinate to learn the needed skills. It also might require regular monitoring and clarification of reporting expectations. It is easy for an eager subordinate to make decisions that are inconsistent with the leader's goals if the leader does not properly monitor the situation.

One area that cannot and should not be delegated is personnel issues. Unless an organization or department is moving toward self-managed teams that have feedback and performance evaluation responsibility, the task of performance management remains the leader's responsibility. For example, it would be inappropriate for a manager to delegate the task of disciplining a tardy employee to a subordinate or to expect the latter to monitor and manage the performance of coworkers. As stated

Table 7-2
Guidelines for Good Delegation

GUIDELINE	DESCRIPTION
Delegate, do not dump	Delegate pleasant and unpleasant tasks; provide followers with a variety of experiences.
Clarify goals and expectations	Provide clear goals and guidelines regarding expectations and limitations.
Provide support and authority	As a task is delegated, provide necessary authority and resources such as time, training, and advice needed to complete the task.
Monitor and provide feedback	Keep track of progress and provide feedback during and after task completion.
Delegate to different followers	Delegate tasks to those who are most motivated to complete them, as well as to those who have potential but no clear track record of performance.

previously, the situation of self-managed teams often changes this guideline. Such changes will be discussed later in the chapter.

Finally, leaders must choose carefully the followers to whom they delegate. The easiest choice for most managers is to delegate to the few people they know will do the job well (the in-group). Although such a position is logical and effective, at least in the short run, a leader must be aware of the in-group/out-group issues presented in Chapter 6. Therefore, leaders must select individuals who, in addition to having shown potential, are also eager and motivated to take on new tasks and have the appropriate skills for the new challenge. A follower who is competent and eager but who has failed recently on one assignment might also be a good choice but could be overlooked if leaders keep relying on their few trusted in-group members. Delegation of tasks to a varied group of followers further provides leaders with a broad view of the performance capabilities of their team or department.

Why Do Leaders Fail to Delegate?

Certain circumstances justify a leader's unwillingness to delegate. In some cases, followers are not be ready for delegation, are already overworked, or have such specialized jobs that they cannot be assigned new tasks. Such situations are rare, however, and the considerable benefits of delegation far outweigh many of the arguments typically presented against it (Kouzes and Posner 1987; Miller and Toulouse 1986). The most commonly used argument against delegation is "I will get it done better and faster myself." Table 7-3 presents the typical excuses and counterarguments for not delegating.

The excuses for not delegating tasks might be valid in the short run. However, by taking a long-term view that considers the leader's personal effectiveness as well as

Table 7-3

Excuses for Not Delegating

EXCUSES	COUNTERARGUMENTS
My followers are not ready.	The leader's job is to get followers prepared to take on new tasks.
My subordinates do not have the necessary skills and knowledge.	The leader's responsibility is to train followers and prepare them for new challenges.
I feel uncomfortable asking my followers to do many of my tasks.	Only a few tasks cannot truly be delegated. Balancing delegation of pleasant and unpleasant tasks is appropriate.
I can do the job quicker myself.	Taking time to train followers frees up time in the long run.
Followers are too busy.	Leaders and followers must learn to manage their workload by setting priorities.
If my followers make a mistake, I am responsible.	Encouraging experimentation and tolerating mistakes is key to learning and development.
My own manager might think I am not working hard.	Doing busywork is not an appropriate use of a leader's time. Delegation allows time to focus on strategic and higher-level activities.

the development of followers, many of the excuses are no longer valid. Effective delegation requires effort and resources such as training, but it also allows leaders to focus on higher-level strategic issues instead of day-to-day routines. One underlying factor that might stop many leaders from delegating is their personality style, their need for control, and their fear of losing it. For example, as discussed in Chapter 3, a Type A's need for control often leads to lack of delegation. Competitiveness also might lead Type A leaders to compete with their followers. Other personal needs, such as a need for power (McClelland 1975), also might cause leaders to want to maintain power over all activities and prevent them from delegating.

Although participation and delegation have been part of management and leadership for many years, they recently have taken on a new form in team-based organizations with the introduction of empowerment and concepts such as super- and self-leadership, which are considered next.

EVOLUTION OF PARTICIPATIVE MANAGEMENT: TEAMS AND SUPERLEADERSHIP

The use of teams in organizations in the United States and many other countries constitutes one of the major trends of the end of the twentieth century and has continued to the present day. Many organizations have made teams a permanent part if not a cornerstone of their structures. Teams create a formal structure through which participation in decision making can be achieved. The use of teams in U.S. and other Western organizations was triggered to a great extent by Japan's economic success and its reliance on teams and participative management (Nahavandi and Aranda 1994). Although teams have not been uniformly successful, a large number of organizations have used and continue to use them as a technique to increase creativity, innovation, and quality.

Characteristics of Teams

Groups have worked together to accomplish organizational goals for many years. However, the concept and use of teams as a central element of decision making and performance are more recent. Table 7-4 outlines the differences between groups and teams.

One of the most celebrated examples of the use of teams is the Johnsonville Sausage Company, where team management and empowerment have provided dramatic results. At Johnsonville Sausage Company, cross-functional teams address the needs of customers, and team members are responsible for solving problems and managing themselves. The results have been quicker response time and more satisfied customers. Other organizations, Ford Motor Company and Shell Oil, also have reaped the benefits of using teams as decision-making and implementation tools. At Roadway Express, a trucking company, the 28,000 employees are encouraged to take on leadership roles. A team of workers from across the company spearheaded an off-site meeting to determine the future strategy of the company (Hammonds 2001c).

Table 7-4

Groups and Teams

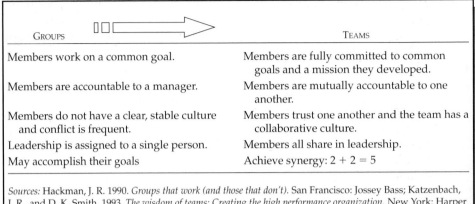

GROUPS	TEAMS
Members work on a common goal.	Members are fully committed to common goals and a mission they developed.
Members are accountable to a manager.	Members are mutually accountable to one another.
Members do not have a clear, stable culture and conflict is frequent.	Members trust one another and the team has a collaborative culture.
Leadership is assigned to a single person.	Members all share in leadership.
May accomplish their goals	Achieve synergy: 2 + 2 = 5

Sources: Hackman, J. R. 1990. *Groups that work (and those that don't).* San Francisco: Jossey Bass; Katzenbach, J. R., and D. K. Smith. 1993. *The wisdom of teams: Creating the high performance organization.* New York: Harper Business.

The first distinguishing characteristic of a team is its members' full commitment to a common goal and approach that they often have developed themselves. Members must agree that the team goal is worthwhile and agree on a general approach for meeting that goal. Such agreement provides the vision and motivation for team members to perform. The second characteristic is mutual accountability. To succeed as a team, members must feel and be accountable to one another and to the organization for the process and outcome of their work. Whereas group members report to the leader or their manager and are accountable to this person, team members take on responsibility and perform because of their commitment to the team.

The third characteristic of a team is a team culture based on trust and collaboration. Whereas group members share norms, team members have a shared culture. Team members are willing to compromise, cooperate, and collaborate to reach their common purpose. However, a collaborative climate does not mean the absence of conflict. Conflict can enhance team creativity and performance if handled constructively. Related to the team culture is shared leadership. Whereas groups have one assigned leader, teams differ by sharing leadership among all members.

Finally, teams develop synergy. Synergy means that team members together achieve more than each individual is capable of doing. Whereas group members combine their efforts to achieve their goal, teams reach higher performance levels.

Self-Managed Teams

Whereas traditional managers and leaders are expected to provide command and control, the role of leaders in teams is to facilitate processes and support team members. The leader sets the general direction and goals; the team members make all other decisions and implement them. This new role for leaders is most obvious in self-managed teams (SMT), meaning teams of employees who have full managerial control over their own work (for some examples, see Barry 1991; Crum and France 1996; Spencer 1995).

WHAT DOES THIS MEAN FOR ME?
Using a Sport Team Model in Management

Organizational behavior expert and Harvard professor Nancy Katz suggests that managers can learn from sports teams how to make teams more effective (Katz 2001). Here are some guidelines based on her work:

- Encourage cooperation and competition. The first leads to cohesion; the second energizes team members to do their best.

- Provide some early wins by assigning smaller, short-term, clearer tasks. The early successes build the team's confidence and create a success spiral.

- Break out of losing streaks through positive thinking, challenging the team to succeed, and focusing team members on outside rather than internal causes for failure.

- Take time to practice; during practice the focus should be on learning and experimentation rather than success.

- Keep the membership stable to develop cohesion and give members time to learn to work together.

- Review performance, particularly mistakes and failures; analyze problems, and learn from them.

Numerous organizations such as Toyota, General Foods, and Procter & Gamble have used self-managed teams successfully for decades. In fact, Procter & Gamble once claimed its self-managed teams were one of the company's trade secrets (Fisher 1993). Self-managed teams have the following six characteristics:

- *Power to manage their work.* Self-managed teams can set goals, plan, staff, schedule, monitor quality, and implement decisions.
- *Members with different expertise and functional experience.* Team members can be from marketing, finance, production, design, and so on. Without a broad range of experience, the team cannot manage all aspects of its work.
- *Absence of an outside manager.* The team does not report to an outside manager. Team members manage themselves, their budget, and their task through shared leadership. Stanley Gault, once chairman of Goodyear, the largest tire manufacturer in the United States, said that "the teams at Goodyear are now telling the boss how to run things. And I must say, I'm not doing half-bad because of it" (Greenwald 1992).
- *The power to implement decisions.* Team members have the power and the resources necessary to implement their decisions.
- *Coordination and cooperation with other teams and individuals affected by the teams' decisions.* Because each team is independent and does not formally report to a manager, the teams themselves rather than managers must coordinate their tasks and activities to assure integration.
- *Team leadership based on facilitation.* Leadership often rotates among members depending on each member's expertise in handling a specific situation. Instead of a leader who tells others what to do, sets goals, or monitors achievement, team leaders remove obstacles for the team and make sure that the team has the

resources it needs. The primary role of the team leader is to facilitate rather than control. Facilitation means that the leader focuses on freeing the team from obstacles to allow it to reach the goals it has set.

The success of the team depends on a number of key factors. First, the members of a team have to be selected carefully for their complementary skills and expertise. The interdependence among the members makes creation of the "right" combination critical. The right combination depends as much on technical skills as on interpersonal skills. Second, the team members need to focus on and be committed to the team goal. For example, individuals from different functional departments such as marketing or production, although selected because of their expertise in particular areas, need to leave the department mind-set behind and focus on the task of the team. Third, the team task must be appropriately complex, and the team has to be provided with the critical resources it needs to perform the task. Finally, the team needs enough power and authority to accomplish its task and implement its ideas. The sources of team power as presented in Chapter 4 are available to the team to allow it to perform its job.

Building an effective team is a time-consuming process that requires interpersonal team-building skills and extensive technical support. The development of trust, a common vision, and the ability to work well together depend on appropriate interpersonal skills. Trust requires a number of factors as presented in Figure 7-2. To build trust, team members must demonstrate integrity, hard work, and mutual respect. They must reward cooperation rather than competition, be fair to one

Figure 7-2
Building Trust

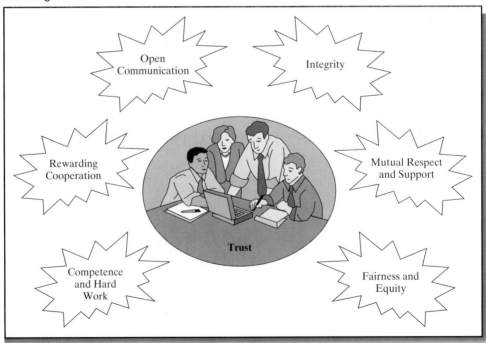

Part III   Current Developments and Applications

another, and communicate openly. They further must believe that their leaders—inside and outside the team—are predictable, have their best interests at heart, and will treat them fairly (Cunningham and MacGregor 2000).

Once the trust and goals are established, tackling complex tasks requires timely technical training. Many of these interpersonal and technical functions traditionally fall on the leader's shoulders. However, leadership in teams is often diffused, a factor that puts further pressure on individual team members to take on new tasks and challenges.

SUPER- AND SELF-LEADERSHIP

One of the applications of participative management and teams is the concept of self-managed teams and superleadership. With the increasing use of teams in organizations, many of the traditional roles of leaders are undergoing change (Lawler 1986). We are empowering individual employees, providing them with training in various areas of business, and expecting them to make many independent decisions. Teams are designed to complement individual employees' skills. Self-managed teams are responsible for continuous assessment and improvement of their own product, the design of their work, and all other work processes that affect them. Leadership often is elected or rotated, and strong pressure is put on individuals to accept responsibility for their decisions and actions.

These changes in the way we operate in many organizations are shifting the focus of attention away from the leader and to the subordinates. Charles Manz and Henry Sims have proposed a model for team leadership that involves self-leadership or superleadership of each team member (Manz 1990, 1992; Manz and Sims 1987, 1991). Superleadership is the process of leading people to lead themselves. As a result, team members are taught and encouraged to make their own decisions and accept responsibility to the point where they no longer need leaders. Super-leadership within teams means that all team members set goals, observe, evaluate, critique, reinforce, and reward one another and themselves. In such an environment, the need for one leader is reduced; team members decide what they need and how to achieve it. Superleadership includes the following elements (for a detailed discussion, see Manz and Neck 1999):

- *Developing positive and motivating thought patterns.* Individuals and teams seek and develop environments that provide positive cues and a supportive and motivating environment.
- *Personal goal setting.* Individuals and teams set their own performance goals and performance expectations.
- *Observation and self-evaluation.* Team members observe their own and other team members' behaviors and provide feedback, critique, and evaluate one another's performance.
- *Self-reinforcement.* Team members provide rewards and support to one another.

The role of leaders is, therefore, primarily to lead others to lead themselves or "to facilitate the self-leadership energy" within each subordinate (Manz and Sims 1991, p. 18). Contrary to views of heroic leadership whereby the leader is expected to provide answers to all questions and to guide, protect, and save subordinates, the concept of super- and self-leadership suggests that leaders must get their subordinates to the point where they do not need their leader much. In effect, through the use of job-design techniques, the development of a team culture, proper performance management, and the modeling of self-leadership, the leader sets up internal and external substitutes for leadership. The right job design and the team are the external substitutes (see Chapter 6). The employees' developing skills and internal motivation serve as internal substitutes for the presence and guidance of a leader (see Exercise 7-2).

In order to be successful, participative management and superleadership require the empowerment of employees (see Chapter 4) and the changing of an organization's culture. One of the key components of the cultural change is redefining the concepts of leadership and followership. Employees who have become superleaders do not require organizing, controlling, and monitoring from their leaders. Such redefinition requires a reconsideration of many of our current definitions of leadership, including the one presented in Chapter 1.

Role of Leaders in a Team Environment

Are leaders becoming obsolete? What happens to leadership when all employees become superleaders and the teams fulfill the traditional functions of leaders? This is a major worry of many managers. Once they implement participation and teams successfully, have they written themselves out of a job? The answers are complex and often depend on the situation and the leader. Some leaders never feel fully comfortable in a team environment, whereas others adapt to it well or even embrace it. Leaders of the first type are likely to feel that they are losing their job and might focus efforts on regaining control. Leaders of the second type might be able to redefine their role and continue contributing to the organization.

The only certainty is that the role of the leader changes in a team environment. Many practitioners (e.g., Katzenbach and Smith 1993) have begun referring to leaders as facilitators and coaches. Leaders are caretakers of their teams, helping them achieve their goals by providing them with instructions, encouragement when needed, and resources. Leader/facilitators still fulfill many of the functions of traditional leaders, but they do so to a lesser extent and only when asked. They assist the teams by obtaining the resources needed to solve problems and to implement solutions, and only interfere when needed. The leader's central activities, therefore, become assessing the team's abilities and skills and helping them develop necessary skills, which often includes getting the right type of training (see Figure 7-3). The team leaders also play the role of conflict and relationship manager while they continue doing real work themselves.

Another role for team leaders is to make the team aware of its boundaries. Many teams fail because they take on too much or ignore organizational realities and constraints. For example, a team of school teachers assigned the role of revising the social studies curriculum for fourth and fifth graders might propose changes that affect other parts of the curriculum and then be disappointed when its recommendations are not fully implemented. The role of the team leader would be to keep the

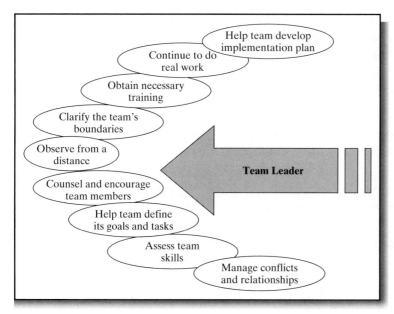

Figure 7-3
New Roles for
Leaders in
a Team
Environment

team focused on its specific task or to integrate the team with others who can help it with its wider recommendations.

An interesting development in the use of teams stems from the view that such structures might not be fully compatible with the Western cultural value of individualism. It has been suggested that teams, although needed as a structural element, are already passé and that the focus needs to shift to individual contributions within teams. The use of teams in the United States and many other Western industrialized nations was spurred by the West's interpretation of Japanese management style. The Japanese have dominated and continue to dominate many sectors of the global economy and give much of the credit for that success to their participative, team-based decision making and management style. It stands to reason, then, that adoption of some of the same management techniques and tools should help the Western industrialized nations regain their global economic positions. However, whereas production and technological tools such as just-in-time (JIT) systems have been implemented successfully in the West, the people and team-management issues have been considerably less successful.

The relative failure of Japanese-style teams in the West and most notably in the United States can be blamed partially on lack of cultural fit. The collectivist Japanese culture fits well within and supports their management styles. The Western cultures by and large are considerably more individualistic, and their values often conflict with team-based approaches. Australians might have come up with a new concept: *Collaborative individualism* could be the buzzword of the future in the West (Limerick 1990). Collaborative individuals are not limited by the boundaries of the group. However, they are cooperative and helpful to their team and organization while

The collectivist Japanese culture fits well within and supports its management styles. The Western cultures by and large are considerably more individualistic and often conflict with team-based approaches.

maintaining their internal motivation and conflict-tolerant skills. Based on a cultural analysis, such an approach could be much more suitable to many Western cultures, particularly those that are vertical individualists, than the Japanese search for consensus and conformity in a team (Nahavandi and Aranda 1994). Australian researchers propose that empathy with an ability to transform organizations and to be proactive with excellent political and conflict management and networking skills, creative thinking, and maturity is at the core of the new competencies needed by future managers. Teams still exist and continue to play a key role, but individuals will be the focus for performance.

SUMMARY AND CONCLUSION

This chapter presents the concepts of participative management and its extension and application to the use of teams in organizations. Although many benefits can be drawn from the use of participative management, its success depends on appropriate application. Cultural and organizational factors should determine the use of participation as a management tool. A basic application of participation is the use of delegation by a leader. Delegation must be implemented carefully and judiciously to ensure fair application; leaders must consider which tasks they should and can delegate and the individuals to whom they are delegating. Thorough feedback and monitoring are also important.

Participation has been formalized in many organizations through the creation of teams. The successful implementation of self-managed teams and superleadership points to the role of teams in revitalizing organizations. As teams continue to be used, their nature and role are changing, as is the role of leadership in a team environment. Despite the need for a contingency view in the use of participative management and teams, teams have become a basic management tool in many parts of the world. More focused attention on cultural factors along with a continued analysis of the success of participative management and teams should lead to continued evolution of the concepts.

Who Gets the Project?

Your department has 15 members who have all been with you for at least 1 year. Although the department is generally cohesive and performs well, you are grooming four "stars" for promotion, because you believe they are the best performers. You have just been handed a new account with a lot of potential, a tight deadline, and the need for considerable grooming and development. The success will not only give the person in charge of the project a lot of visibility, but also could impact your career in the company. Everyone in the department is aware of the importance of the project and several people, including your four stars, have volunteered to take it on. In particular, one of the members with the most tenure and experience (but not one of the four stars) has been pushing to get the project. Given the project's importance, you want this to be handled well and without too much direction from you.

As you are about to delegate the project to your top star, you receive a call from the human resources director telling you that one of the department members has filed an informal complaint against you, accusing you of favoritism. He can't tell you the name, but he wanted you to be aware of potential problems and the fact that he will be conducting informal fact-finding interviews.

1. Who will you assign to the project?
2. Consider the implications of your decision.

REVIEW AND DISCUSSION QUESTIONS

1. What is the role of participation in the development of leadership theory and practice?
2. How does culture affect an organization's ability to implement employee participation?
3. What organizational strategies can be used to help leaders delegate more often and more effectively?
4. Compare and contrast groups and teams. Provide an example of an effective team. What are the elements that contribute to its success?
5. What challenges do leaders face in managing teams?
6. What is the difference between delegation and implementation of self-managed teams?
7. What are the steps to superleadership and self-leadership?
8. How has the role of leaders changed in team environments? What functions remain?
9. Several researchers claim that the application of Japanese-style teams is culturally inappropriate in many Western cultures. Do you agree or disagree with such assertions? Why or why not?

SEARCHING THE WEB

Delegation:
www.tsbj.com/editorial/02090614.htm

The Secret of Great Teams:
drucker.org/leaderbooks/121/winter97/
bennis.html
www.gov.sk.ca/psc/mdcentre/
TL-Definition.htm

Different Types of Teams:
www-hr.ucsd.edu/~staffeducation/guide/
teamdef.html

EXERCISE 7-1: TO DELEGATE OR NOT TO DELEGATE?

This role play is designed to provide you with an opportunity to experience the challenges of delegation as a leader or as a follower. Read the following situation and description of team members.

Situation

You are a team manager in the public relations and marketing department at a major resort, Sunshine Incorporated. Your organization specializes in all-inclusive package vacations and has a reputation for excellent customer service. As a team manager, you are responsible for the supervision and development of four account managers in the corporate area. Your team's role is sales and service to corporate clients.

Your manager, the marketing director, has just handed you a new account that she inherited from another of the resort's partners. The client has been problematic in terms of payment and somewhat unreasonable demands, but it has a lot of potential. It is an entrepreneurial firm that your manager has referred to as "spoiled brats." However, successful handling of this client, you are told, is important. "We don't want to lose them; in fact, we really want them to be happy! Nobody seems to have figured out how, but I'm sure you will come up with something."

The four people in your team are:

Fran Smith: She has been with Sunshine for 4 years. She has a bachelor's degree in marketing from a major state university that she has obtained recently. She has some prior work experience with a restaurant supplier. Fran is a good performer with a lot of ambition, creativity, and motivation. You have assigned her many different tasks and they were all well done. Fran is one of your in-group people and you trust her a lot. You have had many discussions about future promotions, and she has followed your advice well. Fran has seemed to be in a slump for the past 3 months but has not talked to you about it and you have let it go, assuming that it might be a personal issue. Performance is still there, but some of the enthusiasm is gone.

Gerry Narden: Gerry has been with Sunshine for 10 years. He has completed a 2-year degree in business in a community college and got his first job as a desk clerk at the resort. Gerry has worked in many different parts of the resort and started in corporate sales only 6 months ago. He transferred in with outstanding evaluations from all his previous bosses. Gerry is the newest member of the team and has had some ups and downs in sales. One of them almost caused the loss of a major client. You had to intervene and managed to save the account. He seems to have learned from the experience and has been doing well in the past 2 months. You have not, however, given him any major accounts since, although he has been asking repeatedly for more challenge.

Terry Chan: Terry has been with your team for 5 years. Terry has a masters in communications and is a good performer. She has more than 10 years of work experience, most of which has been in sales and customer relations within Sunshine. Terry seems to have a knack for working with some of the big clients who keep coming back to her. She usually does not ask for assignments and is good at bringing in her own. Gerry has needed very little help or management from you and seems to do her own thing successfully.

J. P. Ricci: J. P. has been with the team for more than a year; this is his first job. He has been your major management challenge. A bright, Ivy League graduate with a degree in hotel and restaurant management and marketing, he has considerable sales skills, but J. P. wants to do things his own way. His clients are delighted with him when he puts his heart into things, but motivation seems to be lacking sometimes. Your discussions with J. P. lead you to believe that he is often bored and needs to be challenged. J. P. often talks about trying to find another job that would be a better fit, but he likes the sales and resort environment. He seems to be in search of direction. In spite of all this, he is a good performer and delivers when it counts.

Role Play

After reading the scenario, please wait for further information from your instructor.

WORKSHEET FOR MANAGERS

Who would you select to manage the account? What are your reasons?

Plan the meeting during which you will delegate the task. What do you need to say? What areas do you need to cover? How are you addressing your employees' needs?

WORKSHEET FOR EMPLOYEES

What do you need to do a good job?

Has your manager provided you with clear information about the task and expectations? What is done correctly? What is missing? Do you feel ready and motivated to take on the task?

Exercise 7-2: Strategies for Becoming a Superleader

Changing Behaviors

A. Self-Observation

Identify specific behaviors that are related to becoming a self-leader.

1.

2.

3.

Set specific goals for yourself for each behavior.

1.

2.

3.

Include a time line for each goal.

How will you measure your goals?

B. Set up Opportunities for Rehearsal

Identify settings where you can practice the new behaviors.

1.

2.

3.

Identify and work with individuals who can help you rehearse.

C. Establish Reminders
   Establish reminders in your work environment to encourage the new behaviors.
   1.

   2.

   3.

   List individuals who can help you.
   1.

   2.

   3.

D. Set Up Rewards and Punishments
   List rewards that would encourage you to use self-leadership behaviors. Clarify when each should be used.
   1.

   2.

   3.

   List punishments that would stop unwanted behaviors. Clarify when each should be used.
   1.

   2.

   3.

Changing Cognitive Patterns

A. Focus on Natural Rewards in Tasks
   List aspects of your job that can encourage the self-leadership behaviors naturally.

   1.

   2.

   3.

   Focus on the natural rewards.

B. Establish Constructive Thought Patterns
Look for opportunities rather than obstacles.

Use positive mental imagery.

Reevaluate your priorities, beliefs, and assumptions.

Source: Based on superleadership concepts developed by Manz, C. C., and H. P. Sims, Jr. 1987. Leading workers to lead themselves: The external leadership of self-managing work teams. *Administrative Science Quarterly* 32, 106–129; Manz, C. C., and H. P. Sims, Jr. 1991. Superleadership: Beyond the myth of heroic leadership. *Organizational Dynamics* 19, no. 4, 18–35.

SELF-ASSESSMENT 7-1: DELEGATION SCALE

Using the following scale, indicate how much you agree with the following items.

Strongly disagree	Disagree	Neutral	Agree	Strongly agree
1	2	3	4	5

_____ 1. I can do most jobs better and faster than my subordinates can.

_____ 2. Most of my tasks cannot be delegated to my subordinates.

_____ 3. Most of my subordinates do not have the appropriate level of skills to do the tasks that I could delegate to them.

_____ 4. I feel uncomfortable delegating many of my tasks to my subordinates.

_____ 5. I am responsible for my subordinates' mistakes, so I might as well do the task myself.

_____ 6. If my subordinates do too many of my tasks, I might not be needed any longer.

_____ 7. Explaining things to subordinates and training them often takes too much time.

_____ 8. My subordinates already have too much work to do; they can't handle any more.

_____ 9. If my subordinates do the tasks, I will lose touch and be out of the loop.

_____ 10. I need to know all the details of a task before I can delegate to my subordinates.

Scoring key: Your total score should be between 10 and 50. The higher your score is, the less inclined you are to delegate as you agree with many of the common excuses used by managers for not delegating tasks to their subordinates.

Total: _____

SELF-ASSESSMENT 7-2: ARE YOU A TEAM LEADER?

Rate yourself on each of the following items using the scale provided here:

1	2	3	4	5
Strongly disagree	Somewhat disagree	Neither agree nor disagree	Somewhat agree	Strongly agree

____ 1. I enjoy helping others get their jobs done.
____ 2. Managing others is a full-time job in and of itself.
____ 3. I am good at negotiating for resources.
____ 4. People often come to me to help them with interpersonal conflicts.
____ 5. I tend to be uncomfortable when I am not fully involved in the task that my group is doing.
____ 6. It is hard for me to provide people with positive feedback.
____ 7. I understand organizational politics well.
____ 8. I get nervous when I do not have expertise at a task that my group is performing.
____ 9. Effective leaders need to be fully involved with their team's activities.
____ 10. I am skilled at goal setting.

Scoring key: Reverse score items 2, 5, 6, 8, and 9 (1 = 5, 5 = 1). Add your score on all items. The maximum possible score is 50. The higher your score is, the more team leadership skills you have.   *Total:* _____

C A S E

Leadership in Action

Dian Graves Owen

From her friendly and modest demeanor and her easygoing style, you might have trouble recognizing Dian Graves Owen as the powerful chairman of the board of directors of Owen Healthcare, a company that employs 4,500 people and has revenues of more than $400 million (www.cardinalpps.com; www.texnews.com). Owen Healthcare is the largest U.S. provider of complete hospital pharmacy services including inventory, drugs and all other supplies, computer systems, and human resources help needed to run a pharmacy. The company's mission is "To provide value to our clients through innovative pharmacy and materials services . . . delivered with quality and integrity by dedicated professionals" (www.monster.com). Jean Owen, a pharmacist and Dian's late husband, founded Owen Healthcare in 1969 by contracting with several small hospitals to run their pharmacy.

When Jean Owen was killed in a plane crash in 1976, Dian fought hard to turn around the business. Jean had managed his company with an iron hand, and it was hard for Dian to find her own style of leadership. Finally, she focused on building relationships and relying on others. She sought the help of several trusted associates and slowly changed the way the company was managed. She states:

> I stopped trying to be someone I wasn't. We had very capable people, and I started giving them more authority and control, and I found it a great relief to be able to lay responsibility in others' lap. (Enkelis and Olsen 1995, p. 129)

She adds: "I learned that people thrive on responsibility, and as they grow, they become more valuable to me and to the company" (Enkelis and Olsen 1995, p. 129). For example,

although she previously planned every detail of the conventions her company attended, she gave away that responsibility to others.

Owen's employees have considerable autonomy on how to do their job. Focus is on collegiality and informality, and on keeping formal relationships to a minimum. Dian describes the company's structure: "I prefer to think that we work in concentric circles; activity goes on between equals moving out and in from a center, rather than a chain of command" (Enkelis and Olsen 1995, p. 130). She adds:

> I don't think in terms of rigid divisions of responsibility. Everybody knows what has to be done, and they do it. I can't do all the jobs that these people do—I'm not a pharmacist; I'm not an accountant. I have to trust them. (Enkelis and Olsen 1995, p. 130)

Teams of employees called Quality Teams make the major decisions at Owen's Healthcare:

> We believe so strongly in teamwork because it is a good way for as many people as possible to have a say about the things that affect them. We have made the team approach into a formalized process. (Enkelis and Olsen 1995, p. 130)

These teams define their own problems; find the people to work on them; and set goals, processes, and budgets. Some of the teams are permanent; most last 3 to 6 months and disband when they meet their goals.

Dian Owen's leadership style and her programs have paid off. Profits have been growing steadily, and 90 percent of the company's clients renew their contract with Owen. The company is particularly proud of its 1990 to 1993 100 percent renewal rate. Owen also enjoys strong employee loyalty and tries to maintain it by providing profit-driven bonuses and employee stock ownership plans, which over 10 years have distributed 32 percent of the company's stock to its employees. Dian Owen has been recognized as one of the top businesswomen in the United States (www.northwood.edu). She states "I feel a tremendous obligation to the people who work for Owen Healthcare . . . it is they who really make it go. It sometimes overwhelms me to realize how much trust they put in this company" (Enkelis and Olsen 1995, p. 131). ■

QUESTIONS

1. How would you describe Dian Owen's leadership style?
2. What is the role of participation and teams at Owen Healthcare?

3. In your opinion, why has the focus on participation and teams been successful?

Sources: Enkelis, L., and K. Olsen. 1995. *Portraits of women business leaders: On our own terms.* San Francisco: Berrett Koehler Publishers; Cardinal Health Provider Pharmacy Services, company.monster.com/owenhealth/, accessed April 16, 2002; Cardinal Health Provider Pharmacy Services, www.cardinalpps.com/about_chpps.htm, accessed April 16, 2002; Ray, Steve, "Dian Owen Inducted into Texas Women's Hall of Fame," www.texnews.com/news/owen013197.html, accessed April 16, 2002; Acceptance speech by Dian Graves Owen for Northwood University Outstanding Business Leaders Award, 1996, www.northwood.edu/obl/1996/owen.html.

Chapter 8

Change-Oriented Leadership

> *Be the change that you want to see in the world.*
>
> —Mahatma Ghandi

> *The people who get on in this world are the people who get up and look for circumstances they want, and, if they can't find them, make them.*
>
> —George Bernard Shaw

After studying this chapter, you will be able to:

1. Describe the various leader, follower, cultural, and situational characteristics that contribute to charismatic leadership.
2. Explain the positive and negative impact of charismatic leadership on organizations.
3. Distinguish between transactional and transformational leadership.
4. Understand the key role of contingent rewards and the impact of management by exception.
5. Present the elements of transformational leadership and their impact on followers and organizations.
6. Describe the roles of visionary and exemplary leadership in bringing about change in organizations.

*F*or many people, the concept of leadership conjures up images of political or organizational leaders who accomplish seemingly impossible feats. When asked to name leaders, people often mention Martin

Luther King Jr., Gandhi, and John F. Kennedy. These leaders and others like them exude confidence and engender strong emotional responses in their followers. They change their followers, organizations, and society, and even alter the course of history. These leaders have a special relationship with their followers that goes beyond setting goals, using resources, and conducting business. They have charisma and are set on changing the world.

Although Max Weber introduced the concept of charisma in the early 1920s, it did not enter the scientific study of leadership until the mid-1970s. Since then, researchers have developed the concept of charisma for application to organizational contexts (Conger 1989a; Conger and Kanungo 1987; House 1977) and created several models of leadership that focus on large-scale change in organizations. Many of these models focus on the relationship between leaders and followers and can, therefore, be considered part of the exchange and relationship-development models presented in Chapter 6. However, because of their popularity and increasing research, and because they do not rely fully on contingency approaches, these models are treated separately here. This chapter presents the related models of charismatic, transformational, and visionary leadership and focuses on change-related models of leadership, research findings, and applications of the models.

A BRIEF HISTORY OF CHARISMATIC AND TRANSFORMATIONAL LEADERSHIP AND ITS IMPACT

Although not yet old enough to have a "history," the theories and research focused on transformational and charismatic leadership as used in management and organizational behavior situations have evolved and been refined considerably since their first introduction in the 1970s. The research on charismatic and transformational leadership is credited with bringing much-needed new life and enthusiasm to the field of leadership (Hunt 1999), which around the 1970s and 1980s was strongly criticized for being irrelevant, trivial, and inconsequential (see McCall and Lombardo 1978; Mintzberg 1982).

Several well-established leadership researchers such as Bernard Bass and Robert House shifted their attention to these new models, and many of the young researchers entering the field made charismatic and transformational leadership their area of research. The renewed interest moved the research from purely theoretical and primarily case-oriented research to the much-needed empirical investigations of various constructs (Conger 1999). The models of charismatic and transformational leadership provide several advantages over other views of leadership presented in this book. First, they allow us to look at a different aspect of leaders and their role as inspirational visionaries and builders of organizational cultures (Hunt 1999). Second, they highlight the importance of followers' emotional reactions (Chemers 1977). Finally, they focus on leaders at top levels who are the subject of study in strategic leadership (covered in Chapter 9), thereby allowing for a potential integration of upper echelon research with transformational and charismatic leadership.

The models that are presented in this chapter still need considerable development and are subject to much continued debate, but their predictions and explanations are a first step in addressing a growing need in today's organizations for understanding how leaders orchestrate and manage large-scale change.

CHARISMATIC LEADERSHIP: A RELATIONSHIP BETWEEN LEADERS AND FOLLOWERS

The word *charisma* means "an inspired and divine gift." Those who have the gift are divinely endowed with grace and talent. Charismatic leaders capture the imagination and inspire their followers' devotion and allegiance. We describe political and religious leaders as charismatic, but leaders in business organizations also can be charismatic. Charismatic leaders are defined as "leaders who have a profound emotional effect on their followers" (House 1977). Followers see them not merely as bosses but as role models and heroes who are larger than life.

> Charismatic leaders have a profound emotional effect on their followers. Followers see them not merely as bosses but as role models and heroes who are larger than life.

At MicroStrategy, a company that specializes in converting data into meaningful and useful information and distributes it through wireless devices, employees feed off of their CEO Michael Saylor's passion, dedication, intensity, and confidence (Salter 2000). Howard Charney, the founder of Grand Junction Networks, a producer of digital switches based in California that was bought out by Cisco Systems, engenders similar reactions in his followers. Debra Pelsma, who worked as buyer and planner at Grand Junction, describes her first meeting with Charney: "He was so optimistic, so sincere, so genuine, I decided I'd follow him anywhere" (Dillon 1998, p. 92). Kathryn Gould, a venture capitalist and lead investor in the company, echoes Pelsma's feelings: "He is the kind of guy people walk through walls for" (Dillon 1998, p. 92). Charney's view is simple: "What do people come to work for? To be successful. To be appreciated" (Dillon 1998, p. 94).

Saylor and Charney are charismatic leaders. They inspire their followers, and their followers are in turn loyal to them. This type of relationship, although desirable, is not typical of all leadership situations. The relationship goes beyond a simple exchange; it also involves an intense bond between leaders and their followers. The following sections consider the three elements of charismatic leadership: leader characteristics, follower characteristics, and the leadership situation.

Characteristics of Charismatic Leaders

Charismatic leaders have several common personality and behavioral characteristics (see Table 8-1). Although many of the characteristics—such as self-confidence, energy, and the ability to communicate well—are related to all types of leadership, their combination is what sets apart the charismatic leaders.

Table 8-1
Characteristics of Charismatic Leaders

- High degree of self-confidence
- Strong conviction about ideas
- High energy and enthusiasm levels
- Expressiveness and excellent communication skills
- Active image building and role modeling

One of the defining characteristics of charismatic leaders is their self-confidence in their own abilities and in the correctness and the moral righteousness of their beliefs and actions (Bass 1985). Gandhi's unwavering beliefs about the need for change in India and Martin Luther King Jr.'s single-minded focus on civil rights are two often-cited examples of this aspect of charismatic leaders. The self-confidence is associated with lack of internal conflict. Whereas noncharismatic leaders doubt themselves in the face of failure and criticism, charismatic leaders know they are right and project that confidence. Their high level of confidence in their actions motivates their followers and creates a self-fulfilling prophecy. The more confident the leader is, the more motivated the followers are, and they then carry out the leader's wishes wholeheartedly. Such motivation and hard work increase the chances of success, which provides proof of the leader's righteousness.

Steve Case is the 39-year-old CEO of America Online (AOL); he shows self-confidence and strong conviction in his beliefs. He has made others believe in his vision of connecting everyone through the Internet. One of Case's associates explains:

> In a little company everybody's got to believe. But there needs to be somebody who believes no matter what. That was Steve. Steve believed from the first day that this was going to be a big deal. (Gunther 1998, p. 71)

Many examples of the charismatic leader's self-confidence also can be found in political leaders. Fidel Castro has withstood considerable pressure over the past 40 years and has remained undaunted in his approach. AnSan su Kyi, the leader of the political resistance in Burma, has been under house arrest for many years, yet she is unwavering in proclaiming her agenda for democratic reform. President Gamal Abdul Nasser of Egypt galvanized Arab pride in the 1950s and 1960s, and his view of a united Arab world dominated the psyche and dreams of millions in the Middle East.

Along with a high level of self-confidence, charismatic leaders have high energy levels. They are enthusiastic about their ideas and actions. They are highly expressive, and their nonverbal cues lend dramatic support to the verbal message they deliver with considerable skill. They have exceptional articulation skills that allow them to communicate the content of their ideas and their excitement about them to their subordinates (Conger 1991). Martin Luther King Jr.'s considerable oratory skills provide an example, as do Hitler's. Excellent communication skills allow the charismatic leader to define the mission of the organization or the group in a way that makes it meaningful and relevant to followers. This process of framing puts the goals of the leader in a worthwhile context that is used to draw and motivate followers

(Conger 1991; Fairhurst and Sarr 1996). Charismatic leaders emphasize the group's history and common past, their common identity, and future hopes and common goals (Shamir, Arthur, and House 1994). In addition, charismatic leaders appeal to the emotions of their followers through the use of language, symbols, and imagery.

Charismatic leaders carefully craft their message and present themselves as role models to their followers. They "walk the talk," whether is it through the self-sacrifice that they demand of their followers or the self-control they demonstrate. House and Shamir (1993) note that a large number of charismatic political leaders have spent time in prison, which demonstrates their willingness to take risks to achieve their vision. For example, Gandhi and Nelson Mandella were imprisoned for defending their beliefs. AnSan su Kyi has been under house arrest for many years. Still other charismatic leaders, such as Martin Luther King Jr. role modeling the peaceful resistance he advocated, demonstrate through their actions what they expect of their followers.

Hatim Tyabji, president of Verifone, Incorporated of California, states:

> The first principle of leadership is authenticity: Watch what I do, not what I say. Leadership requires moral authority. You can't have moral authority if you behave differently from your people. If you want your people to be frugal, then don't spend money on perks designed to make your life more comfortable. (Tyabji 1997, p. 98)

Cheong Choong Kong, the CEO of Singapore Airlines who was named *Fortune* magazine's Asia Businessman of the Year, sets such an example of austerity and frugality for his followers. He works in a small office, sometimes flies coach on his own airline, and along with other managers, gave up a raise, inspiring employees to do likewise (Kraar 1999).

The process of role modeling also can be symbolic, as was the case with the well-publicized $1 salary that Lee Iaccoca accepted while receiving considerable income from stock options and other benefits. PepsiCo's CEO Roger Enrico similarly decided to forgo his $900,000 salary in 1998 and instead asked the company's board to spend the money on scholarships for the children of PepsiCo employees (Deogun and Lublin 1998). Whether actual or symbolic, role modeling and powerful verbal messages contribute to the enhanced image of the leader. Cult leaders make use of all these behaviors to create a powerful and self-perpetuating mystique that strengthens their relationship and their hold on followers.

Charismatic leaders are masterful impression managers (Conger 1989a; House 1977). They surround themselves with dramatic and mystical symbols that further enhance the image of the leader as a larger-than-life figure. Bass (1985) cites John F. Kennedy as a case in point. His administration carefully developed the image of Camelot, complete with Guinevere and the knights who were fighting in the battle against communism. The competition to conquer space before the Russians further contributed to the mystical and heroic image of a youthful statesman who struggled to pull the United States out of the stodgy Eisenhower era. The power of these symbols and their resulting emotional bonds is evidenced by the strong sense of loss after President Kennedy's assassination.

Organizational leaders use equally effective symbols to maintain their image. In the case of Steve Case of AOL, the mystique includes being one of the gang. One

AOL employee describes him as follows: "Nothing about him says media mogul—he lunches on turkey sandwiches and Sun Chips, and has the boyish good looks of an aging fraternity brother (Gunther 1998, p. 71).

Overall, considerable agreement has been reached over the characteristics of charismatic leaders (Conger 1999). The next requirement is developing followers who are devoted to the leader.

Characteristics of Followers

Because charismatic leadership results from an interaction and relationship between a leader and followers, the followers of such leaders generally display certain characteristics. Without the leader and the follower characteristics, no charismatic relationship can form. Take away the frenzied followers and Hitler would not have been considered charismatic. The same is true for many cult leaders. Even for positive and constructive charismatic leaders such as Gandhi, followers demonstrate particular characteristics and behaviors (see Table 8-2). First and foremost, followers hold the leader in high esteem. They are strongly devoted to the leader, and an intense emotional bond forms between followers and their charismatic leader. They admire their leader; emulate the leader's behaviors and mannerisms; and are likely to talk, dress, and act like the leader. The intense emotional bond and attraction to the leader create a situation whereby followers will obey the leader without question. They have total confidence in the leader's vision and direction. Once the identification process takes place, complete internalization of the leader's values and aspirations occurs. In addition, some followers' personality traits have been linked to the development of charismatic relationships. In particular, it has been suggested that self-monitoring and self-concept might affect how the charismatic relationship develops (Weierter 1997).

Charismatic leaders are able to connect their followers to their own vision. Researchers have suggested that charismatic leaders change the followers' perception of the nature of what needs to be done. They also offer an appealing vision of the future, develop a common identity, and heighten the followers' self-esteem and sense of self-efficacy (for a review, see Conger 1999). In addition, one of the key components of the emergence of charismatic leaders is for the followers to perceive a need for change because the current state is unacceptable and because they believe that a crisis is either imminent or already exists (Shamir 1991; Trice and Beyer 1993). The final element of charismatic leadership is, therefore, the situation.

Table 8-2
Characteristics of Followers of Charismatic Leaders

- High degree of respect and esteem for the leader
- Loyalty and devotion to the leader
- Affection for the leader
- High performance expectations
- Unquestioning obedience

Based on the assumption that charisma is not only a characteristic of a leader but also a relationship between a leader and followers, researchers Mark Ehrhart and Katherine Klein investigated the "attributes of followers that distinguish the loyal and committed followers of charismatic leaders" (2001, p. 154.). Their research is based on four assumptions. First, followers will respond differently to the same leadership behavior. Second, followers' similarity and attraction to the leader and their need for satisfaction will affect how they react to leadership. Third, individual preferences for a particular type of leadership are likely to predict one's reaction to the leader. Finally, how followers describe and evaluate their leader impacts organizational outcomes such as satisfaction, turnover, and performance.

Ehrhart and Klein measured nine follower characteristics (achievement; risk taking; self-esteem; need for structure; and intrinsic, extrinsic, interpersonal, security, and participation work value) of 267 students and studied their impact on their preference for charismatic, task-oriented, and relationship-oriented leadership styles. The researchers found clear preferences for leadership style, with 50 percent of the students selecting a relationship-oriented leader, 30 percent a charismatic leader, and 20 percent a task-oriented leader. They also found variations in how the same behavior is seen and perceived by different people. Risk taking was the only follower characteristic that was not related to preferences for leadership style. The results further indicate that followers with a strong worker participation value and those low in security work value are most attracted to charismatic leadership, while those who value extrinsic rewards might be most satisfied with relationship-oriented leaders, and those with strong security values prefer task-oriented leaders.

Source: Ehrhart, M. G., and K. J. Klein. 2001. Predicting followers' preferences for charismatic leadership: The influence of follower values and personality. *Leadership Quarterly* 12, no. 2, 153–179.

The Charismatic Situation

A crisis causes followers to look for new solutions. During a time of crisis, followers are ready for change. If an individual is able to capture and represent the needs and aspirations of the group, that individual is likely to become the group leader. In addition, individuals who demonstrate competence and loyalty to a group and its goals are provided with "credit" that they can spend to assume leadership roles. This idiosyncrasy credit allows certain individuals to emerge as leaders and change the direction of the group (Hollander 1979). Because of the strong emotional impact of charismatic leaders, followers provide them with tremendous leeway (credit) to lead the group into new territory.

External Crisis and Turbulence

At the heart of the issue of charismatic leadership is how certain individuals emerge as leaders in leaderless groups or to replace an appointed leader. Many charismatic revolutionary leaders achieve their status without being designated formally. In organizations, although charismatic leaders sometimes are elected or appointed, they often have been recognized already as charismatic leaders by a group of followers. The official appointment is the last step in their rise to power, which often occurs during a time of crisis. Popular political and religious leaders, such as Martin Luther King Jr. or Ronald Reagan, already had won the hearts and minds of their followers, who carried them into formal positions.

Table 8-3 summarizes the external situational elements that contribute to the development of charismatic leadership. Although not all researchers believe that a situation of crisis is necessary for the emergence of charismatic leadership, many suggest that a sense of distress or crisis is necessary for the emergence and *success* of charismatic leaders (Bass 1985; Beyer 1999b; Shamir and Howell 1999). Research by Roberts and Bradley (1988) suggests that situations of crisis provide more latitude for leader initiative such that the person can demonstrate leadership abilities. In crisis situations, charismatic leaders are perceived by followers to be the only ones who can resolve the crisis. Therefore, they emerge in situations where there is a need to articulate change and a new ideological vision, and when followers are ready to be saved or more simply moved in a different direction. With an emotionally charged situation, charismatic leaders enter the field promising a new beginning, radical solutions, and a break from the unwanted values of the past (Boal and Bryron 1987). They use dramatic symbols to illustrate their goals, and point to clear and specific roles that their followers can play in resolving the crisis. As a result, followers are convinced that the charismatic leader is the only one who can help, and followers each become aware of how they can contribute personally.

All the historical charismatic leaders share this element. Consider Cyrus the Great of Persia, who united warring tribes in 1500 B.C.; Napoléon, who galvanized post-revolutionary France; Lakshmi the Maharani of the Indian state of Jansi, who became the symbol of the anticolonial Cipaye revolt of 1857; the fascist dictators of modern European history; and the U.S. civil rights leaders of the 1960s: They all brought a new vision of the future to their eager followers. In all cases, the crises and the perceived need for change prepared the stage for the charismatic leaders' skills.

Internal Organizational Conditions for the Emergence of Charismatic Leadership

In addition to a sense of external crisis, researchers have suggested that several internal organizational conditions also facilitate charismatic leadership (Shamir and Howell 1999).

- *Organizational life cycle:* Charismatic leaders are more likely to emerge and be effective in the early and late stages of an organization's life cycle, when either no set direction is established or change and revival are needed.

Table 8-3
External Elements of Charismatic Situations

- Sense of real or imminent crisis
- Perceived need for change
- Opportunity to articulate ideological goal
- Availability of dramatic symbols
- Opportunity to clearly articulate followers' role in managing the crisis

- *Type of task and reward structure.* Complex, challenging, and ambiguous tasks that require initiative and creativity and where external rewards cannot be clearly tied to performance can be ideal situations for charismatic leaders.
- *Organizational structure and culture.* Flexible and organic structures and non-bureaucratic organizational cultures are likely to encourage charismatic leadership.

Although some evidence is available to support these propositions, empirical testing is needed before they can be established fully as conditions for the emergence of charismatic leadership.

Role of Culture

As you have read throughout this book, culture strongly affects what behaviors and styles are considered appropriate and effective for leaders (Gerstner and Day 1994; Lord and Maher 1991). Therefore, it makes sense that culture would impact charismatic leadership, as well. Interestingly, although considerable research has been conducted about charismatic leadership, few studies have considered cross-cultural issues (Hunt and Conger 1999).

Based on the nature and elements of charismatic leadership, it would stand to reason that cultures that have a strong tradition for prophetic salvation, in particular, would be more amenable to charismatic leadership. For example, the Judeo-Christian beliefs of the coming of the savior create fertile ground for charismatic leaders to emerge and be accepted. Prophets by definition are charismatic saviors. Israel, for example, has this type of strong tradition. Another case in point is the recent rise of Islamic fundamentalism, which typically is tied to a prophetic spiritual leader, as is the case in the Sudan and Iran (Dekmejian and Wyszomirski 1972). The case of Khomeini in Iran illustrates all the elements of a typical charismatic relationship, including leader and follower characteristics, the intense and calculated image management on the part of the leader, and the sense of crisis due to the political climate of Iran in the 1970s (F. Nahavandi 1988; H. Nahavandi 1994).

In cultures that do not have such prophetic traditions, few strong charismatic figures are likely to emerge. For example, in China, although periods of crisis and change certainly have occurred, it appears that the relationship between leader and followers is based more on the social hierarchy and need for order, as is prescribed in the Confucian tradition, than on the intense emotional charismatic bonds that exist in Judeo-Christian religions. Such seems to be the case for one of the few charismatic Chinese leaders, Mao Zedong. Furthermore, the development of a charismatic relationship in a culture such as Japan needs to rely on the leader's development of an image of competence and moral courage, and the securing of respect from followers (Tsurumi 1982); by contrast, in India, charismatic leadership is associated with a religious, almost supernatural state (Singer 1969).

The one exception to the inclusion of culture in the study of charismatic leadership is the GLOBE research program, which focuses specifically on effective leader behaviors and attributes in 60 countries (Den Hartog et al. 1999). The basic assumption of the research project is that ". . . charismatic leadership will be universally reported as facilitating 'outstanding' leadership" (Den Hartog et al. 1999, p. 230). The researchers found that although some attributes are universally endorsed and some are universally negative, several attributes are culturally contingent (see Table 8-4 for a summary). It is important to note that although several of the behaviors associated with charismatic leadership are universally associated with effectiveness, the term *charisma* evokes mixed reactions in different cultures. In other words, being charismatic is seen as both positive and negative.

In addition to characteristics typically associated with charismatic leadership (e.g., positive and dynamic), Table 8-4 also presents other characteristics (e.g., being a team builder and being intelligent) that are not part of charisma. Interestingly, although having a vision is universally associated with leadership, how it is expressed and communicated differs greatly across cultures. For example, Chinese leaders are seen as effective if they communicate their vision in a nonaggressive and soft-spoken manner, while Indians prefer bold and assertive leaders (Den Hartog et al. 1999). Similarly, communicating with followers is valued universally, but the communication style (e.g., level of directness, tone of voice, and so forth) that is considered desirable is highly culture specific. Furthermore, risk taking, an important component of charismatic leadership in the United States, does not contribute to outstanding leadership in other cultures such as Mexico (Martinez and Dorfman 1998).

The Dark Side of Charisma

Although the popular business press is full of examples of inspiring leaders, the potential negative effects of charisma are not fully addressed. Given the charismatic leaders' strong emotional hold on followers, they can abuse that power easily and use it toward inappropriate ends. Researchers have identified several aspects of unethical charismatic leadership (Bass and Steidlmeier 1999; Conger 1990; Howell 1988; Howell and Avolio 1992).

Table 8-4
Cross-Cultural Attributes of Leadership

UNIVERSALLY POSITIVE	UNIVERSALLY NEGATIVE	CULTURALLY CONTINGENT
• Encouraging and positive	• Being a loner	• Risk taking
• Motivational	• Being noncooperative	• Enthusiasm
• Dynamic	• Ruthelss	• How vision is communicated
• Having integrity	• Nonexplicit	• What constitutes good
• Being trustworthy	• Irritable	communication
• Team builder	• Dictatorial	• How much leader is seen
• Decisive		as equal
• Intelligent		
• Communicator		
• Win-win problem solver		

Source: Based on information in Den Hartog, D., R. J. House, P. J. Hanges, and S. A. Ruits-Quintana and associates. 1999. Culture specific and cross-culturally generalizable implicit leadership theories: Are attributes of charismatic/transformational leadership universally endorsed? *Leadership Quarterly* 10, no. 2, 219–256.

The major difference
between ethical and unethical charismatic leaders is
the focus on personal goals
rather than on organiza-
tional goals. Unethical
leaders use their gift and
special relationship with
followers to advance
their vision and to exploit
followers.

The major difference between ethical and unethical charismatic leaders is the unethical leaders' focus on personal goals rather than organizational goals. Unethical leaders use their gift and special relationship with followers to advance their personal vision and to exploit followers; they have an internal and personal orientation. Ethical charismatic leaders use their power to serve others, develop followers, and achieve the common vision. They have an external orientation that is focused on serving their followers (Weierter 1997).

The unethical charismatic leader censures opposing views and engages in one-way communication, whereas the ethical one accepts criticism and remains open to communication from followers. Given the considerable power of some charismatic leaders and their extensive and intense bond with their followers, it is easy to see how the line between ethical and unethical behaviors can be blurred. Leaders who are convinced of their vision, have no doubts about its righteousness, and have the ability to persuade often will do so without concern for others. The characteristics of self-confidence and skillful modeling and persuasion that make a charismatic leader effective also can be the sources of highly destructive outcomes.

Distinguishing between the two types of charismatic leadership further helps explain how negative leadership can develop. Howell (1988) contrasts socialized and personalized charismatic leaders. Socialized leaders focus on satisfying their followers' goals and on developing a message that is congruent with shared values and needs. Personalized leaders rely on getting followers to identify and agree with their personal values and beliefs. Both examples demonstrate all the characteristics of charismatic leaders, their followers, and the situation. However, personalized leadership situations are more prone to abuse.

In addition to the potential for power abuse and corruption, charismatic leaders also might present other liabilities ranging from a flawed vision that is self-serving to unrealistic estimates of the environment (Conger and Kanungo 1998). The charismatic leader's skills at impression management and influence also can become a liability when leaders mislead their followers with exaggerated estimates of their own or their followers' abilities and the chances for success. Other potential liabilities of charismatic leadership include failure to manage details, failure to develop successors, creation of disruptive in- and out-groups, and engagement in disruptive and unconventional behaviors (Conger and Kanungo 1998).

Evaluation and Application

The considerable changes that many organizations have undergone in recent years have created a sense of crisis and resulted in a perceived need for revitalization and change. Therefore, it is no coincidence that the concept of charismatic leadership has dominated U.S. academic and popular views of leadership in recent years. The need to revitalize industrial, educational, health, and governmental institutions has created one of the essential elements for charismatic leadership. We are making considerable demands on our leaders to provide us with revolutionary ideas and are often disappointed when they cannot fulfill those expectations. In fact, our expectations are so high that we are bound to be disappointed.

Researchers have developed a number of different approaches to explain charismatic leadership, ranging from an attributional perspective whereby the leader's behavior and the situation persuade followers to attribute charismatic characteristics to the leader (Conger 1989a; Conger and Kanungo 1987) to self-concept views that focus on explaining how charismatic leaders can influence and motivate their followers (Shamir, House, and Arthur 1993) to psychoanalytic perspectives (Kets de Vries 1993). Much debate has taken place about the sociological and organizational views of charismatic leadership regarding its contents, focus, and its situational antecedents (Bass 1999; Beyer 1999a and b; House 1999; Shamir 1999). Various studies have tested numerous elements of the different views of charismatic leadership, although the results have not always been consistent (for an example, see Shamir et al. 1998). However, continued research is providing strong support for the existence and importance of understanding charismatic relationships and how such leaders impact their followers and their organizations.

The charismatic relationship is a powerful and undeniable part of the most celebrated leadership situations in Western culture. Charismatic leaders and their followers can achieve incredible feats. However, such leadership is not required for an organization to be successful. Indeed, it can be destructive, as is the case of negative charismatic leadership or when a charismatic leader is wrong and drives the organization to failure. Finally, it is important to remember that charismatic leadership is not a cure-all (Bryman 1992; Trice and Byer 1993). In addition, because it is difficult if not impossible to train someone to be a charismatic leader (Trice and Byer 1993), the phenomenon depends on one individual rather than on stable organizational processes that can be put in place once the leader is gone. With all its potential benefits, charismatic leadership is a double-edged sword that requires careful monitoring to avert abuse. Although charismatic leadership has a negative side because of the many destructive charismatic historical figures, transformational leadership, which is presented next, relies on charisma as one element but concentrates on the positive role of leadership in change.

TRANSACTIONAL AND TRANSFORMATIONAL LEADERSHIP

How do leaders create and sustain revolutionary change in organizations? What style of leadership is needed to motivate followers to undertake organizational transformations? Several researchers have proposed transformational leadership concepts to answer these questions, and to describe and explain how leaders succeed in achieving large-scale change in organizations. First developed by Burns (1978), transformational leadership suggests that some leaders, through their personal traits and their relationships with followers, go beyond a simple exchange of resources and productivity.

The leadership models presented in previous chapters focus on the transaction and exchange between leaders and followers. For example, in the Path-Goal Theory, the leader clears obstacles in exchange for follower motivation by providing structure to the task or by being considerate. Such basic exchanges have been labeled transactional leadership and are considered an essential part of leadership. Leaders must understand and manage such exchanges well. However, they need to supplement them with transformational leadership, which focuses on changing followers and organizations.

LEADING CHANGE
Changing the Soft Stuff: The EDS Culture

For much of its early days, Electronic Data Systems (EDS), the company that Ross Perot built, was known for its pioneering moves in information technology, its speed, and its cutting-edge technology. Sometime between the time GM acquired and divested EDS and the time it became independent again, EDS got lost. When Dick Brown became EDS's CEO in 1999, the company was sluggish, lacked identity and focus, and was performing poorly.

Dick Brown started sending the clear message that: "What we do well is focus on the client. I have said to EDS people 'You serve that client better than the client expects to be served'" (Burke and Lingblom 2002). To achieve this goal, Brown focuses on the company culture and its people. He believes: "You can't change a business with numbers. Numbers are the end result. You change a business, by changing the behavior of its people" (Breen, 2001, pp. 108, 112). The old Perot EDS culture was highly individualistic and competitive, but Brown wanted the new EDS to focus on speed, information sharing, and cooperation. Brown is looking for ideas and wants everyone at EDS to make a commitment to serve the customer above all else.

A monthly "performance call" publicly reviews all managers' performance.

> We don't try to embarrass people with those calls, we try to help them. At the same time, facts are facts . . . A commitment is your pledge to get the job done. And that's how we strive to behave as a team. (Breen 2001, p. 113)

Brown's relentless push has paid off. EDS has seen 12 percent to 19 percent increases in various performance measures, and the CEO is now launching new projects to increase the sales team by 50 percent so that it can close new deals estimated to be worth $48 billion (Burke and Lingblom 2002).

Sources: Breen, B. 2001. How EDS got its groove back. *Fast Company* (October), 106–117; Burke, S., and M. Lingblom. 2002. Green light for EDS, www.crn.channelsupersearch.com/news/crn/33678.asp, accessed April 18, 2002.

Transactional Leadership

Transactional leadership is based on the concept of exchange between leaders and followers. The leader provides followers with resources and rewards in exchange for motivation, productivity, and effective task accomplishment. This exchange and the concept of providing contingent rewards is at the heart of much of motivation, leadership, and management theory and practice. Transactional leadership can take two forms.

Contingent Reward

Leaders can be taught to provide contingent rewards, reinforce appropriate behavior, and discourage inappropriate behavior. When well managed, contingent rewards are highly satisfying and beneficial to the leader, the followers, and the organization. The informal and formal performance contracts that often result are also highly desirable and effective in managing performance (Bass 1985).

Management by Exception

Another type of transactional relationship is management by exception (MBE), which is a popular technique with many managers. In such situations, the leader intervenes only when things go wrong. In one type of MBE, labeled "active MBE," leaders monitor follower activities and correct mistakes as they happen (Bass and Avolio 1990a). In another type, labeled "laissez-faire," the leaders are passive and indifferent toward followers and their tasks. In both cases, little positive reinforcement or encouragement is given; the leader relies almost exclusively on discipline and punishment. Some managers confuse this style with empowerment. After all, it does appear that followers have freedom to do as they please, as long as they do not make a mistake. However, such comparisons are not warranted. Encouragement and the creation of a supportive and positive environment in which risk taking is encouraged are at the heart of empowerment. Such an environment does not result from MBE.

Despite the success of transactional relationships in achieving performance, particularly the use of contingent rewards, an exclusive focus on such exchanges and transactions with followers has been blamed for low expectations of followers and minimal performance in organizations (Zaleznik 1990). Furthermore, using MBE, particularly laissez-faire, as a primary leadership style has little impact or a negative impact on follower performance and satisfaction. Transactional contracts do not inspire followers to aim for excellence; rather, they focus on short-term, immediate outcomes. Long-term inspiration requires transformational leadership.

Transformational Leadership

Many leadership scholars and practitioners (Bass 1985, 1990b; Bennis and Nanus 1985; Conger and Kanungo 1998) have proposed that today's organizations need leadership that inspires followers and enables them to enact revolutionary change. Transformational leadership theory proposes that leaders use behaviors that are more complex than initiation of structure and consideration. Based on the observations of many leaders, it is clear that the two dimensions cannot account for the full range of behaviors ascribed to many leaders. Transformational leadership also suggests that the majority of leadership theories focus on the exchange and transaction between leaders and their followers. For example, much attention has been paid in the health care industry to the role of hospital administrators in guiding their organizations in uncertain times. Institutions such as Harbor Health Systems focus on clarifying each person's role in the accomplishment of the organization's mission. Pacific Presbyterian stresses strong leadership commitment to the organization's mission and goals. Young leaders such as Mark Wallace of Texas Children's Hospital are celebrated for their vision, creativity, and ability to inspire followers (Lutz 1992). All of these factors are needed to create a new vision to deal with the dynamic and often-threatening environment that characterizes the health care industry.

Transformational CEOs from the industrial and service sectors are also at the center of attention, and many, such as Jack Welch of GE and Andy Grove of Intel, have become management gurus who provide others with extensive advice.

Transformational leadership includes three factors (see Figure 8-1). These factors and transactional leadership are measured through the Multifactor Leadership Questionnaire (MLQ) (Bass and Avolio 1990b).

Charisma and Inspiration

The concept of charisma described previously is one of the three central elements of transformational leadership (Bass 1985; Bass and Avolio 1993). In fact, much of the recent theory and research about charisma do not differentiate it from transformational leadership and refer to the two concepts at the same time. The charismatic-leadership relationship creates the intense emotional bond between leaders and followers. The result is complete loyalty and trust in, as well as emulation of, the leader. Followers are inspired to implement the leader's vision. The strong loyalty and respect of a charismatic relationship pave the way for undertaking major change.

Intellectual Stimulation

The second factor in transformational leadership is the leader's ability to challenge followers to solve problems. The leaders and the group question existing values and assumptions and search for new answers. By encouraging them to look at problems in new ways and requiring new solutions, the leader pushes followers to perform beyond what they previously considered possible. The charismatic bond provides support and encouragement in this endeavor and prevents followers from feeling isolated. Intellectual stimulation has a strong empowering component, which assures followers of their abilities and capabilities, and enables them to search out new solutions.

Figure 8-1
Transformational Leadership Factors

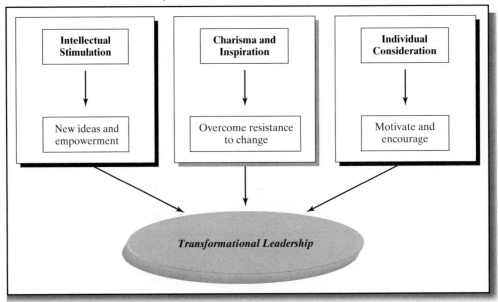

Individual Consideration

The last factor of transformational leadership, the development of a personal relationship with each follower, is closely related to the LMX model presented in Chapter 6 (Howel and Hall-Meranda 1999). The leader treats each follower differently but equitably, providing all with individual attention. As a result, followers feel special, encouraged, and motivated. The leader's individual consideration also allows for matching each follower's skills and abilities to the needs of the organization.

The three factors—charisma and inspiration, intellectual stimulation, and individual consideration—combine to allow the leader to undertake the necessary changes in an organization. The charismatic emotional bond overcomes the psychological and emotional resistance to change. The intellectual stimulation provides the new solutions and innovation, and empowers followers. The individual relationship between leader and follower encourages followers and provides them with additional motivation. The transactional leadership behaviors support the maintenance of the routine aspects of the organization. In terms of the definition of leadership and organizational effectiveness presented in Chapter 1, the transformational leadership behaviors allow for external adaptation, whereas the transactional behaviors maintain internal health.

Evaluation and Application

Several empirical studies have tested the propositions of transformational leadership in a variety of settings (e.g., Podsakoff, MacKenzie, and Bommer 1996; Yammarino and Bass 1990). For example, researchers have found that transformational leadership can help the quality of research and development groups (Keller 1992) and lead to higher follower satisfaction (Ross and Offerman 1997). A number of recent studies also have extended the concept by linking personality attributes to transformational leadership. For example, one study suggests that a personality pattern characterized by high levels of pragmatism and nurturance and low levels of aggression and criticalness is associated with transformational leadership (Ross and Offerman 1997).

Other recent studies have considered transformational leadership theory across gender and cultures. For example, female transformational leaders form a unique relationship with each of their followers, suggesting that women favor an interpersonal-oriented style of leadership (Yammarino et al. 1997). Also, women leaders often exhibit the concern for others, expressiveness, and cooperation (Eagly, Karau, and Makhijani 1995) traits that are associated with transformational leadership.

From a cross-cultural point of view, it appears that ideal leadership characteristics across many countries—such as Canada, South Africa, Israel, Mexico, Sweden, and Singapore—include some transformational leadership elements (Bass 1997). The collectivistic cultures in particular might be most receptive to transformational leadership (Jung, Bass, and Sosik 1995).

Further research is needed, especially in regard to the measurement of transactional and transformational behavior (Yukl 1999). The only empirically derived, tested measure, the MLQ, does not consistently allow for separate identification of the various behaviors (Bycio, Hackett, and Allen 1995; Keller 1992; Seltzer and Bass 1990; Tepper and Percy 1994). Therefore, it is difficult to measure many of the behaviors of charismatic, transformational, and visionary leaders; we continue to rely excessively on anecdotes and case studies. In addition, despite the focus on behaviors, many of the charismatic behaviors have strong dispositional, traitlike elements and are reported to develop early in life (Bass 1985). For example, although it might be easy to instruct a leader about how to provide contingent rewards, teaching the leader to inspire and intellectually stimulate followers might not be as simple. Additionally, as is the case with charismatic leadership, the tendency is to propose transformational leadership as a panacea to organizational problems. However, a stronger contingency approach is needed to identify various contextual organizational variables that might contribute to the effectiveness of transformational leadership (Pawar and Eastman 1997). Yukl (1999) has further suggested that the transformational leadership theory could benefit from clarification of the difference between charismatic and transformation leadership and the mediating processes and situational variables that lead to transformational leadership (Yukl 1999).

Transformational leadership concepts have considerable application to organizational effectiveness and leadership training. Although charismatic leadership sometimes carries negative connotations, transformational leadership generally is perceived as positive. Research findings suggest that organizations can benefit from encouraging their leaders to be less aggressive and more nurturing (Ross and Offerman 1997, p. 1084). Other recommendations for leaders based on transformational leadership models include the following:

- Projecting confidence and optimism about the goals and followers' ability.
- Providing a clear vision.
- Encouraging creativity through empowerment, rewarding experimentation, and tolerance for mistakes.
- Setting high expectations and creating a supportive environment.
- Establishing personal relationships with followers.

The use of transformational leadership can facilitate change in organizations. The next section considers other leadership theories that also have focused on how to bring about change.

CHANGE-ORIENTED AND VISIONARY LEADERSHIP IN THE POPULAR PRESS

The late 1980s saw a considerable resurgence of interest in leadership in the popular business press. These approaches are discussed here briefly because they share the focus on change and the importance of vision with charismatic and transformational leadership. Although, a considerable amount of diversity appears in the books and articles about leadership in the popular business press, several themes emerge:

- *Importance of vision.* Successful and effective leaders provide a clear vision or help followers develop a common vision. In either case, whether stemming from the leader or the followers, vision is key to effective leadership.
- *Empowerment and confidence in followers.* Popular views strongly emphasize empowering followers to allow them to act autonomously and independently

from the leader. This empowerment is possible only if leaders show genuine confidence in their followers.

- *Flexibility and change.* The fast-changing environment requires leaders to focus on flexibility and change in their organization.
- *Teamwork and cooperation.* Successful leaders emphasize teamwork and, maybe more importantly, the development of shared responsibility, as well as the need for trust and cooperation between leaders and followers and among followers.

Each author places different relative emphasis on each of these themes and presents them differently. The leader plays a key role in the development and communication of the vision. Some leaders, for instance, communicate their vision and values through stories. Patrick Kelly, CEO of Physician Sales and Services (PSS), relies on his storytelling skills to remind employees what is important (Weil 1998). Whenever he repeats one of his favorites:

> PSS employees chuckle. . . . And they learn, or relearn, an important lesson: No matter how badly other people treat you, no matter how confident you get about your future, never burn your bridges. (Weil 1998, p. 38)

Researcher Noel Tichy recommends that leaders develop three stories. The first one should tell who the leader is or the "Who I am" story. The second story is about "Who we are." Finally, the leader must have a "Where we are going" story (Weil 1998). Other consultants and practitioners agree that storytelling can be one of the most powerful ways for leaders to communicate their vision to their followers. According to Harvard professor Howard Gardner, "Stories of identity convey values, build esprit de corps, create role models, and reveal how things work around here" (Stewart 1998, p. 165).

The leader's vision is key to creating change, another major theme of leadership in the popular press. A motivating vision is clear and understandable, challenging, idealistic yet achievable, appeals to emotions, and is forward looking. Having a forward-looking vision is essential for transforming organizations and enacting large-scale change. Kouzes and Posner (1995) have proposed one of the most clearly developed models of visionary leadership. In addition to presenting the practices of what the researchers call exemplary leadership (see Figure 8-2), the model considers the followers' points of view and their expectations of leaders (Kouzes and Posner 1993).

Kouzes and Posner (1999) emphasize the importance of reward and recognition—in their words "encouraging the heart"—both key aspects of empowerment, confidence in followers, and development of trust. They specifically suggest that in order to truly motivate and inspire followers, the leader must:

- Set clear standards for behavior and performance that are accepted by all followers.
- Expect the best from followers through a genuine belief in their abilities. This strong belief creates a self-fulfilling prophecy in followers, who will, in turn, perform better.
- Pay attention by being present; walking around; noticing followers; and caring about their behaviors, actions, and results.
- Personalize recognition by not only considering each follower's needs and preferences, but also by making them feel special in the process.

Chapter 8   **Change-Oriented Leadership**   239

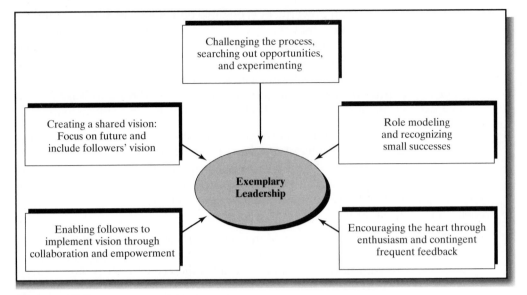

Figure 8-2
Practices of Exemplary Leadership

- Tell a story about followers, events, and performances as a way to motivate and teach.
- Celebrate together. Leaders must look for many opportunities to celebrate the team and the individual's success together.
- Role model the six principles just presented to gain credibility and reinforce the message.

WHAT DOES THIS MEAN FOR ME?
"Encouraging the Heart"

In their book "Encouraging the Heart: A Leader's Guide to Rewarding and Recognizing Others," Kouzes and Posner (1999) provide 150 examples of how leaders can motivate and inspire followers. Their recommendations apply to people in all levels of leadership positions. Below are just a few:

- Take the time to identify and clarify the team's key values with all the members; keep the values current; discuss them often; advertise them; and reward those who implement them.

- Practice smiling and show a positive mental attitude.

- Take the time to pay attention to your followers and teammates and recognize them for what they do well.

- Find creative ways to celebrate; visit a party store; learn from other parties and celebrations; and get everyone involved in planning events.

- Walk your talk!

To be exemplary and visionary, leaders need to commit
themselves to questioning
old beliefs and assumptions
continuously. This process
leads to the creation of a
new common vision.

To be exemplary and visionary, leaders need to commit themselves to continuously questioning old beliefs and assumptions.
This process leads to the creation of a new common vision.
Through empowerment, encouragement, and proper role modeling, leaders can motivate followers to implement the vision. The
driving force behind a leader's ability to fulfill this commitment is
their credibility (Kouzes and Posner 1993). By asking followers
about the characteristics they admire most and expect from their leaders, Kouzes and
Posner have identified honesty, the ability to be forward looking, and the capacity to
be inspiring and competent as the pillars of a leader's credibility. A leader's ability to
change followers and the organization depends on their credibility.

Kathy Taggares, president of K.T.'s Kitchens, a California-based food-processing
company, is a leader who has built her credibility. She claims that she has few of the
business skills that many people in her company have. However, she explains, "The
reason I'm sitting in the president's seat and they aren't is because I am gutsy, I am
tenacious, I stir things up, and I am a very, very hard worker" (Enkelis and Olsen
1995, p. 30). When she took over the business, she had to convince many reluctant
employees of her abilities. She states:

> Being tough wasn't the most important thing. What really brought them
> around, I think, is that they saw how hard I worked, and they could see I
> didn't set myself above them. I did the same physical work they did.
> (Enkelis and Olsen 1995, p. 34)

Her active role modeling and her willingness to let her followers do their job,
both of which are key elements of exemplary leadership, have helped Taggares build
a $26 million company that employed close to 500 people in 1994.

Evaluation and Application

The popular, change-oriented visionary leadership approaches allow us to explain
one of the most interesting and visible sides of leadership. They let us talk about the
interesting leaders, those whom everyone would agree are the "real" leaders. It satis-
fies our need to find and explain heroes. This search—maybe this wish—for heroic
leadership seems to be part of the fabric of many cultures. As with charismatic leadership, the intuitive appeal of visionary leadership concepts is undeniable. Despite
some survey-based studies, however, these approaches generally lack the empirical
research needed to establish their validity and to clarify and refine their propositions.

As with the other models presented in this chapter, one of the major limitations
of visionary theories is their apparent suggestion that there is one best way to lead.
None of the theories proposes a contingency view that considers task, organizational, and follower characteristics. It is clear that visionary leadership is needed in
times of crisis, but the effect of such leadership in times when consolidation and status quo are needed is not as clear. Change-oriented leadership, by definition, would
fit in times of change; the role of such a leader when change is not the focus is not
clear. Anecdotes of the disastrous effects of change-oriented leaders in times when
change is not needed are common and point to the limitations of visionary leadership. The current presentations of visionary leaders do not address these limitations.

Additionally, no research has been done on the fate of organizations and employees who either do not buy into the leader's vision or who buy into an inappropriate vision. Many historical and political examples can be found, though. The extent to which similar events would occur in organizations needs to be explored.

Despite these shortcomings, the models provide interesting key guidelines. Accordingly, leaders must have passion, develop their credibility, develop and clarify their vision, share power with their followers, and—perhaps most importantly—role model all the attributes that they expect their followers to have. Overall, the concepts presented in this chapter are responsible for a revival of interest in leadership. They have popularized the study of leadership and are changing the field so that leadership is considered from a dynamic and organizational viewpoint. The focus on small groups and task and relationship orientation is needed; supplementing this focus with a more-encompassing view can only benefit the study of leadership.

SUMMARY AND CONCLUSION

This chapter focuses on recent theories of charismatic and transformational leadership and their impact on leadership practice. Although the notion of charisma has been a central element of leadership for many years, recent scientific approaches to the concept have allowed for more thorough descriptions of the process. In particular, current approaches view charismatic leadership as a relationship between leaders and followers, rather than as a combination of leadership traits and behaviors. In order for the charismatic leadership relationship to occur, leaders need to have certain traits and behaviors, followers have to demonstrate particular traits and frames of mind, and the situation has to have an element of crisis. The combination of these three factors allows for the emergence of charismatic leadership.

Charismatic leadership is one of the elements in the transformational leadership model. The model suggests that the transactional views of leadership, which focus on developing an exchange and transaction contract between leaders and followers, must be supplemented with behaviors that lead to organizational transformation. Transformational leadership provides vision, inspiration, and the intense emotions required to enact such large-scale changes in organizations. Charismatic, transformational, and other change-oriented leadership concepts have contributed to the demystification and understanding of leadership processes. They have broad appeal and provide an intuitive understanding of leadership that is applicable to large-scale leadership situations. They are also responsible for a resurgence in the interest in leadership. Due to their relatively recent formation, the concepts still require much refinement, and their use in training leaders needs further development, particularly with regard to identification of various situations under which change-oriented leadership might be more appropriate and more effective.

Standing Up to a Charismatic but Unethical Leader

You are one of the "lucky" people who work with a leader who demonstrates considerable personal charisma. She has a grand vision of the future, communicates with passion, inspires her followers, and makes them feel special. However, because of prior knowledge and experience with her, you are one of the few people who is aware that she is disingenuous, is focused on her personal agenda and career, would not hesitate to sacrifice all her followers for her own benefit, and is ruthless with those who disagree with her. You know that it is only a matter of time before her followers suffer because of her lack of concern and extreme self-interest.

1. Should you share your concerns with other department members? With her supervisor?
2. What are the consequences of your action or inaction?
3. What course of action would you choose? Why?

REVIEW AND DISCUSSION QUESTIONS

1. What are the factors that have given rise to the development of change-oriented leadership theories?
2. Describe the elements of charismatic leadership.
3. What are the cultural constraints on the development of charismatic leadership?
4. Describe the elements of transactional leadership.
5. How is management by exception different from empowerment?
6. Describe the elements of transformational leadership and its role in enacting organizational change.
7. Describe the fundamentals of exemplary leadership and the role of credibility in a leader's effectiveness.
8. What are the major shortcomings of change-oriented leadership theories?
9. What are the major contributions of change-oriented theories to our understanding of leadership?

SEARCHING THE WEB

Leadership Quarterly **Web Site:**
  ilr.ba.ttu.edu/lq.htm

Bibliography of Transformational Leadership:
  www.ndu.edu/icaf/departments/center/
  TL_Bibliography.htm

Managing Change:
  drucker.org/leaderbooks/L2L/summer99/
  kanter.html

  www.advantagepoint.com/articles/change/
  art7.html

EXERCISE 8-1: DO YOU KNOW A CHARISMATIC LEADER?

Identify a leader you consider to be highly effective. This person can be in your work organization, or a leader in your civic, sports, educational, or religious organization.

Step 1: Describe the Leader

Rate the leader you selected on the following items using the scale shown here.

1	2	3	4
Never	Occasionally	Often	Always

_____ 1. The leader shows a high degree of self-confidence.
_____ 2. The leader does not show any doubt about his or her ideas.
_____ 3. The leader has a clear, well-articulated vision.
_____ 4. The leader has a high energy level.
_____ 5. The leader shows a lot of enthusiasm about the work to be done.
_____ 6. The leader is emotionally expressive.
_____ 7. The leader expresses his or her ideas well.
_____ 8. The leader is articulate.
_____ 9. The leader also does all that he or she requires of the followers.
_____10. The leader role models the desired behaviors and "walks the talk."

Scoring key: Add up your scores for all 10 items. The maximum possible score is 40. The higher your leader's score is, the more he or she demonstrates charismatic characteristics.

Total: _____

Step 2: Describe Followers' Reactions and Behaviors

Rate the leader's followers (including yourself) on the following items, using the scale shown here.

1	2	3	4
Never	Occasionally	Often	Always

_____ 1. The followers respect the leader.
_____ 2. The followers hold the leader in high esteem.
_____ 3. The followers are loyal and devoted to the leader.
_____ 4. The followers like the leader.
_____ 5. The followers believe in their own capability for exceptional performance.
_____ 6. The followers are enthusiastic about the work to be done.
_____ 7. The followers follow the leader's directions eagerly.

Scoring key: Add up your rating for all seven items. The maximum possible score is 28. The higher the followers' scores are, the more they demonstrate the characteristics of followers of charismatic leaders.

Total: _____

Step 3: Describe the Situation

Consider the situation that the leader and follower face in their day-to-day activities. Rate the situation on the following items using the scale shown here.

1	2	3	4
Never	Occasionally	Often	Always

____ 1. Our team/organization needs to change.
____ 2. We seem to go from crisis to crisis.
____ 3. We could do many things better around here.
____ 4. We do not seem to know what we are all about.
____ 5. We have not explored many possible opportunities.
____ 6. Many of us are not performing to our fullest potential.

Scoring key: Add up your rating for all six items. The maximum possible score is 24. The higher your group's score is, the more you are ready for change and face a crisis situation.

Total: _____

Step 4: Putting It All Together

Using the scores from the three previous measures, consider whether:
  1. Your leader has the personal characteristics of a charismatic leader.

  2. The group exhibits the behaviors typically associated with charismatic leadership.

  3. The group faces a crisis situation where there is a perceived need for change.

Based on these three questions, to what extent is the leader you selected charismatic?

1	2	3
Not at all	Has some but not all the elements	To a great extent

Step 5: Discussion

* What are the factors that explain your leader's effectiveness?

* What do you foresee for the future if the situation changes?

EXERCISE 8-2: CHARISMATIC SPEECH

One of the characteristics of charismatic leaders is their ability to articulate their ideas and vision in an inspiring manner. These articulation skills might come easier to some than to others, but they can be learned if practiced.

An inspiring message includes two elements: (1) proper framing of ideas to give them a powerful context, and (2) use of various rhetorical techniques to support the message.

Elements of Framing:

- Amplify values and beliefs.
- Bring out the importance of the mission.
- Clarify the need to accomplish the mission.
- Focus on the efficacy of the mission.

Rhetorical Techniques:

- Use of metaphors, analogies, and brief stories.
- Gearing language to the audience.
- Repetition.
- Rhythm.
- Alliteration.
- Nonverbal message.

Write a short speech that presents your goals (personal or for your team or organization). Revise and practice the message using charismatic speech methods.

Source: This exercise is based on concepts developed by Conger, J. A. 1989a; Conger, J. A. 1991. Inspiring others: The language of leadership. *Academy of Management Executive* 5, no. 1, 31–45.

SELF-ASSESSMENT 8-1: BUILDING CREDIBILITY

One of the key elements of exemplary and visionary leadership is the leader's credibility. Having credibility allows a leader to undertake the necessary changes with sincerity and with followers' trust. Following are the elements of credibility. Rate yourself on each of the items using the following scale:

1	2	3	4
Never	Occasionally	Often	Always

_____ 1. I state my position clearly.
_____ 2. My coworkers and subordinates always know where I stand.
_____ 3. I listen to other people's opinions carefully and respectfully.
_____ 4. I accept disagreement from my coworkers and followers.
_____ 5. I try to integrate my point of view with that of others.
_____ 6. I encourage and practice constructive feedback.
_____ 7. I encourage and practice cooperation.
_____ 8. I build consensus out of differing views.
_____ 9. I develop my coworkers' and subordinates' skills.
_____ 10. I provide frequent positive feedback and encouragement.
_____ 11. I hold myself and others accountable for actions.
_____ 12. I practice what I preach.

Scoring key: Add up your rating for all 12 items. The maximum score is 48. A higher score indicates demonstrations of behaviors that build credibility.

Total: _____

Self-Analysis and Action Plan

* Are there any items on which you have a low score? If yes, those are areas that you need to target in order to build your credibility.

    Items with low score:

* What can I do about them? Focus on clear and specific behaviors. Develop short-term and long-term goals. When will you know that you have improved? How will you measure yourself?

Source: This exercise is based partially on concepts developed by: Kouzes, J. M., and B. Z. Posner. 1993. *Credibility: How leaders gain and lose it, why people demand it.* San Francisco: Jossey-Bass; Kouzes, J. M., and B. Z. Posner, 1995. *The leadership challenge.* San Francisco: Jossey-Bass.

CASE

Leadership in Action

Andrea Jung Orchestrates Avon's Makeover

Avon is a venerable company with a history that spans two centuries. It was global before business became "globalized"; it served and employed women before diversity became a key factor in business; it was customer focused before the concept became an organizational mantra; and it has been successful longer than most organizations have been. Interestingly enough, the company that almost exclusively served women through its cosmetics did not have a female executive until recently. Andrea Jung, Avon's first female executive, was appointed CEO in 1999 and chairman in 2001. She faces the daunting task of moving a traditional, door-to-door sales company to the high-tech Internet world without alienating its loyal sales force—the "Avon Ladies" (Sellers 2000). With all its past success, Avon was getting sluggish and showing its age.

Just the fact that so few women can be found in the top ranks of major companies worldwide makes Jung part of a small club. Her company is also the global leader in direct sales of beauty products (Brady 2001), and it posted record sales in 2001. In addition, the company raised $7 million to aid children affected by the September 11, 2001, terrorist attacks in the United States (avoncompany.com/about/pressroom), and was also one of the key corporate sponsors of "Race for Cure" to support the fight against breast cancer. Jung was able to achieve such impressive results through dogged determination and unwavering confidence in her strategy, which involves the slow introduction of the Internet and other retail sales, and a gradual blending of new retail methods with the traditional direct sales. She strongly believes that the global force of 3.4 million independent Avon

Ladies is the backbone of the company. She demonstrated her commitment to them by increasing the number and incentives for the direct sales representatives.

Kurt Schansinger, a financial analyst at Merrill Lynch, describes Jung as having a "... strong vision, high standards, deep knowledge of the business, and enough confidence to delegate key tasks ..." (Brady 2001). These attributes are mentioned often when people talk about Jung. Born into a highly educated Chinese immigrant family—her father is an architect and her mother was Canada's first female chemical engineer—Jung always was expected to succeed. She received a Princeton education, graduating magna cum laude, and speaks fluent Mandarin and Cantonese as well as some French. When she joined Bloomingdale's, her parents did not originally approve of their daughter lowering herself to become a retailer. However, their concerns did not stop her. Jung states: "They did not understand just what I was doing by going into retailing. After I started, though, it got into my blood" (www.goldsea.com, p. 1).

After Bloomingdale's, Jung followed her mentor Vass to I. Magnin and later to Neiman Marcus. Jung credits Vass with teaching her the art of tactful aggression, a style that matches her cultural roots (www.goldsea.com, p. 2). Jung joined Avon partly because of the corporate culture and partly because of the fact that women form a quarter of the company's board of directors, which appealed to her. She says: "I'm very selective about the companies I work for. I started at Bloomingdale's because it was committed to developing women. When I went to I. Magnin in San Francisco, it was to accompany a female CEO, and because there's a strong Asian population in that city..." (www.goldsea.com, p. 3).

Jung enjoys building consensus among her team and making sure everyone's voice is heard. She makes an extra effort to listen to her team members' suggestions and ideas. When her global marketing team was having difficulty finding an appealing name for a new facial cream, she engaged everyone in the discussion. Joking about integrating everyone's ideas, she states: "It was like naming a child after your mother, your husband's mother, your grandmother, and your great aunt" (Morris 1997, p. 79). Her constant smile and upbeat approach and attitude set the tone for her company and send a message of confidence and success. Describing her feelings about Avon, Jung says:

> I have a love for this business. I have an enormous amount of passion for it. Since I'm a mother and a wife, I have to have passion or the frustration would win out. But I love managing people. The product is second to managing the people. And marketing to consumers is so challenging because it is evolving constantly. (www.goldsea. com, p. 3) ■

QUESTIONS

1. What are the key elements of Andrea Jung's leadership style?

2. How closely does she match elements of charismatic and transformational leadership?

Sources: www.avoncompany.com/about/pressroom, accessed April 16, 2002; Brady, D. A makeover has Avon looking good, www.businessweek.com/bwdaily/dnflash/jan2001/nf20020122_8624.htm, accessed April 16, 2002; "Executive Sea," goldsea.com/WW/Jungandrea/jungandrea.html; Morris, B. 1997. If women ran the world it would look a lot like Avon. *Fortune* (July), 21; Sellers, P. 2000. Big, hairy, audacious goals don't work—Just ask P&G. *Fortune* (April 3), 38–44.

Chapter 9

The Upper-Echelon View: Strategic Leadership

> *Setting an example is not the main means of influencing another; it is the only means.*
>
> —*Albert Einstein*

After studying this chapter, you will be able to:

1. Differentiate between micro and upper-echelon leadership.
2. Describe the domain and roles of strategic leaders in the management of an organization.
3. Identify the external and internal factors that impact strategic leaders' discretion.
4. List the individual characteristics of strategic leaders and their impact on their style.
5. Contrast the four strategic leadership types and discuss the role of culture and gender in strategic leadership.
6. Explain the processes through which strategic leaders manage their organization.
7. Review issues of executive compensation and accountability.

The press in business, public, and health sectors is replete with examples of leaders. Many publications and professional associations have yearly awards for the best leaders in their industry. The health care industry awards a "best health care administrator award"; best and worst city mayors are ranked regularly, as are best and worst business leaders. Based on the amount of attention given to top executives, one can deduce that practitioners clearly believe that the top leader of an organization is important, but the academic interest in the effect of leaders on organizational elements such as culture, strategy, and structure is relatively new. With the exception of some of the change-oriented leadership models discussed in Chapter 8, none of the leadership theories presented so far in this book directly address the role and impact of upper-echelon leaders. These issues are typically the domain of strategic management. However, until recently, research in strategy focused more on the content and types of strategies leaders implement rather than on the leadership process itself. This chapter will clarify the differences between micro and upper-echelon (macro) strategic leadership and consider individual characteristics of strategic leaders and the processes through which they impact their organization.

DIFFERENCES BETWEEN MICRO AND UPPER-ECHELON STRATEGIC LEADERSHIP

The reviews of the role of upper-echelon leadership in organizations suggest that the practitioners' efforts at understanding executives are justified (see Finkelstein and Hambrick 1996; Hambrick and Mason 1984; Nahavandi and Malekzadeh 1993a). Although the research results are somewhat fragmented, they show that the CEO is key to organizational performance. Many of the leadership concepts and processes presented in previous chapters operate regardless of the level of the leader. For example, the basic definition of leadership and leadership effectiveness can be transferred from small groups to upper echelons with only minor adjustments. Upper-echelon leaders are still the people who guide others in goal achievement, and their effectiveness depends on maintaining internal health and external adaptability. Therefore, the major differences between micro and macro leadership are not in the nature of the process but rather in the level and scope of leadership. We call upper-echelon leaders "strategic leaders" because they impact the whole organization. Strategic leadership is a leader's ability to anticipate events, and maintain flexibility and a long-term perspective in order to guide the organization (Christensen 1997). Table 9-1 summarizes the differences between micro and strategic leadership.

Strategic leadership is a leader's ability to anticipate events, and maintain flexibility and a long-term perspective to guide the organization.

One of the first differences between micro and strategic leadership involves identifying who the leader is. In the case of micro leadership, the person leading the group, team, or department is clearly the leader. In the case of strategic leadership, the issue is often not that simple (Finkelstein and Hambrick 1996). The leader of the organization might be the president, CEO, or chief operating officer (COO), or it could be a top management team (TMT) made up of division heads and vice presidents. In some cases, the relevant strategic leadership is a governance body such as the board of directors, board of regents, or supervisors.

Table 9-1
Differences Between Micro and Strategic Leadership

	MICRO (SMALL GROUP)	STRATEGIC (UPPER ECHELON)
Who is the leader?	One person heading a group, team, or department	A person heading a whole organization with a variety of titles (president, CEO, COO), top management team (TMT), governance body such as board of directors
Scope	Small group, team, or department	Entire organization
Focus	Internal	External
Effectiveness criteria	Productivity, quality, employee satisfaction and motivation, turnover, absenteeism	Stock prices and other financial measures, stakeholder satisfaction

Any of these individuals or groups might be the senior executives who make strategic choices for the organization. Research indicates that the makeup and characteristics of the TMT relate to factors such as degree of globalization (Carpenter and Fredrickson 2001).

A second difference in leadership at the two levels is the scope of the leader's impact. Whereas most micro leadership is concerned with small groups or small departments, upper-echelon leaders have jurisdiction over entire organizations that include many smaller groups and departments. As a result of the broader scope, upper-echelon leaders have discretion and power over many decisions. For example, when a city mayor makes a decision, thousands, and in some cases millions, are affected. When the CEO of GM and his TMT decide to downsize, more than 300,000 employees are at risk, not to mention thousands of suppliers and the employees' families and communities. By comparison, the scope of micro leaders' decisions is limited to a smaller number of individuals.

A third difference between the two groups is their focus. The micro leaders' focus is typically internal to the organization and includes factors that affect their teams or departments. Part of their job might involve dealing with external constituents, as may be the case with a customer representative or a sales manager, or they might be under pressure to take on a more strategic view even in their small department. Overall, though, they do not need an external view in order to perform their job. In comparison, the job of the upper-echelon leader requires almost equal attention to internal and external factors. Dealing with outside constituents, whether they are stockholders, governmental agencies and officials, or customers and clients, is central to the function of high-level executives.

The effectiveness criteria are also different for the two groups. Although in a general sense, they are both effective when they achieve their goals, micro leaders focus on department productivity, quality of products and services, and employee morale. Effectiveness for the upper-echelon leader is measured by overall organizational performance, stock prices, and satisfaction of outside constituents. The hospital administrator has to integrate internal productivity issues with overall performance. The CEO of a major corporation does not focus on turnover of employees as a measure of

WHAT DOES THIS MEAN FOR ME?
Moving to Upper Management

Being a leader in the upper levels of an organization requires the acquisition of new skills and behaviors. As you make the transition to upper management, keep the following in mind:

- Look at the big picture and think long term. The focus at upper-management levels is on conceptual skills and strategic thinking.

- Make a conscious effort to acquire knowledge and experience in all areas of the

organization. A broad understanding of all the different functions of the organization is essential.

- Seek out international assignments. International experience is becoming indispensable to upper-echelon leaders.

- Build and carefully maintain a strong network. Coalitions inside and outside the organization are essential for top management success.

personal effectiveness. Instead, the criteria are overall return on investment and the corporation's growth.

THE DOMAIN AND IMPACT OF STRATEGIC LEADERSHIP

What is the role of senior executives? Do they simply provide direction or do they stay involved in the day-to-day operations of their organization? The answer depends in part on the leader's style and personality. However, six strategic forces depicted in Figure 9-1 are the primary domain of strategic leadership (Malekzadeh 1995). Culture is defined as a common set of beliefs and assumptions shared by members of an organization (Schein 1985). Structure is comprised of the basic design dimensions (centralization, formalization, integration, and span of control) that organize the human resources of an organization (Pugh et al. 1968). The environment includes all the outside forces that have the potential to affect the organization. Technology is the process by which inputs are transformed into outputs, and leadership includes managers and supervisors at all levels.

Any strategic effort requires a balance and fit among the strategic forces. With a good fit, the organization has a higher potential to be effective.

Any strategic effort requires a balance and fit among the strategic forces. When the fit is good, the organization has a greater potential to be effective (Nahavandi and Malekzadeh 1999). Consider the example of Jagged Edge Mountain Gear (JEMG), a Colorado-based company that specializes in fashionable mountaineering clothing. Twin sisters Margaret and Paula Quenemoen founded the company in 1993 based on the Asian philosophy that focuses on the journey and process (Nahavandi and Malekzadeh 1999, pp. 108–109). JEMG's goal is to become a nationally recognized competitor in their industry. However, the Quenemoens state, "We are our own competition. We do what we think is right" (Nahavandi and Malekzadeh 1999, p. 108). To achieve their goal, the sisters have attracted a group of passionate mountain enthusiasts who perform the many business functions while remaining dedicated to cold-

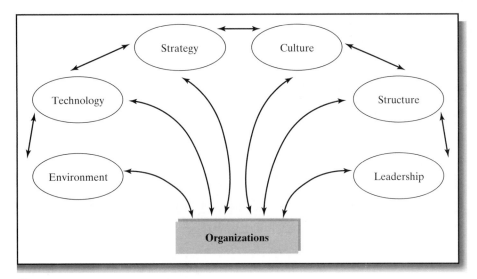

Figure 9-1
The Domain of Strategic Leaders: The Six Strategic Forces

weather, extreme sports. The JEMG owners, managers, and employees work together and play together. The culture of the organization is informal and exudes the members' passion for their sports. The structure, although formally stated, remains informal, with a heavy reliance on participation and empowerment. In addition, because of the company's relative isolation in Telluride, everybody depends on information technology to stay in touch with the marketing division located in Salt Lake City and their suppliers in Massachusetts, Tennessee, and China. The success of JEMG is attributable to a great extent to a fit among the six strategic forces.

The simultaneous management of the six forces is the essence of strategic management (Malekzadeh 1995). The upper-echelon leader's role is to balance these various factors and set the direction for the organization. Once a direction is selected, internal forces (e.g., culture, structure, and leadership) come into play once more in order to move the organization toward its selected path.

Role of Strategic Leaders

Strategic leaders are the ones in charge of setting and changing the environment, culture, strategy, structure, leadership, and technology of an organization and motivating employees to implement the decisions. Their role is to devise or formulate the vision and strategy for their organization and to implement those strategies; they play the dual role of strategy formulator and implementer (Nahavandi and Malekzadeh 1993a). If an organization has not drafted a strategy or is looking for major changes and strategic redirection, the leaders have a vital role in formulating the direction of the organization based on their reading of the environment. If, on the other hand, the organization has a well-established, successful strategy already in place, the leaders become a key factor in implementing that strategy. The dual role of strategic leaders is depicted in Figure 9-2.

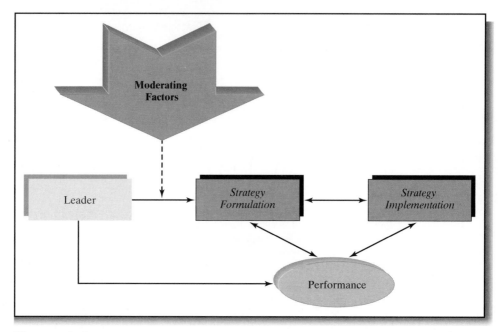

Figure 9-2
The Dual Role of Upper-Echelon Leaders

Although they play a central role in the creation and maintenance of major organizational elements, the top managers' influence often is moderated by a number of organizational and environmental factors. Therefore, although leaders are highly influential in many aspects of organizational decision making, many circumstances and variables limit a leader's discretion. The next section considers these factors.

Executive Discretion: Moderating Factors of the Role of Leaders

Upper-echelon leaders do not have unlimited power to impact their organization. The research about the limits of their power has come under the label of managerial or executive discretion (Finkelstein and Hambrick 1996; Hambrick and Finkelstein 1987). Table 9-2 presents the factors that moderate a leader's discretion. They are divided into external environmental and internal organizational factors. Both sets operate to limit the direct or indirect impact of senior executives on their organization.

External Environmental Factors

Several researchers have suggested that the leader's role becomes more prominent when organizations face an uncertain environment (Gupta 1988; Hall 1977; Hambrick and Finkelstein 1987). For example, in highly dynamic industries such as high technology, computers, or airlines, top managers have to scan and interpret their environment actively and make strategic decisions based on their interpreta-

Table 9-2

Moderators of Executive Discretion

• *External environmental factors*	Environment uncertainty
	Type of industry
	Market growth
	Legal constraints
• *Internal organizational factors*	Stability
	Size and structure
	Culture
	Stage of organizational development
	Presence, power, and makeup of TMT

tions. Such activities provide many opportunities for a leader to affect the organization. Charlie Feld, founder and CEO of the Feld Group, a technology and management consulting company that specializes in turnaround strategies, believes that the leader's vision and priority setting are key to surviving a crisis (Maruca 2001). Other external forces include market growth and legal constraints. In fast-growing markets, strategic leaders have considerable discretion to set and change the course of their organization (Haleblian and Finkelstein 1993). However, legal constraints, such as environmental laws, health and safety regulations, and international trade barriers, limit the discretion of leaders. In such environments, many of their decisions already are made for them, leaving less room for action.

Consider the case of utility companies that, up until a few years ago, faced a stable and calm environment. As competition increases and the government deregulates the industry, their leaders are becoming more prominent. Similarly, the leaders of the computer industry, such as John Chambers (Cisco Systems), Margaret Whitman (eBay), and Michael Dell (Dell Computers), have become household names, as have leaders in many of the Internet companies, such as AOL's Steve Case and Amazon.com's Jeff Bezos.

Internal Organizational Factors

When organizations face internal uncertainty, organizational members question existing practices and decisions and rely more heavily on the leader to provide direction and guidance. In routine situations, organizational rules and regulations and a well-established culture in effect become substitutes for leadership (Kerr and Jermier 1978). One example of a situation in which leaders are heavily relied upon would be during a threatened or actual merger. The employees are likely to seek direction from their CEO, whose every word and action will be interpreted as a signal and whose attitude toward the merger will be a role model for the employees. Professor Mike Useem, director of the Center for Leadership and Change at the University of Pennsylvania's Wharton School of Business, suggests that a leader's calm and confidence is a key factor in managing during times of crisis (Maruca, 2001). The sense of crisis provides the stage for leaders to increase their impact or to demonstrate charismatic leadership behaviors (see Chapter 8), which influence followers to a high degree.

Size and structure are the second set of internal moderators of discretion. The larger an organization is, the more likely it is that decision making is decentralized. As an organization grows, the impact of the top managers on day-to-day operations declines. In small organizations, the desires of a top manager for a certain type of culture and strategy are likely to be reflected in the actual operations of an organization. However, in large organizations, the distance between the leader and other organizational levels and departments leads to a decline in the immediate effect of the leaders. For example, the U.S. Postal Service is the largest employer in the world, with more than 650,000 employees. The postmaster's influence is diffused through numerous layers of bureaucracy and probably is not felt by local post office employees. This filtering also could be one reason it is difficult to change large organizations. Even the most charismatic, visionary leader might have trouble reaching all employees to establish a personal bond and energize them to seek and accept change.

One of the causes of internal and external uncertainty is the organization's life cycle or stage of development (Miller 1987; Nahavandi and Malekzadeh 1993a). When an organization is young and in its early stages of development, the impact of a leader's personality and decisions is pervasive. The personality and style of the leader/entrepreneur are reflected in all aspects of the organization. The younger an organization is, the more likely it is that its culture, strategies, and structure are a reflection of its leader's preferences. As the organization matures and grows, the leader's influence decreases and is replaced by the presence of a strong culture and a variety of well-established, successful routines. It is often at this stage that the founders of an organization leave and move on to new ventures. The leader's influence, however, becomes strong once again when the organization faces decline. The lack of success and the perceived need to revitalize the organization increase the reliance on the top managers. They once again have the opportunity to shape the organization. Carly Fiorina of Hewlett-Packard (HP) and several of her executives including Ann Livermore, president of HP Services, have been the center of attention inside and outside the company, partly because HP is in need of redirection and revitalization. Although the HP culture is hard to change (Boyle 2001), Fiorina has implemented major changes, believing that "A company is a system—you have to have the courage and capability to tackle everything at once" (Sellers 2000, p. 133).

Mickey Drexler, chief executive of Gap, Incorporated, is responsible for much of the company's success in the late 1990s. One former Gap employee states: "Mickey is omnipotent. There is nobody who is his equal. There is nobody who is near his equal" (Munk 1998). Drexler has considerable control and impact over his organization. He makes decisions regarding even minute details of the products. Because the Gap is relatively new and at the same time experiencing a revival, the leader's influence is pervasive. Another example of the leader's impact in the early stages of an organization's life is Oprah Winfrey—the first African-American and the third woman to own a television and film production studio with more than $100 million in sales—who runs an organization that reflects her high-energy, supportive style (Sellers 1998, 2000).

The last moderator of power and influence of top managers of an organization is the presence, power, and homogeneity of a top management team (Hambrick 1987). As noted at the beginning of the chapter, upper-echelon leadership often involves working within a team. If an organization does not have a TMT or if it is weak, the impact of its CEO is likely to be more direct. If, on the other hand, the organization is managed by a powerful TMT, such a team will moderate the power and discretion of the individual leader. An interesting twist is the degree to which the TMT is similar to the leader. Much research indicates that leaders often pick board of director members and other top advisors who are similar to them. The more similar the TMT is to the leader, the greater the power of the leader is (Miller 1987).

Many organizations take into account the importance of heterogeneity in the makeup of the TMT or board of directors. When Mercedes, the German automobile manufacturer, built a plant in Vance, Alabama, the heart of the Deep South, the executive leaders deliberately pieced together a diverse team of executives. It included managers with Detroit automobile experience, several who had worked for Japanese plants in North America, and four Germans (Martin 1997). The team was designed to provide the best possible mix of experience for running a successful foreign automaker in the United States.

These external and internal moderating factors limit the power and discretion of strategic leaders and can prevent the leader from making a direct impact on the organization. The next section considers the key relevant, individual characteristics of upper-echelon leaders.

LEADERSHIP ON THE CUTTING EDGE
The Complexity of Leadership Succession

Because selection of a new CEO can have considerable impact in the life and performance of an organization, and because unplanned succession can be highly disruptive, companies go to great lengths to identify "heirs apparent" well in advance of actual succession. Many of these "heirs" leave the company, and only a few ever reach the promised position. Albert Cannella and Wei Shen studied the factors that affect either the exit or the promotion of the heirs (2001). The researchers suggest that leadership succession is a highly political event that involves significant power struggles and negotiation among the incumbent CEO, the heir apparent, and the board of directors. They hypothesized that the balance of power among these three parties along with firm performance will influence the process and outcome of the succession.

Cannella and Shen (2001) used archival data from 168 U.S. manufacturing firms to conduct their study. They found that incumbent CEOs have considerable power and can influence the exit of heirs, particularly when their firm is performing well. The power of the board of directors decreases the likelihood of the heir apparent exiting when the firm is performing well, but increases the likelihood of exit when firm performance is below average. The results indicate that ". . . powerful CEOs are reluctant to relinquish their power and thus may strive to postpone heir apparent promotion" (p. 266), particularly when the firm is performing well. Based on the results of this study, although the heirs' longer tenure in the organization appears to help them avoid dismissal, they do not have much control over the succession. The study supports the view that CEO succession is a highly complex process.

Source: Cannella, A. A., Jr., and W. Shen. 2001. *Academy of Management Journal* 44, no. 2, 252–270.

CHARACTERISTICS OF UPPER-ECHELON LEADERS

What impact do executives' personality and other individual characteristics have on their style and the way they run the organization? Are some characteristics or combinations of characteristics more relevant for upper-echelon leadership? Information about upper-echelon leadership characteristics is somewhat disjointed. Research about micro leadership presented throughout this book has identified several dimensions that are key to predicting and understanding small-group leadership; the task and relationship dimensions, in particular, have dominated much of leadership theory for the past 40 to 50 years. However, despite the success of those dimensions, they do not necessarily have predictive value when dealing with upper-echelon leadership (Day and Lord 1988). A number of different studies have identified the individual characteristics of upper-echelon leaders.

Demographic and Personality Traits

Older CEOs have been found to be more risk averse (Alluto and Hrebeniak 1975), and insider CEOs (as opposed to those who are brought in from the outside) attempt to maintain the status quo and are, therefore, less likely to change the organization (Kotin and Sharaf 1976; Pfeffer 1983). Researchers also have considered the impact of an upper manager's functional background on an organization's strategic choices (Song 1982), and a body of research has focused on various personality characteristics. Among the most successful is the concept of locus of control (see Chapter 3). Managers with internal locus of control emphasize research and development (R&D) and frequent product changes. They also tend to be more innovative than those with an external locus of control (Anderson, Hellriegel, and Slocum 1977).

Another measure that has been used is the Myers Briggs Type Indicator (MBTI) (see Chapter 3). The overall pattern of results suggests that different MBTI types perceive risk differently and, as a result, select different strategies. Most of the leader's personal characteristics studied have some impact on organizational decision making, although the effect is not always strong. Although different measures and constructs are used, two common themes that run through the research about individual characteristics of strategic leaders are the degree to which they seek challenge and their need for control (Nahavandi and Malekzadeh 1993a).

> The two common themes that run through the research about individual characteristics of strategic leaders are the degree to which they seek challenge and their need for control.

Challenge Seeking

A number of researchers have considered the upper-echelon leader's openness to change to be an important factor of strategic leadership. Upper-echelon management's entrepreneurship (Covin and Slevin 1988), openness to change and innovation, futurity (Miller and Freisen 1982), and risk taking (Khandwalla 1976) are all part of this theme. The common thread among these constructs is the degree to which they seek challenge. How much is the leader willing to take risks? How much will the leader be willing to swim in uncharted waters? How much does the leader lean toward tried-and-true strategies and procedures? The more challenge-seeking person is likely to engage in risky strategies and undertake new and original endeavors (Nahavandi and Malekzadeh 1993a). A leader who does not seek challenges will be risk averse and stick with well-established and previously proven methods. The challenge-seeking dimension is most relevant in the way a leader formulates strategy. For example, one leader might pursue a highly risky product and design strategy that will help produce and market such a product by accepting a high level of failure risk.

Challenge-seeking executives often are celebrated in the current climate of crisis in many U.S. institutions. Livio DeSimone of 3M, Jack Welch formerly of GE, and Carol Bartz of Autodesk, Incorporated, although they have different management styles in other areas, share this constant push to innovate. Jill Barad, past president and CEO of Mattel, managed to break the glass ceiling because of her unrelenting pursuit of bigger challenges and her risk taking. Darla Moore, who is featured in the case at the end of Chapter 4, has a reputation for being daring. On the other side of the Atlantic, Luca di Montezemolo, chief executive of Ferrari; Jean-Marie Messier of Europe's Vivendi, Canal +, and Seagram; and Noel Goutard of France's Valeo are similarly known for their willingness and ability to change their organizations drastically.

Need for Control

The second theme in research about CEO characteristics is the leader's need for control, which refers to how willing the leader is to give up control. The degree of need for control is reflected in the extent of delegation and follower participation in decision making and implementation of strategy. Other indicators are the degree of centralization and formalization or encouragement, and the degree of tolerance for diversity of opinion and procedures. Issues such as the degree of focus on process and interpersonal orientation (Gupta 1984), tolerance for and encouragement of participation and openness, and what one researcher has called organicity, which generally refers to openness and flexibility, (Khandwalla 1976) are all part of this theme.

The leader with a high need for control is likely to create an organization that is centralized, with low delegation and low focus on process (Nahavandi and Malekzadeh 1993a, 1993b). The culture will be tight, and focus will be on uniformity and conformity. The leader with a low need for control decentralizes the organization and delegates decision-making responsibilities. Such a leader encourages an open and adaptable culture, with a focus on the integration of diverse ideas rather than conformity to a common idea. The culture will encourage employee involvement and tolerance for diversity of thought and styles (Nahavandi and Malekzadeh 1993a).

There appears to be no pattern regarding how controlling the upper echelons of successful organizations are, despite the empowerment trends. In some cases, such as the CEO and TMT of Johnson & Johnson, decentralization and autonomy of various units are built into the credo of the organization. Similarly, Genentech's Kirk Raab strongly believes in hiring the best employees and leaving them alone, as does John Bryan, CEO of Sara Lee, who fights hard to run the company as a series of small businesses. On the other end of the control spectrum are Mickey Drexler of the Gap and Göran Lindahl, chief executive of Swiss-Swedish ABB.

An interesting potential impact of a CEO's need for control is the implementation of cultural diversity programs in an organization. If the CEO focuses on uniform approaches and unique cultures, little room exists for cultural diversity. On the other hand, if diversity is one of the issues that the high-control CEO focuses on, the organization is likely to implement diversity programs aggressively in order to achieve the uniform goals set by the CEO. Such a situation appears to have taken place at GE, where Jack Welch pushed cultural diversity and the advancement of women as one of his personal goals. His high-control style was partly responsible for the success of such policies. Herb Stokes, the outspoken CEO of Alliance Relocation Services LLC, is equally relentless about diversity issues. He targets specific minority groups when hiring employees and will not budge until he gets his way (Hofman 2001). Answering hints of discrimination, he states:

> I'm not discriminating at all. I made a conscious decision that I wanted a diverse company, so I recruit from sources—employment agencies, placement companies—that are going to give me diverse people. (Hofman 2001, p. 73)

Strategic Leadership Types

The two themes of challenge seeking and need for control impact leaders' decision-making and managerial styles and the way they manage the various strategic forces (Nahavandi and Malekzadeh 1993a, 1993b). First, the upper-echelon leader has to understand and interpret the environment of the organization. Second, as the primary decision maker, the leader selects the strategy for the organization. Third, the leader plays a crucial role in the implementation of the chosen strategy through the creation and encouragement of a certain culture and structure, and the selection of leaders and managers throughout the organization.

Challenge seeking and need for control combine to yield four strategic leadership types (see Figure 9-3). Each type represents an extreme case of strategic management style, and they handle the strategic forces in a manner consistent with their basic tendencies and preferences. Given the pressure toward empowerment, employee participation, and the perceived need by many to be unconventional and innovative in all aspects of an organization, it might appear that some types of leaders are more desirable than others. The participative innovator (PI), in particular, could be perceived as ideal. Such an assumption, however, is inaccurate; different leadership styles fit different organizations based on their long-term strategic needs.

Descriptions of Types and Impact on Organizations

The first strategic type is the high-control innovator (HCI). The HCI leader is a challenge seeker who likes to maintain tight control over organizational functioning. This type of leader sees opportunities in the environment and is willing to use technological advancements to achieve goals. HCIs look for risky and innovative strategies at the corporate and business levels that involve navigating uncharted territories and entering new markets or new industries. (See Table 9-3 for a summary of leaders' impact on an organization and how they perceive and manage the six strategic forces.)

As opposed to the need for innovation when concerned with external factors, HCIs tend to be conservative in the management of their organization. The HCI leader has a high need for control that leads to the creation of a highly controlled culture in

DESIRE FOR CONTROL

High Control   Low Control

	High Control	Low Control
High Challenge Seeking	***High-Control Innovator (HCI)*** Challenge-seeking leader who maintains tight control of the organization	***Participative Innovator (PI)*** Challenge-seeking leader who delegates control of the organization
Low Challenge Seeking	***Status Quo Guardian (SQG)*** Challenge-averse leader who maintains tight control of the organization	***Status Quo Guardian (SQG)*** Challenge-averse leader who delegates control of the organization

CHALLENGE SEEKING

Figure 9-3
Four Strategic Leadership Types

which adherence to common goals and procedures is encouraged and rewarded. Decision making is likely to be centralized, with the leader delegating few if any of the major decisions. The ideal organization for an HCI leader is one that is innovative and focused. The employees have a strong common bond and believe in "their way" of managing. Mickey Drexler, the Gap executive discussed previously, provides an example of an HCI. Although he has been innovative and takes risks in his strategies and marketing, he keeps a tight control over his organization. His COO states: "Mickey's always looking for a way to improve. He is always on the road, always talking to people in stores" (Munk 1998, p. 82). Another Gap manager notes: "Nothing gets by Mickey. His attention to detail is extraordinary. He looks at threads, buttons, everything. He's difficult and very demanding. He can attack" (Munk 1998, p. 71).

Unlike the HCI, the status quo guardian (SQG) does not seek challenge; however, like the HCI, SQGs want to maintain control (see Figure 9-3). This type of leader needs control over the internal functioning of the organization and is risk averse. SQGs perceive their environment as threatening and have a tendency to want to protect their organization from its impact. They do not seek new and innovative strategies, but rather stick to tried and well-tested strategies (Nahavandi and Malekzadeh 1993b). The organization run by an SQG leader is not likely to be an industry leader in new-product development and innovation. However, it might be known for efficiency and low cost.

The ideal organization for an SQG leader is highly focused and conservative with a tight, well-defined culture that expects employees and managers to conform to existing practices and procedures. Decision making is highly centralized, with the SQG leader keeping informed and involved in the majority of decisions. Tootsie Roll Industries, Incorporated, is a privately held company with considerable name recognition that is run by SQG leaders: Ellen Gordon and her husband Melvin, along with four other executives, have full control of all operations. Tootsie Roll has been named

Table 9-3

The Impact of Strategic Leadership Types on the Six Strategic Forces

LEADER	PERCEPTION OF ENVIRONMENT	TECHNOLOGY	STRATEGY	CULTURE	STRUCTURE	LEADERSHIP
HCI	Presence of many opportunities for growth and threats from others	Innovation and use of high technology	High risk; product innovation; stick to core	Strong dominant culture with few subcultures	Centralized decision making by a few people	Leaders and managers with similar styles and views
SQG	Many threats; desire to protect organization from outsiders	Little focus on innovation unless it helps control	Low risk; few innovations; focus on efficiency	Strong dominant culture; low tolerance for diversity	Centralized decision making by a few people	Leaders and managers with similar styles and views
PI	Many opportunities; tendency to open organization to outside	Encouragement of experimentation; wide use of technology	High risk; product innovation; open to new areas	Fluid main culture; many subcultures; high tolerance for diversity	Decentralized decision making to lowest levels; empowerment and participation	Leaders and managers with many diverse styles and views
PM	Threats and tendency to protect organization from outside	Moderate use of technological innovation	Low risk; few innovations; focus on efficiency	Fluid culture with focus on "no change"; tolerance for diversity	Decentralized decision making; participation	Leaders and managers with many diverse styles and views

Source: Partially based on information in Nahavandi, A., and A. R. Malekzadeh. 1993a. Leader style in strategy and organizational performance: An integrative framework. *Journal of Management Studies* 30, no. 3, 405–425; Nahavandi, A., and A. R. Malekzadeh. 1993b. *Organizational culture in the management of mergers.* New York: Quorum Books.

repeatedly as one of the best-run small companies in the United States. Much of the credit for its success goes to the Gordons for their single-minded focus on their business and their benevolent, authority-oriented styles. The company has managed to focus on the candy-making business for 100 years, and through a number of defensive moves, has warded off acquisition attempts. With a narrow strategy and tight controls, the Gordons encourage openness and feedback from employees and continue to build a strong, conservative culture.

The participative innovator (PI) is diametrically opposed to the SQG. Whereas the SQG values control and low-risk strategies, the PI seeks challenge and innovation on the outside and creates a loose, highly open, and participative culture and structure inside the organization. PIs view the environment as offering many opportunities and are open to outside influences that could bring change in all areas, including technology. Similar to the HCI, the PI is a challenge seeker and is likely to select strategies that are high risk. An organization run by a PI is often known for being at the cutting edge of technology, management innovation, and creativity.

The ideal organization for a PI leader is open and decentralized, with many of the decisions made at the lowest possible level, because the leader's low need for control allows for delegation of many of the decisions. The culture is loose, with much tolerance for diversity of thought and practice. The only common defining element might be tolerance of diversity—a "vive la difference" mentality. Employees are encouraged to create their own procedures and are given much autonomy to implement their decisions. The key to PI leadership is allowing employees and managers to develop their own structure and come up with the ideas that lead to innovative products, services, and processes.

Ricardo Semler (see Chapter 6) is celebrated for his willingness to give up control and empower his employees while implementing innovative management strategies (Colvin 2001b). Roy Wetterstrom, an entrepreneur who has created several businesses, is a high risk taker, but he also believes that "to make a big strategic shift, you'll need to take a breather from day-to-day stuff" (Hofman 2000, p. 58) and push responsibility down the chain of command. John Chambers, CEO of Cisco Systems, often introduces himself as the "corporate overhead," serves ice cream to his employees, is open to ideas, is willing to adapt, and relies heavily on others to make decisions (Kupfer 1998). One Cisco employee describes the culture: "John has instilled a culture in which it's not a sign of weakness but a sign of strength to say, 'I can't do everything myself'" (Kupfer 1998, p. 86).

The last type of strategic leader, the process manager (PM), has the internal elements of PI leadership and the external elements of SQG leadership. The PM leader prefers conservative strategies that stick to the tried and tested. PMs are likely to shy away from risky innovation. However, the PM's low need for control is likely to engender diversity and openness within the organization. Employees are not required to adhere to common goals and culture. As such, they have autonomy, and day-to-day operations are not highly standardized; the basic condition for decision making is not to create undue risk for the organization.

As the former president of American Express and RJR Nabisco, and CEO of IBM since 1993, Lou Gerstner has a well-established and enviable track record as a strategic leader. He joined IBM at a time when the company was facing one of the most serious crises of its history. Gerstner is a cautious leader. While at RJR Nabisco, he opened the way for reconsideration of many internal processes. He is intelligent and has exceptional analytical skills, but he is careful about change. He strongly believes that change cannot happen unless it is balanced with stabilization (Rogers 1994), and he is particularly skilled at letting his expectations be known. His approach is to improve existing processes slowly. He has changed some elements of IBM and is proud of the company's slow and steady progress. He has been called an incrementalist rather than a revolutionary who has not made big mistakes but is moving too slowly.

All types of successful and effective leaders can be found in organizations. The need to revitalize our organizations is likely to be the reason we are celebrating innovators. The health care industry's award to best administrators regularly goes to innovators. The most-admired business executives are those who push their busi-

LEADING CHANGE
Sari Baldauf's Fighting Spirit

"We need to be extremely aware and extremely agile" states Sari Baldauf, president of Nokia Networks, the division of Nokia that offers systems and infrastructure for analogs and digital telecommunications networks (Guyon 1999). With a relatively small stature, particularly for a Finn, a personal touch, along with considerable experience and credit for contributing to Nokia becoming one of the most well-known brands in the world, Sari Baldauf is considered one of Europe's most powerful businesswomen (online.wsj.com).

Baldauf had spent 8 years building Nokia's current network business when she took a break to study languages and literature. She returned to become executive vice president of Nokia's Asia Pacific operation. In 1998, Jorma Ollila, CEO of Nokia, appointed Baldauf as president of Nokia Networks with the tough assignment of helping Nokia catch up with rivals Erickson and Motorola (online.wsj.com). Nokia and Baldauf have been highly success-

ful. Nokia is one of the world's best-known brands, with *Nokia* being synonymous with *mobile phone* in many parts of the world (Guyon 1999). Although most of its rivals struggled in the early 2000s, Nokia continued to produce amazing results due to efficient manufacturing and great marketing (People to Watch 2001).

As part of Nokia's close-knit, nine-member executive board, Baldauf has been instrumental to the company's success. She is keenly aware that flexibility and speed are key to success in her industry. She states: "We all have a fast market-adjusted rhythm in our spinal reflexes, and so we have ourselves been able to influence the rapid development occurring in the industry." She credits Nokia's teams for the company's success. Baldauf believes that cooperation with universities, networking within the industry, and continuously improving the quality of education of Nokia employees are key to the company being able to stay ahead in a fast-paced, fast-moving industry.

Sources: www.career-space.com/what's_new/prnttns.htm; Guyon, J. October 1999. Next up for cell phones, www.business2.com/articles/mag/1,1640,5787,00.html, accessed April 16, 2002; Europe's 25 most successful businesswomen, online.wsj.com/article_email/0,,SB1014757702301666600,00.html, accessed March 4, 2002; People to watch 2001. 2001. *Fortune* (January 8), 34; Fox, J. Sari Baldauf, 45, www.business2.com/articles/mag/print/0,1643,8648,FF.html.

nesses through change. However, many uncelebrated SQG and PM leaders are managing highly effective and efficient organizations. For example, the leaders of the much-publicized Lincoln Electric Company have consistently been SQGs or PMs. Their organization is a model for using financial incentives in successfully managing performance. Our current tendency to appreciate only change could make us overlook some highly effective managers and leaders.

Strategic Leadership: Culture and Gender

Given the cross-cultural differences in micro leadership style and the importance and impact of culture on leadership behaviors, one would expect that strategic leadership also differs across cultures to some extent. Cultural values, in particular, can be expected to impact a top manager's decisions and style (Finkelstein and Hambrick 1996).

Effect of Culture

Although little recent empirical research has been conducted about the direct effect of culture on executive style, considerable anecdotal evidence suggests similarities and differences across cultures. As organizations are becoming more global, their strategic leaders are also increasingly global, a factor that can attenuate cross-cultural differences. Consider that L'Oreal, the French cosmetics company, is headed by Lindsay Own-Jones, who is Welsh. Irishman Tony O'Reilly runs the all-American Heinz, Swiss Nestle is headed by a German, and Rajat Gupta, an Indian, is head of the consulting firm of McKinsey. Other companies actively seek to build diverse and multicultural TMTs. For example, half of the senior managers at Citibank and Procter & Gamble are not from the United States (Fisher 1997).

Models of cultures such as those proposed by Trompenaars (1994) also suggest that strategic leadership differs from one country to another. For example, being part of the *cadre* (French word for "management") in France means having fairly distinct characteristics (Barsoux and Lawrence 1991). In the United States, upper-echelon managers are from different social classes with many different skills and backgrounds, but the French upper-echelon leaders are much more homogeneous. In a high power-distance culture in which leaders are ascribed much authority and many powers, the cadre comes almost exclusively from the upper social classes. Nearly all have graduated from a few top technical universities (Grandes Ecoles), where entry depends as much on social standing as it does on intellectual superiority. These schools have a strong military influence and continue to be male dominated. Their goal is to train highly intellectual, highly disciplined students who develop close ties and support each other well beyond their years in school. The French cadre is, therefore, characterized by intellectual brilliance, ability to analyze and synthesize problems, and excellent communication skills. Contrary to the case with U.S. leaders, the cadre's focus is not on practical issues or the development of interpersonal skills. With high-power distance, there is little need to convince subordinates of the leadership's ideas (Laurent 1983). The cadre is expected to be highly intelligent, and its decisions are not questioned.

Many of the members of French upper management have considerable experience in the public and governmental sectors. This allows them to forge government-business relationships that do not exist in countries such as the United States. Interestingly, graduates of the Grandes Ecoles would not consider working for those who have received regular university education. This factor perpetuates the homogeneity of the cadre, which in turn creates a group of like-minded executives who agree on many industrial and political issues. By the same token, this like-mindedness can lead to lack of innovation, as the focus on intellect at the expense of action can cause poor implementation.

Effect of Gender

Another area of interest is potential gender differences. Unfortunately, little research has been conducted about gender differences in strategic leadership. It is evident that many of the top-level female executives in traditional organizations have succeeded because their style mirrors that of their male counterparts. As Linda Hoffman, a managing partner at Coopers & Lybrand, states, "Many of the things you must do to succeed are more comfortable for men than women" (Himelstein and Anderson-Forest 1997, p. 68). Nonetheless, the more recent accounts of female executives and business owners and their focus on openness, participation, and interactive leadership provide some basis to make deductions about gender differences. It appears that the feminine style of leadership is generally low control. Advertising company Ogilvy & Mather CEO Shelly Lazarus asserts: "Power is more important to men. Men like to issue orders. They like to feel powerful. I get no thrill out of being powerful" (Sellers 1998, p. 80). Similarly, Parmount's Sherry Lansing is famous for her nurturing style, charm, and ability to show empathy (Sellers 1998). Gail McGovern, president of Fidelity Investments, observes that: ". . . real power is influence. My observation is that women tend to be better in positions where they can be influential (Sellers, 2000, p. 148).

Whether they are challenge seekers or risk averse, many upper-echelon women leaders, such as those described in the research by Sally Helgesen (1990), encourage diversity of thought and employee empowerment. Their supportive style allows employees to contribute to decision making. In addition, the web structure that some women leaders are reputed to use is flat, with well-informed leaders at the center and without centralized decision making.

As is the case with micro leadership, the type of strategic leadership that is needed depends on the type of environment the organization faces, the industry to which it belongs, and the internal culture and structure that it currently has. Therefore, leaders define and influence strategic forces, and their style also needs to match existing ones. If an organization is in a highly stable industry with few competitors, the need for innovation and openness might not be as great. The appropriate focus in such circumstances would be on efficiency. For such an organization, a highly participative and innovative strategic leadership style might not be appropriate.

How Do Executives Affect Their Organization?

Regardless of the type of leadership at the top of an organization, the processes through which strategic leaders impact and influence the organization are similar. As the chief decision makers and the people in charge of providing general guidelines for implementation of the strategies, top executives influence their organizations in a variety of ways (see Figure 9-4).

Direct Decisions

Leaders' decisions regarding various aspects of the organization shape the course of their organization. The choices regarding the vision and mission for an organization influence all aspects of an organization's functioning. The vision and mission affect the culture of an organization by determining what the basic assumptions are, what is important, what needs to be attended to first, and what is considered to be of lesser value. Similarly, the choice of strategy is considered to be the almost-exclusive domain of top management (Gupta 1986).

In addition to the vision, mission, culture, and strategy, the decisions to adopt a new structure, adjust an existing one, or make any changes in the formal interrelationship among employees of an organization rest primarily with top management (Miller and Droge 1986; Nahavandi 1993; Yasai-Ardekani 1986, 1989). The leader can determine the structure of the organization through direct decisions on the type of structure or indirectly through the way employees share and use information. Mickey Drexler of the Gap never uses e-mail and does not write memos. He likes to leave voice messages and communicate face to face. His employees have learned to check their voice mail on a regular basis and be ready for his questions at any time (Munk 1998). A leader who consistently communicates only through formal reporting channels sets up a different structure than one who crosses hierarchical lines and encourages others to do so, as well.

Figure 9-4
The Processes Leaders Use to Impact Their Organizations

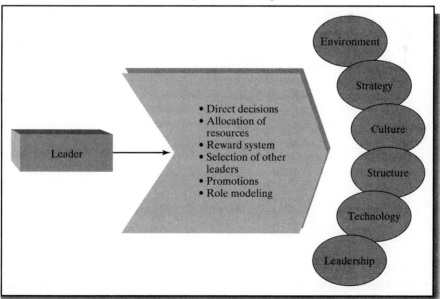

Allocation of Resources and Control Over the Reward System

In addition to direct decisions, one of the most powerful effects of top managers on their organization is through the allocation of resources and the control they have over the reward system (Kerr and Slocum 1987; Schein 1985). A top executive is the final decision maker on allocation of resources to departments or individuals. If leaders want to encourage continued innovation and creativity, they might decide that the R&D and training departments of the organization will get the lion's share of the resources. Such allocations reinforce certain goals and actions, support a particular organizational culture and strategy, and create structures that facilitate desired outcomes and discourage undesirable ones (Kets De Vries and Miller 1986; Miller 1987). Consider that Jeff Bezos, CEO of the successful on-line bookseller Amazon.com, is most worried about upstart competitors who have innovative ideas and cutting edge technology. He has, therefore, decided to allocate a large portion of his organization's resources to updating technology (Martin 1996).

The formal and informal reward systems also can have a powerful impact on the culture of an organization and on the behavior of its members (Schein 1985). For example, top managers can shape the culture of their organization by rewarding conformity to unique norms and standards of behavior at the expense of diversity of behaviors and opinions (Nahavandi and Malekzadeh 1988). This process could take place not only through encouragement of certain behaviors but also through the selection of other top managers and the promotion of those who adhere to the leader's culture. Such a process is likely to take place regardless of the leader's style of strategic leadership. For instance, an HCI will be most comfortable with other HCIs, whereas a PI will prefer other managers with a similar style in key positions. A comparable process is likely to take place on an individual employee level. Employees whose actions fit the vision, mission, and culture of the organization are more likely to be rewarded. These processes create domino effects that further lead an organization to reflect the style and preferences of its leader.

Setting the Norms and Modeling

Whereas rewarding certain types of behaviors and decisions is an overt action on the part of the leader, modeling behaviors and setting certain decision standards and norms are more indirect ways of impacting organizations. In addition to making decisions, the top managers can set the parameters by which others make decisions. For example, CEOs might tell their vice presidents that they will go along with their choice of a new product while also providing them with clear guidelines on which types of products are appropriate and which types of markets the organization should enter. By setting such standards, even without making a direct decision, the CEO still can be assured that the vice presidents will make the "right" decision.

Another subtle way in which leaders affect their organization is by the types of behavior they model (Nahavandi and Malekzadeh 1993a; Schein 1985). A top manager who believes that physical fitness is important might engage in vigorous exercise and invite members of the TMT to join in. Irishman Feargal Quinn, founder and president of Superquinn, a chain of supermarkets, has gained a reputation as the "pope of customer service" (LaBarre 2001b, p. 90). He focuses obsessively on making sure his customers come back—an obsession that he transfers to his employees. Another area in which role modeling can have a powerful impact is in ethics. Stan Shih, CEO of Acer, set the tone for his organization by suggesting that there are no alternatives to integrity and honesty (Kraar 1995). Bob Moffat, head of IBM's personal computers, demonstrates the need for hard work by spending 15 to 16 hours a day at the office (Fishman 2001).

Direct decisions, allocation of resources and rewards, setting of decision norms, and modeling are some of the ways through which a leader impacts the organization. Through these various processes, leaders can make an organization be the reflection of their style and preferences. They also provide strategic leaders with considerable power and influence. Such power requires some accountability, which is considered in the next section.

STRATEGIC LEADERS' ACCOUNTABILITY

CEOs and TMTs around the world have considerable power and influence over people's lives. Their actions affect the economic health of countries and citizens. For this burden, CEOs are well rewarded financially and achieve considerable status. The topic of executive compensation, another governance mechanism, has attracted considerable attention. In 2001, executive salaries and stock options in the largest companies in the United States exceeded $10 million, a 16 percent increase over the previous year (Abelson 2001). CEO compensation packages, which include salary, bonuses, and stock options, have more than doubled since 1995 when companies paid their executives an average of $4.4 million (Abelson 2001). However, during the same years, on the whole, other white- and blue-collar workers in the United States saw less than a 4 percent increase in their income. A more telling figure is the ratio between the CEO's and workers' pay. Whereas the ratio in the United States was 30:1 in the 1960s, it was close to 100:1 in the mid-1990s (Uchitelle 1996).

Even ousted CEOs fare well. When toy maker Mattel ousted Jill Barad because of the company's poor performance, she received a $26.4 million payout and supplemental retirement worth $1 million. In addition, the board forgave her $4.2 million stock-related loan, the balance on a $3 million home loan, and covered the $3.3 million tax hit that resulted from the forgiven loans (Strauss 2001). Gillette paid CEO Michael Hawley $8.7 million when the board fired him after only 18 months on the job. Ralston Purina awarded its ex-CEO shares worth $16.2 million (Strauss 2001).

Interestingly, the salary of CEOs in other industrialized countries does not even come close to that of their U.S. counterparts. Japanese and European executives earn between one-half to one-tenth that of comparable U.S. CEOs. These differences could be explained by stating that U.S. executives, as evidenced by a strong U.S. economy, are simply better and more effective than their counterparts all over the world; however, the issue is not that simple. Theoretically, boards of directors determine the CEO's compensation relative to company performance; the better the financial performance of the company is, the higher the CEO's compensation is. Therefore, CEO compensation can be an effective tool for motivating and controlling managers. However, several highly publicized cases are at least one indication that CEO compensation is not always tied to their company's financial performance. For example, Maytag and Commodore International experienced serious financial losses in the late eighties, but their CEOs' compensation increased by 38 percent and 40 percent, respectively (Serwer 1993). Many executives get pay raises that are considerably higher than their company's performance levels would indicate (Delacroix and Saudagaran 1991). Similarly, in 1996, when AT&T was laying off more than 40,000 workers, its CEO's compensation package exceeded $16 million (Puri 1997).

Clearly, company performance is not the only determinant of CEO compensation. So why are U.S. executives worth so much? (See Table 9-4 for a summary.) One factor that seems to explain the size of executive pay in the United States is the size of the organization (for a review, see Finkelstein and Hambrick 1988, 1996). The larger the organization is, the larger the CEO's compensation package is, regardless of performance. Another factor seems to be the competition for hiring CEOs. As organizations outbid one another, salaries continue to increase. For example, Conseco, having fired its CEO and being in financial crisis, still paid former GE Capital executive Gary Wendt a $45 million cash signing bonus to forfeit his GE options and become their CEO (Colvin 2001a).

Organizations in which top managers have more discretion also tend to have higher pay (Finkelstein and Boyd 1998). Several other factors further impact executive pay. For instance, research shows that top-management pay and company performance are more aligned when the company's board of directors is dominated by members from outside the organization (Conyon and Peck 1998). Other research considering the impact of internationalization has found that increased internationalization is related to higher CEO pay (Sanders and Carpenter 1998). Some have suggested that the high demands put on CEOs and the instability of their positions must be balanced with high salaries. These high salaries have become standard in U.S. industry, and there appears to be no end to the trend. The result is the creation of a new, powerful U.S. managerial class and a widening of the gap between high and low levels of organizations.

Many of the highly paid top executives have become popular heroes whose names are part of our everyday life. Based on economic and organizational theory, environmental forces will push a nonperforming leader to be replaced. Ideally, elected federal, state, and city officials who do not perform are not reelected. Similarly, the board of directors replaces a CEO who does not manage well. The prin-

Table 9-4
Factors That Affect Executive Compensation

Firm size	The larger the firm is, the higher the compensation amount is.
Industry competition	Companies often outbid one another to hire top executives.
CEO power and discretion	The greater the power of the CEO is, the greater the compensation package is.
Internationalization	Increased internationalization is related to higher executive pay.
High stress and instability	CEO jobs are considered high stress and, therefore, require high compensation.

cipal of a school with poor student academic performance and a high dropout rate would be fired by the school board. These ideal situations do not seem to be common, however. Many powerful leaders are not being held accountable for their actions. They continue to hold positions of power and influence regardless of their organization's poor performance, ethical abuses, and social irresponsibility. It is not common in the United States for a company CEO or public officials to resign when they fail to live up to the promises they made. When their organizations cause major disasters, the CEOs escape unscathed. The CEO of Exxon accepted none of the responsibility for the *Valdez* fiasco. After the Bhopal disaster, with several thousand dead and hundreds of thousands injured, the CEO of Union Carbide was not replaced. Even in the case of Enron, it took considerable public outcry and pressure before Kenneth Lay resigned. Our elected officials continue to represent us poorly. It took years of mismanagement before any GM president was fired. Even then, he was replaced by a member of the inner circle that had supported him.

For the benefit of organizational and social functioning and well-being, it is essential that the tremendous power, influence, and status of CEOs be accompanied by accountability and responsibility to their various constituents. Such accountability exists on paper but is hardly ever executed. The power and impact of upper-echelon leaders are undeniable. However, their credibility and ability to further impact their organizations can increase only with more accountability.

SUMMARY AND CONCLUSION

Many of the same processes apply to the upper levels as to the small-group levels of leadership. However, upper-echelon leadership adds a new level of complexity to the process by focusing the leader on a whole organization rather than a small group or department and by giving the leader discretion with far-reaching impacts over decisions. In addition, upper-echelon leaders focus on external constituencies as well as the internal environment, and in so doing are required to lead with a team of other executives.

An integrated approach to upper-echelon leadership considers the leader to be a formulator and implementer of strategy. Therefore, in addition to considering the need to match the leader to existing strategy and other organizational elements, the integrated approach also considers the role of the leader's individual characteristics and style in the selection of various organizational elements and the implementation of decisions. The matching concept, which views the CEO primarily as an implementer of existing strategy, is useful when considering the effect of the leader when the organization is selecting a leader to implement a newly charted course.

Two major themes run through the diverse research about top-management characteristics. The first theme is the leader's degree of challenge seeking and preference for risk and innovation. The second is the leader's need for control over the organization. The combination of these two themes yields four types of strategic leaders: HCI, SQG, PI, and PM. These four types each have different preferences for the direction and management of their organization. They exert their influence through direct decisions, allocation of resources and rewards, and the setting of norms and the modeling of desired behaviors. Through these processes, strategic leaders gain considerable power and influence. Such power is accompanied by generous compensation packages. However, accountability for the actions of top executives is still limited.

Overall, the area of strategic leadership provides a different and important perspective to the study of leadership. Strategic leaders face many challenges that micro leaders do not have to deal with. The study of strategic leaders is also a fertile area for integrative research linking micro- and macrofactors.

BOD and CEOs

Public corporations are led by CEOs and other upper-echelon leaders who, in turn, report to shareholders and boards of directors (BODs). Interestingly, while the board oversees the CEOs, decides on terms of employment and salaries and monitors their performance, the CEOs are, more often than not, the people who nominate board members. The justification is that CEOs are well placed to know what type of expertise they need on the board and should have a BOD they can work with. The relationship between the BOD and the CEOs is a complex and interesting one.

1. What are the potential ethical and conflict-of-interest issues arising from CEO involvement in the selection of board members?
2. How can these issues be addressed?

REVIEW AND DISCUSSION QUESTIONS

1. How are current changes in organizations affecting the differences between micro and macro leadership?
2. What are the strategic forces in organizations?
3. What is the role of the upper echelon in managing the strategic forces in the formulation and implementation of strategy?
4. Provide examples for each of the moderating factors on the impact of leadership in organizations.
5. What are the major themes in various constructs used to describe upper-echelon leaders?
6. Describe each of the four strategic leadership types. Provide examples of each type.
7. How do culture and gender affect strategic leadership?
8. Describe each of the processes used by leaders to influence strategic forces in their organizations. Which of the processes is most important? Why?
9. What is the upper echelon's responsibility in organizational actions and performance?

SEARCHING THE WEB

Developing Strategic Leaders:
  www.ndu.edu/inss/books/strategic/
  pt2ch7.html
Information about Strategic Management and Strategic Leadership:
  knowledge.wharton.upenn.edu/category.
  cfm?catid=7

Grupo M Web Site:
  www.grupom.com.do/

EXERCISE 9-1: UNDERSTANDING STRATEGIC FORCES

This exercise is designed to help you understand the role of leaders in managing the six strategic forces of environment, strategy, culture, structure, technology, and leadership presented in the chapter.

The Scenario

You are a member of a school board for a medium-sized middle (junior high) school in a major western city. The city has experienced tremendous growth in the past 5 years; as a result, the student body has increased in size by 20 percent without much change in facilities and a relatively limited increase in funding. The classrooms are overcrowded, much of the equipment is old, teachers have limited resources with which to enrich the curriculum, and no clear sense of direction is evident. During the same time period, the school has slowly developed one of the poorest records for student academic performance and dropout rate.

Prior to the past few years, however, the school had a well-established reputation as one of the most creative and academically sound schools in the city. Traditionally, parent involvement and interest in the school have varied greatly. Similarly, the faculty are diverse in their approach, tenure, and backgrounds, but the majority have demonstrated dedication to their students and are committed to the improvement of the school.

Due to a number of recent threats of lawsuits from parents over equal opportunity issues, several violent incidents among the students, and the poor academic performance, the principal was just asked to resign. Many parents, teachers, and board members blamed her for a laissez faire attitude and what appeared to be a total lack of direction and focus. Problems and complaints simply were not addressed and no plan appeared to be in place for dealing with the changes that the school was experiencing.

After a 2-month, multistate regional search and interviews with a number of finalists, the school board has narrowed its search for the new principal to two candidates.

The Candidates

J. B. Davison is 55 years old and has a doctorate in education administration with a bachelor of arts and a master of arts in education. He has been the principal at two other schools, where he was successful in focusing on basic academic skills, traditional approaches, discipline, and encouragement of success. Prior to moving to school administration, he was a history and social studies teacher. The board is impressed with his clear headedness and no-nonsense approach to education. He readily admits that he is conservative and traditional, and considers himself to be a father figure to the students. He runs a tight ship and is involved in every aspect of his school.

Jerry Popovich is 40 years old. She also has a master's and doctorate in education administration with an undergraduate degree in computer science. She worked in the computer industry for several years prior to starting to teach science and math. She has been an assistant principal in one other school and is currently the principal of an urban middle school on the West Coast. She has been successful at involving many business and community members in her current school. The board is impressed with her creativity and her ability to find novel approaches to problem solving. She considers one of her major strengths to be the ability to involve many constituents in decision making. She describes herself as a facilitator in the education process.

Understanding Strategic Forces Worksheet: Comparing the Candidates

In helping you decide on which person to recommend, consider how each would handle and balance the six strategic management forces of environment, strategy, culture, structure, technology, and leadership.

Strategic Forces	J. B. Davison	Jerry Popovich
Environment		
Strategy		
Culture		
Structure		
Technology		
Leadership		

Discussion Items

How are the two candidates different?

What explains the differences between them?

Your Choice

Who would you recommend for the job? Why?

EXERCISE 9-2: YOUR ORGANIZATION

This exercise is designed to illustrate the potential impact of an upper-echelon leader on the organization. Before starting this exercise, clearly define the department, team, or organization that you are rating. Your instructor also might provide you with several vignettes to use in your evaluation.

Rate your organization or team on the following items, using the scale shown here:

1	2	3	4	5
Strongly disagree	Somewhat disagree	Neither agree nor disagree	Somewhat agree	Strongly agree

_____ **1.** Decision making in my organization is centralized.
_____ **2.** My organization has a strong, thick culture.
_____ **3.** We are always coming up with new ways of doing things.
_____ **4.** A few people make most of the important decisions.
_____ **5.** My organization has many subgroups and cliques.
_____ **6.** Our primary concern is efficiency.
_____ **7.** We are known for our ability to innovate.
_____ **8.** We are open to differing points of views.
_____ **9.** Employees are empowered to make many decisions without checking with management.
_____ **10.** We have not changed our course much in the past few years.
_____ **11.** We take many risks.
_____ **12.** Many rules and procedures are utilized in completing our tasks.
_____ **13.** People are encouraged to do their own thing.

Scoring key: Reverse score items 5, 6, 8, 9, and 13 (1 = 5, 2 = 4, 3 = 3, 4 = 2, 5 = 1)

Organizational Structure: Add items 1, 4, 9, and 12. Maximum score is 20. A higher score indicates a more centralized, control-oriented structure.

Total: _____

Organizational Culture: Add items 2, 5, 8, and 13. Maximum score is 20. A higher score indicates a unicultural organization where diversity is not encouraged.

Total: _____

Strategy: Add items 3, 6, 7, 10, and 11. Maximum score is 25. A higher score indicates risk taking and innovation.

Total: _____

Discussion Issues

Based on your organization's score on the structure, culture, and strategy scales, what would you predict the organization's leaders' strategic leadership style to be?

EXERCISE 9-3: INFLUENCE PROCESSES

This exercise is designed to help you identify the processes that upper-echelon leaders use to impact their organization and most particularly its culture. After reading each of the following scenarios, identify the processes that the leaders and TMT are using to impact the organization.

Brain Toys Executives

Stanley Wang, the CEO of Brain Toys, joined the organization a few years before the founder, J. C. Green, decided to retire. It became clear early on that Stanley was destined to rise fast. With a bachelor of science degree in engineering and graphic design, a masters in business administration, and several years of experience in computer software design, he fit right in with the Brain Toys culture. He was bright, witty, analytical, and competitive. J. C. took a liking to him and put him in charge of several high-visibility projects with potential for high impact and big budgets. Stanley performed every time. Within the first 2 years, Stanley had won all the internal awards that Brain Toys gave its managers. Several of his peers maliciously credited Stanley's love of running rather than his technical and managerial competence as the reason for his success. Stanley ran with the boss every day before work, and they trained for many races together.

The Soft-Touch Leader

Leslie Marks was proud of her accomplishment as one of the few executives in the male-dominated information technology field. As the president of Uniform Data Link, she describes herself as a "soft-touch" leader. "I just don't believe in heavy-handed leadership. People have to be able to express themselves and that is when you get the best out of them. Our best ideas come from all levels." She keeps an open door for all employees and has moved her office from the third floor to the first. She often comes to work in jeans and spends a lot of time with the engineers brainstorming on technical problems. She has changed many of the evaluation and promotion procedures and has asked several less-educated but highly experienced employees to work with her on important projects.

The Hospital Economist

J. Hadad graduated with a doctorate in economics and health care administration from a major southwestern university, and after many years of work in various health care organizations, Hadad was named the top administrator of a major Phoenix hospital. As an economist and a strong believer in fair pay, Hadad has focused much time with the human resource managers, revamping the hospital's compensation and benefit plan. The old system based on seniority was all but dismantled and replaced with a pay-for-performance system that ties all employees' pay, including the physicians', partially to the hospital's financial performance. The plan allows for some flexibility for 2 years, whereby employees are not penalized for poor performance but are rewarded only for good financial health. After 2 years, they share in the good and the bad. Most of the hospital's employees complain that Hadad seems to care about nothing else. Many also note a major change in everybody's behaviors.

Influence Process Worksheet

Influence Method	Stanley Wang	Leslie Marks	Joseph Hadad
Direct decisions			
Allocation of resources			
Reward system			
Selection and promotion of other leaders			
Role modeling			

SELF-ASSESSMENT 9-1: WHAT IS YOUR STRATEGIC LEADERSHIP TYPE?

This exercise is a self-rating based on the four strategic leadership types presented in the chapter. You also can use the scale to rate your organizational leaders.

For each of the following items, please rate yourself using the following scale. (You can also use the items to rate a leader in your organization.)

0	1	2	3
Never	Sometimes	Often	Always

_____ 1. I enjoy working on routine tasks.
_____ 2. I am looking for new ways of doing things.
_____ 3. I have trouble delegating tasks to my subordinates.
_____ 4. I like my subordinates to share the same values and beliefs.
_____ 5. Change makes me uncomfortable.
_____ 6. I encourage my subordinates to participate in decision making.
_____ 7. It is hard for me to get things done when there are many contrasting opinions.
_____ 8. I enjoy working on new tasks.
_____ 9. I feel comfortable giving power away to my subordinates.
_____ 10. I consider myself to be a risk taker.

Scoring key: Reverse scores for items 1, 5, 6, 7, and 9 (0 = 3, 1 = 2, 2 = 1, 3 = 0).

Challenge-Seeking Score: Add items 1, 2, 5, 8, and 10. Your score will be between 0 and 15.

Total: _____ Transfer the score to the challenge-seeking line (vertical line) in the accompanying grid.

Need for Control Score: Add items 3, 4, 6, 7, and 9. Your score will be between 0 and 15.

Total: _____ Transfer the score to the control line (horizontal line) in the accompanying grid.

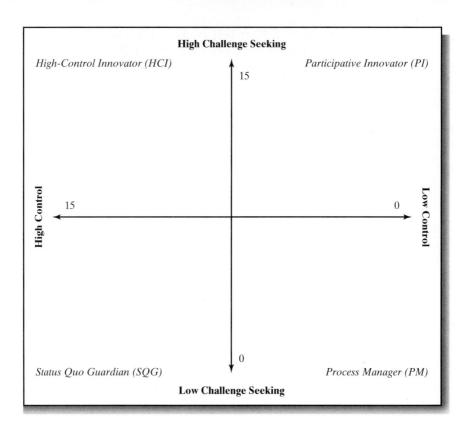

What Is Your Strategic Leadership Type?

Where do your two scores intersect? For example, if you have a score of 5 on control and 10 on challenge seeking, your scores indicate that you are a participative innovator.

C A S E

Leadership in Action

Fernando Capellán Is Mixing a Social Agenda and Business Success

The mention of a Central American garment factory is likely to evoke the image of a sweatshop with dreadful work conditions, worker exploitation, and child labor. Grupo M successfully dispels all these stereotypes. With 26 factories employing 13,000 people, Grupo M is the largest private employer in the Dominican Republic (grupom.com.do). The company makes garments for designers such as Tommy Hillfiger and Ralph Lauren. It does so at great profit and while advancing a social agenda that is a model for companies all over the developing world. "To dress the world with quality—stitch by stitch" is the company motto (grupom.com.do).

Fernando Capellán, founder and president, created Grupo M in 1986 to contribute to his hometown of Santiago and to his nation. He states:

> When I make decisions, first I think of the company and the people who work for me. But then I think of Santiago. I'm committed to this town. These are my people; this is where I was born. (Dahle 2000, p. 256)

He also knows that he needs to slowly change the unstructured agricultural culture that his workers are used to, where life is dictated by the rhythms of nature rather than the needs of a business. "If it's raining nobody works, If it's windy, nobody works . . . The other days work is over by 10 A.M., because the sun is too hot. We are going through a change in mentality" (Dahle 2000, p. 258). In addition to running Grupo M, Capellán is also a social business activist, the president of the National Free Zones Association (ADOZONA), and recipient of the 1996 distinguished "Leadership of the Year Award" from the Bobbin Group in recognition of his innovative business success (www.webaid.net).

Grupo M and Capellán's fame are well deserved. Because of the company literacy program started in 1987, almost all employees can read. Their children attend a free day care; they can take English language courses, visit the company medical clinic, fix their cars at the company garage, eat breakfast at work every morning, and take the company shuttle bus to and from work—all free! (www.utopies.com). All new sewing machine operators get a 6-month training program to develop their writing skills, and learn about personal health, safety, communication skills, and other job skills (usemb. gov.do). Capellán's sister, Mercedes Capellán de Lama, former company physician and current executive, believes that all these programs are responsible for the amazingly low 1 percent yearly turnover rate (Dahle 2000).

This way of doing business comes naturally to the Capelláns:

> We have proven that you don't have to run a factory like a sweatshop in order to be profitable and to grow. In fact we believe that we have been able to innovate, to expand, and to do what we have done because of the way that we treat our people. (Dahl 2000, p. 256)

Grupo M's labor costs are higher than those of most garment factories around the world. However, by using new technology and a modular production process instead of the traditional assembly line, and because of their unique culture, they produce much higher-quality products and do so much more efficiently (Dahle 2000).

"Good ideas can come from anywhere. Our customers have taught us new methods of quality control. But the best ideas often come from the sewing-machine operators themselves," says Fernando Capellán (Dahle 2000, p. 268). He has learned to listen to his workers through biweekly meetings and to work cooperatively with his management team, which meets daily over lunch. He also is not satisfied with simply producing what his customers send him. He is constantly looking for new fabrics, new work methods, new areas of business, and ways to solve his customers' problems (Dahle 2000). He believes that unless he stays ahead, looking for new ideas, his business could become obsolete: "The industry is going to fade away faster than most people think it will. We have to be ready to diversify" (Dahle 2000, p. 270). Instead of exploiting cheap labor, Grupo M invests in its people, trains and educates them, treats them with dignity, and reaps the benefits in profits. Angel Lorenzo, a shift supervisor at Grupo M, states: "My work is my life. It's the reason that I can support my children and have a home, so I take it very seriously" (Dahle 2000, p. 256). ■

QUESTIONS

1. What strategic forces does Fernando Capellán have to consider in his job as president of Grupo M?
2. How would you describe Capellán's strategic leadership style?
3. What challenges does he face? How is he addressing them?

Sources: www.grupom.com.do/flash-eng/index-flash-eng.html, accessed April 16, 2002; www.webaid. net/forums/messages/group.htm; "Ambassador Manett praises Grupo M's progressive labor practices," www.usemb.gov.do/prelease/1102002.htm, accessed April 18, 2002; Dahle, C. 2000. The new fabric of success. *Fast Company* (June), 252–270.

Part

IV

Looking Toward the Future

*P*art IV summarizes our current knowledge of the field of leadership and considers the emerging trends that are likely to shape the future.

This book has been devoted to providing you with an in-depth look at the field of leadership, the existing research, and its practical implications. Scientific methods have helped us learn a great deal about leadership. Experience has also taught us much. Our past and our current knowledge base will guide us toward continued understanding of who leaders are, what makes them effective, and how we can all learn to lead better. The last chapter of the book summarizes our current knowledge and considers where the field might be going in the future.

Chapter 10

Looking Toward the Future: What Will We Be When We Grow Up?

> *If you truly want to understand something, change it.*

—KURT LEWIN

After studying this chapter, you will be able to:

1. Summarize the information and knowledge that you acquired from this book and outline areas that need further clarification.
2. Explain the changes in the leadership context.
3. Distinguish between previous and current definitions of leadership.
4. Understand the challenges that will face leaders in the future.

Leadership is a complex process. Scholars and philosophers have studied leaders throughout human civilization. Researchers have studied the field of leadership using various scientific methods for almost a century. Leaders themselves and those practitioners who help them put all the knowledge to work have come up with their own insights and solutions. All that information helps us understand leadership better. Some aspects are captured well by science; others require insight and intuition.

WHAT WE KNOW AND WHAT WE DON'T KNOW

Thousands of studies about leadership have been conducted. They have taught us a lot. We know much more about leaders and leadership than many of our disagreements and debates would indicate.

We have learned many lessons from history. Although a great amount of diversity is found in even the definition of leadership, there is agreement that leadership is a group phenomenon—no leaders can exist without followers—and that a leader influences and guides others to achieve goals. Finally, leadership assumes a hierarchy, with the leader at the top. We also agree that leadership effectiveness depends on maintaining internal health, as well as external adaptability. Despite the simplicity of these definitions, the actual work of effective leadership is considerably more difficult.

What Do We Know?

In trying to understand leadership, we have focused on traits and behaviors, and finally have accepted that in order to understand leadership, we need a more complex contingency viewpoint. Our past research about traits proposed simplistic approaches; many of the current views either consider a combination of traits or include situational contingencies. We do know that on the average, leaders have more energy, intelligence, motivation, and self-confidence than followers (House and Aditya 1997). However, we also know that no individual trait or even set of traits is enough to predict who will be a leader and when they will be effective.

We understand the role of power in leadership. We are aware of its importance in achieving goals and its potential for corruption. We recognize situational patterns that can make power a detriment rather than a positive tool to a leader. As a result, we are redefining what is considered the appropriate distribution of power in organizations in order to take advantage of its motivational and productive potential.

We have learned about the importance of understanding situational characteristics. We do not look at leadership in a vacuum any longer; we take into consideration the task, the organization, and the followers and their needs. Our current views of leadership are deeply grounded in the concept of contingency. Many of our theories identify situational and individual contingency factors that make a one-size-fits-all leadership style inappropriate. Through the application of various theories, we are able to teach leaders to adjust their own behaviors, change their leadership situation, and make better use of their followers in order to become more effective. We can teach leaders to become better decision makers. We have identified situations in which leaders lose their impact and can show them how to let their followers function without them. We know that leaders are subject to the same biases as the rest of us when it comes to understanding their own and their followers' behaviors, and we can help them overcome some of their biases.

As a result of the need to revitalize institutions worldwide, we have begun to accept the use of teams, understand their role in individualistic cultures, and determine how to use them better. We are reconsidering the role of leaders in a team environment. We know when leaders should and should not use teams, and we can train them to delegate better. The research on task design and leadership substitutes helps us set up autonomous and self-managed teams. We are considering the leadership potential within each follower rather than focusing on the leader alone. Much of our current thinking is focused on how to enact change in organizations. To that end, many of our current views have looked at the change masters of our times and identified their styles and behaviors. Whether it is through charismatic, transformational, visionary, or exemplary leadership, we have become keenly aware of the motivational power of leaders and the importance of the emotional bond between leader and follower.

We have begun to understand the importance of upper-echelon leadership and have mapped out the differences between micro and strategic leadership. We are developing frameworks to help us understand the upper-echelon leaders and the particular challenges that they face.

Although we hope for the universality of our ideas, we have come to realize their cultural limits. The increased globalization of our economy and our changing social structures are teaching us that simple answers to cross-cultural issues are not possible. We have learned that culture, whether it is national, ethnic, or gender-based, impacts the way leaders behave, as well as followers' expectations of their leaders. Such knowledge has made us appropriately cautious about applying our theories to diverse groups and about our own approaches when facing diversity.

> Culture, whether it is national, ethnic, or gender based, impact the way leaders behave, as well as followers' expectations of their leaders. Such knowledge has made us appropriately cautious about applying our theories to diverse groups and about our own approaches when facing diversity.

What Don't We Know?

In spite of our knowledge, there is also much we do not know. The following areas of future investigation should keep many researchers busy for years to come.

Traits Revisited

First, we still need to learn more about leaders' individual characteristics and personality traits. We still must understand better under what circumstances traits explain leader behavior and how several traits and individual characteristics might interact. For example, self-monitoring has been found to impact the extent to which leaders behave in ways that are consistent with their traits. The past few years have seen a resurgence in the interest in leadership skills, and new models are showing considerable promise and point to cognitive abilities as an interesting area of research. Furthermore, in spite of the extensive research on charismatic and transformational leadership, our understanding of the elements of charismatic and other change-oriented characteristics is still lacking.

The Organizational Context

A second area where our knowledge needs further development is in understanding the organizational context in which leaders operate. The micro-leadership research focuses on small groups, teams, and departments but does not consider the broad organizational context. The strategic leadership approach considers the organizational context, but research in the area is still relatively new. Furthermore, the areas of micro and strategic leadership are not well integrated, and little cross-fertilization occurs between them. The theories of charismatic and transformational leadership are particularly well placed for such an integration.

Understanding the organizational context can help us in several ways. First, the organizational context can clarify the impact of individual differences. Personality theorists have for many years suggested that when situational demands are strong, people respond to them instead of acting based on their own tendencies (Mischel 1973). Strong organizational cultures and inflexible structures, for instance, could provide such situational demands and limit the extent to which leaders act on their own tendencies. Such a suggestion also has been made in the case of charismatic leaders. Second, leadership, even at the micro level, simply does not occur in a vacuum. Organizational processes affect leaders at all levels. This is particularly relevant with the current changes in our organizations. Leadership research, by and large, continues to ignore the organizational context beyond consideration of follower and task characteristics.

Finally, understanding the organizational context can help clarify ongoing debates about the difference between leadership and management (Zaleznik 1990). In a recent review, House and Aditya (1997) suggest that the potential lack of impact of traditional leadership research on organizational and social leadership could be due to micro leadership's inordinate focus on management and supervision, rather than strategic leadership. Consideration of the organizational context and processes in analyzing micro-leadership processes might help address this concern.

Cross-Cultural Leadership

Current leadership research considers the potential impact of culture. Several prominent leadership researchers (e.g., Chemers, Oskamp, and Costanzo 1995) and leadership journals such as *Leadership Quarterly* have focused on the role of culture and its importance. Researchers have considered diversity and cross-cultural international topics. The GLOBE project (discussed in Chapter 8) is likely to make considerable contributions to our understanding of cross-cultural issues in leadership.

The question is whether we are doing enough. Some scholars argue that our current theories still are based primarily on male Western leaders (Chen and Van Velsor 1996; Ayman 1993). There is clearly room for considerably more research in the area, particularly when culture is defined to include gender, because research generally does not focus on female leaders.

One of the key themes in the inclusion of culture in leadership research is the issue of "emic" and "etic" approaches. Emic research focuses on understanding a particular culture, whereas etic research attempts to generalize across different cultures. Both types of research are needed to understand leadership across cultures. Other areas that require further development include whether leadership exists in all cultures (Peterson and Hunt 1997), whether contingency concepts vary, what ideal leadership is in different cultures (Triandis 1993), and how to lead culturally diverse groups and organizations (Mai-Dalton 1993).

The need for continued research is guided partly by gaps in our existing knowledge and partly by changes occurring in the leadership context. These are considered next.

CHANGES IN THE LEADERSHIP CONTEXT AND ITS CONSEQUENCES

The world of leaders is changing rapidly. The old cliché that change is the only constant has never been more applicable. Several major changes affect the way we lead organizations (see Table 10-1).

Changing Context

Organization forms and structures are changing. The traditional nineteenth-century and early twentieth-century hierarchies and work processes have been challenged. Due to continued restructuring and financial pressures, organizations have fewer levels and often rely on team-based structures to accomplish their goals. Many also have broken down internal barriers to create boundaryless organizations or are relying on outsourcing, consultants, and outside contractors to perform work typically done by internal employees. Many of us can work at home and be connected to our coworkers and customers anywhere in the world. We work away from our managers and leaders. Employees are relying more on each other and their own knowledge and less on their organization's formal structures.

Companies such as Rosenbluth International, the world's third-largest travel service company, have restructured into what the president calls a family farm structure (Walker 1997). The company is broken down into 100 units, each with their own region and their own clients. Decision making is localized, and the headquarters provides direction. The different cells stay connected through the use of sophisticated

Table 10-1
Changes in Organizations

CHANGES	DESCRIPTION
Structural changes	New structural forms; use of teams; continued push toward empowerment; telecommuting
Changing demographics	Cultural diversity in the United States; aging workforce in the United States and most other Western countries; generational differences
Globalization	Increased cross-cultural encounters; multinational teams; multinational leaders
New work ethic	Disappearing loyalty; changing values about work; push for work and life balance
Learning and knowledge	Knowledge workers; focus on learning organizations
Technology and access to information	New technology; increased information; increased speed of information flow; new ways of accessing and sharing information
Emphasis on flexibility	Flexible structures that can adapt quickly; individual flexibility
Fast-paced change	Internal and external uncertainty due to constant change

technology that allows instant access to data and to people. The company is also proud of its family culture. Rosenbluth states, "We're a company built on friendship" (Walker 1997, p. 120). He believes friendship prevents coworkers from letting each other down and lets them accomplish anything.

Changing demographics and globalization, topics discussed throughout the book, are two other major changes in organizations. Employees from different cultures and generations now work side by side. Although they respond to the same basic principles of leadership, they have different values, different preferences for leadership, and different needs. Some require more structure and direction, and others demand autonomy. Some expect their leaders to be supportive and caring; others simply want to be provided with direction to do their jobs. Some prefer indirect and soft-spoken leaders; others prefer their leaders to be assertive. The employees from different cultures and different generations do not all value work the same way and do not seek the same goals.

The emphasis on learning and the presence of what are called knowledge workers are other factors that are changing the organizational context. These new employees are highly skilled and have considerable knowledge and information at their fingertips. They often can contract out their skills to organizations as independent contractors. Their loyalty is to themselves and their profession—not to any organization, its vision, and its leaders. These knowledge workers do not fit well into traditional structures, but organizations can benefit from them in times of change because they provide flexibility.

The temporary workforce, technology, and globalization are reshaping information in organizations. Whereas access to information was once the well-guarded domain of leaders, information is now widely available. If organizations until the 1980s carefully managed, planned, and regulated access to information, they cannot do so any longer. Access to information at all levels is becoming increasingly essential in the search for quality, efficiency, and survival. Finally, the pace of change is increasing, making forecasting difficult and requiring continued flexibility.

So what is left for a leader to do? What does it mean to be a leader? How does a leader influence individuals and groups within an organization, help them in the establishment of goals, and guide them toward achievement of those goals? With flattening hierarchies, the use of teams, and the presence of knowledge workers often in faraway places connected through information technology, leaders are no longer certain about their position, their authority, or even who reports to them.

Consequences

The case of AES Corporation, an independent producer of electrical power headquartered in Arlington, Virginia, provides an excellent illustration of the changes and consequences of the new organizational context. The company does business all over the world, including Hungary, China, Brazil, and Kazakhstan (Markels 1998). To remain competitive and be successful, the company uses a radical management and business model that relies on employee participation, empowerment, flexibility, and learning. Oscar Prieto, AES director of Brazilian operations, explains: "We broke all the rules. No overtime. No bosses. No time records. No shift schedules. No assigned responsibilities. No administration. And guess what? It worked" (Markels 1998,

p. 165). The company mission statement is that work should be "fun, fulfilling, and exciting" (Markels 1998, p. 160). Roger Sant, AES cofounder and chairman, believes that the fun comes from intellectual challenge, interacting with others, and learning through struggles and mistakes. Dennis Bakke, AES's other cofounder and CEO, declares: "We're all creative, capable of making decisions, trustworthy, able to learn, and perhaps most important, fallible. We all want to be part of a community and use our skills to make a difference in the world" (Markels 1998, p. 160).

Based on these principles, AES empowers its employees to make decisions. Leaders provide advice and serve as consultants to the teams, who then make decisions. For example, Alessandra Marinheiro, a 24-year-old, entry-level financial analyst who became project manager, found herself responsible for more than $2 billion in acquisitions only 1 year after joining the company (Markels 1998). She feels confident taking on the challenge because of the training the company provides her in all aspects of the business, and because of the support of her team members and the confidence the leaders express in her abilities.

AES is an example of how organizations and their leaders are addressing the changes that are coming their way. Table 10-2 summarizes the consequences of such changes to leadership. Leaders have to accept new roles, whether as team facilitator or consultant to a team. They have to provide training and support, and allow their followers to make decisions. One of the major consequences of these changes is to shift attention away from leaders to followers. Marcus Buckingham, who has conducted the Gallup survey on leadership in organizations (LaBarre, 2001a), points out that leaders must realize that they are not the most important people in their organization. He further recommends that leaders must shift away from trying to change their followers and instead focus on helping them become more of who they already are. A recent book about followers provides a model of followership and guidance for today's followers to stand up to and for their leaders (Chaleff 1995). Its focus is differentiating between followers and subordinates and emphasizing that a follower, like a leader, is "a steward of the resources an

Leaders have to accept new roles, whether as team facilitator or consultant to a team.

Table 10-2
Changes and Consequences for Leaders

CHANGES	CONSEQUENCES FOR LEADERSHIP
Structural	New roles for leaders; emphasis on followers and teamwork
Demographic	Understanding differences and cultural factors
Globalization	Understanding culture and international, global issues
New work ethic	Accommodating working styles and generational differences
Learning	Continuous training; leading knowledge workers
Technology	Staying up to date; change in sources of power; integrating technology in effective leadership
Flexibility	Learning to manage change
Constant and fast-paced change	Staying current and flexible

organization can draw on to carry out its work. The resources of a group include its leaders. Thus, a follower is a leader's steward every bit as much as the leader is the follower's steward" (Chaleff 1995, p. 13).

Many other researchers and practitioners also have addressed the new roles for leaders (see, for example, Block 1993; Davis, Schoorman, and Donaldson 1997; Greenleaf 1998; Wheatley 1994). The common theme of much of this work is to change leaders from individuals at the top of the hierarchy with considerable power and control to individuals who serve others and continue to be productive themselves. The new leaders are committed to helping others grow. Additionally, organizations need to lose some of their rigidity and become more fluid systems in which the focus is on the whole and on relationships among people rather than on maintaining order and control. The leader's role is one of guidance and support. In the case of Greenleaf's servant-leader, the role is to provide service to others, an activity that allows the leader to develop, nurture, and help others become healthier and wiser, and prepare them to become servant-leaders, as well (Greenleaf 1998).

Another impact of the structural change is the need for teamwork and cooperation. Beyond the fact that participation builds commitment and creativity, so much of what we do is so complex that without full cooperation and collaboration, most work could not be done. Consider how the scientists at the Monterey Bay Aquarium Research Institute (MBARI) funded by David Packard, Silicon Valley legend and of Hewlett-Packard fame, work together to explore the world in the deep ocean (Warner 2001). Packard created a mandate, cast in bronze in MBARI's lobby, for scientists and engineers to work on an equal footing in a spirit of collaboration. When Marcia McNutt became the institute's CEO several years ago, she did not see much collaboration. Through her own deep conviction about the need for collaboration and her creation of a series of work setting policies that encouraged collaboration and equality, MBARI is closer to achieving Packard's mandate. George Malby, a MBARI engineer, states: "We have a natural respect for each other. We have no reason to judge each other. We just have questions we want to ask and answer" (Warner 2001, p. 132).

A major consequence of organizational changes for leaders is the need to understand culture and its impact on followers and organizations. For example, the model that AES has developed for its organization is clearly and distinctly North American. It fits a low power-distance culture in which authority is decentralized and ambiguity is encouraged and welcomed. One of the challenges AES leaders face is whether they can implement their model in countries such as China and Hungary. Several test cases in Brazil should provide them with some indication. In a company northwest of Sao Paulo, the change caused massive layoffs as well as technological upgrade. Oscar Prieto has been able to find local leaders who agree with AES's philosophy and has used them as change agents. The non-U.S. employees are in shock. Prieto explains: "Brazilians want to know exactly how much money they are going to have at the end of the month. And they want to know that they're never going to have to work on Sundays" (Markels 1998, p. 165). The AES management system cannot provide such certainty, but the company leadership is undaunted. Prieto says: "If you treat human beings fairly, they will respond as adults. It's a matter of believing in people" (Markels 1998, p. 165).

A universal model of leadership appears to be working for AES, but many other organizations and their leaders are learning to adjust their practices to fit other cultures. For example, John Mumford, head of British Petroleum's Thailand division, found that solving morale problems and enticing employee input required special attention to the Thai high power-distance culture. The company started a monthly birthday luncheon to allow employees and managers from all levels to interact freely—something they would not do without a company-sponsored event (Murray 1997).

Tomorrow's leaders face the challenge of redefining themselves to continue to provide the direction, guidance, and nurturing that all followers need.

LOOKING TO THE FUTURE

Leadership as we traditionally know it—command and control—does not address the rapid social, cultural, and organizational changes that are occurring globally. The lean, efficiency-minded, and flexible organizations of tomorrow leave little room for a privileged managerial class. They cannot afford to have a large number of people whose jobs are simply to supervise others. Although it is difficult to predict the future, several themes emerge based on our past and current research about leadership, analysis of organizational practices, and predictions about social and cultural factors.

- Future leaders must adopt a service mentality toward internal and external stakeholders. By serving followers, leaders help them develop and in turn serve their outside constituents and stakeholders. In this process, leaders must be willing to give up the traditional views of "all-powerful bosses." One key aspect of the service mentality is integrity and honesty toward all stakeholders.
- Future leaders must have a global perspective and a keen awareness of cultural factors. With increased cultural diversity, the changing workforce, and globalization, the ability to understand and interact with other cultures in a non-judgmental fashion is essential. It is impossible for any one person to know all the cultures with which he or she might come in contact. What is possible is asking questions, listening to the answers, and refraining from judgment. Contact with diverse groups is a powerful aid in this process.
- Future leaders must understand organizations and how they function from an integrated perspective. They must know their team and department but also acquire strategic skills that allow them to view their organization as a whole.
- Future leaders must remain flexible and open to new experiences and welcome and manage change. Leaders in the twenty-first century must be willing to experiment, push the limits of their assumptions, and consider the inconceivable.
- Future leaders must commit to continuous learning, training, and practice in order to acquire and retain the multitude of skills and tools necessary to lead their organizations. Without such skills, they will not have the flexibility they need to be effective. The leadership models discussed in this book are only some of the tools leaders need. They can help teach a leader what resources to use and how to use them. Other necessary skills are self-awareness and self-knowledge, interpersonal and communication skills, the ability to work with teams, negotiation and conflict management skills, mastery of technology and information technology, and knowledge of political behaviors.

- Future leaders must be able to achieve balance and manage their own careers. Organizations provide opportunities but do not guarantee employment. Continuing on an already-established trend, tomorrow's leaders must actively take charge of their career and balance and integrate it with their personal lives.

Despite all that we know, we are far from fully understanding leadership. Our considerable knowledge is being challenged continuously. Given that leadership is a social phenomenon, it is by its very nature subject to constant change. Searching for definitive answers might be foolish. The defining characteristic of our modern organizations is fluidity and change. Kurt Lewin's simple quote at the beginning of this chapter defines the state of leadership today: If you truly want to understand something, change it.

REFERENCES

Abelson, R. 2001. CEO packages at major firms are still rising. *Arizona Republic*, 19 February, sec. D1, D3.

Abrashoff, D. M. 2001. Giving up control to gain command. www.watsonwyatt.com/strategyat work/articles/2001/2001_05_tl.asp, accessed April 15, 2002.

Ackerson, L. 1942. *Children's behavior problems: Relative importance and intercorrelations among traits*. Chicago: University of Chicago Press.

Adler, N. J. 1991. *International dimensions of organizational behavior*. 2d ed. Boston: PWS-Kent.

Alderfer, C. P. 1969. An empirical test of a new theory of human needs, *Organizational Behavior and Human Performance*, 4: 142–175.

Alessi SPA: The leading company in design. 2002. www.alessikitchenware.com/alessi2.htm, accessed January 24, 2002.

Allen, T. H. 1981. Situational management roles: A conceptual model. *Dissertation Abstracts International* no. 42, 2A: 465.

Alluto, J. A., and L. G. Hrebeniak. 1975. Research on commitment to employing organizations: Preliminary findings on a study of managers graduating from engineering and MBA programs. Paper presented at the National Academy of Management Annual Conference, August, New Orleans.

Anders, G. 2001a. John Chambers, After the deluge. *Fast Company* (July): 100–111.

Anders, G. 2001b. Slack off. *Fast Company* (August): 27–30.

Anders, G. 2002. Roche's new scientific method. *Fast Company* (January): 60–67.

Anderson, C. 1997. Values-based management. *Academy of Management Executive* 11, no. 4: 25–46.

Anderson, C. R., D. Hellriegel, and J. W. Slocum. 1977. Managerial response to environmentally induced stress. *Academy of Management Journal*, 20, no. 2: 260–272.

Anderson, C. R., and C. E. Schneier. 1978. Locus of control, leader behavior and leader performance among management students. *Academy of Management Journal* 21: 690–698.

Anderson, T. D. 1998. *Transforming leadership* (2d edition), Boca Raton, FL: St. Lucie Press.

Andrews, P., and S. Manes. 1993. *Gates*. New York: Doubleday.

Ash, M. K. 1981. *Mary Kay*. New York: Harper and Row.

Astley, W. G., and P. S. Sachdeva. 1984. Structural sources of intraorganizational power: A theoretical synthesis. *Academy of Management Review* 9: 104–113.

Aune, R. K., and L. L. Waters. 1994. Cultural differences in deception: Motivation to deceive in Samoans and North Americans. *International Journal of Intercultural Relations* 18: 159–172.

Ayman, R. 1993. Leadership perception: The role of gender and culture. In *Leadership theory and research: Perspectives and directions*, edited by M. M. Chemers and R. Ayman. New York: Academic Press, 137–166.

Ayman, R. and M. M. Chemers. 1983. Relationship of supervisory behavior ratings to work group effectiveness and subordinate satisfaction. *Journal of Applied Psychology* 68: 338–341.

———. 1991. The effect of leadership match on subordinate satisfaction in Mexican organizations: Some moderating influences of self-monitoring. *International Review of Applied Psychology* 40: 299–314.

Ayman, R., M. M. Chemers, and F. E. Fiedler. 1995. The contingency model of leadership effectiveness: Its levels of analysis. *Leadership Quarterly* 6, no. 2: 147–167.

Ayman-Nolley, S., R. Ayman, and J. Becker. 1993. Gender affects children's drawings of a leader. Paper presented at the annual meeting of the American Psychological Association, August, Chicago.

Ballon, M. 1998. Extreme managing, *Inc.*, (July): 60–72.

Bandura A. 1977. Self-efficacy: Toward a unifying theory of behavioral change. *Psychological Review* 84: 191–215.

Banking's best-paid woman, money.cnn.com/1998/06/17/fortune/fortune_promo/, accessed February 28, 2002.

Baron, R. A. 1989. Personality and organizational conflict: Effects of the Type A behavior pattern and self-monitoring. *Organizational Behavior and Human Decision Processes* 44: 281–296.

Baron, R. A., J. H. Neuman, and D. Geddes. 1999. Social and personal determinants of workplace aggression: Evidence for the impact of perceived injustice and the Type A behavior pattern. *Aggressive Behavior* 25, no. 4: 281–296.

Barrick, M. R., and M. Mount. 1991. The five big personality dimensions and job performance: A meta-analysis. *Personnel Psychology* 44, no. 1: 1–76.

Barrick, M. R., and M. Mount. 1993. Autonomy as a moderator of the relationship between the Big Five personality dimensions and job performance. *Journal of Applied Psychology* 78: 111–118.

Barry, D. 1991. Managing the bossless team. *Organizational Dynamics* 19, no. 4: 31–47.

Barsoux, J. L., and P. Lawrence. 1991. The making of a French manager. *Harvard Business Review* (July-August): 58–67.

Bartlett, C. A., and S. Ghoshal. 1989. *Managing across borders, the transnational solution.* Boston: Harvard Business School Press.

———. 1992. Managing across borders: New organizational responses. *Sloan Management Review* 28, no. 9: 3–13.

Bass, B. M. 1960. *Leadership, psychology, and organizational behavior.* New York: Harper and Row.

———. 1981. *Stogdill's handbook of leadership.* New York: Free Press.

———. 1985. *Leadership and performance beyond expectations.* New York: Free Press.

———. 1990a. *Bass and Stogdill's handbook of leadership.* 3d ed. New York: Free Press.

———. 1990b. From transactional to transformational leadership: Learning to share the vision. *Organizational Dynamics* 18, no. 3: 19–36.

———. 1997. Does the transactional-transformational leadership paradigm transcend organizational and national boundaries? *American Psychologist* 52, no. 3: 130–139.

———. 1999. On the taming of charisma: A reply to Janice Beyer. *Leadership Quarterly* 10, no. 4: 541–553.

Bass, B. M. and B. J. Avolio. 1990a. Developing transformational leadership: 1992 and beyond. *Journal of European Industrial Training* 14: 21–27.

———. 1990b. *Manual for the multifactor leadership questionnaire.* Palo Alto, CA: Consulting Psychologist Press.

———. 1993. Transformational leadership: A response to critiques. In *Leadership theory and research: Perspectives and directions*, edited by M. M. Chemers and R. Ayman. San Diego, CA: Academic Press, 49–80.

Bass, B. M. and P. Steidlmeier. 1999. Ethics, character, and authentic transformational leadership behavior. *Leadership Quarterly* 10, no. 2: 181–217.

Bass, B. M., E. R. Valenzi, D. L. Farrow, and R. J. Solomon. 1975. Management styles associated with organizational, task, and interpersonal contingencies. *Journal of Applied Psychology* 60: 720–729.

Bauer, T. N., and S. G. Greene. 1996. Development of the leader-member exchange: A longitudinal test. *Academy of Management Journal*, 39, no. 6: 1538–1567.

Becker, J., R. Ayman, and K. Korabik. 1994. Gender and self/subordinate discrepancies in perceptions of leadership: Understanding the impact of behavioral content, organizational context, and self-monitoring. Working paper. Chicago: Illinois Institute of Technology.

Bedeian, A. G., and A. A. Armenakis. 1998. The cesspool syndrome: How dreck floats to the top of declining organizations. *Academy of Management Executive* 12, no. 1: 58–67.

Bennis, W. G. 1992. *Leaders on leadership.* Boston: Harvard Business Review Books.

Bennis, W. G., and B. Nanus. 1985. *Leaders: The strategies for taking charge.* New York: Harper and Row.

Bethune, G., and S. Huler. 1998. *From worst to first: Behind the scenes of a remarkable comeback.* New York: John Wiley & Sons Inc.

Bettis, R. A., and C. K. Prahalad. 1995. The dominant logic: Retrospective and extension. *Strategic Management Journal* 16: 5–14.

Beyer, J. M. 1999a. Taming and promoting charisma to change organizations. *Leadership Quarterly* 10, no. 2: 307–330.

Beyer, J. M. 1999b. Two approaches to studying charismatic leadership: Competing or complementary. *Leadership Quarterly* 10, no. 4: 575–588.

Bianco, A. and P. L. Moore. 2001. "Downfall." *Business Week* (March 5): 82–91.

Bigoness, W. J. and G. L. Blakely. 1996. A cross-national study of managerial values. *Journal of International Business Studies* 27, no. 4: 739–752.

Bird, C. 1940. *Social psychology.* New York: Appleton.

Block, P. 1987. *The empowered manager.* San Francisco: Jossey-Bass.

———. 1993. *Stewardship: Choosing service over self-interest.* San Francisco: Berrett-Koehler.

Blumberg, H. H. 2001. The common ground of natural language and social interaction in personality description. *Journal of Research in Personality* 35, no. 3: 289–312.

Boal, K. B., and J. M. Bryron. 1987. Charismatic leadership: A phenomenological and structural approach. In *Emerging leadership vistas,* edited by J. G. Hunt, B. R. Baliga, H. P. Dachler, and C. A. Schriesheim. Lexington, MA: D.C. Heath, 11–28.

Boden, M. A. 1994. What is creativity? In *Dimensions of creativity,* edited by M. A. Boden. Cambridge, MA: MIT Press, 75–117.

Bowers, D. G., and S. E. Seashore. 1966. Predicting organizational effectiveness with a four-factor theory of leadership. *Administrative Science Quarterly* 11: 238–263.

Boyle, M. 2001. How the workplace was won. *Fortune* (January 8): 139–146.

Bray, D. W., and D. L. Grant. 1966. The assessment center in the measurement of potential for business management. *Psychological Monographs* 80, no. 17: No. 625.

Breen, B. 2001. How EDS got its groove back. *Fast Company* (October): 106–117.

Broverman, I., S. Vogel, D. Broverman, F. Clarkson, P. Rosenkrantz. 1975. Sex-role stereotypes: A current appraisal. *Journal of Social Issues* 28: 29–78.

Brower, H. H., F. D. Schoorman, and H. H. Tan. 2000. A model of relational leadership: The integration of trust and leader-member exchange. *Leadership Quarterly* 11, no. 2: 227–250.

Brown, M. C. 1982. Administrative succession and organizational performance: The succession effect. *Administrative Science Quarterly* 29: 245–273.

Bruce, J. S. 1986. The intuitive pragmatists: Conversations with chief executive officers (special report). Greensboro, NC: Center for Creative Leadership.

Bryant, A. 1995. Worker ownership was no paradise. *International Herald Tribune* 23 March, sec. 16.

Bryman, A. 1992. *Charisma and leadership.* London: Sage.

Buchanan, L. 1999. The smartest little company in America. *Inc.* (January): 43–54.

Buchanan, L. 2001. Managing one-to-one. *Inc.* (October 16): 82–88.

Burke, S., and M. Lingblom. Green light for EDS. www.crn.com/Section/CoverStory.asp?ArticleID=33678, accessed April 16, 2002.

Burke, W., E. A. Richley, and L. DeAngelis. 1985. Changing leadership and planning processes at the Lewis Research Center, National Aeronautics and Space Administration. *Human Resource Management* 24, no. 1: 81–90.

Burns, J. M. 1978. *Leadership.* New York: Harper and Row.

Bycio, P., R. D. Hackett, and J. S. Allen. 1995. Further assessments of Bass's (1985) conceptualization of transactional and transformational leadership. *Journal of Applied Psychology* 80: 468–478.

Caggiano, C. 1998. Psycho path. *Inc.* (July): 77–85.

Caligiuri, P. M. 2000. The Big Five personality characteristics as predictors of expatriate's desire to terminate the assignments and supervisor-rated performance. *Personnel Psychology* 53, no. 1: 67–88.

Canabou, C. 2001. Have kid, won't travel. *Fast Company* (October): 48.

Canabou, C., and A. Overholt. 2001. Smart steps. *Fast Company* (March): 98.

Cannella, A. A., Jr., and W. Shen. (2001). *Academy of Management Journal*, 44, no. 2: 252–270.

Carbonara, P. 1998. Mervyn's calls in the SWAT team. *Fast Company* (April–May): 54.

Carey, S. 1998. US Air "peon" team pilots start-up of low-fare airline. *The Wall Street Journal*, 24 March, sec. B1, B2.

Carlyle, T. 1907. *Heroes and hero worship*. Boston; Adams.

Carpenter, M. A., and J. W. Fredrickson. 2001. Top management teams, global strategic postures, and the moderating role of uncertainty. *Academy of Management Journal* 44, no. 3: 533–545.

Cartwright, D. C. 1965. Influence, leadership, control. In *Handbook of organizations*, edited by J. G. March. Chicago: Rand McNally.

Carvell, T. 1998. By the way, your staff hates you. *Fortune* 138, no. 6: 200–212.

Casimir, G. 2001. Combinative aspects of leadership style: The ordering and temporal spacing of leadership behaviors. *Leadership Quarterly* 12, no. 3: 245–278.

Castaneda, M., and A. Nahavandi. 1991. Link of manager behavior to supervisor performance rating and subordinate satisfaction. *Group and Organizational Studies* 16, no. 4: 357–366.

Chaleff, I. 1995. *The courageous follower: Standing up, to, and for our leaders*. San Francisco: Berrett-Koehler.

Charan, R., and Covin G. 2001. Making a clean handoff. *Fortune* (September 17): 72.

Chatman, J. A., and F. J. Flynn. 2001. The influence of demographic heterogeneity on the emergence and consequences of cooperative norms in work teams. *Academy of Management Journal* 44, no. 5: 956–974.

Chemers, M. M. 1969. Cross-cultural training as a means for improving situational favorableness. *Human Relations* 22: 531–546.

———. 1993. An integrative theory of leadership. In *Leadership theory and research: Perspectives and directions*, edited by M. M. Chemers and R. Ayman. New York: Academic Press, 293–320.

———. 1997. *An integrative theory of leadership.* Mahwah, NJ: Lawrence Erlbaum Associates.

Chemers, M. M., R. B. Hays, F. Rhodewalt, and J. Wysocki. 1985. A person environment analysis of job stress: A contingency model explanation. *Journal of Personality and Social Psychology* 3: 628–635.

Chemers, M. M., S. Oskamp, and M. A. Costanzo. 1995. *Diversity in organizations.* Thousand Oaks, CA: Sage.

Chemers, M. M., and G. J. Skrzypek. 1972. An experimental test of the contingency model of leadership effectiveness. *Journal of Personality and Social Psychology* 24: 172–177.

Chen, C. C., and E. Van Velsor. 1996. New direction for research and practice in diversity leadership. *Leadership Quarterly* 7: 285–302.

Chen, M. 1995. *Asian management systems: Chinese, Japanese, and Korean styles of business.* London: Routledge.

Cherrington, D. J., S. J. Condies, and J. L. England. 1979. Age and work values. *Academy of Management Journal* (September): 617–623.

Cherry, J., and J. Fraedrich. 2000. An empirical investigation of locus of control and the structure of moral reasoning: Examining ethic decision-making processes of sales managers. *Journal of Personal Selling and Sales Management* 20, no. 3: 173–188.

Christensen, L. M. 1997. Making strategy: Learning by doing. *Harvard Business Review* 75, no. 6: 141–156.

Christie, R., and F. L. Geis. 1970. *Studies in Machiavellianism.* New York: Academic Press.

Ciarrochi, J. V., A. Y. C. Chan, and P. Caputi. 2000. A critical evaluation of the emotional intelligence construct. *Personality and Individual Differences* 28, no. 3: 539–561.

Cleyman, K. L., S. M. Jex, and K. G. Lover. 1993. Employee grievances: An application of the leader-member exchange model. Paper presented at the 9th Annual Meeting of the Society of Industrial and Organizational Psychology, Nashville, TN.

Colella, A., and Varma, A. 2001. The impact of subordinate disability on leader-member exchange relationships. *Academy of Management Journal* 44, no. 2: 304–315.

Colvin, G. 2001a. The great CEO pay heist. *Fortune* (June 25): www.fortune.com, accessed on February 12, 2002.

———. 2001b. The anti-control freak. *Fortune* (November 26): 60.

Conger, J. A. 1989a. *The charismatic leader: Behind the mystique of exceptional leadership.* San Francisco: Jossey-Bass.

———. 1989b. Leadership: The art of empowering others. *Academy of Management Executive* 3, no. 1: 17–24.

———. 1990. The dark side of leadership. *Organizational Dynamics* 19: 44–55.

———. 1991. Inspiring others: The language of leadership. *Academy of Management Executive* 5, no. 1: 31–45.

———. 1992. *Learning to lead: The art of transforming managers into leaders.* San Francisco: Jossey-Bass.

———. 1999. Charismatic and transformational leadership in organizations: An insider's perspective on these developing streams of research. *Leadership Quarterly* 10, no. 2: 145–179.

Conger, J. A., and R. N. Kanungo. 1987. Toward a behavioral theory of charismatic leadership in organizational settings. *Academy of Management* 12: 637–647.

———. 1988. The empowerment process: Integrating theory and practice. *Academy of Management Review,* 13, no. 3: 471–482.

———. 1998. *Charismatic leadership in organizations.* Thousand Oaks, CA: Sage Publications.

Conger, J. A., G. M. Spreitzer, and E. E. Lawler, III. 1999. *The leader's change handbook: An essential guide to setting direction and taking action.* San Francisco: Jossey-Bass.

Conyon, M. J., and S. I. Peck. 1998. Board control, remuneration committees, and top management compensation. *Academy of Management Journal* 41, no. 2: 146–157.

Cook, K. W., C. A. Vance, and P. E. Spector. 2000. The relation of candidate personality with selection interview outcomes. *Journal of Applied Social Psychology* 304, no. 4: 867–885.

Cornwell, J. M. 1983. A meta-analysis of selected trait research in the leadership literature. Paper presented at the Southeastern Psychological Association, August, Atlanta, GA.

Corral, S., and E. Calvete. Machiavellianism: Dimensionality of the March IV and its relation to self-monitoring in a Spanish sample. *Spanish Journal of Psychology* 3, no. 1: 3–13.

Covey, S. R. 1989. *The seven habits of highly effective people.* New York: Fireside Books.

Covin, J. G., and D. P. Slevin. 1988. The influence of organization structure on the utility of an entrepreneurial top management style. *Journal of Management Studies* 25, no. 3: 217–234.

Crouch, A., and P. Yetton. 1987. Manager behavior, leadership style, and subordinate performance: An empirical extension of Vroom-Yetton conflict rule. *Organizational Behavior and Human Decision Processes* 39: 384–396.

Crum, S., and H. France. 1996. Teamwork brings breakthrough improvements in quality and climate. *Quality Progress* 29, no. 3: 39–43.

Cunningham, J. B., and J. MacGregor. 2000. Trust and the design of work: Complementary constructs in satisfaction and performance. *Human Relations* 53, no. 12: 1575–1591.

Cyert, R. M., and J. G. March. 1963. *A behavioral theory of the firm.* Upper Saddle River, NJ: Prentice Hall.

Dahle, C. 2000. Updating the agenda. *Fast Company* (April): 206–208.

Daniels, C. 2001. Does this man need a shrink? *Fortune* (February 5): 205–208.

Dansereau, F. Jr., G. B. Graen, and W. J. Haga. 1975. A vertical dyad linkage approach to leadership within formal organizations: A longitudinal investigation of the role making process. *Organizational Behavior and Human Performance* 13: 46–78.

Davis, J. H., F. D. Schoorman, and L. Donaldson. 1997. Toward a stewardship theory of management. *Academy of Management Review* 22: 20–47.

Day, D. V., and R. G. Lord. 1988. Executive leadership and organizational performance:

References

Suggestions for a new theory and methodology. *Journal of Management* 14: 453–464.

De Bono, E. 1992. *Serious creativity: Using the power of lateral thinking to create new ideas.* New York: Harper Business.

Dekmejian, R. H., and M. J. Wyszomirski. 1972. Charismatic leadership in Islam: The Mahdi of the Sudan. *Comparative Studies in Society and History* 14: 193–214.

Delacroix, J., and S. M. Saudagaran. 1991. Munificent compensations as disincentives: The case of American CEOs. *Human Relations* 44, no. 7: 665–679.

Delbecq, A. 2001. "Evil" manifested in destructive individual behavior: A senior leadership challenge. *Journal of Management Inquiry* 10, no. 3: 221–226.

Den Hartog, D., R. J. House, P. J. Hanges, S. A. Ruits-Quintana and associates. 1999. Culture specific and cross-culturally generalizable implicit leadership theories: Are attributes of charismatic/transformational leadership universally endorsed? *Leadership Quarterly* 10, no. 2: 219–256.

Deogun, N. and J. S. Lublin. 1998. PepsiCo's Enrico forgoes 1998 salary, asks firm's board to fund scholarship. *The Wall Street Journal,* 25 March, sec. A1.

Digman, J. M. 1990. Personality structure: Emergence of the five-factor model. *Annual Review of Psychology* 41: 417–440.

Dillon, P. 1998. Is selling out "selling out"? *Fast Company* (February–March): 92.

Dobbins, G. H., W. S. Long, E. J. Dedrick, and T. C. Clemons. 1990. The role of self-monitoring and gender on leader emergence: A laboratory and field study. *Journal of Management* 16, no. 3: 609–618.

Donaldson, T. 1994. Global business must mind its morals. *New York Times*, 13 February, sec. F11.

Donaldson-Briggs, A. L. 2002. Embracing the "F" word, www.managementfirst.com/articles/failure.htm; www.alessi.com/history, accessed January 24, 2002.

Donnelly, S. B. 2001. Blue skies for Jetblue. *Time Magazine* (July 10).

Dorfman, P. W., J. P. Howell, S. Hibino, J. K. Lee, U. Tate, and A. Bautista. 1997. Leadership in Western and Asian countries: Commonalities and differences in effective leadership processes across cultures. *Leadership Quarterly,* 8, no. 3: 233–274.

Dorsey, D. 2000. Change factory. *Fast Company* (June): 210–224.

Dose, J. J. 1999. The relationship between work values similarity and team-member and leader-member exchange relationships. *Group Dynamics,* 3, no. 1: 20–32.

Downey, H. K., J. E. Sheridan, and J. W. Slocum, Jr. 1975. Analysis of relationships among leader behavior, subordinate job performance and satisfaction: A Path-goal approach. *Academy of Management Journal* 18: 253–262.

Drath, W. 2001. *The deep blue sea: Rethinking the source of leadership.* San Francisco: Jossey-Bass.

Duarte, N. T., J. R. Goodson, and N. R. Klich. 1994. Effects of dyadic quality and duration on performance appraisal. *Academy of Management Journal* 37: 499–521.

Duff, C. 1993. "Jack the Ripper": A CEO for a new era prospers by practicing the art of firing. *The Wall Street Journal,* 11 January, sec. A1, A4.

Eagly, A. H., S. J. Karau, and M. G. Makhijani. 1995. Gender and the effectiveness of leaders: A meta-analysis. *Psychological Bulletin* 117: 125–145.

Early, C., and E. Mosakowski. 1996. Experimental international management research. In *Handbook for international management research,* edited by B. J. Punnett and O. Shenkar, Oxford: Blackwell, 83–114.

Erhart, M. G., and K. J. Klein. 2001. Prediction followers' preferences for charismatic leadership: The influence of follower values and personality. *Leadership Quarterly,* 12, no. 2: 153–179.

Ekvall, G., and L. Ryhammer. 1999. The creative climate: Its determinants and effects at a Swedish university. *Creativity Research Journal* 12, no. 4: 303–310.

Ellerbee, L. 1999. My biggest mistake. *Inc.* (January): 81.

Enkelis, L., and K. Olsen. 1995. *Portraits of women business leaders: On our own terms.* San Francisco: Berrett-Koehler.

Ettorre, B. 1994. Why overseas bribery won't last. *Management Review* 83, no. 6: 20–24.

Evans, M. G. 1996. R. J. House's Path-goal theory of leader effectiveness. *Leadership Quarterly* 7, no. 3: 305–309.

Fairhurst, G. T., and R. A. Sarr. 1996. *The art of framing: Managing the language of leadership.* San Francisco: Jossey-Bass.

Farh, J. L., P. M. Podsakoff, and B. S. Cheng. 1987. Culture free leadership effectiveness versus moderators of leadership behavior: An extension and test of Kerr and Jermier's "substitutes for leadership" model in Taiwan. *Journal of International Business Studies* 18, no. 3: 43–60.

Farnham, A. 1993. Mary Kay's lessons in leadership. *Fortune* 128, no. 6: 68–76.

Fenn, D. 1998. Built for speed. *Inc.* (September): 61–71.

Fiedler, F. E. 1967. *A theory of leadership effectiveness.* New York: McGraw-Hill.

———. 1978. The contingency model and the dynamics of the leadership process. In *Advances in experimental social psychology.* Vol. 2, edited by L. Berkowitz. New York: Academic Press, 59–112.

———. 1992. The role and meaning of leadership experience. In *Impact of leadership*, edited by K. E. Clark, M. B. Clark, and D. P. Campbell. Greensboro, NC. Center for Creative Leadership, 95–105.

———. 1993. The leadership situation and the black box in contingency theories. In *Leadership theory and research: Perspectives and directions,* edited by M. M. Chemers and R. Ayman. New York: Academic Press, 2–28.

———. 1995. Cognitive resources and leadership performance. *Applied Psychology: An International Review* 44, no. 1: 5–28.

Fiedler, F. E., and M. M. Chemers. 1974. *Leadership and effective management.* Glenview, IL: Scott-Foresman.

———. 1984. *Improving leadership effectiveness: The leader match concept.* 2d ed. New York: John Wiley.

Fiedler, F. E., and J. E. Garcia. 1987a. *Improving leadership effectiveness: Cognitive resources and organizational performance.* New York: John Wiley.

———. 1987b. *New approaches to leadership: Cognitive resources and organizational performance.* New York: John Wiley.

Fisher, A. 1997. The world's most admired companies. *Fortune* 136, no. 8: 232.

———. 1998. Success secret: A high emotional IQ. *Fortune* 138, no. 8: 293–298.

Fisher, K. 1993. *Leading self-directed work teams.* New York: McGraw-Hill.

Fishman, C. 2001a. A dose of change. *Fast Company* (August): 50–52.

———. 2001b. Who's fast: Leader—Bob Moffat. *Fast Company* (November): 98–104.

Finkelstein, S., and B. K. Boyd. 1998. How much does the CEO matter? The role of managerial discretion in the setting of CEO compensation. *Academy of Management Journal* 41: 179–199.

Finkelstein, S., and D. C. Hambrick. 1988. Chief executive compensation: A synthesis and reconciliation. *Strategic Management Journal* 9: 543–558.

———. 1990. Top management team tenure and organizational outcomes: The moderating role of managerial discretion. *Administrative Science Quarterly* 35: 484–503.

———. 1996. *Strategic leadership: Top executives and their effects on organizations.* Minneapolis-St. Paul: West Publishing.

Fleishman, E. A. 1953. The measurement of leadership attitudes in industry. *Journal of Applied Psychology* 37: 153–158.

Fleishman, E. A., and E. F. Harris. 1962. Patterns of leadership behavior related to employee grievance and turnover. *Personnel Psychology* 15: 43–56.

Folger, J. L., P. M. Podsakoff, and B. S. Cheng. 1987. Culture-free leadership effectiveness versus moderators of leadership behavior: An extension and test of Kerr and Jermier's "substitutes for leadership" model in Taiwan. *Journal of International Business Studies* (Fall): 43–60.

Folpe, J. 1999. *Fortune's* 50 most powerful women. *Fortune*; (www.business2.com/

References

articles/mag/print/0,1643,5757,FF.html), accessed October 10, 2001.

French, J. R. P., and B. H. Raven. 1968. *The basis of social power*. In *Group dynamics*. 3d ed., edited by D. Cartwright and A. Zander. New York: Harper and Row, 259–269.

Frey, R. 1003. Empowerment or else. *Harvard Business Review* (September–October): 80–94.

Friedland, J., and J. Millman. 1998. Led by a young heir, Mexico's Televisa puts new stress on profits. *The Wall Street Journal*, 10 July, sec. A1, A8.

Frink, D. D., and G. R. Ferris. 1999. The moderating effects of accountability on the conscientiousness performance relationship. *Journal of Business and Psychology* 13, no. 4: 515–524.

Fromartz, S. 1998. The right staff. *Inc.* 20 (October): 125–132.

Furnham, A., and P. Stringfield. 1993. Personality and occupational behavior: Myers-Briggs Type Indicator correlates of managerial practices in two cultures. *Human Relations* 46, no. 7: 827–848.

Galton, R. 1869. *Hereditary genius*. New York: Appleton.

Gardner, J. W. 1986. The task of leadership (Leadership Paper No. 2). Washington, DC: Independent Sector.

George, J. M. 2000. Emotions and leadership: The role of emotional intelligence. *Human Relations* 53, no. 8: 1027–1055.

George, W. 2001. Medtronic's chairman William George on how mission-driven companies create long-term shareholder value. *Academy of Management Executive* 15, no. 4: 39–47.

Gerstner, C. R., and D. V. Day. 1994. Cross-cultural comparison of leadership prototypes. *Leadership Quarterly* 5: 121–134.

Ghiselli, E. E. 1963. Intelligence and managerial success. *Psychological Reports* 12: 898.

Gibson, F. W. 1992. Leader abilities and group performance as a function of stress. In *Impact of leadership*, edited by K. E. Clark, M. B. Clark, and D. P. Campbell. Greensboro, NC: Center for Creative Leadership, 333–343.

Gimein, M. 2001. Smart is not enough. *Fortune* (January): 124–136.

Glass, D. C. 1983. Behavioral, cardiovascular, and neuroendocrine responses. *International Review of Applied Psychology* 32: 137–151.

Goldstein, I. L. 1986. *Training in organizations: Needs Assessment, Development, and Evaluation*. Monterey, CA: Brooks/Cole.

Goldstein, L. 2000. Whatever space works for you. *Fortune* (July 10): 269–270.

Goleman, D. 1995. *Emotional intelligence: Why it can matter more than IQ*. New York: Bantam Books.

Goleman, D. 1998. *Working with emotional intelligence*. New York: Bantam Books.

Goleman, D., R. E. Boyatzis, and A. McKee. 2002. *Primal Leadership: Realizing the Power of Emotional Intelligence*. Boston: Harvard Business School Press.

Gomez, C., B. L. Kirkman, and D. L. Shapiro. 2000. The impact of collectivism and in-group/out-group membership on the evaluation generosity of team members. *Academy of Management Journal* 46, no. 6: 1097–1106.

Government in Mexico: Baby steps towards change. 2001. *The Economist* (December 1): 35–36.

Graeff, C. L. 1983. The situational leadership theory: A critical review. *Academy of Management Review* 8: 285–296.

Graen, G. B., and J. R. Cashman. 1975. A role making model of leadership in formal organizations: A developmental approach. In *Leadership Frontiers*, edited by J. G. Hunt and L. L. Larson. Kent, OH: Kent State University Press, 143–165.

Graen, G. B., and W. Shiemann. 1978. Leader-member agreement: A vertical dyad linkage approach. *Journal of Applied Psychology* 63: 206–212.

Graen, G. B. and M. Uhl-Bien. 1991. The transformation of work group professionals into self-managing and partially self-designing contributors: Toward a theory of leadership-making. *Journal of Management Systems*, 3, no. 3: 33–48.

———. 1995. Relationship-based approach to leadership: Development of Leader-member exchange (LMX) theory of leadership over 25 years: Applying a multi-level-multi-domain perspective. *Leadership Quarterly* 6: 219–247.

Green, S. G., and T. Mitchell. 1979. Attributional processes of leaders in a leader-member interactions. *Organizational Behavior and Human Performance* 23: 429–458.

Greenleaf, R. K. 1998. *The power of servant leadership.* San Francisco: Berrett-Koehler.

Greenwald, J. 1992. Is Mr. Nice guy back? *Time* (January 27): 43.

Griffin, R. W. 1979. Task design determinants of effective leader behavior. *Academy of Management Review* 4: 215–224.

Gronn, P. 1999. Substituting for leadership: The neglected role of the leadership couple. *Leadership Quarterly* 10, no. 1: 41–62.

Grove, A. 1996. *Only the paranoid survive: How to exploit the crisis that challenges every company and career.* New York: Doubleday.

Grove, A. S. 1986. Tapping into the leader who lies within us. *The Wall Street Journal,* April 22, sec. B1, col. 3.

Guerra, J. 2001. In a former life. *Inc.* (July): 84.

Gunther, M. 1998. The Internet is Mr. Case's neighborhood. *Fortune* 137, no. 6: 68–80.

Gupta, A. K. 1984. Contingency linkages between strategy and general manager characteristics: A conceptual examination. *Academy of Management Review* 9, no. 3: 399–412.

———. 1986. Matching managers to strategies: Point and counterpoint. *Human Resource Management* 25, no. 2: 215–234.

———. 1988. Contingency perspectives on strategic leadership: Current knowledge and future research directions. In *The executive effect: Concepts and methods for studying top managers,* edited by D. C Hambrick. Greenwich, CT: JAI Press, 141–178.

Hackman, J. R. (editor) 1990. *Groups that work (and those that don't): Creating conditions for effective teamwork.* San Francisco: Jossey-Bass.

Hackman, J. R., and G. R. Oldham. 1980. *Work redesign.* Reading, MA: Addison-Wesley.

Haleblian, J., and S. Finkelstein. 1993. Top management team size, CEO dominance, and firm performance: The moderating roles of environmental turbulence and discretion. *Academy of Management Journal* 36: 844–863.

Haley, U., and S. A. Stumpf. 1989. Cognitive traits in strategic decision making: Linking theories of personality and cognition. *Journal of Management Studies* 26: 467–477.

Hall, E. T. 1973. *The silent language.* Garden City, NY: Anchor Press, Doubleday.

———. 1976. *Beyond culture.* Garden City, NY: Anchor Press, Doubleday.

Hall, R. N. 1977. *Organizations, structure, and process.* 2d ed. Upper Saddle River, NJ: Prentice Hall.

Halpin, A. W., and B. J. Winer, 1957. A factorial study of the leader behavior descriptions. In *Leader behavior: Its description and measurement,* edited by R. M. Stogdill and A. E. Coons. Columbus: The Ohio State University, Bureau of Business Research.

Hambrick, D. C. 1987. The top management team: Key to strategic success. *California Management Review* 29: 88–108.

Hambrick, D. C., and S. Finkelstein. 1987. Managerial discretion: A bridge between polar views of organization. In *Research in organizational behavior.* Vol. 9, edited by L. L. Cummings and B. L. Staw. Greenwich, CT: JAI Press, 349–406.

Hambrick, D. C. and P. A. Mason. 1984. Upper echelon: The organization as a reflection of its top management. *Academy of Management Review* 9: 193–206.

Hammer, M., and J. Champy. 1993. *Reengineering the corporation: A manifesto for business revolution.* New York: Harper Business.

Hammonds, K. H. 2000. Grassroots leadership: Ford Motor Co. *Fast Company* (April): 138–152.

———. 2001a. How do you structure success? *Fast Company* (April): 58.

———. 2001b. "The not-so-quick fix." *Fast Company* (July) www.fastcompany.com/lead_feature/mulcahy.html, accessed on April 21, 2002.

———. 2001c. Leaders for the long haul. *Fast Company* (July): 56–58.

———. 2001d. Continental's turnaround pilot. *Fast Company* (December): 96–101.

Hammonds, K. H. 2002. Planned parenthood's 25-year plan. *Fast Company* (February): 55–56.

Hampden-Turner, C. M., F. Trompenaars, and D. Lewis. (Illustrator) 2000. *Building*

References

Cross-Cultural Competence: How to Create Wealth from Conflicting Values. Yale and London: Yale University Press.

Hannan M. T., and J. H. Freeman. 1977. The population ecology of organizations. *American Journal of Sociology* 82: 929–964.

Hardy, C. 1985. The nature of unobtrusive power. *Journal of Management Studies* 22: 384–399.

Hayes, T., H. Roehm, and J. Catellano. 1994. Personality correlates of success in total quality manufacturing. *Journal of Business and Psychology* 8, no. 4: 397–411.

Helgesen, S. 1990. The female advantage: Women's way of leadership. New York: Doubleday, Currency.

Hemphill, J. K., and A. E. Coons. 1957. Development of the Leader Behavior Description Questionnaire. In *Leader behavior: Its description and measurement.* Edited by R. M. Stogdill and A. E. Coons. Columbus: The Ohio State University, Bureau of Business Research.

Henderson, J. P., and P. Nutt. 1980. The influence of decision style on decision-making behavior. *Management Science* 26: 371–386.

Hershey, P., and K. H. Blanchard. 1977. *Management of organizational behavior.* 3d. ed. Upper Saddle River, NJ: Prentice Hall.

Hickson, D. J., C. R. Hinings, C. A. Lee, R. E. Scheneck, and J. M. Pennings. 1971. A strategic contingencies theory of intra-organizational power. *Administrative Science Quarterly* 16: 216–229.

Himelstein, L., and S. A. Forest. 1997. Breaking through. *Business Week* (February 17): 64–70.

Hirsch, J. S. 1993. New hotel clerks provide more than keys. *The Wall Street Journal,* 5 March, sec. B1 and B2.

Hofman, M. 2000. The metamorphosis. *Inc.* Tech 2000, no. 1: 53–60.

———. 2001. It takes all kinds. *Inc.* (July): 70–75.

Hofmann, D. A., and F. P. Morgeson. 1999. Safety-related behavior as a social exchange: The role of perceived organizational support and leader-member exchange. *Journal of Applied Psychology* 84, no. 2: 286–296.

Hofstede, G. 1980. *Culture's consequences.* Beverly Hills, CA: Sage Publications.

———. 1992. *Culture and organizations.* London: McGraw-Hill.

———. 1993. Cultural constraints in management theories. *Academy of Management Review* 7, no. 1: 81–94.

———. 1996. An American in Paris: The influence of nationality on organization theories. *Organization Studies* 17, no. 3: 525–537.

———. 1997. *Culture and Organizations: Software of the mind—Intercultural cooperation and its importance for survival.* New York: McGraw-Hill.

———. 2001.*Culture's Consequences: Comparing Values, Behaviors, Institutions, and Organizations Across Nations.* Beverly Hills, CA: Sage Publications.

Hollander, E. P. 1979. Leadership and social exchange processes. In *Social change: Advances in theory and research,* edited by K. Gergen, M. S. Greenberg, and R. H. Willis. New York: Winston-John Wiley.

Homans, G. C. 1950. *The human group.* New York: Harcourt, Brace.

Hooijberg, R., and J. Choi. 1999. From Austria to the United States and from evaluating therapists to developing cognitive resources theory: An interview with Fred Fiedler. *Leadership Quarterly* 10, no. 4: 653–665.

Horton, T. R. 1986. *What works for me.* New York: Random House.

House, R. J. 1971. A path-goal theory of leader effectiveness. *Administrative Science Quarterly* 16: 321–339.

———. 1977. A 1976 theory of charismatic leadership. In *Leadership: The cutting edge,* edited by J. G. Hunt and L. L. Larson. Carbondale: Southern Illinois University Press, 189–204.

———. 1996. Path-goal theory of leadership: Lessons, legacy, and a reformulated theory. *Leadership Quarterly* 7: 323–352.

———. 1999. Weber and the neo-charismatic leadership paradigm: A response to Beyer. *Leadership Quarterly* 10, no. 4: 563–574.

House, R. J., and R. N. Aditya. 1997. The social scientific study of leadership: Quo Vadis? *Journal of Management* 23: 409–473.

House, R. J., and G. Dessler. 1974. The path-goal theory of leadership: Some post hoc and a priori tests. In *Contingency approaches to leadership* edited by J. G. Hunt and L. L. Larson. Carbondale, IL: Southern Illinois University Press, 29–55.

House, R. J., and A. C. Filley. 1971. Leadership style, hierarchical influence, and the satisfaction of subordinate role expectations: A test of Likert's influence proposition. *Journal of Applied Psychology* 55: 422–432.

House, R. J., and T. R. Mitchell. 1974. Path-goal theory of leadership. *Contemporary Business* 3 Fall: 81–98.

House, R. J., and B. Shamir. 1993. Toward the integration of transformational, charismatic and visionary leadership. In *Leadership theory and research: Perspective and directions*, edited by M. M. Chemers and R. Ayman. New York: Academic Press, 81–107.

Howell, J. M. 1988. Two faces of charisma: Socialized and personalized leadership in organizations. In *Charismatic leadership: The illusive factor in organizational effectiveness*, edited by J. Conger and R. Kanungo. San Francisco: Jossey-Bass, 213–236.

Howell, J. M., and B. J. Avolio. 1992. The ethics of charismatic leadership: Submission or liberation. *Academy of Management Executive* 6, no. 2: 43–54.

Howell, J. P. 1997. "Substitutes for leadership: Their meaning and measurement"—an historical assessment. *Leadership Quarterly* 8, no. 2: 113–116.

Howell, J. P., D. E. Bowen, P. W. Dorfman, S. Kerr, and P. M. Podsakoff. 1990. Substitutes for leadership: Effective alternatives to ineffective leadership. *Organizational Dynamics* 19: 21–38.

Howell, J. M., and K. E. Hall-Merenda. 1999. The ties that bind: The impact of leader-member exchange, transformational and transactional leadership, and distance on predicting follower performance. *Journal of Applied Psychology* 84, no. 5: 680–694.

Hunt, J. G. 1999. Transformational/charismatic leadership's transformation of the field: An historical essay. *Leadership Quarterly* 10, no. 2: 129–144.

Hunt, J. G., and J. A. Conger. 1999. From where we sit: An assessment of transformational and charismatic leadership research. *Leadership quarterly* 10, no. 3, 335–343.

Hymowitz, C. 1988a. Five main reasons why managers fail. *The Wall Street Journal*, 2 May, sec. B1.

———. 1998b. Some managers are more than bosses—they're leaders too. *The Wall Street Journal*, 8 November, sec. B1.

Imperato, G. 1998. Joyce Wycoff. *Fast Company* (December): 142.

Jaffe, E. D., I. D. Nebenzahl, and H. Gotesdyner. 1989. Machiavellianism, task orientation, and team effectiveness revisited. *Psychological Reports* 64, no. 3: 819–824.

Jago, A. G., and V. H. Vroom. 1980. An evaluation of two alternatives to the Vroom/Yetton normative model. *Academy of Management Journal* 23: 347–355.

James, W. 1880. Great men, great thoughts and their environment. *Atlantic Monthly* 46: 441–459.

Jawahar, I. M. 2001. Attitudes, self-monitoring, and appraisal behavior. *Journal of Applied Psychology* 86, no. 5: 875–883.

Jenkins, W. O. 1947. A review of leadership studies with particular reference to military problems. *Psychological Bulletin* 44: 54–79.

Johns, G. 1978. Task moderators of the relationship between leadership style and subordinate responses. *Academy of Management Journal* 21: 319–325.

Johnson, M. 1996. Still a man's world at the top, survey says. *Arizona Republic*, 18 October, sec. E1, E2.

Johnson, R. S. 1997. Motown: What's going on? *Fortune* 136, no. 10: 133–140.

Jones. E. E., and K. E. Davis. 1965. From acts to dispositions: The attribution process in person perception. In *Advances in experimental social psychology*. Vol. 2, edited by L. Berkowitz, 219–266.

Jones, S. 1998. Emergency surgery for MedPartners. *Business Week* (March 9): 81.

Judge, P. C. 2001. Suddenly the world changes. *Fast Company* (December): 131–132.

References

Judge, T. A., C. A. Higgins, C. J. Thoresen, and M. R. Barrick. 1999. The big five personality traits, general mental ability, and career success across the life span. *Personnel Psychology* 52, no. 3: 621–652.

Jung, D. I., B. M. Bass and J. Sosik. 1995. Collectivism and transformational leadership. *Journal of Management Inquiry* 2:3–18.

Kahn, J. 1998. The world's most admired companies. *Fortune* 138, no. 8: 218.

Kanter, R. M., and R. I. Corn. 1993. Do cultural differences make a business difference? Contextual factors affecting cross-cultural relationship success. *Journal of Management Development* 13, no. 2: 5–23.

Katz, D., and R. L. Kahn. 1966. *The social psychology of organization.* New York: Wiley.

Katz, N. 2001. Sport teams as a model for workplace teams: Lessons and liabilities. *Academy of Management Executive* 15, no. 3: 56–67.

Katzenbach, J. R., and D. K. Smith. 1993. *The wisdom of teams: Creating the high-performance organization.* New York: Harper Business.

Kaufman, L. 2001. Question of style in Warnaco's Fall. *New York Times,* May 6, sec 3, p. 1.

Keller, L. M., T. J. Bouchard, Jr., R. D. Arvey, N. L. Segal, and R. V. Dawis. 1992. Work values: Genetic and environmental influences. *Journal of Applied Psychology* 77: 79–88.

Keller, R. T. 1992. Transformational leadership and the performance of research and development project groups. *Journal of Management* 18: 489–501.

Kelley, H. H. 1967. Attribution theory in social psychology. In *Nebraska symposium on motivation 1967,* edited by D. Levine. Lincoln: University of Nebraska press, 192–238.

Kennedy, J. K. Jr. 1982. Middle LPC leaders and the contingency model of leadership effectiveness. *Organizational Behavior and Human Performance* 30: 1–14.

Kennedy, M. M. 1997. What it means to lead. *Fast Company* (February–March): 98.

Kerr, J., and J. W. Slocum. 1987. Managing corporate culture through reward systems. *Academy of Management Executive* 1: 99–108.

Kerr, S., and J. M. Jermier. 1978. Substitutes for leadership: Their meaning and measurement.

Organizational Behavior and Human Performance 22: 395–403.

Kets de Vries, M. F. R. 1993. Leaders, fools, and imposters: Essays on the psychology of leadership. San Francisco: Jossey-Bass.

Kets de Vries, M. F. R., and D. Miller. 1986. Personality, culture, and organizations. *Academy of Management Review* 11: 266–279.

Khandwalla, P. N. 1976. Some top management styles, their context, and performance. *Organization and Administrative Science* 74: 21–52.

Kipnis, D. 1972. Does power corrupt? *Journal of Personality and Social Psychology* 24: 33–41.

Kipnis, D., S. M. Schmidt, and I. Wilkinson. 1980. Why do I like thee: Is it your performance or my orders? *Journal of Applied Psychology* 66: 324–328.

Kirkpatric, D. 1997. He wants all your business—and he's starting to get it. *Fortune* 135, no. 10: 58–68.

Kirkpatrick, S. A., and E. A. Locke. 1991. Leadership: Do traits matter? Academy of Management Executive 5, no. 2: 48–60.

Kirschenbaum, J. 2001. Failure is glorious. *Fast Company* (October): 35–38.

Klein, H. J., and J. S. Kim. 1998. A field study of the influence of situational constraints, leaders-member exchange, and goal commitment on performance. *Academy of Management Journal* 41: 88–95.

Komaki, J. 1986. Toward effective supervision: An operant analysis and comparison of managers at work. *Journal of Applied Psychology* 71: 270–278.

Kotin, J., and M. Sharaf. 1976. Management succession and administrative style. *Psychiatry* 30: 237–248.

Kotter, J. P. 1985. *Power and influence.* New York: Free Press.

———. 1990. *A force for change: How leadership differs from management.* New York: Free Press.

———. 1996. *Leading change.* Boston: Harvard Business School Press.

Kouzes, J. M., and B. Z. Posner. 1987. *The leadership challenge: How to get extraordinary things done in organizations.* San Francisco: Jossey-Bass.

———. 1993. Credibility: How leaders gain and lose it, why people demand it. San Francisco: Jossey-Bass.

———. 1995. *The leadership challenge.* San Francisco: Jossey-Bass.

———. 1999. *Encouraging the heart: A leader's guide to rewarding and recognizing others.* San Francisco: Jossey-Bass.

Kraar, L. 1994. The overseas Chinese: Lessons from the world's most dynamic capitalists. *Fortune* 130, no. 9: 91–114.

———. 1995. Acer's edge: PC to go. *Fortune* 132, no. 9: 187–204.

———. 1999.Asia's businessman of the year. *Fortune* 139, no. 2: 27.

Krech, D., and R. S. Crutchfield. 1948. *Theory and problems of social psychology.* New York: McGraw-Hill.

Kriss, E. 1998. So you want to be an *Inc.* 500 CEO? *Inc.* October 20: 25–26.

Kupfer, A. 1998. The real king of the Internet. *Fortune* 138, no. 5: 84–93.

Kurtz, D. L., L. E. Boone, and C. P. Fleenor. 1989. *CEO: Who gets to the top in America?* East Lansing: Michigan State University Press.

Labarre, P. 1998. These leaders are having a moment. *Fast Company* (October): 86–88.

———. 1999. Grassroots leadership. *Fast Company* (April): 115–129.

———. 2001a. Marcus Buckingham thinks your boss has an attitude problem. *Fast Company* (August): 88–98.

———. 2001b. Leader Feargal Quinn. *Fast Company* (November): 89–94.

Laurent, A. 1983. The cultural diversity of Western conceptions of management. *International Studies of Management and Organizations* 13, nos. 1–2: 75–96.

Lawler, E. E. III 1986. *High involvement management.* San Francisco: Jossey-Bass.

Lawler, E. E. III, and S. A. Mohrman. 1987. Quality circles: After the honeymoon. *Organizational Dynamics* (Spring): 42–54.

Lawler, E. E. III, S. A. Mohrman, and G. E. Ledford, Jr. 1995. *Creating high performance organizations: Practices and results of employee involvement and total quality management in* Fortune *1000 companies.* San Francisco: Jossey-Bass.

Lennox, R. D., and Wolfe, R. N. 1984. Revision of the self-monitoring scale. *Journal of Personality and Social Psychology* (June): 1361.

Levering, R., and M. Moskowitz. 2001. The 100 best companies to work for. *Fortune* (January 8): 166.

Lewin, K., and R. Lippit. 1938. An experimental approach to the study of autocracy and democracy: A preliminary note. *Sociometry* 1: 292–300.

Lewin, K., R. Lippit, and R. K. White. 1939. Patterns of aggressive behavior in experimentally created social climates. *Journal of Social Psychology* 10: 271–301.

Liden, R. C., and G. Graen. 1980. Generalizability of the vertical dyad linkage model of leadership. *Academy of Management Journal* 23:451–465.

Lieber, R. B. 1998. Why employees love these companies. *Fortune* 137, no. 1: 73.

Lieberson, S., and J. F. O'Connor. 1972. Leadership and organization performance: A study of large corporations. *American Sociological Review* 37, no. 2: 117–130.

Limerick, D. C. 1990. Managers of meaning: From Bob Geldof's Band Aid to Australian CEOs. *Organizational Dynamics* 18, no. 4: 22–33.

Lord, R. G., C. L. De Vader, and G. M. Alliger. 1986. A meta-analysis of the relation between personality traits and leadership perceptions: An application of validity generalization procedures. *Journal of Applied Psychology* 71: 402–410.

Lord, R. G., and K. J. Maher. 1991. *Leadership and information processing.* London: Routledge.

Luthans, F. 1989. Successful vs. effective managers. *Academy of Management Executive* 2, no. 2: 127–132.

Luthans, F., and D. L. Lockwood. 1984. Toward an observation system for measuring leader behavior in natural settings. In *Leaders and managers: Internal perspectives on managerial behavior and leadership,* edited by J. G. Hunt, D. Hosking, C. A Schreishrim, and R. Stewart. New York: Pergamon Press, 117–141.

Lutz, S. 1992. A "lifetime" of accomplishments by age 38. *Modern Healthcare* (March 2): 41–44.

References

Mai-Dalton, R. 1993. Managing cultural diversity on the individual, group, and organizational levels. In *Leadership theory and research: Perspective and directions,* edited by M. M. Chemers and R. Ayman. New York: Academic Press, 189–215.

Maier, N. R. F. 1963. *Problem solving discussion and conferences: Leadership methods and skills.* New York: McGraw-Hill.

Malaysia, 2002. www.cia.gov/cia/publications/factbook/geos/my.html, accessed April 21, 2002.

Malekzadeh, A. 1995. How leaders manage the six strategic forces. Manuscript.

Manz, C. C. 1990. How to become a super-leader. *Executive Excellence* (June): 10–12.

———. 1992. Self-leading work teams: Moving beyond self-management myths. *Human Relations* 11: 1119–1140.

Manz, C. C., and C. Neck. 1999. *Mastering self-leadership: Empowering yourself for personal excellence.* 2d edition. Upper Saddle River, NJ: Prentice Hall.

Manz, C. C., and H. P. Sims, Jr. 1987. Leading workers to lead themselves: The external leadership of self-managing work teams. *Administrative Science Quarterly* 32: 106–129.

———. 1991. Superleadership: Beyond the myth of heroic leadership. *Organizational Dynamics* 19, no. 4: 18–35.

Markels, A. 1998. Power to the people. *Fast Company* (February–March): 155–165.

Marsick, V. J., E. Turner, and L. Cederholm. 1989. International as a team. *Management Review* 78, no. 3: 46–49.

Martin, J. 1997. Mercedes: Made in Alabama. *Fortune* 136, no. 1: 150–158.

Martin, M. H. 1996. The next big thing: A bookstore? *Fortune* 134, no. 11: 168–170.

Martinez, S., and P. W. Dorfman. 1998. The Mexican entrepreneur: An ethnographic study of the Mexican empressario. *International Studies in Management and Organizations* 28 (summer): 97–123.

Maruca, R. F. 2001. Masters of disaster. *Fast Company* (April): 81–96.

Massey, M. E. 1986. The past: What you are is where you were when. Schaumburg, IL: Video Publishing House.

Mathur, A., Y. Zhang, and J. P. Meelankavil. 2001. Critical managerial motivational factors: A cross-cultural analysis of four culturally divergent countries. *International Journal Cross-Cultural Management* 1, no. 2: 251–267.

McAllister, D. J. 1995. Affect- and cognition-based trust as foundations for interpersonal cooperation in organizations. *Academy of Management Journal* 38: 24–59.

McCall, M. W., and M. M. Lombardo. 1978. *Leadership: Where else can we go?* Durham, NC: Duke University Press.

———. 1983. Off the track: Why and how successful executives get derailed. Technical Report No. 21, Center for Creative Leadership, Greensboro, NC.

McCauley, L. 2000. Unit of one: Don't burn out. *Fast Company* (May): 101–132.

McClelland, D. C. 1975. *Power: The inner experience.* New York: Irvington.

McClintick, M. 1997. The bank scandal that keeps growing. *Fortune* 136, no. 1: 36–38.

McCrae, R. R. 1993. Moderated analyses of longitudinal personality stability. *Journal of Personality and Social Psychology* 65, no. 3: 577–585.

McGarvey, C. 2002. Christian business woman Mary Kay Ash dies, www.christianity.com . . . ,PTID1000%7CCHD10%1179700,00.html, accessed February 28, 2002.

Meindl, J. R., and S. B. Ehrlick. 1987. The romance of leadership and the evaluation of organizational performance. *Academy of Management Journal* 30: 90–109.

Menon, S. T. 2001. Employee empowerment: An integrative psychological approach. *Applied Psychology: An International Review* 50, no. 1: 153–180.

Meyerson, M. 1997. What it means to lead. *Fast Company* (February–March): 99.

Mieszkowski K. 1998. Barbara Waugh. *Fast Company* (December): 146–154.

Miller, D. M. 1987. The genesis of configuration. *Academy of Management Review* 12: 686–701.

Miller, D. M., and C. Droge. 1986. Psychological and traditional determinants of structure. *Administrative Science Quarterly* 31: 539–560.

Miller, D. M., and P. H. Freisen. 1982. Structural change and performance: Quantum vs.

piecemeal-incremental approaches. *Academy of Management Journal* 25: 867–892.

Miller, D. M., M. F. R. Kets de Vries, and J. M. Toulouse, 1982. Top executive locus of control and its relationship to strategy-making, structure, and environment. *Academy of Management Journal* 25, no. 2: 237–253.

Miller, D. M., E. R. Lack, and S. Asroff. 1985. Preference for control and the coronary-prone behavior pattern: "I'd rather do it myself." *Journal of Personality and Social Psychology* 49: 492–499.

Miller, D. M., and J. Toulouse. 1986. Chief executive personality and corporate strategy and structure in small firms. *Management Science* 32:1389–1409.

Miner, J. B., and N. R. Smith. 1982. Decline and stabilization of managerial motivation over a 20-year period. *Journal of Applied Psychology* (June): 298.

Mintzberg, H. 1973. *The nature of managerial work*. New York: Harper and Row.

Mischel, W. 1973. *Towards a cognitive social learning reconceptualization of personality. Psychological Review* 80: 252–283.

Misumi, J. 1985. *The behavioral science of leadership*. Ann Arbor: University of Michigan Press.

Misumi, J., and M. F. Peterson. 1985. The performance-maintenance (PM) theory of leadership: Review of a Japanese research program. *Administrative Science Quarterly* 30: 198–223.

Mitchell, T. R., and R. E. Wood. 1980. Supervisor's responses to subordinate poor performance: A test of an attributional model. *Organizational Behavior and Human Performance* 25: 123–138.

Moore, T. 1987. Personality tests are back. *Fortune* 121, no. 5: 30, 74–82.

Morris, B. 2000. This Ford is different: Idealist on board. *Fortune* (April 30): 123–136.

Moxley, R. S. 2000. *Leadership and spirit: Breathing new vitality and energy into individuals and organizations*. San Francisco: Jossey-Bass.

Muio, A. 1999. Mint condition. *Fast Company* (December): 330.

Mumford, M. D., S. J. Zaccaro, M. S. Connelly, and M. A. Marks. 2000. Leadership skills: Conclusions and Future directions. *Leadership Quarterly* 11, no. 1: 155–170.

Mumford, M. D., S. J. Zaccaro, F. D. Harding, T. O Jacobs, and E. A. Fleishman. 2000. Leadership skills for a changing world: Solving complex and social problems. *Leadership Quarterly* 11, no. 1: 11–35.

Mumford, M. D., S. J. Zaccaro, J. F. Johnson, M. Diana, J. A. Gilbert, and K. V. Threlfall. 2000. Patterns of leader characteristics: Implications for performance and development. *Leadership Quarterly* 11, no. 1: 115–133.

Munk, N. 1998. Gap gets it. *Fortune* 138, no. 3: 68–82.

Munter, M. 1993. Cross-cultural communication for managers. *Business Horizons* (May–June): 69–78.

Murphy, S. E., and E. A. Ensher. 1999. The effects of leaders and subordinate characteristics in the development of leader-member exchange quality. *Journal of Applied Social Psychology* 29, no. 7: 1371–1394.

Murray, S. 1997. BP alters atmosphere amid turnaround. *The Wall Street Journal*, 17 September, sec. A19.

Nahavandi, A. 1983. The effect of personal and situational factors on satisfaction with leadership. Ph.D. diss. University of Utah, Salt Lake City.

———. 1993. Integrating leadership and strategic management in organizational theory. *Canadian Journal of Administrative Sciences* 10, no. 4: 297–307.

Nahavandi, A., and E. Aranda. 1994. Restructuring teams for the re-engineered organization. *Academy of Management Executive* 8, no. 4: 58–68.

Nahavandi. A., and A. R. Malekzadeh. 1988. Acculturation in mergers and acquisitions. *Academy of Management Review* 13: 79–90.

———. 1993a. Leader style in strategy and organizational performance: An integrative framework. *Journal of Management Studies* 30, no. 3: 405–425.

———. 1993b. *Organizational culture in the management of mergers*. New York: Quorum Books.

References

―――. 1999. *Organizaional behavior: The person-organization fit.* Upper Saddle River, NJ: Prentice Hall.

Nahavandi, A., P. J. Mizzi, and A. R. Malekzadeh. 1992. Executives' Type A personality as a determinant of environmental perception and firm strategy. *Journal of Social Psychology* 13, no. 1: 59–68.

Nahavandi, F. 1988. *Aux sources de la revolution iranienne.* Paris: Editions L'Harmattan.

Nahavandi, H. 1994. *Le voile dechire de l'Islamisme.* Paris: Premiere Ligne.

Nelton, S. 1997. Leadership for the new age. *Nation's Business* (May): 18–27.

Newsome, S., A. L. Day, and V. M. Catano. 2000. Assessing the predictive validity of emotional intelligence. *Personality and Individual Differences* 29, no. 6: 1005–1016.

Newstetter, W. I., M. J. Feldstein, and T. M. Newcomb. 1938. *Group adjustment.* Cleveland: Western Reserve University Press.

Nicholls, J. R. 1985. A new approach to situational leadership. *Leadership and Organization Development Journal* 6, no. 4: 2–7.

1997 Economic Census Minority- and Women-Owned Businesses, United States, www.census.gov/epcd/mwb97/us/us.html, accessed February 5, 2002.

Nocera, J. 2000. I remember Microsoft. *Fortune* (July 10): 114–136.

Norman, W. T. 1963. Toward an adequate taxonomy of personality attributes: Replicated factor structure in peer nomination personality ratings. *Journal of Abnormal and Social Psychology* 66: 547–583.

Nutt, P. 1986. Decision style and strategic decisions of top executives. *Technological Forecasting and Social Change* 30: 39–62.

―――. 1988. The effects of culture on decision making. *OMEGA International Journal of Management Science* 16: 553–567.

Offermann, L. R., C. J. Schroyer, and S. K. Green. 1998. Leader attributions for subordinate performance: Consequences for subsequent leader interaction behaviors and ratings. *Journal of Applied Social Psychology* 28, no. 13: 1125–1139.

Olofson, C. 1998. The end of authority. *Fast Company* (November): 74.

Ones, D. S., and C. Viswesvaran. 1999. Relative importance of personality dimensions of expatriate selection: A policy capturing study. *Human Performance* 12, no. 3–4: 275–294.

O'Reilly, B. 1994. J & J is on a roll. *Fortune* 130, no. 13: 178–192.

―――. 1995. Agee in exile. *Fortune* 131, no. 10: 51–74.

Overholt, A. 2001. Unit of one: Open to women. *Fast Company* (August): 66.

Paine Weber. 2000. www.ubspaineweber.com/PWIC/CDA/main/1,1194,SE745-EN 745,00.hmtl, March 4, 2002.

Panitz, E. 1989. Psychometric investigation of the MACH IV scale measuring Machiavellianism. *Psychological Reports* 64, no. 3: 963–968.

Pawar, B. S., and K. K. Eastman. 1997. The nature and implications of contextual influences on transformational leadership: a conceptual examination. *Academy of Management Review* 22: 80–109.

Pelled, L. H., and K. R. Xin. 1997. Birds of a feather: Leader-member demographic similarity and organizational attachment in Mexico. *Leadership Quarterly* 8: 433–450.

―――. 2000. Relationship demography and relationship quality in two cultures. *Organization Studies* 21, no. 6: 1077–1094.

People to watch 2001. 2001 *Fortune* January 8; 34.

Peters, L. H., D. D. Hartke, and J. T. Pohlmann. 1985. Fiedler's contingency theory of leadership: An application of the meta-analysis procedure of Schmitt and Hunter. *Psychological Bulletin* 97: 274–285.

Peterson, M. F., and J. G. Hunt. 1997. International perspective on international leadership. *Leadership Quarterly* 8: 203–231.

Pettigrew, A. 1973. *The politics of organizational decision making.* London: Tavistock.

Pfeffer, J. 1981. *Power in organizations.* Marshfield, MA: Pitman.

―――. 1983. Organizational demography. In *Research in organizational behavior,* edited by L. L. Cummings and B. W. Staw. Greenwich, CT: JAI Press, 299–357.

——. 1998. *The human equation: Building profits by putting people first*. Cambridge: Harvard Business School Press.

Planned Parenthood. 2002. www.planned parenthood.org/vision2025/index.html, accessed January 24, 2002.

Podsakoff, P. M., and S. B. MacKenzie. 1994. An examination of the psychometric properties and nomological validity of some revised and reduced "substitutes for leadership" scales. *Journal of Applied Psychology* 79: 702–713.

Podsakoff, P. M., and S. B. MacKenzie. 1996. Kerr and Jermier's substitutes for leadership model: Background, empirical assessment, and suggestions for future research. *Leadership Quarterly* 8: 117–125.

——. 1997. Kerr and Jermier's substitutes for leadership model: Background, empirical assessment, and suggestions for future research. *Leadership Quarterly* 8: 117–125.

——. 1998. An examination of substitutes for leadership within a levels-of-analysis framework. In *Leadership: The multiple-level approaches: Contemporary and alternative. Monographs in organizational behavior and industrial relations,* edited by F. Dansereau and F. J. Yammarino. Vol. 24, part B, pp. 215–284.

Podsakoff, P. M., S. B. MacKenzie, M. Ahearne, and W. H. Bommer. 1995. Searching for a needle in a haystack: Trying to identify the illusive moderators of leadership behaviors. *Journal of Management* 21: 423–470.

Podsakoff, P. M., S. B. MacKenzie, and W. H. Bommer. 1996. Transformational leadership behaviors and substitutes for leadership as determinants of employee satisfaction, commitment, trust, and organizational citizenship behaviors. *Journal of Management* 22: 259–298.

Poggioli, S. 1998. Turkish feminism. National Public Radio, 7 March, Weekend Edition.

Politics in Venezuela: To the barricades. 2001.*The Economist* (November 24): 38.

Porter, L. W., and E. E Lawler. 1968. *Managerial attitudes and performance*. Homewood, IL: Irwin-Dorsey.

Prendergast, C. 1993. The theory of "Yes Men." *American Economic Review* 83, no. 4: 757–770.

Puffer, S. M. 1994. Understanding the bear: A portrait of Russian business leaders. *Academy of Management Executive* 8, no. 1: 41–54.

Pugh, D. S., D. J. Hickson, C. R. Hinings, and C. Turner. 1968. Dimensions of organization structure. *Administrative Science Quarterly* 13: 65–105.

Puri, S. 1997. The problem with stock options: Pay for underperformance, *Fortune* (December 8): 52–56.

Rahim, M. A., D. Antonioni, K. Krumov, and S. Ilieva. 2000. Power, conflict, and effectiveness: A cross-cultural study in the United States and Bulgaria. *European Psychologist,* 5, no. 1: 28–33.

Ralston, D. A., D. J. Gustafson, F. M. Cheung, and R. H. Terpstra. 1993. Differences in managerial values: A study of U.S., Hong Kong, and PRC managers. *Journal of International Business Studies* 2: 249–275.

Ralston, D. A., D. J. Gustafson, R. H Terpstra, D. H. Holt, F. M. Cheung, and B. A. Ribbens. 1993. The impact of managerial values on decision-making behavior: A comparison of the United States and Hong Kong. *Asia Pacific Journal of Management* 10, no. 1: 21–37.

Rattan, S. 1993. Why busters hate boomers. *Fortune* 128, no. 8: 56–70.

Rice, R. 1978a. Construct validity of the least preferred coworker. *Psychological Bulletin* 85: 1199–1237.

——. 1978b. Psychometric properties of the esteem for least preferred coworker (LPC) scale. *Academy of Management Review* 3: 106–118.

Roberts, N. C., and R. T. Bradley. 1988. Transforming leadership: A process of collective action. *Human Relations* 38: 1023–1046.

Roberts, P. 1998. We are one company, no matter where we are. *Fast Company* (April–May): 125.

Rogers, A. 1994. Is he too cautious to save IBM? *Fortune* 130, no. 7: 78–88.

Rokeach, M. 1973. *The nature of human values*. New York: Free Press.

Rosenfeld, J. 2000. Here's an idea. *Fast Company* (April): 102.

Rosenman, R. H., and M. Friedman. 1974. Neurogenic factors in pathogenesis of coronary heart disease. *Medical Clinics of North America* 58: 269–279.

References

Rosier, R. H. 1994, 1995. *The competency model handbook,* Vol. 1 and 2, Boston, MA: Linkage.

Ross, S. M., and L. R. Offerman. 1997. Transformational leaders: Measurement of personality attributes and work group performance. *Personality and Social Psychology Bulletin* 23: 1978–1086.

Rotter, J. B. 1966. Generalized expectancies for internal versus external control of reinforcement. *Psychological Monographs* 80 (1, Whole No. 609).

———. 1971. External control and internal control. *Psychology Today* (June): 42.

Row, H. 1998. Dan Hanson. *Fast Company* (December): 192.

Rubin, H. 2000. Booooring!!! *Fast Company* (June): 228–248.

Russell, A. M. 1990. The end of the big bad boss. *Working Woman* (March): 79.

Rust, J. 1999. Discriminant validity of the "Big Five" personality traits in employment settings. *Social Behavior and Personality* 27, no. 1: 99–108.

Rychlak, J. F. 1963. Personality correlates of leadership among first level managers. *Psychological Reports* 12: 43–52.

Safilios-Rothschild, C. 1977. *Love, sex, and sex roles.* Upper Saddle River, NJ: Prentice Hall.

Salancik, G. R., and J. Pfeffer. 1977a. Constraints on administrator discretion: The limited influence of mayors in city budgets. *Organizational Dynamics* 12, no. 4: 475–496.

———. 1977b. Who gets power—and how they hold onto it: A strategic-contingency model of power. *Organizational Dynamics* (Winter): 3–21.

Salter, C. 2000a. We believe in an ignorant world. Our mission is to purge that ignorance. *Fast Company* (April): 190–202.

———. 2000b. What's your mission statement? *Fast Company* (July): 48–50.

Sanders, W. M. G., and M. A. Carpenter. 1998. Internationalization and firm governance: The roles of CEO compensation, top team composition, and board structure. *Academy of Management Journal* 41: 158–178.

Scandura, T. 1999. Rethinking leader-member exchange: An organizational justice perspective. *Leadership Quarterly* 10, no. 1: 25–40.

Schein, E. H. 1985. *Organizational culture and leadership.* San Francisco: Jossey-Bass.

Schlender, B. 1997. On the road with Chairman Bill. *Fortune* 135, no. 10: 72–81.

———. 1998. The Bill and Warren show. *Fortune* 138, no. 2: 48–64.

Schriesheim, C. A., S. L. Castro, and C. C. Cogliser. 1999. Leader-member exchange (LMX) research: A comprehensive review of theory, measurement, and data-analytic practices. *Leadership Quarterly* 10, no. 1: 63–113.

Schriesheim, C. A., S. L. Castro, and F. J. Yammarino. 2000. Investigating contingencies: An examination of the impact of span of supervision and upward controllingness on leader-member exchange using traditional and multivariate within- and between-entities analysis. *Journal of Applied Psychology* 85, no. 5: 659–677.

Schriesheim, C. A., and S. Kerr. 1974. Psychometric properties of The Ohio State University Leadership scales. *Psychological Bulletin* 81: 756–765.

———. 1977. R.I.P. LPC: A response to Fiedler. In *Leadership: The cutting edge,* edited by J. G. Hunt and L. L. Larson. Carbondale: Southern Illinois University Press, 51–56.

Schwartz, N. D. 2001. What's in the cards for Amex? *Fortune* (January 22): 58–70.

Schwartz, T. 2000. How do you feel? *Fast Company* (June 2000): 297–313.

Schwarzzwald, J., M. Koslowsky, and V. Agassi. 2001. Captain's leadership style and police officers' compliance to power bases. *European Journal of Work and Organizational Psychology* 10, no. 3: 273–290.

Sellers, P. 1996. Cocktails at Charlotte's with Martha and Darla. *Fortune* 134, no. 3: 56–57.

———. 1997. Don't mess with Darla. *Fortune* 136, no. 5: 62–72.

———. 1998. The 50 most powerful women in American business. *Fortune* 138, no. 7: 76–98.

———. 2000. The 50 most powerful women in business. *Fortune* (October 16): 131–160.

———. 2000. Big, hairy, audacious goals don't work—just ask P & G, *Fortune* (April 3): 39–44.

Seltzer, J., and B. M. Bass. 1990. Transformational leadership: Beyond initiation of structure and consideration. *Journal of Management* 16: 693–703.

Seltzer, J., and R. E. Numerof. 1988. Supervisory leadership and subordinate burnout. *Academy of Management Journal* 31: 439–446.

Semler, R. 1989. Managing without managers. *Harvard Business Review* 67, no. 5: 76–84.

———. 1993. *Maverick!, The success story behind the world's most unusual workplace.* London: Century.

Serwer, A. E. 1993. Payday! Payday! *Fortune* 127, no. 12: 102–111.

———. 1996. Mr. Price is on the line. *Fortune* 134, no. 11: 70–88.

Shamir, B. 1991. The charismatic relationship: Alternative explanations and predictions. *Leadership Quarterly* 2: 81–104.

———. 1999. Taming of charisma for better understanding and greater usefulness: A response to Beyer. *Leadership Quarterly* 10, no. 4, 555–562.

Shamir, B., M. B. Arthur, and R. J. House. 1994. The rhetoric of charismatic leadership: A theoretical extension, a case study and implications for research. *Leadership Quarterly* 5: 25–42.

Shamir, B., R. J. House, and M. B. Arthur. 1993. The motivational effects of charismatic leadership. A self-concept based theory. *Organization Science* 4: 1–17.

Shamir, B., and J. M. Howell. 1999. Organizational and contextual influence on the emergence and effectiveness of charismatic leadership. *Leadership Quarterly* 10, no. 2: 257–283.

Shamir, B., E. Zakay, E. Breinin, and M. Popper. 1998. Correlates of charismatic leaders' behavior in military units: Subordinates' attitudes, unit characteristics, and superiors' appraisals of leader performance. *Academy of Management Journal* 41: 387–409.

Sherman, S. 1994. Leaders learn to heed the voice within. *Fortune* 130, no. 4: 92–100.

Siebert, S. E., M. L. Kraimer. 2001. The five-factor model of personality and career success. *Journal of Vocational Behavior* 58, no. 1: 1–21.

Sightler, K. W., and M. G. Wilson. 2001. Correlates of the imposter phenomenon among undergraduate entrepreneurs. *Psychological Reports* 88, no. 3: 679–689.

Singer, P. 1969. Toward a re-evaluation of the concept of charisma with reference to India. *Journal of Social Research* 12, no. 2: 13–25.

Slocum, J. W., Jr., and Hellreigel, D. 1983. A look at how managers' minds work. *Business Horizons* (July–August): 58–68.

Smith, T. W., and F. Rhodewalt. 1986. On states, traits, and processes: A transactional alternative to the individual difference assumption in Type A behavior and psychological reactivity. *Journal of Research in Personality* 20: 229–251.

Snyder, M. 1974. The self-monitoring of expressive behavior. *Journal of Personality and Social Psychology* 30: 526–537.

Song, J. H. 1982. Diversification strategies and the experience of top executives of large firms. *Strategic Management Journal* 3: 377–380.

Sosik, J. J., and L. E. Megerian. 1999. Understanding leader emotional intelligence and performance: The role of self-other agreement on transformation leadership perceptions. *Group and Organization Management* 24, no. 3: 367–390.

Sparks, D. 1994. Ming the Merciless. *FW* (June 21): 26–27.

Sparrowe, R. T., and R. C. Liden. 1997. Process and structure in leader-member exchange. *Academy of Management Review* 22, no. 2: 522–552.

Spector, B. 1987. Transformational leadership: The new challenge for U.S. unions. *Human Resource Management* 26: 3–16.

Spector, P. E. 1982. Behavior in organizations as a function of employee's locus of control. *Psychological Bulletin* 91, no. 3: 482–497.

Spencer, R. J. 1995. Success with self-managed teams and partnering. *The Journal for Quality and Participation* 18, no. 4: 48–54.

Sternberg, R. J., and T. I. Lubart. 1995. *Defying the crowd: Cultivating creativity in a culture of conformity.* New York: Free Press.

Stewart, T. A. 1998. Why leadership matters. *Fortune* 137, no. 4: 82.

References

————. 1998. The cunning plots of leadership. *Fortune* 138, no. 5: 165–166.

Stewart-Belle, S., and J. A. Lust. 1999. Career movement of female employees holding lower-level positions: An analysis of the impact of the Type A behavior pattern. *Journal of Business and Psychology* 14, no. 1: 187–197.

Stinson, J. E., and T. W. Johnson. 1975. The path-goal theory of leadership: A partial test and suggested refinement. *Academy of Management Journal* 18: 242–252.

Stogdill, R. M. 1948. Personal factors associated with leadership: A survey of the literature. *Journal of Psychology* 25: 35–71.

————. 1974. *Handbook of leadership*. New York: Free Press.

Strauss, G. 2001. Forget brass rings—Execs grad for gold. *USA Today,* 20 March, 1B and 2B.

Strube, M. J., and J. E. Garcia. 1981. A meta-analytical investigation of Fiedler's contingency model of leadership effectiveness. *Psychological Bulletin* 90: 307–321.

Strube, M. J., C. W. Turner, D. Cerro, J. Stevens, and F. Hinchey. 1984. Interpersonal aggression and the Type A coronary-prone behavior pattern: A theoretical distinction and practical implications. *Journal of Personality and Social Psychology* 47: 839–847.

Strube, M. J., and C. Werner. 1985. Relinquishment of control and the Type A behavior pattern. *Journal of Personality and Social Psychology* 48: 688–701.

Swan, K. 2000. Difference is power. *Fast Company* (July): 258–266.

Szilagyi, A. D., and H. P. Sims. 1974. An exploration of the path-goal theory of leadership in a health care environment. *Academy of Management Journal* 17: 622–634.

Tannenbaum, A. S., and R. A. Cooke. 1974. Control and participation. *Journal of Contemporary Business* 3, no. 4: 35–46.

Taylor, A. III. 1999. The Germans take charge. *Fortune* 139, no. 1: 92–96.

Teagarden, M. B., M. C. Butler, and M. A. Von Glinow. 1992. Mexico's Maquiladora industry: Where strategic human resource management makes a difference. *Organizational Dynamics* 20, no. 3: 34–47.

Tepper, B. J., and P. M. Percy. 1994. Structural validity of the multifactor leadership questionnaire. *Educational and Psychological Measurement* 54: 734–744.

Thomas, A. B. 1988. Does leadership make a difference to organizational performance? *Administrative Science Quarterly* 33: 388–400.

Tjosvold, D., W. C. Wedley, and R. H. G. Field. 1986. Constructive controversy: The Vroom-Yetton model and managerial decision-making. *Journal of Occupational Behavior* 7: 125–138.

Tomlinson, R. 2000. Europe's new business elite. *Fortune* (April 3): 177–184.

The top 25 managers of the year. 2002. *Business Week* (January 14): 53–72.

Townsend, J., J. S. Phillips, and T. J. Elkins. 2000. Employee retaliation: The neglected consequence of poor leader-member exchange relations. *Journal of Occupational Health Psychology* 5, no. 4: 457–463.

Transparency International. 2001. www.global corruptionreport.org/press.htm, accessed February 19, 2002.

Trevelyan, R. 2001. The paradox of autonomy: A case of academic research scientists. *Human Relations* 54, no. 4: 495–525.

Triandis, H. C. 1993. The contingency model in cross-cultural perspective. In *Leadership theory and research: Perspectives and directions,* edited by M. M. Chemers and R. Ayman. New York: Academic Press, 167–188.

————. 1995. *Individualism and collectivism.* Boulder, CO: Westview Press.

Triandis, H. C., P. Carnevale, M. Gelfand, C. Robert, S. A. Wasti, T. Probst, E. S. Kashima, T. Dragonas, D. Chan, X. P. Chen, U. Kim, C. de Dreu, E. van de Vliert, S. Iwao, K. Ohbuchi, and P. Schmitz. 2001. Culture and deception in business negotiations: A multilevel analysis. *Internationbal Journal of Cross-Cultural Management* 1, no. 1: 73–90.

Trice, H. M., and J. M. Beyer. 1993. *The cultures of work organizations.* Upper Saddle River, NJ: Prentice Hall.

Trompenaars, A., C. M. Hampden-Turner, and F. Trompenaars. 1997. *Riding the waves of culture: Understanding diversity in global business.* Chicago: McGraw-Hill.

Trompenaars, A, and C. M. Hampden-Turner. 2001. *21 leaders for the 21st century.* Chicago: McGraw-Hill.

Trompenaars, F. 1994. *Riding the waves of culture: Understanding culture and diversity in business.* London: Nicholas Brealey.

Tropila, D., and B. H. Kleiner. 1994. *Equal Opportunities International* 13, no. 1/2: 1–6.

Tsui, A. S., and C. A. O'Reilly. 1989. Beyond simple demographic effects: The importance of relationship demography in superior-subordinates dyads. *Academy of Management Journal* 32: 402–423.

Tsurumi, R. 1982. American origins of Japanese productivity: The Hawthorne experiment rejected. *Pacific Basin Quarterly* (Spring/Summer) 7: 14–15.

Turnley, W. H., and M. C. Bolino. 2001. Achieving desired images while avoiding undesired images: Exploring the role of self-monitoring in impression management. *Journal of Applied Psychology* 86, no. 2: 351–360.

Tyabji, H. 1997. What it means to lead. *Fast Company* (February–March): 98.

Uchitelle, L. 1996. Performance pay: 1995 bonus year for executives, *Houston Chronicle,* 30 March, sec. C3.

Useem, J. 2001. It's all yours Jeff. Now what? *Fortune* (September 17): 64–68.

Useem, M. 2001. *Leading up: How to lead your boss so you both win.* New York: Crown Business/Random House.

Vecchio, R. P. 1983. Assessing the validity of Fiedler's contingency model of leadership effectiveness: A closer look at Strube and Garcia. *Psychological Bulletin* 93: 404–408.

Venezuela. 2002. Report on *Morning Edition,* National Public Radio, 28 January.

Vroom, V. H. 1964. *Work and motivation.* New York: Wiley and Sons.

Vroom, V. H., and A. G. Jago. 1988. *The new leadership: Managing participation in organizations.* Upper Saddle River, NJ: Prentice Hall.

Vroom, V. H., and P. W. Yetton. 1973. *Leadership and decision making.* Pittsburgh: University of Pittsburgh Press.

Wakababayashi, M., G. B. Graen, M. R. Graen, and M. C. Graen. 1988. Japanese management progress: Mobility into middle management. *Journal of Applied Psychology* 73: 217–227.

Walker, R. 1997. Back to the farm. *Fast Company* (February–March): 110–122.

Walsh, T. 1996. CEOs: Greenspan by a landslide. *Fortune,* 133, no. 5: 43.

Warner, R. 2001. where is the next frontier of innovation? *Fast Company* (September): 128–132.

Wayne, S. J., M. Shore, R. C. Liden. 1997. Perceived organizational support and leader-member exchange: A social exchange perspective. *Academy of Management Journal* 40, no. 1: 82–111.

Webber, A. 2000. Will companies ever learn? *Fast Company* (October): 275–282.

Weber, D. O. 1990. Grace under pressure . . . The emerging leaders, 1990. *Health Care Forum Journal* (May–June): 51–64.

Weierter, S. J. M. 1997. Who wants to play follow the leader? A theory of charismatic relationships based on routinized charisma and follower characteristics. *Leadership Quarterly* 8, no. 2: 171–193.

Weil, E. 1998. Every leader tells a story. *Fast Company* (June–July): 38–40.

Weiner, N., and T. A. Mahoney. 1981. A model of corporate performance as a function of environment, organization, and leadership influences. *Academy of Management Journal* 24: 453–470.

Weiss, H. M., and S. Adler. 1984. Personality in organizational research. In *Research in organizational behavior.* Vol. 6, edited by B. Staw and L. Cummings. Greenwich, CT: JAI Press, 1–50.

Welles, E. 1998. Ben's big flop. *Inc.* (September): 40–57.

Wheatley, M. J. 1994. *Leadership and the new science: Learning about organization from an orderly universe.* San Francisco: Berrett-Koehler.

Whitford, D. 2001. A human place to work. *Fortune* (January 8): 108–122.

Wofford, J. C., and L. Z. Liska. 1993. Path-goal theories of leadership: A meta analysis. *Journal of Management* 19: 858–876.

Yammarino, F. J., and B. M. Bass. 1990. Long-term forecasting of transformational leadership and its effects among Naval officers: Some preliminary findings. In *Measures of leadership,* edited by K. E. Clark and M. B. Clark. Greensboro, NC: Center for Creative Leadership, 151–169.

Yammarino, F. J., A. J. Dubinsky, L. B. Comer, and M. A. Jolson. 1997. Women and transformational and contingency reward leadership: A multiple-levels-of-analysis perspective. *Academy of Management Journal* 40: 205–222.

Yasai-Ardekani, M. 1986. Structural adaptations to environments. *Academy of Management Review* 11: 9–21.

———. 1989. Effects of environmental scarcity and munificence on the relationship of context to organizational structure. *Academy of Management Journal* 32: 131–156.

Yukl, G. 1970. Leader LPC score: Attitude dimensions and behavioral correlates. *Journal of Social Psychology* 80: 207–212.

———. 1999. An evaluation of conceptual weaknesses in transformational and charismatic leadership theories. *Leadership Quarterly* 10, no. 2: 285–305.

Yukl, G., and C. M. Falbe. 1990. Influence tactics in upward, downward, and lateral influence attempts. *Journal of Applied Psychology* 75: 132–140.

———. 1991. The importance of different power sources in downward and lateral relations. *Journal of Applied Psychology* 76: 416–423.

Zaleznik, A. 1990. The leadership gap. *Academy of Management Executive* 4, no. 1: 7–22.

Zander, A. 1983. The value of belonging to a group in Japan. *Small Group Behavior* 14: 7–8.

Zhou, J., and J. M. George. 2001. When job dissatisfaction leads to creativity: Encouraging the expression of voice. *Academy of Management Journal* 44, no. 4: 682–696.

AUTHOR INDEX

Burke, W., 23
Burns, J. M., 233
Butler, M. C., 99
Bycio, P., 237

C

Caggiano, C., 76, 80
Caligiuri, P. M., 71
Calvete, E., 78
Canabou, C., 4, 9, 79
Cannella, A. A., Jr., 259
Caputi, P., 67
Carbonara, P., 104
Carey, S., 195
Carlyle, T., 33
Carpenter, M. A., 253, 272
Cartwright, D. C., 4
Carvell, T., 40, 65–66
Cashman, J. R., 170
Casimir, B., 37
Castro, S. L., 169
Catano, V. M., 67
Catellano, J., 71
Cederholm, L., 200
Chaleff, I., 295, 296
Chan, A. Y. C., 67
Charan, R., 20
Chatman, J. A., 198
Chemers, M. M., 37, 124, 125, 126, 127, 128,
    130, 131, 133, 142, 146, 153, 157, 161,
    223, 292
Chen, C. C., 292
Chen, M., 199
Cheng, B. S., 173
Cherrington, D. J., 64
Cherry, J., 72
Cheung, F. M., 79
Choi, J., 140
Christensen, L. M., 252
Christie, R., 78, 93
Ciarrochi, J. V., 67
Cleyman, K. L., 167
Cogliser, C. C., 169
Colella, A., 169
Colvin, 173, 265, 272

Condies, S. J., 64
Conger, J. A., 58, 76, 113, 223, 225, 226, 227,
    230, 231, 232, 233, 235, 247
Connelly, M. S., 41
Conyon, M. J., 111, 272
Cook, K. W., 60
Cooke, R. A., 98, 112
Coons, A. E., 36
Corn, R. I., 199
Cornwell, J. M., 65
Corral, S., 78
Costanzo, M. A., 292
Covey, S. R., 80
Covin, G., 20
Covin, J. G., 260
Craig, T. J., 141
Crouch, A., 138
Crowley, A., 159
Crum, S., 204
Crutchfield, R. S., 4
Cunningham, J. B., 207
Cyert, R. M., 21

D

Dahle, C., 189, 285–286
Daniels, C., 80
Dansereau, F., Jr., 166
Davis, J. H., 100, 101, 115, 296
Davis, K. E., 164
Day, A. L., 67
Day, D. V., 23, 230, 260
DeAngelis, L., 23
De Bono, E., 68
Dekmejian, R. H., 230
Delacroix, J., 272
Delbecq, A., 111
Den Hartog, D., 230, 231
Deogun, N., 226
Dessler, G., 161
De Vader, C. L., 65
Digman, J. M., 70
Dillon, P., 224
Dobbins, G. H., 75, 76
Donaldson, L., 100, 101, 115, 296
Donaldson, T., 64

Greenwald, J., 205
Griffin, R. W., 162
Gronn, P., 173
Grove, A., 71
Grove, A. S., 16
Guerra, J., 195
Gunther, M., 225, 227
Gupta, A. K., 256, 261, 269
Gustafson, D. J., 79
Guyon, J., 266

H

Hackett, R. D., 237
Hackman, J. R., 42, 200, 204
Haga, W. J., 166
Halbig, C., 159
Haleblian, J., 257
Haley, U., 78
Hall, E. T., 8, 10, 256
Hall-Merenda, K. E., 237
Halpin, A. W., 36
Hambrick, D. C., 22, 252, 256, 258, 267, 272
Hammonds, K. H., 21, 40, 45, 76, 94–95, 129, 194, 203
Hampden-Turner, C. M., 12
Hanges, P. J., 231
Hannan, M. T., 21
Harding, F. D., 34
Hardy, C., 106
Harris, E. F., 37
Hartke, D. D., 133
Hayes, T., 71
Helgesen, S., 17, 268
Hellriegel, D., 72, 92, 260
Hemphill, J. K., 36
Henderson, J. P., 78
Hershey, P., 174
Hickson, D. J., 104, 105
Himelstein, L., 46, 47, 268
Hofman, M., 262, 265
Hofmann, D. A., 167
Hofstede, G., 10–11, 62, 99, 199
Hollander, E. P., 228
Homans, G. C., 4
Hooijberg, R., 140

Horton, T. R., 68
House, R. J., 5, 37, 161, 162, 163, 175, 223, 224, 226, 231, 233, 290, 292
Howell, J. M., 229, 231, 232, 237
Howell, J. P., 173
Hrebeniak, L. G., 260
Huler, S., 94–95
Hunt, J. G., 223, 230, 292
Hymowitz, C., 15, 79

I

Imperato, G., 4

J

Jaffe, E. D., 78
Jago, A. G., 134–138
James, W., 33
Jawahar, I. M., 75
Jenkins, W. O., 34
Jermier, J. M., 172, 257
Jex, S. M., 167
Johns, G., 163
Johnson, J. F., 41, 69
Johnson, M., 46
Johnson, R. S., 109
Johnson, T. W., 162
Jones, E. E., 164
Jones, S., 109
Judge, T. A., 71
Jung, D. I., 237

K

Kahn, J., 44
Kahn, R. L., 4
Kanter, R. M., 199
Kanungo, R. N., 113, 223, 232, 233, 235
Karau, S. J., 237
Katz, D., 4
Katz, N., 205
Katzenbach, J. R., 106, 204, 208
Kaufman, L., 6
Keller, L. M., 59
Keller, R. T., 237
Kelley, H. H., 164

Kennedy, J. K., Jr., 132
Kennedy, M. M., 127
Kerr, J., 19, 270
Kerr, S., 132, 163, 172, 257
Kets de Vries, M. F. R., 72, 233, 270
Khandwalla, P. N., 260, 261
Kim, J. S., 166
Kipnis, D., 102, 108
Kirkman, B. L., 12
Kirkpatric, D., 159
Kirkpatrick, S. A., 39, 40, 72, 75
Kirschenbaum, J., 31
Klein, H. J., 166
Klein, K. J., 228
Kleiner, B. H., 17
Klich, N. R., 166
Komaki, J., 17
Korabik, K., 76
Koslowsky, M., 101
Kotin, J., 260
Kotter, J. P., 16, 103
Kouzes, J. M., 39, 58, 202, 239, 240, 241, 248
Kraar, L., 99, 226, 271
Kraimer, M. L., 71
Krech, D., 4
Kriss, E., 42
Kupfer, A., 265
Kurtz, D. L., 40–41

L

Labarre, P., 48, 113, 188–189, 270, 295
Lack, E. R., 74
Laurent, A., 99, 267
Lawler, E. E., III, 98, 112, 115, 161, 194, 195
Lawrence, P., 267
Ledford, G. E., Jr., 115, 194, 195
Lennox, R. D., 90
Levering, R., 174
Lewin, K., 35, 123, 289
Lewis, D., 12
Liden, R. C., 166, 167
Lieber, R. B., 98
Lieberson, S., 22, 23
Limerick, D. C., 209
Lingblom, M., 234

Lippit, R., 35, 123
Liska, L. Z., 163
Locke, E. A., 39, 40, 72, 75
Lockwood, D. L., 17
Lombardo, M. M., 79, 223
Lord, R. G., 23, 65, 230, 260
Love, K. G., 167
Lubart, T. I., 68
Lublin, J. S., 226
Lust, J. A., 74
Luthans, F., 5, 17, 48, 78, 79
Lutz, S., 235

M

MacGregor, J., 207
MacKenzie, S. B., 173, 237
Maher, K. J., 230
Mahoney, T. A., 23
Mai-Dalton, R., 292
Maier, N. R. F., 138
Makhijani, M. G., 237
Malekzadeh, A., 254, 255
Malekzadeh, A. R., 18, 74, 106, 252, 254, 255, 258, 260, 261, 262, 263, 264, 270
Manes, S., 159
Manz, C. C., 207, 217
March, J. G., 21
Markels, A., 294–295, 296
Marsick, V. J., 200
Martin, J., 259
Martin, M. H., 270
Martinez, S., 231
Maruca, R. F., 257
Mason, P. A., 252
Massey, M. E., 64
Mathur, A., 63
McAllister, D. J., 169
McCall, M. W., 79, 223
McCauley, L., 171
McClelland, D. C., 203
McClintick, M., 107
McCrae, R. R., 60
McGarvey, C., 158–159
McKee, A., 66
Meelankavil, J. P., 63

Megerian, L. E., 67
Meindl, J. R., 21, 22
Menon, S. T., 112
Meyerson, M., 127
Mieszkowski, K., 5
Miller, D., 270
Miller, D. M., 72, 74, 202, 258, 259, 260, 269, 270
Millman, J., 40
Miner, J. B., 42
Mintzberg, H., 17, 26, 223
Mischel, W., 60, 292
Misumi, J., 37, 142
Mitchell, T., 164
Mitchell, T. R., 161, 162, 163, 164
Mizzi, P. J., 74
Mohrman, S. A., 98, 112, 115, 194, 195
Moore, P. L., 21, 40
Morgeson, F. P., 167
Morris, B., 46, 250
Mosakowski, E., 141
Moskowitz, M., 174
Mount, M., 60, 70, 71
Moxley, R. A., 39
Muio, A., 44
Mumford, M. D., 34, 41, 69
Munk, N., 258, 263, 269
Munter, M., 10
Murphy, S. E., 169
Murray, S., 297

N

Nahavandi, A., 18, 42, 74, 106, 133, 203, 210, 252, 254, 255, 258, 260, 261, 262, 263, 264, 269, 270
Nahavandi, F., 230
Nahavandi, H., 230
Nanus, B., 40, 112, 235
Nebenzahl, I. D., 78
Neck, C., 207
Nelton, S., 79
Neuman, J. H., 74
Newcomb, T. M., 34
Newsome, S., 67
Newstetter, W. I., 34

Nicholls, J. R., 175
Norman, W. T., 70
Numerof, R. E., 37
Nutt, P., 78

O

O'Connor, J. F., 22, 23
Offermann, L. R., 164, 237, 238
Oldham, G. R., 200
Olofson, C., 114
Olsen, K., 220–221, 241
Ones, D. S., 71
O'Reilly, B., 109
O'Reilly, C. A., 169
Oskamp, S., 292
Overholt, A., 4, 18, 80

P

Panitz, E., 78
Pawar, B. S., 238
Peck, S. I., 111, 272
Pelled, L. H., 170
Peng, T. K., 141
Percy, P. M., 237
Peters, L. H., 133
Peters, T., 39
Peterson, M. F., 37, 292
Pettigrew, A., 106
Pfeffer, J., 21, 22, 48, 104, 106, 260
Phillips, J. S., 167
Podsakoff, P. M., 163, 173, 237
Poggioli, S., 46
Pohlmann, J. T., 133
Porter, L. W., 161
Posner, B. Z., 39, 58, 202, 239, 240, 241, 248
Prahalad, C. K., 10
Prendergast, C., 108, 110
Puffer, S. M., 40
Pugh, D. S., 254
Puri, S., 272

R

Rahim, M. A., 99
Ralston, D. A., 79

Rattan, S., 46, 63, 64
Raven, B. H., 100
Ray, S., 221
Rhodewalt, F., 73
Rice, R., 126, 127, 133
Richley, E. A., 23
Roberts, N. C., 229
Roberts, P., 98
Roehm, H., 71
Rogers, A., 266
Rokeach, M., 60, 85
Rosenfeld, J., 194
Rosenman, R. H., 73
Rosier, R. H., 87
Ross, S. M., 237, 238
Rotter, J. B., 72, 88
Row, H., 67
Rubin, H., 68
Ruits-Quintana, S. A., 231
Russell, A. M., 80
Rust, J., 70
Rychlak, J. F., 34
Ryhammer, L., 68

S

Sachdeva, P. S., 107
Safilios-Rothschild, C., 8
Salancik, G. R., 21, 22, 104
Salter, C., 5, 224
Sanders, W. M. G., 272
Sarr, R. A., 226
Saudagaran, S. M., 272
Scandura, T., 170
Schein, E. H., 9, 18, 254, 270
Schlender, B., 71, 158–159
Schmidt, S. M., 102
Schneier, C. E., 72
Schoorman, F. D., 100, 101, 115, 169, 296
Schriesheim, C. A., 132, 163, 169
Schroyer, C. J., 164
Schwartz, N. D., 67
Schwartz, T., 67
Schwarzzwald, J., 101
Seashore, S. E., 36
Seibert, S. E., 71

Sellers, P., 18, 42, 121–122, 249–250, 258, 268
Seltzer, J., 37, 237
Semler, R., 173
Serwer, A. E., 5, 272
Shamir, B., 226, 227, 229, 233
Shapiro, D. L., 12
Sharaf, M., 260
Shen, W., 259
Sheridan, J. E., 163
Sherman, S., 80
Shiemann, W., 166
Shore, M., 167
Sightler, K. W., 72
Sims, H. P., Jr., 163, 207, 217
Singer, P., 230
Skrzypek, G. J., 126
Slevin, D. P., 260
Slocum, J. W., Jr., 19, 72, 92, 163, 260, 270
Smith, D. K., 106, 204, 208
Smith, N. R., 42
Smith, T. W., 73
Snyder, M., 75
Song, J. H., 260
Sosik, J., 237
Sosik, J. J., 67
Sparks, D., 47
Sparrowe, R. T., 167
Spector, P. E., 60, 72
Spencer, R. J., 204
Steidlmeier, P., 231
Sternberg, R. J., 68
Stewart, T. A., 71, 239
Stewart-Belle, S., 74
Stinson, J. E., 162
Stogdill, R. M., 34, 37, 39
Strauss, G., 271
Stringfield, P., 76, 77
Strube, M. J., 73, 74, 133
Stumpf, S. A., 78
Swan, K., 47
Szilagyi, A. D., 163

T

Tan, H. H., 169
Tannenbaum, A. S., 98, 112

Taylor, A., III, 170
Teagarden, M. B., 99
Tepper, B. J., 237
Terpstra, R. H., 79
Thomas, A. B., 23
Tjosvold, D., 138
Tomlinson, R., 40, 74
Toulouse, J., 202
Toulouse, J. M., 72
Townsend, J., 167
Trevelyan, R., 173
Triandis, H. C., 11, 65, 142, 292
Trice, H. M., 227, 233
Trompenaars, A., 12
Trompenaars, F., 12, 13–14, 168,
    199, 267
Tropila, D., 17
Tsui, A. S., 169
Tsurumi, R., 230
Turner, E., 200
Turnley, W. H., 75
Tyabji, H., 226

U

Uchitelle, L., 271
Uhl-Bien, M., 166, 168
Useem, J., 20
Useem, M., 18

V

Vance, C. A., 60
Van Velsor, E., 292
Varma, A., 169
Vecchio, R. P., 132
Viswesvaran, C., 71
Von Glinow, M. A., 99
Vroom, V. H., 134–138, 161, 256

W

Wakababayashi, M., 167
Walker, R., 293, 294

Walsh, T., 100
Warner, R., 296
Waterman, R., 39
Waters, L. L., 65
Wayne, S. J., 167
Webber, A., 69
Weber, D. O., 44
Wedley, W. C., 138
Weierter, S. J. M., 227, 232
Weil, E., 239
Weiner, N., 23
Weiss, H. M., 60
Welles, E., 18
Werner, C., 73
Wheatley, M. J., 296
White, R., 159
White, R. K., 35, 123
Whitford, D., 174
Wilkinson, I., 102
Wilson, M. G., 72
Winer, B. J., 36
Wofford, J. C., 163
Wolfe, R. N., 90
Wood, R. E., 164
Wyszomirski, M. J., 230

X

Xin, K. R., 170

Y

Yammarino, F. J., 169, 237
Yasai-Ardekani, M., 269
Yetton, P. W., 134–138, 256
Yukl, G., 100, 102, 132, 237, 238

Z

Zaccaro, S. J., 34, 41, 69
Zaleznik, A., 15–16, 235, 292
Zander, A., 199
Zhang, Y., 63
Zhou, J., 68

SUBJECT INDEX

A

ABB, 40, 261
Ability, 60, 65–69
Abramson, Roger, 9, 18, 74
Abrashoff, Michael, 188–189
Accountability, of strategic leaders, 271–273
Acer, 271
Achievement-oriented leadership, 162
Acton, Lord, 96
AES Corporation, 294–297
Agee, Philip, 109
Agreeableness, 71
Alaska Airlines, 195
Alessi, Alberto, 31
Alessi, Giovanni, 31
Alessi SPA, 31
Alexander, Pam, 79
Alliance Relocation Services LLC, 262
Amazon.com, 257, 270
American Express, 21, 67, 265
American Golf, 195
America Online (AOL), 225, 226–227, 257
AnSan su Kyi, 225, 226
Apple, 40
Asea Brown Boveri, 44
Ash, Mary Kay, 158
Atlantic Group Furniture Procurement and
      Project Management, Inc., 9, 74
AT&T, 80, 171, 272
Attributional models, 163–164
   limitations and applications, 165
Autocratic leader decision style, 134, 138
Autodesk, 15, 261
Avon, 249–250

B

Babiss, Lee, 114
Bador, Nancy, 17–18

Bakke, Dennis, 295
Baldauf, Sari, 266
Barad, Jill, 261, 271
Bartz, Carol, 15, 261
Behavior era (mid-1940s to early 1970s) of
      leadership theory, 34–37
Bezos, Jeff, 257, 270
Bhopal disaster, 273
Bias, 165
   avoiding, 166, 170–171
Big Five Personality Dimensions, 70–72
Bristol Myers, 80
British Petroleum, 297
Brown, Dick, 234
Bryan, John, 261

C

Canal +, 261
Canon, 40
Capellán, Fernando, 285–286
Career Strategies, 127
Carter, Jimmy, 131
Case, Steve, 225, 226–227, 257
Castro, Fidel, 225
Center of Creative Leadership, 76, 79
Centrality, 105
Chambers, John, 80, 257, 265
Change-oriented leadership
   Andrea Jung Orchestrates Avon's
      Makeover (case), 249–250
   in the popular press, 238–242
   See also Charismatic leadership;
      Transactional leadership;
      Transformational leadership
Charismatic leadership
   characteristics of followers, 227–228
   characteristics of leaders, 224–227
   dark side, 231–232
   evaluation and application, 232–233

Delegation
  benefits, 200–201
  failure of leaders in, 202–203
  guidelines, 201–202
Dell Computers, 80, 257
Dell, Michael, 257
Delphi Automotive Systems, 196
Delta Express, 195
DeMarco, Tom, 74
Demographic trends
  among upper-echelon leaders, 260–262
  in the United States, 46, 47
Dependence and substitutability, 105–106
DeSimone, Livio, 261
Diehl, Philip, 44
Differences
  See Individual differences
di Montezemolo, Luca, 261
Directive leadership, 161–162
Disabilities, quality of exchange and, 169
Disney, 40
Diversity, 46, 262
  disability and quality of exchange, 169
Drexler, Mickey, 258, 261, 263, 269
Duffield, David, 98, 102
Dunlap, Al, 47

E

Eastern Airlines, 197
e-Bay, 257
Education, level of employees', 46–47
Effectiveness, 5–6
Eiffel Tower cultures, 13–14
Einstein, Albert, 251
Eisner, Michael, 40
Electronic Data Systems (EDS), 234
Ellerbee, Linda, 112
Emotional intelligence, 66–67
Emotional stability, 71
Empowerment
  impact of, 115
  steps to
    leadership factors, 112–113
    organizational factors, 113–114
Enrico, Roger, 226
Enron, 40, 106, 273

Environment, 59
Erickson, 266
Ethics
  charismatic leaders and, 231–232
  values and, 64–65
Ethnic culture, 8–10
Exchange and relationship development
      and management, 160
  attributional models, 163–16
  Caring Navy Commander, The (case),
      188–189
  Leader-Member Exchange (LMX),
      166–171
  Path-Goal Theory, 161–16
  Situational Leadership Model, 174–175
  Substitutes for Leadership Model,
      171–174
Executive discretion
  external environmental factors, 256–257
  internal organizational factors, 257–259
Executives, power sources of top, 106–107
Expectancy model of motivation, 161
Expert power, 101
External crisis, 228–229
Extraversion, 71
Exxon, 273

F

Family cultures, 13–14
Favoritism, 168
Feld, Charlie, 257
Feld Group, 257
Feldt, Gloria, 45
Ferrari, 261
Fiedler, Fred, 37–38, 125
  See also Contingency models
Fiorina, Carly, 258
Ford, Bill, Jr., 46
Ford Motor Company, 194, 203
Ford Motor Credit Company, 129
Fox, Vincente, 9–10

G

Gandhi, Mahatma, 222, 223, 225, 226, 227
Gangwal, Rakesh, 195

Gap, Incorporated, 258, 261, 263, 269
Gates, Bill, 71, 158–159
Gault, Stanley, 205
GE Capital, 272
Gender
    leadership roles and, 17–18
    strategic leadership and, 268
Genentech, 261
General Electric (GE), 20, 80, 107, 235–236,
        261, 262
General Foods, 205
General Motors, 171, 273
George, Bill, 174
Gerra, Joe, 195
Gerstner, Lou, 265–266
Gillette, 271
Gioia, Nancy, 194
Global competition, 44, 46
Goleman, Daniel, 66
Goodyear, 205
Gordon, Ellen, 263, 265
Gordon, Melvin, 263, 265
Gould, Kathryn, 224
Goutard, Noel, 261
Grand Junction Networks, 224
Greenfield, Jerry, 18
Greenspan, Alan, 100–102
Grogan, Barbara, 17–18
Group culture, 8–10
Group leader decision style, 134
Grove, Andy, 71, 235–236
Grundhofer, John, 47
Grupo M, 285–286
Grupo Televisa SA, 40
Guided missile cultures, 13
Gulf & Western, 107
Gupta, Rajat, 267

H

Hartnett, Jack, 55
Hawley, Michael, 271
Hay Group, 44
HealthSouth Corporation, 109
Heinz, 267
Helgesen, Sally, 17, 268

Heredity, 59
Hesselbein, Francis, 17–18
Heterogeneity, 198
Hewlett-Packard, 71, 80, 258, 296
Heyde, Mary Ellen, 194
High-context and low-context cultural
        framework, 10
High-control innovator (HCI),
        262–263
Hofstede, Geert, 10–12, 99
Hofstede's dimensions, 10–12
Hollady Park Medical Center, 44
Hostility, 74
Hymowitz, Carol, 15

I

Iaccoca, Lee, 226
IBM, 19, 47, 171, 265, 271
Incubator cultures, 13
Individual consideration, 237
Individual differences, 80–81
    abilities and skills
        creativity, 68
        intelligence and emotional intelli-
            gence, 65–67
        skills, 68–69
    elements of characteristics, 58–59
        individual characteristics set the
            limits, 61
        multiple perspectives and the impact of
            the situation, 60–61
        using, 80–81
    values, 61
        culture and, 62–64
        ethics and, 64–65
Individualism/collectivism, 11–12
Individuality, 62
Individual power, 100–103
Influence tactics, 102–103
In-group status, 166–167, 171
Innovation Network, 4
Inspiration and charisma, 236
Intel, 71, 235–236
Intellectual stimulation, 236
Intelligence, 65–66

O

Ogilvy & Mather, 268
Ogilvy Public Relations World-
       wide, 79
Ohio State Leadership Studies, 36–37
Ollila, Jorma, 266
Openness to experience, 71
O'Reilly, Tony, 267
Organizational culture, 9–10
   creation and maintenance of, by leaders,
       18–20
   cross-cultural (figure), 13
Organizational structure
   power in
       centrality, 105
       dependence and substitutability,
           105–106
       uncertainty, 104–105
Organizations, learning in, 69
Out-group status, 167–168
Owen, Dian Graves, 220–221
Owen Healthcare, 220–221
Own-Jones, Lindsay, 267
Oxygen Media, 18

P

Packard, David, 296
Paramount, 268
Participative innovator (PI), 265
Participative leadership, 162
Participative management and leading
       teams, 193
   criteria for participation, 196–198
   culture and, 199–200
   delegation
       benefits of, 200–201
       failure of leaders in, 202–203
       guidelines for, 201–202
   Dian Graves Owen (case), 220–221
   self-leadership, 207–208
   superleadership, 207
   teams
       characteristics of, 203–204
       leaders, role of, in, 208–210
       self-managed, 204–207

when to use participation, 194–195
   See also Teams
Path-Goal Theory, 37
   framework, 161–162
   limitations and applications, 162
Pelsma, Debra, 224
PeopleSoft, 98, 102
PepsiCo, 80, 226
Perot, Ross, 234
Perot Systems, 127
Personality, 59–60
Personality traits
   among upper-echelon leaders, 260–262
   Big Five Personality Dimensions, 70–72
   Bonnie Reitz—Helping to Fly
       Continental (case), 94
   leaders who fail, 79–80
   locus of control, 72–73
   Machiavellian personality, 78–79
   Myers Briggs Type Indicator, 76–78
   self-monitoring, 75–76
   Type A, 73–75
Peterson, David, 9
Planned Parenthood Federation of
       America, 45
Platt, Lew, 71
Political changes worldwide, 44
Polyphasic behaviors, 73–74
Popular press, change-oriented and vision-
       ary leadership in, 238–242
Position power, 101, 128
Power
   abuse of, 170, 232
   corruption, 107
       causes, 108–109
       consequences, 109–110
       cycle (figure), 108
       evil leadership, 111
       solutions, 110–111
   empowerment
       impact of, 115
       steps to, 112–114
   how to use wisely, 103
   Most Powerful Woman in Banking, The
       (case), 121
   in organizations
       consequences of using, 97–98

self-managed, 204–207
sport team model for management, 205
Texas Children's Hospital, 235
Theory X, 194
Theory Y, 194
3M, 14, 261
Time urgency, 73
Tootsie Roll Industries, 263, 265
Toyota of Japan, 44, 205
Trait era (late 1800s to mid-1940s) of
    leadership theory, 33–34, 35
Transactional leadership, 233
  contingent reward, 234
  management by exception (MBE), 235
Transformational leadership, 233, 235
  charisma and inspiration, 236
  evaluation and application, 237–238
  history and impact of, 223–224
  individual consideration, 237
  intellectual stimulation, 236
Triandis, Harry, 11–12
Trompenaars, Fons, 12–14
Trompenaars's dimensions of culture,
    12–14
Tuck, Richard, 9
Turbulence, 228–229
Tyabji, Hatim, 226
Type A personality, 73–75, 203
Type B personality, 73

U

Uncertainty, 104–105
Union Carbide, 273
Upper-echelon strategic leadership, 251
  accountability, 271–273
  characteristics of leaders
    culture, 267–268
    demographic and personality traits,
      260–262
    gender, 268
    types, 262–267
  distinguished from micro leadership,
    252–253
  domain and impact of, 254
    executive discretion, 256–259

role of leaders, 255–256
  Fernando Capellán Is Mixing a Social
    Agenda and Business Success
    (case), 285–286
  how executives affect the organiza-
    tion, 268
    allocation of resources and control of
      the reward system, 270
    direct decisions, 269
    setting the norms and modeling,
      270–271
  leadership succession, 259
US AirWays, 195
U.S. Intel, 44
U.S. National Aeronautics and Space
    Administration (NASA), 13

V

Vagelos, Roy, 113
Valdez, 273
Valeo, 261
Values, 60, 61
  culture and, 62–64
  ethics and, 64–65
  generation-based differences
    (table), 64
Verifone, Incorporated, 226
Vertical Dyad Linkage Model, 166
Vivendi, 261
Vroom, Victor, 134

W

Wachner, Linda, 6
Wallace, Mark, 235
Waugh, Barbara, 5
Weber, Max, 223
Welch, Jack, 20, 107, 235–236, 261, 262
Wendt, Gary, 272
Westberg, Jon, 9
Wetterstrom, Roy, 265
Whitman, Margaret, 257
Widerotter, Maggie, 170–171
Winfrey, Oprah, 258
Wink Communication, 170–171